CAMBRIDGE GREEK AND LATIN CLASSICS

T0382021

EURIPIDES
CYCLOPS

EDITED BY

RICHARD HUNTER

University of Cambridge

REBECCA LAEMMLE

University of Cambridge

Shaftesbury Road, Cambridge CB2 8EA, United Kingdom

One Liberty Plaza, 20th Floor, New York, NY 10006, USA

477 Williamstown Road, Port Melbourne, VIC 3207, Australia

314–321, 3rd Floor, Plot 3, Splendor Forum, Jasola District Centre, New Delhi – 110025, India

103 Penang Road, #05–06/07, Visioncrest Commercial, Singapore 238467

Cambridge University Press is part of Cambridge University Press & Assessment,
a department of the University of Cambridge.

We share the University's mission to contribute to society through the pursuit of
education, learning and research at the highest international levels of excellence.

www.cambridge.org
Information on this title: www.cambridge.org/9781108399999

DOI: 10.1017/9781108227148

First published 2020

A catalogue record for this publication is available from the British Library

Library of Congress Cataloging-in-Publication data
Names: Eurpides, author. | Hunter, R. L. (Richard L.), editor. |
Laemmle, Rebecca, editor.
Title: Cyclops / Euripides ; edited by Richard Hunter, University of
Cambridge ; Rebecca Laemmle, University of Cambridge.
Other titles: Cyclops. English | Cambridge Greek and Latin classics.
Description: Cambridge ; New York : Cambridge University Press, 2020. |
Series: Cambridge Greek and Latin classics | Includes bibliographical
references and indexes.
Identifiers: LCCN 2020019040 (print) | LCCN 2020019041 (ebook) |
ISBN 9781316510513 (hardback) | ISBN 9781108227148 (ebook)
Subjects: LCSH: Cyclopes (Greek mythology)–Drama. | Euripides. Cyclops.
Classification: LCC PA3973.C9 H95 2020 (print) | LCC PA3973.C9 (ebook) |
DDC 882/.01–dc23
LC record available at https://lccn.loc.gov/2020019040
LC ebook record available at https://lccn.loc.gov/2020019041

ISBN   978-1-316-51051-3   Hardback
ISBN   978-1-108-39999-9   Paperback

For
Pat Easterling

CONTENTS

ACKNOWLEDGEMENTS

In preparing this edition, we have incurred a number of debts which we here very gratefully acknowledge. Neil Hopkinson read earlier versions of both the Introduction and the Commentary and identified much that needed clarification. James Diggle read the Commentary with his characteristic care, and his notes both saved us from error and made us rethink in many places. Our debt to him is, of course, far deeper than this; without his Oxford Classical Text of Euripides to guide us, we would probably never even have begun this project. Cédric Scheidegger Laemmle put his finger on much that needed rewriting, while engaging in hours of *Cyclops*-chatter with remarkably good grace. We hope that our debt to earlier commentators on the *Cyclops*, notably Richard Seaford and Werner Biehl, will be obvious to those interested, and we regret that we were unable to take account of the edition of *Cyclops* by Bernd Seidensticker (Berlin 2020), whose earlier work has shed so much light on satyr-drama.

This book is dedicated to Pat Easterling, as a very small return for all she has taught us about ancient drama and for the example she has set.

REFERENCES AND ABBREVIATIONS

All dates are BC, unless otherwise indicated. References to plays of Euripides are by title or standard abbreviation only. Unless stated otherwise, references to fragments of tragedy follow *TrGF*, to fragments of comedy *PCG*, to Hesiod Merkelbach–West, to Sappho and Alcaeus Voigt, and to Callimachus Pfeiffer. Standard abbreviations for other collections and editions of texts and for works of reference are used, but the following may be noted:

Beekes   R. Beekes, *Etymological Dictionary of Greek*, Leiden 2010
CA   J.U. Powell, *Collectanea Alexandrina*, Oxford 1925
CEG   P.A. Hansen, *Carmina epigraphica Graeca*, 2 vols., Berlin 1983, 1989
CGCG   E. van Emde Boas, A. Rijksbaron, L. Huitink and M. de Bakker, *The Cambridge Grammar of Classical Greek*, Cambridge 2019
DGE   F.R. Adrados *et al.*, *Diccionario Griego-Español*, Madrid 1980–
D–K   H. Diels and W. Kranz, *Die Fragmente der Vorsokratiker*, 6th ed., Berlin 1951
DNO   S. Kansteiner, K. Hallof, L. Lehmann, B. Seidensticker and K. Stemmer eds., *Der neue Overbeck*, Berlin 2014
FGE   D.L. Page, *Further Greek Epigrams*, Cambridge 1981
FGrHist   F. Jacoby, *Die Fragmente der griechischen Historiker*, Berlin 1923–1930, Leiden 1940–1958
GG   *Grammatici Graeci*, Leipzig 1883–1894
GP   A.S.F. Gow and D.L. Page, *The Greek Anthology: The Garland of Philip*, I–II, Cambridge 1968
*GP*²   J.D. Denniston, *The Greek Particles*, 2nd ed., Oxford 1954
GVI   W. Peek, *Griechische Vers-Inschriften* I, Berlin 1955
HE   A.S.F. Gow and D.L. Page, *The Greek Anthology: Hellenistic Epigrams*, Cambridge 1965
IG   *Inscriptiones Graecae*, Berlin 1873–
K–B   R. Kühner, *Ausführliche Grammatik der griechischen Sprache*, I, 3rd ed., revised by F. Blass, Hannover 1890–1892
K–G   R. Kühner, *Ausführliche Grammatik der griechischen Sprache*, II, 3rd ed., revised by B. Gerth, Hannover and Leipzig 1898–1904
KPS   P. Krumeich, N. Pechstein and B. Seidensticker, *Das griechische Satyrspiel*, Darmstadt 1999

LfgrE	*Lexikon des frühgriechischen Epos*, Göttingen 1979–2010
LIMC	*Lexicon Iconographicum Mythologiae Classicae*, Zurich 1981–1999
OSC	P. O'Sullivan and C. Collard, *Euripides, Cyclops and Major Fragments of Greek Satyric Drama*, Oxford 2013
PCG	R. Kassel and C. Austin, *Poetae Comici Graeci*, Berlin 1983–2001
PMG	D.L. Page, *Poetae melici Graeci*, Oxford 1962
RE	A. Pauly, G. Wissowa and W. Kroll *et al.* eds., *Real-Encyclopädie der classischen Altertumswissenschaft*, Stuttgart and Munich 1893–1978
SGO	R. Merkelbach and J. Stauber, *Steinepigramme aus dem griechischen Osten*, Munich 1998–2004
SH	H. Lloyd-Jones and P. Parsons, *Supplementum Hellenisticum*, Berlin and New York 1983
Smyth	H.W. Smyth, *Greek Grammar*, Cambridge, MA 1920
TrGF	R. Kannicht, B. Snell and S. Radt, *Tragicorum Graecorum Fragmenta*, Göttingen, 1971–2004

PLATES

1a Attic red-figure volute-*kratēr*, c. 400 BC, the 'Pronomos Vase', 'A-side'.
National Archaeological Museum of Naples H 3240

1b 'Pronomos Vase', 'B-side'

2 Lucanian red-figure calyx-*kratēr*, late fifth century BC. British Museum
inv. 1947.7-14.18

INTRODUCTION

1 EURIPIDES

Hellenistic and Byzantine sources[1] place Euripides' birth either in 485/4, also the year of Aeschylus' first victory,[2] or more usually in 480/79, the year of the Greek victory at Salamis; the explicit synchronicity with other significant events in Athenian dramatic and political history enjoins caution, but neither date is inherently implausible and neither is likely to be very far wrong. We are also told that Euripides first competed in the tragic contest in 455 and won his first victory in 442/1. Biographical sources report that, late in life (probably 407), he accepted an invitation to the court of King Archelaos in Macedonia, and he died there after a relatively brief stay; modern scholarship is divided as to the credit to be given to these accounts.[3] At any event, Aristophanes' *Frogs*, produced at the Lenaian festival in winter 405, suggests that Euripides' death was very recent, as was Sophocles' (406). The *Bacchae* and the *Iphigeneia at Aulis* appear to have been staged posthumously in Athens by Euripides' son.[4]

The *Frogs* also attests to Euripides' stature as a tragic poet, as does an ancient anecdote that, after news of Euripides' death, Sophocles appeared at the next ceremonial *proagōn* (presumably in 406) dressed in a dark cloak of mourning, his actors and choreuts did not wear garlands as was normal, and this scene caused the people to weep.[5] The preserved information, which will go back eventually to the public dramatic records or *didaskaliai*, that Euripides was granted a chorus, i.e. allowed to compete in the dramatic contests, twenty-two times between 455 and his move to Macedonia, confirms his public stature. It is much harder to know what conclusions to draw from the fact that during his life he won first prize at the City Dionysia only four times (Sophocles

---

[1] The sources are most conveniently collected in Vol. I of Kannicht's edition of the fragments in *TrGF* and (with English translation) in Kovacs 1994: 2–141. Particularly important for later sources may have been the *On Euripides* of Philochorus (c. 340–260 BC), cf. *FGrHist* 328 F 217–22 (with Jacoby's commentary).

[2] So very probably the earliest independent witness, the *Marmor Parium*, Eur. T 10a.

[3] For the sceptical case cf. Scullion 2003; for the importance of Macedonia to Euripides' *Nachleben* in the fourth and third centuries cf. Hanink 2008.

[4] The evidence is a scholium to Ar. *Frogs* 67 = DID C 22 Snell; cf. below p. 46.

[5] The *proagōn* appears to have been a ceremonial appearance of the competitors some days before the dramatic contest, at which the poets would announce the subjects of the plays to be staged at the festival, cf. Pickard-Cambridge 1968: 67–8, Csapo and Slater 1995: 109–10.

had eighteen victories), particularly as dramatists were judged not for single plays but for a group of three tragedies and a satyr-play ('tetra-logies').[6] What we can say, however, is that a great deal of evidence points to the ever-increasing popularity and influence of his dramas after his death, both in reperformances all over the Greek world and as texts to be read; as the very significant number of papyri of otherwise lost plays of Euripides attests, the fourth century and beyond was the real period of his 'victory'.[7]

According to the preserved *Lives* of the poet, Alexandrian scholars knew the titles of ninety-two plays of Euripides, texts of seventy-eight of which had survived to be included in the Library. Three of these were tragedies of debated authenticity, and the number will also have included the surviving *Rhesos,* an all but certainly fourth-century play by an unknown dramatist which had taken the place of the authentic (but lost) Euripidean *Rhesos.* Of these seventy-eight, eight were satyr-dramas, of which one, perhaps the *Sisyphos,* was of debated authenticity.[8] Given that satyr-plays should have accounted for one-quarter of Euripides' output (perhaps some seventeen plays in total),[9] eight is a very small number. In 438, the fourth play with which Euripides competed was *Alcestis,* which is not a satyr-play; the author of the Alexandrian *hypothesis* who described it as σατυρικώτερον 'because, unlike tragedies, it ends in joy and pleasure ... which is more appropriate to comedy' may perhaps have felt that the fact that Euripides did not include a satyr-play in his tetralogy of that year called for comment.[10] Whatever the implications of this ancient judgement, it has led modern scholars regularly to seek a

[6] Cf. further below p. 24. We use the unqualified term 'tetralogy' to refer to such groups of four plays, regardless of whether or not they dealt with parts of the same story.

[7] In 387/6, the performance (out of competition) of an 'old drama' was added to the City Dionysia; the chance preservation of an inscription (*IG* II² 2320, Millis and Olson 2012: 61-90) shows that in three successive years (341, 340, 339) the 'old tragedy' which was chosen for reperformance was Euripidean.

[8] Kannicht concludes that the eight satyr-plays extant in Alexandria were *Autolykos* I, *Autolykos* II, *Bousiris, Eurystheus, Cyclops, Sisyphos, Skiron,* and *Syleus*; others have held that there was only one satyric *Autolykos* (cf., e.g., Pechstein 1998: 33-40). Another of the uncertainties concerns the title *Epe(i)os,* which is preserved only on the so-called *Marmor Albanum* from Rome (T 6); Kannicht regards this either as a simple error or as the title of a satyr-play which had not reached Alexandria. Cf. further below p. 3, and for more detailed discussion cf. Kannicht 1996, Jouan and Van Looy 1998: xi-xvi, Pechstein 1998: 19-34.

[9] Cf. below pp. 3-4.

[10] Whether this sentence of the *hypothesis* goes back to Aristophanes of Byzantium is disputed among modern scholars, but there is a similar observation in the *hypothesis* to the *Orestes*: τὸ δρᾶμα κωμικωτέραν ἔχει τὴν καταστροφήν. This parallel has led to doubt as to whether the observation about the 'satyric' nature of the *Alcestis* has

'satyric' flavour for that play in the role of Heracles and, in particular, the servant's description of his drunken feasting and Heracles' subsequent expressions of a hedonist *carpe diem* view of life (*Alcestis* 747–802); both these motifs find parallels in the behaviour of the Cyclops in *Cyclops*.[11] Even so, the satyrless *Alcestis* is not a satyr-drama, and there is at least no good reason to think that the pattern of Euripides' four plays in 438 was a regular occurrence. Unless it was, however, the case that Euripides wrote far fewer satyr-dramas than was to be expected, there seem to be two possible explanations for the very low attested figure for his satyric output.

The attested numbers of satyr-plays for Aeschylus and Sophocles are also considerably smaller than expected, and here a good case can be made for believing that more of the attested titles for these dramatists were in fact satyr-plays than is recorded;[12] unlike the case with Euripides, however, there are no surviving notices which record knowledge of Aeschylean or Sophoclean plays which never reached Alexandria. The standard way of referring to a satyr-play in, say, a list of titles was to add σάτυροι or σατυρικός -ή -όν (*uel sim.*) to the title, and this addition could easily get dropped in transmission; we can in fact see this process at work in several instances. This does not, however, seem very probable for the rather different situation of Euripides' surviving titles, and it is perhaps more likely that another explanation should be sought. The most obvious is that satyr-dramas formed the lion's share of the fourteen or so plays which did not reach Alexandria; we know that was the case with the *Theristai*, the satyr-drama which was staged with *Medea* (according to the *hypothesis*).[13] If so, a number of factors may have contributed. One may have been the very popularity of some of Euripides' tragedies, now regularly reperformed as single plays without the accompanying satyr-plays, some of which perhaps gradually faded into such obscurity that texts were no longer available to be deposited in the public archives under Lycurgus and from there to be transmitted to Alexandria. Interest in satyr-play more generally seems to

anything to do with the fact that the play was performed in fourth place, cf., e.g., Fantuzzi 2014: 227.

[11] In Euripides' satyric *Syleus* Heracles was sold as a slave to Syleus, a monstrous son of Poseidon, whom he killed after dining on his cattle and drinking copiously of his wine, cf. the evidence for the play in *TrGF*, Laemmle 2013: 252 n. 16. In his summary of the play (Eur. T 221b) Tzetzes associates such behaviour with the nature of satyr-drama, cf. below p. 49 n.167.

[12] Cf. Radt 1982: 190–4.

[13] Kirchhoff's suggestion that the title of a satyr-play is recorded as 'not preserved' in the fragmentary Aristophanean *hypothesis* of *Phoinissai* is attractive. Two other possibilities are the *Epe(i)os* (cf. above n. 8) and the *Lamia* (see Kannicht's introduction to fr. 472m).

have waned for a variety of reasons in the course of the fourth century,[14] and those aspects of Euripidean tragedy most responsible for the dramatist's fame – the plotting, the monologues and monodies for actors, the pathos – would inevitably be less prominent in satyr-drama than in tragedy.

2 THE *CYCLOPS* ON STAGE

The first performance of *Cyclops* was certainly not the first dramatisation of the events of *Odyssey* 9, and not even the first satyric dramatisation.[15] Whereas we can trace in close detail Euripides' engagement with the Homeric text, we may take it as certain that *Cyclops* also alludes to, and makes use of, previous dramatisations of the Cyclops-story, which will have been more or less familiar to at least some of the audience; in this case, however, our appreciation of such inter-dramatic play is restricted by the wretchedly few fragments of such other plays that have survived, and we must rely far too often on speculation and assessments of probability.

Aristias of Phlious, whose father Pratinas was identified in antiquity as the 'first inventor' of satyr-play (*TrGF* I 4 T1), staged a satyric *Cyclops* at Athens in (roughly) the middle part of the fifth century. The one surviving fragment of interest well illustrates some of the difficulties we face in piecing together how Euripides has used the dramatic tradition. In fr. 4, the Cyclops says to Odysseus ἀπώλεσας τὸν οἶνον ἐπιχέας ὕδωρ, 'you ruined the wine by pouring in water', which strongly suggests that already in that play the ruse by which Odysseus makes the Cyclops drunk had been represented in terms of contemporary sympotic practice, a theme which is so prominent in Euripides' play (cf. further 558n.). That fragment is cited by Athenaeus, whose predilection for passages concerning dining and drinking means that it is difficult to draw large-scale conclusions from this isolated verse.

Much the same is true of the three one-verse fragments of the comic *Cyclops* of Epicharmus of Syracuse, the earliest dramatic representation of the story of which we know. Drinking and dining seem to have played an important part in that play also,[16] and this may remind us of the importance of the reputation of Sicilian cuisine and cooking to Euripides' satyric presentation of the Cyclops. Fr. 72 of Epicharmus' play, φέρ' ἐγχέας ἐς τὸ σκύφος, suggests a sympotic scene very like that which we find in *Cyclops* (cf. 568n.), and it is an attractive suggestion that fr. 71, χορδαί τε ἁδύ, ναὶ

---

[14] Cf. Laemmle 2014: 926–9, below pp. 34–5; by at least 341/0 only one satyr-play was performed, and outside the contest proper, at the Great Dionysia.

[15] For a helpful survey of 'the Cyclops on stage' cf. Mastromarco 1998.

[16] Cf. nn. on 390–1, 568.

μὰ Δία, χὼ κωλεός, 'the sausages are delicious, by Zeus, as is the haunch', was spoken by the Cyclops about his cannibal meals; if so, Epicharmus' Cyclops anticipated both Euripides' Polyphemos and representations by Athenian comic poets who turned the Homeric monster into something of a discerning gourmet.[17] It is, however, only a guess that Polyphemos is the speaker, and the context is entirely unknown. Nevertheless, Epicharmus' importance cannot be judged only on the scraps of his play which have survived or on the near certainty that the Syracusan poet set his play, as Euripides was to do, in the region of Mount Etna.[18] However influential Epicharmus' comedy may have been at Athens,[19] the fragments as a whole display a persistent parodic engagement with the authority of Homer,[20] and it is not improbable (to say no more) that Epicharmus preceded (and presumably influenced) Euripides in the presentation of a version that undercut Odysseus' self-serving Homeric narration. Drinking and dining are also the subjects of the very scanty fragments of Callias' comic *Cyclopes* (434 BC), again preserved largely in Athenaeus;[21] there thus seems to have been a particular and persistent mode in which comedy presented the events of *Odyssey* 9, and Euripides will have been the heir of this.

Perhaps the most important comic version of the events of *Odyssey* 9 to appear on the Athenian stage, and certainly the one from which the most intriguing fragments survive, is the Ὀδυσσῆς (literally, 'Odysseuses') of Cratinus, perhaps roughly contemporary with Callias' *Cyclopes*.[22] The fragments reveal again the comic penchant for representing the events of *Odyssey* 9 through the lens of contemporary sympotic performance, but we now have the chance to identify specific elements of the travestied Homeric model, and several of the fragments find striking analogies in *Cyclops*. In one fragment (fr. 145), τῇ νῦν πῖθι λαβὼν ἤδη, καὶ τοὔνομά μ' εὐθὺς ἐρώτα, 'Here now, take this and drink it, and straightaway ask me my name', we see Odysseus forcing the Cyclops to follow the Homeric script; in Homer, as in Euripides (vv. 548–9), the Cyclops, unprompted, asks Odysseus his name. As in Euripides (cf. 141–3n.), however, Maron, the Homeric priest of Apollo, is used as a metonymy for the wine itself, perhaps by the Cyclops (fr. 146). In one fragment (fr. 147) the Cyclops asks

[17] Cf., e.g., Mastromarco 1998: 34.
[18] Thucyd. 6.2.1 identifies the Cyclopes as early dwellers in a part of Sicily, cf. 20n.
[19] For a recent suggestive account cf. Willi 2015.
[20] Cf., e.g., Willi 2012b. On the language of Epicharmus and its relation to Homer see also Cassio 2002, esp. 70–3.
[21] Cf. Imperio 1998: 204–17.
[22] On Cratinus' comedy see esp. Bakola 2010: 235–46; earlier bibliography is listed in Kassel and Austin's introductory note to the fragments in *PCG*. Kaibel 1895 has been particularly influential, but is now rather out of date.

Odysseus where he saw 'the man, the dear son of Laertes'; like Euripides' Silenos, Cratinus' Cyclops apparently knows the opening verse of the *Odyssey* (cf. 104n.). We may speculate that this fragment derives from a scene, not like those at the end of the Homeric episode and *Cyclops*, where the now-blinded Cyclops learns Odysseus' real name and is forced to remember the long-buried prophecy of Telemos, but rather one in which 'No man' claims to have seen Odysseus on his travels, just as the Homeric hero tells Eumaeus and Penelope of his alleged sightings of Odysseus. As in Euripides, the Homeric monster has also become something of a cook and gourmet (fr. 150), but what is very striking is that the Cyclops speaks some verses at least in hexameters (fr. 150, perhaps fr. 149) and with some decidedly epic phraseology (note the sarcastic ἐρίηρας ἑταίρους, fr. 150.1);[23] Cratinus' comic form thus allowed a greater openness and flexibility than do the relatively strict scenic structures of Euripidean drama. Another fragment, οἱ δ᾽ ἀλυσκάζουσιν ὑπὸ ταῖς κλινίσιν, 'and they seek to hide under the couches' (fr. 148), suggests perhaps a messenger-speech (by Odysseus?) telling of the Cyclops' attack on some of his comrades;[24] if so, then Odysseus' speech at *Cyclops* 382–436 (cf. esp. 407–8) had at least one comic precedent, and it may be that the cave of Cratinus' Cyclops too had many more 'mod cons' than did his Homeric predecessor.[25]

Even more striking than these comic reworkings of Homeric scenes seems to have been the opening of Cratinus' play in which Odysseus and his comrades, who probably formed the chorus,[26] seem to have entered the theatre in a boat, driven on to the Cyclops' land by an approaching storm, described in suitably Homeric terms (νέφος οὐράνιον, fr. 143); whether or not the storm itself was somehow represented, or merely described, we cannot say, but this must have been a notable dramaturgical stroke. It is tempting to think that there was some kind of visual echo of the

[23] Cf. 377–8n. on φίλους ἑταίρους.
[24] There is perhaps here a memory of *Od.* 9.457 (the Cyclops to his ram) εἰπεῖν ὅππηι κεῖνος ἐμὸν μένος ἠλασκάζει.
[25] Cf., e.g., Mastromarco 1998: 38–40. ἀλυσκάζειν is another item from the Homeric lexicon.
[26] The fact that in *Cyclops* Odysseus and his men enter immediately after the parodos reinforces our sense that the satyrs are here 'out of place', in a story to which they do not belong and for which there was an obvious alternative chorus. In Homer, Odysseus took 12 crew members with him (*Od.* 9.195), and if he entered at *Cycl.* 96 with roughly that number, this too would suggest how they have been displaced from their choral role, regardless of whether the satyr-chorus consisted of 12 or 15 choreuts, cf. below pp. 28–9. Cratinus' chorus presumably numbered 24, as was apparently normal for Old Comedy.

ship-cart which was such a noteworthy feature of Dionysiac ritual.[27] The representation (however minimalist) of a Homeric storm must have been a remarkable experiment in turning even the most apparently intractable elements of Homeric narrative into drama, and it was one which was to have a rich *Nachleben* in ancient theatre (cf., e.g., Plautus, *Rudens*). In Homer, Odysseus and his men are not driven by a storm to take shelter on the Cyclops' island; rather, they beach smoothly on nearby 'Goat Island' without even noticing that they are approaching land (9.146–50). In *Cyclops* Odysseus claims that he and his men were driven to the Cyclops' island by storm-winds (ἀνέμων θύελλαι 109, cf. n. ad loc.), and although he there clearly evokes the Homeric 'bag of winds', there is perhaps also a memory of the motif of Cratinus' comedy.

No doubt other plays too made use of scenes and motifs drawn from *Odyssey* 9 and its dramatic progeny. If we only had a play-title and brief plot-summary, we would, for example, never guess that Aristophanes' *Wasps* contains a relatively extended reworking of the escape of Odysseus and his men from the cave.[28] Philocleon, desperate to escape from the house despite the watchful eye of his son Bdelycleon, hides under a donkey which he claims should be sold, and the scene in which he enters the stage (vv. 179–96) replays the escape of Odysseus and his men, 'No-man' joke and all, in farcical mode; thus, for example, Bdelycleon's concerned query to the donkey, 'Dear donkey, why are you weeping? Is it because you will be sold today …?' (vv. 179–81), picks up the Cyclops' famous address to his ram at *Od.* 9.447–60, κριὲ πέπον κτλ. Of perhaps greater interest with regard to *Cyclops* is the play with the language of food in vv. 193–5 ('a belly-cut of well-aged juryman'); Philocleon presents his son as not merely a cannibal Cyclops, but also (perhaps) as one with a refined interest in the quality and nature of his meals.[29] It is tempting to think that we catch here an echo of what seems to have been, well before the production of *Wasps*, the standard presentation of the events of *Odyssey* 9: the Cyclops as cook and gourmet, an image which was to play an important role in *Cyclops*.

The story of the Cyclops was not the only one of Odysseus' adventures which was dramatised in all three dramatic forms, Sicilian comedy, Athenian satyr-play and comedy; the hero's encounter with Circe seems to have been another such episode.[30] The story of the Cyclops did, however,

---

[27] Wilamowitz 1920: 15 assumes that Dionysos' ship was actually used (as perhaps it was) for the entrance and exit of the chorus.

[28] To the standard commentaries add Davies 1990; for further parallels with *Wasps* cf. 492–3n.

[29] Cf. Biles and Olson 2015 n. on vv. 193–5.

[30] Aeschylus, Deinolochus (Epicharmus' son, pupil or rival, according to various testimonia), and the fourth-century comic poets Anaxilas and Ephippus, all

also enjoy another, semi-dramatic existence in the world of lyric poetry and performance at the end of the fifth century and the beginning of the fourth.[31] Timotheus of Miletus, perhaps the greatest exponent of the so-called 'New Music', composed (and presumably performed) a 'Cyclops' nome (*PMG* 780–3), which seems to have involved not just narrative, but also impersonated direct speech (*PMG* 781); Timotheus' nome may have been roughly contemporary with Euripides' *Cyclops*. The only surviving fragment of any length suggests that here again sympotic themes were prominent:

> ἔγχευε δ' ἐν μὲν δέπας κίσσινον μελαίνας
> σταγόνος ἀμβρότας ἀφρῶι βρυάζον,
> εἴκοσιν δὲ μέτρ' ἐνέχευ', ἀνέμισγε
> δ' αἷμα Βακχίου νεορρύτοισιν
> δακρύοισι Νυμφᾶν

Timotheus, PMG 780

He poured in a single ivy-wood cup brimming with the foam of dark, ambrosial drops, and also poured twenty measures over it, and mixed the blood of the Bacchic one with the newly shed tears of the Nymphs.

Whether this is a description of Odysseus mixing wine for the Cyclops or of Maron's habitual practice,[32] it stays quite close to the Homeric text, here transposed to the 'dithyrambic' idiom of contemporary lyric,[33] and perhaps suggests an audience (or at least part of one) who do know the detail of *Odyssey* 9 well.

Of great interest also in the context of *Cyclops* is *Cyclops or Galateia* of Philoxenus of Cythera, although this composition certainly postdated *Cyclops*; this dithyramb, the narrative of which was set, like *Cyclops*, on Sicily, became particularly famous for its presentation of the Cyclops' love for the nymph Galateia.[34] To judge from a quasi-parody in Aristophanes'

---

wrote *Circe* dramas. It is instructive about our difficulties in this area that the one fragment of Ephippus' play (fr. 11), preserved in Athenaeus, concerns the ratio of water to be mixed with the wine; it is easy enough to guess that Circe is here entertaining Odysseus, but the fragment would be perfectly at home in a *Cyclops* comedy.

[31] For what follows cf. particularly Power 2013.

[32] Cf. Hordern: 2002: 110; κίσσινον would seem to point to the Cyclops (cf. 390–1n.), but that is not a completely decisive indication.

[33] Cf. Hunter 1983: 19–20, LeVen 2014: 160–78, esp. 176–8.

[34] On Philoxenus' dithyramb cf. 475n., 503–10n., Hunter 1999: 216–17, Power 2013: 250–6, LeVen 2014: 233–42.

Wealth 290–301, in one part of the dithyramb Philoxenus represented the Cyclops holding a modern kithara and imitating the sound of its strings by the exclamation θρεττανελο. The parody in *Wealth* suggests a 'bucolic' song, as the Cyclops serenaded his flocks; there is no good reason to think of any influence from the parodos of *Cyclops* in either Philoxenus or Aristophanes,[35] but these songs might, conversely, point us towards some of the lyric tradition which actually lies behind the Euripidean parodos. It is very likely that Philoxenus' dithyramb was an important influence on fourth-century comedies by Antiphanes, Nicochares and Alexis concerned with the love of the Cyclops for Galateia.

3 THE *ODYSSEY* AND THE *CYCLOPS*

Odysseus' narration of his encounter with the Cyclops near the beginning of the *apologoi* was in antiquity one of the most familiar episodes of the *Odyssey* and it has remained to this day one of the episodes, perhaps indeed *the* episode, which defines the epic and its hero 'of much μῆτις'. It was, however, also one of Odysseus' tales which, along with, for example, the *nekuia* of Book 11, earned Odysseus a reputation as an archetypal liar and boaster, an ἀλαζών.[36] In *On the Sublime* Longinus characterises parts of the *Odyssey* (and particularly Odysseus' narrative to the Phaeacians) as μυθώδη καὶ ἄπιστα, 'full of *muthos* and unbelievable' (*Subl.* 9.13), and *Cyclops* itself bears witness to this tradition when Odysseus describes the events in the cave almost identically as οὐ πιστά, μύθοις εἰκότ' οὐδ' ἔργοις βροτῶν (v. 376, cf. nn. ad loc.).[37] Homer himself seems to anticipate this negative reception for the *apologoi* when he has Alcinous declare to Odysseus that the Phaeacians do *not* consider him a liar and a deceiver, because of the manner of his telling:

σοὶ δ' ἔπι μὲν μορφὴ ἐπέων, ἔνι δὲ φρένες ἐσθλαί,
μῦθον δ' ὡς ὅτ' ἀοιδὸς ἐπισταμένως κατέλεξας

Homer, *Odyssey* 11.367–8

There is a shapeliness in your words and excellent sense, and you tell your story (*muthos*) with understanding, like a bard

---

[35] Cf., however, 475n. for a possible borrowing by Philoxenus from *Cyclops*.

[36] Cf. Montiglio 2011: 125. The 'facts' of the cannibalism and subsequent blinding of the Cyclops were, however, usually exempted from this criticism, as they are validated in the poem by the narrator and the gods.

[37] At *Tristia* 1.5. 49–50 Ovid, echoing *Od.* 1.4, claims that his sufferings will not be believed: *multaque credibili tulimus maiora ratamque,/ quamuis acciderint, non habitura fidem.*

For Alcinous, the way in which Odysseus tells his story guarantees the truth of the extraordinary adventures he relates. Here, however, was the very nub of the matter for the post-Homeric tradition: in Homer, Odysseus' tale is indeed just that, a tale told in the first person (all other potential witnesses are either dead or uncontactable), and it is Odysseus alone upon whom we must rely for much of the detail of 'what actually happened'. Euripides' *Cyclops* both bears witness to, and was very likely formative for, an exegetical tradition which persistently wondered whether Odysseus was telling the truth and how things might 'really' have happened, if we had reports which did not emanate from the hero himself. Most of our evidence for that tradition comes from much later in antiquity and the Byzantine period – the Greek literature of the Roman empire, the scholia on Homer and the Homeric commentaries of Eustathius – but Euripides' satyr-drama is itself in part a wry commentary on the events of *Odyssey* 9, and one whose spirit finds some of its closest parallels in that later tradition.

Despite Odysseus' apparent admission that in not following the advice of his comrades simply to rob the Cyclops' cave and retreat to the boat he had made a bad mistake (*Od.* 9.224–9), both ancient and modern audiences have found it easy enough to identify aspects of Odysseus' narration in *Odyssey* 9 which seem designed to cast Odysseus in a good light and/ or at least stretch credulity. Odysseus reports, for example, that when his comrades drew lots as to which of them would assist with the blinding, the four were chosen by lot 'whom I myself would have wanted to choose' and that he himself joined them as a fifth (vv. 331–5).[38] The scene clearly led to discussion in antiquity. The scholium on v. 331 reports criticism that it was inappropriate to entrust such a matter to the chances of the lot, a criticism apparently answered (the text of the scholium is lacunose) by the observation that no one would in fact willingly undertake such a task. Someone who did, however, do just that was Odysseus. The scholium on v. 335 draws our attention to how Odysseus puts himself 'in harm's way' 'without thinking (αὐτομάτως) and without hesitation'; here, then, some ancient readers did not fail to see the real 'hero' of this tale. In *Cyclops*, by contrast, the satyrs make much of the question as to which of them will handle the fiery torch together with Odysseus (vv. 483–6, 630–45); here there is no talk of the lot – it is just assumed that Odysseus will give the command. In the end, of course, no satyr comes anywhere near the 'serious action', but it is at least worth asking whether Euripides' employment

[38] Plato seems to have fun with this scene at *Rep.* 10.620c3–d2: Odysseus in the Underworld is allotted the very last choice of soul, finds that of a humble ἀπράγμων, and says that this is what he would have chosen, even if the lot had given him first choice.

of the motif implicitly recognises the improbability of Odysseus' Homeric narration that his comrades drew lots for this 'privilege' and that the lot produced just the result that Odysseus would have chosen anyway. In his discussion of the Homeric scene, Eustathius (below p.49) finds Odysseus' account an excellent one – the lot was the only possible method, as a choice imposed by Odysseus would have created resentment and division among the comrades – but he also notes the operation of luck (εὐτυχῶς ... εὐτυχεῖ), not just in how the lot turned out, but also in the fact that none of the comrades chosen by lot were included in the Cyclops' immediately following meal (*Hom.* 1631.16–21). Behind Eustathius' praise of the narrative we sense that other reactions to Odysseus' story were possible.

Eustathius sees the operation of chance elsewhere in the narrative also. It was extraordinarily lucky for the Greeks that the Cyclops decided to bring all the sheep, including the rams, into the cave on the fateful night, and Odysseus' explanation for this action, 'he either had some foreboding, or a god ordered him to do it' (9.339), is in fact an expression of Odysseus' wonderment at his own good fortune, for he was 'amazingly fortunate' in being able to use the sheep to escape (θαυμάσας τὸ τῆς τύχης ... εὐτύχισε ... θεσπέσιον, *Hom.* 1631.49–52). Here, too, we sense that other inferences from Odysseus' narrative were both possible and had in fact been drawn; Euripides, whose Cyclops inhabits a steading with rather different spatial arrangements, does not need to draw attention to this particular detail, though he does have fun with the Homeric motif of the sheep tied together (cf. below pp. 14–15). Less striking from our point of view may be Eustathius' subsequent observation that Odysseus was also lucky in that the drunken Cyclops collapsed on his back (v. 371), thus making him an easy target for the blinding, although drunks usually collapse face first (*Hom.* 1635.15–18).[39] Even if Eustathius is here to some extent the victim of his own reading of ancient texts, it is another example of an attitude to Odysseus' narration which looks to the probability of its crucial moments; the defenders of Odysseus' truthfulness know that they had their work cut out, and the operation of chance was an extremely useful explanatory resource.

If some aspects of the Homeric Odysseus' narration have stretched the credulity of many readers, ancient and modern, some other aspects of his narration might seem to have been refashioned in the light of what he claims actually happened, as some of the 'ethnographical' detail of the early part of the tale evidently is (e.g., 9.106–15, 187–92).[40] In vv. 213–15, for example, Odysseus says that he took with him a bag of supplies and a

---

[39] Cf. Arist. frr. 666, 671 Gigon, Ath. 1.34a–b, 10.447a–b.
[40] Cf., e.g., de Jong 2001: 232, 237.

large skin of Maron's powerful wine, 'as my manly heart suspected from the first (αὐτίκα) that it would encounter a man clothed in great might, a wild man, who knew neither justice nor ordinances'. Odysseus' alleged foresight here is in fact only explicable in the light of how events actually unfold: the wine is needed to make the Cyclops drunk. The scholia preserve traces of ancient readings which perhaps reflect some unease at this narrative fissure: food and wine are, so we are told, the natural things to take for dealings with 'shepherds and uncivilised men' (scholia on *Od.* 9.195–6). Scholia often preserve readings which seek to find familiar, 'naturalistic' explanations for epic behaviour, but here we may sense a reading of 'what really happened' which seeks to make allowance for Odysseus' self-glorification. It is not that there is a deep factual divide between the explanations of Odysseus and the scholia; rather, the explanations of the latter draw our attention to the self-congratulatory language in which Odysseus clothes his decisions.

In *Cyclops* Odysseus and his men come to the cave because they are looking for fresh water and supplies, and the wine they bring with them is intended as exchange goods (v. 139). The pattern may remind us of very many narratives of colonisation and the confrontation with 'other' societies,[41] but it is also close enough to the explanations of the scholia to make us wonder whether the difference from the *Odyssey* draws attention precisely to the exaggerated expression of Odysseus' alleged motivation. 'What might *really* have happened between Odysseus and the Cyclops?' is the question which *Cyclops* sets out to dramatise, and it can do this with a generous dose of irony because we are no longer at the mercy of Odysseus' own narration. Much of the fun of *Cyclops* is that all the characters, including even the Cyclops, know 'the Homeric script' and apparently allude to it with great freedom,[42] but just as important for the spirit of the play is the (alternative) reality which it opposes to the Homeric Odysseus' narration.

Nowhere is this seen so clearly as in the passage which formally comes closest to the Homeric first-person narration, namely Odysseus' 'messenger-speech' at *Cyclops* 382–436. In Homer, the Cyclops collapses stretched out after his first meal of Odysseus' companions, and Odysseus claims that his first impulse was the heroic one:

---

[41] The Greeks introduce wine to a land which did not know it before, just as Europeans brought alcohol (and unknown diseases) to the 'new worlds' of the Americas and Australia. There seems, however, little warrant for describing the Odysseus of *Cyclops* as 'the representative of imperialism' (von Reden 1995: 141).

[42] Cf. Kassel 1991: 191-8, Hunter 2009: 59–63, Laemmle 2013: 335–50, citing earlier bibliography.

τὸν μὲν ἐγὼ βούλευσα κατὰ μεγαλήτορα θυμὸν
ἆσσον ἰών, ξίφος ὀξὺ ἐρυσσάμενος παρὰ μηροῦ,   300
οὐτάμεναι πρὸς στῆθος, ὅθι φρένες ἧπαρ ἔχουσι,
χείρ᾽ ἐπιμασσάμενος· ἕτερος δέ με θυμὸς ἔρυκεν.
αὐτοῦ γάρ κε καὶ ἄμμες ἀπωλόμεθ᾽ αἰπὺν ὄλεθρον·
οὐ γάρ κεν δυνάμεσθα θυράων ὑψηλάων
χερσὶν ἀπώσασθαι λίθον ὄβριμον, ὃν προσέθηκεν.   305
ὣς τότε μὲν στενάχοντες ἐμείναμεν Ἠῶ δῖαν.

Homer, *Odyssey* 9.299–306

In my greatness of spirit I planned to draw my sharp sword from
my side, and coming close to him to stab him in the chest, feeling
with my hand for where the midriff conceals the liver. A second
thought however held me back, for we too would have perished
in certain death there and then; we would not have been able
to use our hands to heave back the huge stone from the lofty
entrance where he had placed it. Thus at that time we lamented
and waited for glorious dawn.

On the following day, after two more of his comrades have been devoured,
Odysseus hatches his plan (βουλή, 9.318) to make the Cyclops drunk and
to blind him. The scholia comment on how the narration foregrounds the
hero's μεγαλοψυχία and εὐτολμία (scholia on *Od.* 9.317, 345). In *Cyclops*,
however, things are somewhat different. In the first place, there is no
great door-stone to prevent Odysseus and his men escaping; Odysseus can
apparently come and go more or less as he pleases.[43] It is often thought
that this difference from Homer, together with the apparent awkwardness it necessitates ('Why don't the Greeks and the satyrs just escape?'),
was imposed upon Euripides by the practicalities of drama; there may be
some truth in this, but if so, Euripides has made a positive virtue out of
the necessity.[44] The absence of the door-stone allows several aspects of the
Homeric narration to be called into question; one result is that there is no

[43] The Homeric scholia are interested in how the door-stone operates in the narrative: the Cyclops does not normally close his cave during the day because he
knows that no other Cyclops is going to steal from him, and this is a sign of the
δικαιοσύνη of Cyclopean society (schol. on 9. 225). The scholia on v. 240 apparently reflect an objection to Homer's narrative: why does the Cyclops leave the cave
open when it is empty, but closes the door when he is inside (i.e. at night)? One
answer seems to reflect Odysseus' narrative – to keep the Greeks trapped – and
another the 'normal' Cyclopean situation – to keep the rams from coming in to
get at the ewes.

[44] The play in fact leaves unclear what has prevented the satyrs from escaping
before now; perhaps our familiarity with the motif of 'satyrs in servitude' (cf., e.g.,
Seaford 1984: 33–6, Laemmle 2013: 436) distracts us from asking this question.

equivalent in *Cyclops* for the heroic impulse of *Od.* 9.299–306, an impulse for which of course the Homeric Odysseus is the sole witness. In *Cyclops* Odysseus, as in Homer (*Od.* 9.345–6), does claim that he stood closer to the Cyclops than did his terrified companions, but his actions seem anything but 'heroic':

ἐγὼ δ' ὁ τλήμων δάκρυ' ἀπ' ὀφθαλμῶν χέων
ἐχριμπτόμην Κύκλωπι κἀδιακόνουν.

Euripides, *Cyclops* 405–6

There had not been a word of such demeaning 'service' in Homer, although it is true that the Euripidean monster has a much greater need of a *sous-chef* than does his Homeric counterpart, for whom cooking plays no part in his dining practices. In *Cyclops* the idea of getting the Cyclops drunk comes to Odysseus as τι θεῖον, 'a god-sent impulse' (411), whereas in Homer it is said to be the result of the hero's plotting for revenge (*Od.* 9.316). Odysseus' plan is still of course a cunning one (cf. 449, 476), but the drama gives far less prominence to the hero's μῆτις than does the hero himself in Homer, in part because the characters and the audience know (roughly) what is going to happen.

Perhaps no part of the Homeric Cyclops-episode was as familiar in antiquity as the escape from the cave clinging to the bellies of sheep which had been strapped together. This was very much Odysseus' planning:

ἥδε δέ μοι κατὰ θυμὸν ἀρίστη φαίνετο βουλή·
ἄρσενες ὄϊες ἦσαν ἐϋτρεφέες δασύμαλλοι,   425
καλοί τε μεγάλοι τε, ἰοδνεφὲς εἶρος ἔχοντες·
τῆις ἀκέων συνέεργον ἐϋστρεφέεσσι λύγοισι,
τῆις ἔπι Κύκλωψ εὗδε πέλωρ, ἀθεμίστια εἰδώς,
σύντρεις αἰνύμενος· ὁ μὲν ἐν μέσωι ἄνδρα φέρεσκε,
τὼ δ' ἑτέρω ἑκάτερθεν ἴτην σώοντες ἑταίρους.

Homer, *Odyssey* 9.424–30

To my spirit the best plan seemed as follows. There were some rams there, sturdy, thick-fleeced animals, handsome and large, with dark wool; in silence I began to tie them together with the plaited withies on which the monstrous and lawless Cyclops used to sleep. I bound them in threes, so that the one in the middle would carry a man, whereas the two on either side would keep my comrades safe.

No such subterfuge is necessary in *Cyclops*, but Euripides nevertheless finds a pointed re-use for this Homeric scene. When Silenos re-emerges from the cave with the sheep and cheese which he is going to exchange for Odysseus' wine, the sheep are 'bound together' just as in Homer. In case we miss the point, the Cyclops is made to remark on it when he appears:

ὁρῶ γέ τοι τούσδ' ἄρνας ἐξ ἄντρων ἐμῶν
στρεπταῖς λύγοισι σῶμα συμπεπλεγμένους

Euripides, *Cyclops* 224–5

There is humorous irony in the fact that it is the Cyclops who echoes the words of the scheming Odysseus in Homer, but the re-use of the motif again suggests that perhaps not everything 'really happened' as Odysseus reports in *Odyssey* 9 (cf. 225n.). The Cyclops' sheep – or, at least, his lambs – were indeed tied together, but just to make their transport to the ships easier, not as part of a fantastical escape-plot. Once again, there is a suggestion that Homer's Odysseus is somewhat cavalier in his handling of the truth.

Cyclops also exploits the apparent loose ends in the Homeric episode. In introducing the Cyclopes, the Homeric Odysseus had stressed their solitariness and lack of community:

τοῖσιν δ' οὔτ' ἀγοραὶ βουληφόροι οὔτε θέμιστες,
ἀλλ' οἵ γ' ὑψηλῶν ὀρέων ναίουσι κάρηνα
ἐν σπέεσι γλαφυροῖσι, θεμιστεύει δὲ ἕκαστος
παίδων ἠδ' ἀλόχων, οὐδ' ἀλλήλων ἀλέγουσι.

Homer, *Odyssey* 9.112–15

They have no gatherings which make plans nor ordinances, but they dwell on the peaks of lofty mountains in hollow caves; each man governs his children and wife, and they give no thought to each other.

It is at least somewhat surprising, then, that immediately after the blinding the Cyclops shouts loudly for his fellow-Cyclopes who instantly come to his aid in the belief that he is being robbed or attacked (*Od.* 9.399–406); even more surprising might be the fact that, when he answers their queries, the Cyclops addresses them with ὦ φίλοι (v. 408). Apart from the play with μῆτις, Odysseus' feigned name Οὖτις only makes sense in fact in anticipation precisely of such a scene in which the other Cyclopes come to Polyphemos' aid. In *Cyclops* Silenos paints a picture of Cyclops-society which is, in this respect, not very different from the Homeric Odysseus' account:

Οδ. τίνες δ' ἔχουσι γαῖαν; ἦ θηρῶν γένος;
Σι. Κύκλωπες, ἄντρ' ἔχοντες, οὐ στέγας δόμων.

Οδ. τίνος κλύοντες; ἢ δεδήμευται κράτος;
Σι. μονάδες·⁴⁵ ἀκούει δ᾽ οὐδὲν οὐδεὶς οὐδενός.

Euripides, *Cyclops* 117–20

It is not strictly inconsistent with this picture that the first thing that the
drunken Polyphemos wants to do is to go on a *kōmos* 'to his brother-
Cyclopes' (445–6) and that he wants to share the wine so as to be 'more
useful to his *philoi*' (533, cf. 532–3n.), but the Cyclops' surprisingly
communal instincts once again call attention to implausibilities in the
Homeric narrative. Nothing in fact is more implausible than the conversation which the Homeric Cyclops holds (through the closed cave-door)
with the colleagues who have come to help him:

τοὺς δ᾽ αὖτ᾽ ἐξ ἄντρου προσέφη κρατερὸς Πολύφημος·
"ὦ φίλοι, Οὖτίς με κτείνει δόλωι οὐδὲ βίηφιν."
οἱ δ᾽ ἀπαμειβόμενοι ἔπεα πτερόεντ᾽ ἀγόρευον·
"εἰ μὲν δὴ μή τίς σε βιάζεται οἶον ἐόντα,   410
νοῦσόν γ᾽ οὔ πως ἔστι Διὸς μεγάλου ἀλέασθαι,
ἀλλὰ σύ γ᾽ εὔχεο πατρὶ Ποσειδάωνι ἄνακτι."

Homer, *Odyssey* 9.407–12⁴⁶

Mighty Polyphemos addressed them from within the cave: 'My
friends, No-one is killing me through guile, not through force.'
They answered him with winged words: 'If then no one is doing
you violence and you are alone, there is no way to escape an illness
of great Zeus; you must pray to your father, Lord Poseidon'.

Euripides both avoids and points to this implausibility by putting his version of this exchange at the end of the play, where the chorus, who are
in on the scheme, take the role of the Homeric Cyclopes (vv. 672–5); the
only one who is fooled is the Cyclops himself. The Οὖτις-scheme is therefore much less important in *Cyclops* than in Homer – it is almost included
just because any version of the Cyclops-story would have to have it; this
is in keeping with the general tendency of the drama to downplay the
planning and stratagems which dominate the Homeric narrative.⁴⁷ Wine
is all you need.

---

⁴⁵ For μονάδες rather than the transmitted νομάδες cf. 120n.
⁴⁶ The scholia on 9.410 observe that the Cyclops does well (εἰκότως) not to answer his fellow-Cyclopes, as he would have had to point out that Οὖτις was in fact
the name of the man who had attacked him.
⁴⁷ Cf., e.g., Konstan 1990: 222.

Cyclops offers a recasting of the Homeric story which amounts in fact to an interpretation, a 'critical reading', of it. The complete absence of wine from Cyclops-society, a striking difference from *Odyssey* 9, means that its introduction and destructive effect upon the Cyclops become, more sharply, another variation on the very familiar narrative and dramatic theme of the introduction of Dionysos' rites to a land or city which did not practise them before.[48] The theme is most familiar to us from Euripides' *Bacchae*, but many versions survive; the narrative structure is already present in the *Homeric Hymn to Dionysos* and in Dionysos' earliest appearance in extant Greek literature, the story of Lycurgus' opposition to the god at *Iliad* 6.130–40.[49] As the *Homeric Hymn* makes clear, the theme is intimately linked to the persistent idea of Dionysos as a latecomer, a god who intrudes into a world where a divine pantheon is already established. If satyr-drama restores a proper place for the god in the dramatic performances over which he presides,[50] *Cyclops* also puts the god back into the Homeric story where his wine apparently had had pride of place, but even that had been associated with Apollo, rather than Dionysos (*Od.* 9.196–201, cf. 141–3n.). Some later readers of Homer found this fact puzzling (cf. scholia on *Od.* 9.198). Whether or not this puzzlement had already been expressed in Euripides' day we do not know, but the very small place given to Dionysos in the Homeric poems has been a subject of considerable interest to modern scholarship.[51] *Cyclops* shows that the god in whose honour the drama is performed played in fact a central (if unacknowledged) role in one of Homer's most famous stories.

The relationship between 'ordinary' sympotic pleasures of wine-drinking and the ecstatic, maenadic worship of the god is central to any consideration of the place of Dionysos in Greek culture; it occupies, for example, an important place in Euripides' *Bacchae* (e.g. vv. 375–85, 769–74). If the satyrs carry with them a (slightly faded) resonance of the Dionysiac *kōmos* and of ecstatic worship in the mountains (cf. 38–40, 68–72), it is the pleasures of the symposium which are the form of 'Dionysiac rite' which takes centre-stage in *Cyclops*.[52] The emphasis upon wine as itself 'the god' (521–7) and upon the need for the Cyclops to learn how to conduct the god's rites, i.e. the symposium, makes clear

---

[48] Cf. esp. Rossi 1971a, Hunter 2009: 65–7, below p. 45.

[49] It is striking that Zeus first punished Lycurgus with blindness (*Il.* 6.139), as the Cyclops is to be punished.

[50] Cf. below p. 26.

[51] The name of Dionysos makes just five appearances (in four passages) in Homer: *Il.* 6.132–7, 14.325, *Od.* 11.325, 24.74; for discussion cf. Privitera 1970, Burkert 1985: 162–3, Seaford 1993: 142–6, Davies 2000, Schlesier 2011a.

[52] For sympotic scenes in comedy cf. Bowie 1997.

that it is indeed the 'worship' of the god which is being introduced to
the land of the Cyclops. The sad presence of satyrs in a land without wine
and dancing (123–4) is a visual symbol of what this land needs; in *Cyclops*,
no less than in *Bacchae*, Dionysos will become ἐμφανὴς δαίμων (*Ba.* 22)
through the introduction of his rites. Just as Pentheus in *Bacchae* must be
educated in the god's rites and become a perverted imitation of a maenad as part of the god's plan to make him the vehicle through which the
god demonstrates his power, so the Cyclops is taught some of the practices of the symposium, but he is made by Odysseus and Silenos to deny
its true, communal essence by drinking alone;[53] that misuse is to prove
his undoing, as he becomes another in the long line of θεόμαχοι whose
opposition to the god brings disastrous results. His apparent knowledge
of Dionysiac cult and terminology at *Cyclops* 204–5 (and cf. 445–6), a
knowledge perhaps gleaned from the captive satyrs, might seem to sit
strangely with the ignorance of 521–9, but this brings the narrative pattern of the play into sharp relief: Odysseus and Silenos put his opposition
to Dionysos on display and he is punished in a way singularly appropriate
to that god. As for the satyrs, the familiar motif of their joyless servitude
and ultimate liberation[54] here reinforces this pattern of the introduction
of Dionysos: at the end of the play they escape to serve him as he wishes
to be served.

At the level of verbal detail, Euripides echoes Homeric terminology
and verses, and not just those of *Odyssey* 9, throughout *Cyclops*.[55] The
Homeric flavour of the language reinforces the sense that we are watching events which are very familiar to us; in particular, the Cyclops' grue-
some meals and his subsequent blinding call forth close reworkings of
the Homeric model.[56] Far from seeking to conceal the Homeric narrative which underlies his drama, Euripides revels in the knowledge
shared by characters and audience of that model.[57] When Silenos teases
Odysseus upon learning of his identity with an echo of the opening word
of the *Odyssey* (104n.), he plays in part the role of a 'typical' (Athenian)
spectator, who knows not only the *Odyssey* but also Odysseus' subsequent,
and less glorious, portrayals on the Attic stage. Silenos' perspective here

---

[53] Cf. Seaford 1981: 272–4, Voelke 2001: 201–2, Hunter 2006: 76.
[54] Cf. above 13 n. 44.
[55] The commentary records all significant instances; cf. also Wetzel 1965. One
notable feature of the 'Homeric texture' of *Cyclops* is the number of words found
in the play which occur only once in Homer (so-called 'Homeric *hapax legomena*'),
cf. Laemmle 2013: 69–70 (with earlier literature); here *Cyclops* anticipates another
way in which later Greek poetry engaged with Homer.
[56] Cf., e.g., 410, 456, 460–4 nn.
[57] For *Cyclops* as 'palimpsestic' drama cf., e.g., Napolitano 2005.

in some way resembles that of Dionysos during the tragic contest in Aristophanes' *Frogs*.[58] Silenos had already 'announced' his familiarity with the Homeric text in the prologue, when he follows his risibly fictitious account of his 'heroic' exploits in the Gigantomachy (5–9) with a tale of how the satyrs reached Sicily, which appropriates (and flagrantly predates) Odysseus' own account of his return in *Odyssey* 9 (cf. 18n.). Old Silenos is here the repository not just of dramatic memory (cf. 1–10n., 38–9n.) but also of its epic forebear.

The existence of a Homeric 'script' allows foreknowledge of dramatic events. Thus, for example, when the time for action arrives, Odysseus knows what will happen:

> Οδ.   ἄγε δή, Διονύσου παῖδες, εὐγενῆ τέκνα,
> ἔνδον μὲν ἀνήρ· τῶι δ' ὕπνωι παρειμένος
> τάχ' ἐξ ἀναιδοῦς φάρυγος ὠθήσει κρέα.

Euripides, *Cyclops* 590–2

He knows that this will happen because it happened in Homer (*Od.* 9.371–4). The most remarkable example of such foreknowledge is Odysseus' simile to describe his future blinding of the Cyclops (460–4) which offers a close rewriting, with significant variations,[59] of the famous ship-building simile with which the Homeric Odysseus recalls how he blinded the Cyclops in the past (*Od.* 9.383–90). Odysseus will follow the Homeric script, but if he can imagine this as future action, is there also a suggestion that in *Odyssey* 9 it was just as imaginary? The Homeric Odysseus is never more like a bard than in the two successive similes with which he describes the Cyclops' blinding (*Od.* 9.384–6, 391–3). Similes do not merely make actions more vivid and imaginable (through ἐνάργεια), they (perhaps paradoxically) carry conviction and have πιθανόν τι, as a Greek critic might say, or are an 'effect of the real', in more modern terms; if something can be elaborately described in such a way, it *must have* happened.[60] To use this mode to describe something which has not yet happened inverts the poetic mode; when there is also a famous model-simile lying behind it, the self-consciousness of this trope is very strongly marked. In *Cyclops* in fact the Cyclops is blinded offstage and we are none the wiser as to what has actually happened; perhaps the satyrs' Orphic spell (646–8) really did make the stake act on its own.

---

[58] Silenos resembles the Aristophanic Dionysos in other ways, too: deceitfulness (262–9), cowardice (cf. also Soph. *Ichn.* 205–9) and a certain buffoonishness also fit the comic god.

[59] Cf. 460–4n.   [60] Cf. further Hunter 2006: chapter 3.

If play with the Homeric script is one way in which temporal levels become blurred in the course of *Cyclops*, so also is the strong admixture of elements which clearly look to post-Homeric cultural phenomena. Odysseus borrows from a rhetoric born of the Persian Wars to seek to persuade the Cyclops that the Trojan War was worth fighting (cf. 290–1n.), and many of the audience will have realised the 'chronological impossibility' of a Cyclops trained to sing in the language and metre of Anacreon (cf. 484–518n.). Some of those elements involve what comes close to a kind of Euripidean self-parody, which exploits the audience's knowledge of themes of Euripidean drama. When the satyrs ask Odysseus whether the Greek leaders took it in turns to 'bang' Helen and abuse her as a traitor, the audience will recognise a satyric version of themes familiar in the mouth of Euripidean characters (cf. 181–6n.); Euripides may even exploit his comic persona as a misogynist (cf. 186–7n.). Such themes belong not just to a world 'after Homer' (irrespective of how the cyclic epic poems which told of the fall of Troy were viewed), but are also familiar as 'epic themes' treated in a 'contemporary' manner. The dramatisation of an entire episode from the Homeric poems – of which *Cyclops* is the only certain Euripidean example[61] – is a particularly marked way of exposing the relationship between epic and drama and between Homer and the tragic poets. We are made to see the analogy between the relationship of *Cyclops* to that of *Odyssey* 9 and of Euripides to Homer; Euripides invests both with a wry humour.

Nowhere is the mixing of temporal levels and the rewriting of Homer in a more contemporary mode clearer than in the depiction of the Cyclops. Euripides' Cyclops is not only something of a 'foodie' (cf., e.g., 218, 244–6, 403–4), with an interest in cooking appropriate to his Sicilian homeland, but his view of his position in the world, expressed in answer to Odysseus' pleas (316–47), draws, as has long been recognised, not just on contemporary ideas and stage-representations of tyrants, but also on arguments against convention most familiar to us from Plato's later representation of figures such as Callicles in the *Gorgias*.[62] The speech has also more than a little in common with the famous (and roughly contemporary) speech of Sisyphos, very probably from a satyr-play, about human progress and the invention of gods as a weapon of social control (*TrGF* 43 F 19); Sisyphos, however, was notoriously clever (cf. 104n.), whereas

---

[61] Cf., e.g., Radt 1982: 197–8; the extant *Rhesos* is here regarded as the fourth-century work of an unknown dramatist. It is very unfortunate that we are in no position to compare Euripides' adaptation of the Cyclops-story with, say, one of the *Circe*-dramas (above p. 7) or the *Proteus* of Aeschylus, the satyr-play of the *Oresteia*, if indeed that play dealt with the Homeric version of the return of Menelaos, cf. Griffith 2015: 57–70.

[62] Cf. 338–9n., Konstan 1990: 215, Hunter 2009: 67–71.

the Homeric Cyclops, at least, was no intellectual. In broad terms, the Euripidean speech may be seen as a Cyclopean version, typically self-centred in its orientation, of fifth-century accounts of the development of human civilisation and of cultural progress, such as those of Prometheus in the Aeschylean *Prometheus Bound* (vv. 442–71) and of Theseus in Euripides, *Supplices* 195–218; in the Cyclops' own eye, there is no development and no divine assistance, merely a perpetual order of things in which he has all he will ever need. The Cyclops preaches self-sufficiency based on wealth (315–17) and the exploitation of inevitable, natural processes, such as the fact that 'grass grows' (332–3); this self-sufficiency permits scorn for the gods and for human νόμοι (338–9) as unnecessary complications and restraints upon the indulgence of desires by 'the strongest'. This speech not only allows the Cyclops to mouth some very modern sentiments, but also wryly draws out how close those sentiments can be made to seem to Homer's picture of the monster. In Homer, the Cyclops is governed (so he claims) solely by his bodily desires and his θυμός (*Od.* 9.278), and it is this which allows him to ignore Zeus and the conventional protection which the god is said to offer to suppliants. By 'translating' this Homeric picture into a more modern and sophisticated idiom, Euripides anticipates later allegorical readings of the Cyclops-episode as a clash between reason and the appetites and/or passions;[63] whether or not *Cyclops* also reflects late fifth-century discussion and interpretation of the Homeric Cyclops-episode our evidence does not allow us to say, but it hardly seems unlikely.

4 *CYCLOPS* AND SATYR-PLAY

Cyclops is the only satyr-play which survives in full; papyri have, however, yielded significant fragments of satyr-dramas of Aeschylus (*Diktyoulkoi, Theōroi*) and Sophocles (*Inachos* and, above all, *Ichneutai*), and we are able to grasp something of the range and possibilities of the genre, even if its detailed history inevitably remains beyond our grasp.

Part at least of ancient tradition regarded Aeschylus as the finest composer of satyr-dramas, along with the alleged 'first inventor' of the genre, Pratinas of Phleious (near Corinth) and his son Aristias (cf. Paus. 2.13.6 = Aesch. T 125b); these names push the alleged heyday of satyr-drama back to the very beginning of the fifth or even to the late sixth century: whatever the date of *Cyclops* (below pp. 39–48), satyr-drama had a very

---

[63] Cf., e.g., Hunter 2009: 53-4, citing 'Heraclitus', *Hom. Probl.* 70 and Eustathius *Hom.* 1622.56-64.

long history (and presumably evolution) before this play was produced. When, sometime near the middle of the fifth century, dramatic contests were introduced at the Lenaian festival in Athens (held in mid-winter), there was no room found for satyr-drama; this may be a sign that it was already then recognised as a survival from an earlier set of circumstances. However that may be, the origin of the form presumably lay in the second half of the sixth century, but beyond that all is very largely speculation. No ancient text has given rise to more of that speculation in this context than Aristotle's laconic statements about the early history of tragedy:

> Aeschylus innovated by raising the number of actors from one to two, reduced the choral parts and made speech play the leading role. Three actors and scene-painting came with Sophocles. A further factor was grandeur (μέγεθος): after a period of slight plots and laughable diction, owing to a development from a satyric ethos (διὰ τὸ ἐκ σατυρικοῦ μεταβαλεῖν), it was at a late stage that tragedy acquired dignity, and its metre became the iambic trimeter instead of the trochaic tetrameter. To begin with they used the tetrameter because the poetry was satyric and more associated with dancing (διὰ τὸ σατυρικὴν καὶ ὀρχηστικωτέραν εἶναι τὴν ποίησιν), but when spoken dialogue was introduced, tragedy's own nature discovered the appropriate metre.
>
> Aristotle, *Poetics* 1449a16–24 (trans. S. Halliwell, adapted)

Although there is no other mention of satyr-drama in the *Poetics*, Aristotle's two uses of σατυρικός are most naturally taken to mean 'in the manner of satyr-play', which Aristotle perhaps connected with the dithyrambic performances to which he traced the origin of tragedy (1449a10). It is significant that Aristotle states that 'something satyric' was present at the earliest days of tragedy and then was gradually left behind, for ancient theorising (in the wake of Aristotle) about the history of the dramatic genres seems to have seen in satyr-drama a way of keeping 'something about Dionysos' in the tragic festivals:

> Originally when writing in honour of Dionysos they competed with pieces which were called satyric (σατυρικά). Later they changed to the writing of tragedies and gradually turned to plots and stories (μῦθοι καὶ ἱστορίαι) and no longer made mention of Dionysos. This is the origin of the saying 'Nothing to do with Dionysos'. Chamaileon writes similarly in his work *On Thespis*.
>
> *Suda* o 806 = Chamaileon fr. 38 W² (trans. Pickard-Cambridge, adapted)[64]

---

[64] Cf. Pickard-Cambridge 1962: 124–6.

'Nothing to do with Dionysos'. When, the choruses being accustomed from the beginning to sing the dithyramb to Dionysos, later the poets abandoned this custom and began to write *Ajaxes* and *Centaurs*. Therefore the spectators said in mockery, 'Nothing to do with Dionysos'. For this reason they decided later to introduce satyr-plays (οἱ σάτυροι) as a prelude (προεισάγειν),[65] in order that they might not seem to be forgetting the god.

Zenobius 5.40 (trans. Pickard-Cambridge)

Whatever credit one might wish to give Chamaileon, a pupil of Aristotle, and the other sources which lie behind these notices about early dithyramb and drama, at least one important 'fact' about satyr-drama emerges from them. Satyrs of the classical period are Dionysiac creatures – they appear in the god's retinue, the Dionysiac *thiasos* (cf. *Cycl.* 39–40), throughout classical literature and art – and as long as the satyric chorus performs at the City Dionysia, then the god will always have a very explicit place in performed drama, and one which was both fixed in its regularity and formed the culmination of each tragic offering.[66] It is, however, a precarious place, one that draws attention both to the god and to the god's absence, and that paradox goes, as we shall see, to the heart of satyr-play.[67]

The defining generic characteristic of satyr-play is the chorus of eponymous satyrs, οἱ σάτυροι,[68] the equine but largely anthropomorphic creatures, at home in the wilds of nature and ever in pursuit of wine and nymphs. This dramatic chorus presumably grew out of earlier

---

[65] This may refer to the later practice, attested for the Great Dionysia at least for 342/1, of producing a single satyr-play 'out of competition' before the tragedies (cf. below p. 24), but the matter is disputed, cf., e.g., Sansone 2015: 10–11.

[66] Cf., e.g., Easterling 1997b: 38; for satyr-drama in the fourth place cf. below n. 70.

[67] What follows derives in part from Laemmle 2019a. When Eur.'s son presented *Iphigeneia at Aulis, Alkmaion* and *Bacchae* at the City Dionysia after his father's death (cf. above p. 1), there was no satyr-play; very many reasons could be offered for this, but it is at least worth noting that after a performance of *Bacchae* there was no need to seek to re-introduce Dionysos to his own festival through satyr-play, cf. Laemmle 2013: 350. For the similarities of *Bacchae* and *Cyclops* cf. below p. 46.

[68] οἱ σάτυροι is also the best-attested name for the genre: the title of the only known ancient monograph on satyr-play, by Chamaileon, was Περὶ σατύρων (fr. 37 W2). Cf. further Ar. *Thesm.* 157, Diog. Laert. 2.133, 140, 9.110, Laemmle 2013: 20 n. 3. It is generally accepted that, by the classical period at least, there was no clear distinction between σάτυροι and σιληνοί; the former word seems to derive originally from the Doric Peloponnese, the latter from Attica. For Silenos, the 'father' of the satyrs, see below p. 33. Satyrs do sometimes seem to have formed the chorus of comedy, most famously for us in Cratinus' *Dionysalexandros*, which must have allowed for much 'cross-generic play', cf. Bakola 2010: 82–117, Storey 2005, Laemmle 2013: 44–6.

semi-dramatic performances in which men dressed as satyrs, but whatever
the origins of the form, it seems that, with some exceptions,[69] throughout
the fifth century at least, each of the three tragedians who were granted
a chorus competed at the Great Dionysia with three tragedies and a (relatively short) satyr-drama.[70] Whereas for Aeschylus the production of
tetralogies on the same story (e.g. the *Oresteia*) was very common, though
not by any means a fixed rule, this does not seem to have been the case
for Sophocles and Euripides, just as they did not regularly present three
tragedies from the same myth. We may suspect that satyr-plays sometimes
picked up themes and dramatic patterns, even perhaps individual words,
from the tragedies with which they were presented, even when the plots
had nothing to do with each other,[71] but our evidence is simply not sufficient to allow any clear picture to emerge. What is clear, however, is that
the permanent identity of the chorus, presenting itself as both a single
entity and a collective,[72] marks a crucial difference of satyr-play from both
tragedy and comedy; in the other two dramatic genres the chorus represents groups relevant to the story being performed: elders of Argos, the
Danaids, captive Trojan women, birds, clouds, Odysseus' comrades,[73]
women celebrating the Thesmophoria, etc. The contrasting permanent identity of the satyric chorus marks the shared ground between all

---

[69] Cf. above pp. 2–3 on the *Alcestis*.

[70] The hard evidence that the satyr-play was always performed in fourth position
is in fact very thin, and Sansone 2015 argues for a radical revision of the received
wisdom; there are, however, no compelling reasons (beyond normal caution) to
adopt Sansone's scepticism. The fact that, in the connected tetralogies of which
we know, the satyr-play often dealt with events which were chronologically prior
to those of the tragedies is certainly open to other explanations, cf. Coo 2019.
Although the case cannot carry probative weight, the fact that Alcibiades' 'satyric
and silenic drama' in Pl. *Symp.* (222b3–4) comes last of the speeches and offers a
very different tone from the speeches which have preceded carries at least a very
powerful suggestive force; with Alcibiades, Dionysos, who had earlier been margin-
alised from the symposium over which he is supposed to reign (176b1–e10), returns with unmissable force, just as satyr-drama seems to have restored the god to
his rightful place after tragedies supposedly performed in his honour, but which
were, if not 'nothing to do with Dionysos', at least not obviously dramatisations of
Dionysiac myth. So, too, Dionysos only explicitly enters Xenophon's *Symposium*
at the very end (with the Ariadne-mime). Austin and Olson 2004: lxiv suggest
that the final scene of escape from the Scythian archer in Ar. *Thesm.* 'could ... be
read as the satyr play that rounds out the set of three explicit tragic parodies that
precede it', cf. below pp. 40–1.

[71] Cf. below pp. 43–4 on possible evocations of the *Hypsipyle* in the opening of
Cycl.

[72] Cf. 187n. One marker of this doubleness is the rapid alternation of singular
and plural verbs with reference to the chorus, cf. 212–13, 427–8, 465, 643–4.

[73] Cf. above pp. 5–7 on Cratinus' *Odysseis*.

satyr-plays, which constitute a series to which every tragedian contributes: every single satyr-play offers a new adventure of the Dionysiac *thiasos* in a chain which never seems to end. Just as Silenos at the beginning of *Cyclops* links and contrasts the present plight of the satyrs with their past adventures and service to the god, so at the very end the chorus escape to continue that service, i.e. to reappear as the satyr-chorus in the next satyr-play.

In *Cyclops* the chorus are cut off both from their god and his wine, at least until Odysseus arrives; their servitude to the Cyclops forbids normal Dionysiac activity. This was in fact a standard scenario of satyr-play, which never quite offers the Dionysiac revelry and merriment associated with the god's *thiasos*. The satyrs of the Athenian stage are adventurous wayfarers, hapless castaways, captives, or disloyal deserters; they are separated from (or even abandon) their god, but they are never quite without him. Dionysos' presence looms large in the plots of satyr-play, as both promise and threat, but it is never fully realised. That the god for whom the satyrs long is both present and absent seems to have been a recurrent, almost a defining, idea of the genre. As such, satyr-play seems to capture and indeed dramatise the ambivalence about the god's presence which accounts of the genre's early history seem to be designed to explain (cf. above pp. 22–3). The story of Odysseus and the Cyclops fits this model perfectly: already in Homer, wine was central to the story of *Odyssey* 9, but Dionysos himself was nowhere to be seen.[74]

The satyrs of Greek myth and iconography sing and dance in the mountains and the countryside, surrounded by wild animals and plants; they drink wine, wear fawnskins and are crowned with ivy; in their hands, they carry the *thyrsos* or musical instruments; they chase nymphs, dance with them, and praise their god, Dionysos. In satyr-play, as far as we can tell, they do not. Their 'normal condition', this happy rustic, Dionysiac freedom, is constantly evoked in the plays, but it is invariably addressed as a problem. What satyrs normally do (or what they should be doing) is in satyr-play impossible, endangered, or forbidden; they still perform vigorous, mimetic dances (cf. 37n.), rush around individually or in small groups suggestive of 'freedom', and can never keep quiet or still, but even this nervous energy is always short-lived and repressed – it is a pale shadow of 'the real thing' and seen to be that. Instead of their accustomed pursuits, the satyrs of the Attic stage are standardly compelled to adopt 'new roles', often under the sway of a master other than Dionysos, and in mythological settings to which satyrs do not traditionally belong: the satyrs may become athletes, bridegrooms, labourers of various kinds (particularly

[74] Cf. above p. 17.

painful for these workshy creatures), or fishermen,[75] but they are rarely successful in these new activities. The shepherd-satyrs of *Cyclops* conform to this standard pattern very well.

This repeated plot of satyr-drama must be seen within the context of a structural pattern that underlies the most prominent Dionysiac myths. From the myth of Lycurgus, which is present already in the *Iliad* (6.130–40), to the establishment of the god's cult in Thebes against the resistance of Pentheus dramatised in Euripides' *Bacchae*, Dionysiac mythology is dominated by 'myths of resistance': the god is met with resistance, which he eventually overcomes by establishing his cult and demonstrating that he is a full part of a system that has at first tried to deny and exclude him. Here, too, as we have already noted,[76] *Cyclops* fits a typical Dionysiac, as well as satyric, pattern. The alienation from Dionysos that animates the plots of satyr-drama adopts and enacts this basic trope of Dionysiac mythology, while at the same time satyr-drama playfully imitates and re-enacts the tendency written in the history of tragedy to exclude or marginalise the god; in the long run, however, the god is not to be denied, and every satyr-drama reinstates him both to the tetralogy (connected or unconnected) of which it is a part and to the dramatic festival in his honour in a wider sense.[77]

Satyr-play very probably reinstated the god to his festival in another quite visible manner.[78] Although it cannot be proved, it seems overwhelmingly likely that the same Athenian citizens who had performed as the choruses of the preceding tragedies took the role of the satyr-chorus; the human choreuts thus physically embodied the return of the god to the dramas in his honour. Later sources report that Sophocles first increased the number of the tragic chorus from 12 to 15 (Soph. T1.4, T2), and it is a reasonable inference from this that the chorus of *Cyclops* consisted of 15 members, one of whom acted as κορυφαῖος and spoke the trimeters assigned to the chorus. So too, it is often speculated that Sophocles' introduction of the third actor (cf. Arist. *Poetics* 1449a18, cited above) allowed Silenos, the father of the satyrs and presumably originally their leader and spokes-satyr, to distance himself from the chorus and essentially to become a third actor in satyr-drama, to match the actors now available to tragedy. In *Cyclops* there is no doubt that he plays such a role, both connected to, but set apart from, the chorus; he is on stage before they are,

---

[75] For a fuller list cf. Laemmle 2013: 207–9, and for the relevant iconography Lissarrague 2013: 210–15, Heinemann 2016: 325–425.

[76] Cf. above p. 17.   [77] Cf. Laemmle 2007 and 2013: chapter 4.

[78] Throughout this book we assume that *Cycl.* was first performed at the Athenian Great Dionysia; this is, however, an unprovable assumption. Pat Easterling has rightly suggested that the possibility of a (? first) performance in Sicily cannot be ruled out, cf. Easterling 1994: 79–80.

exchanges sharp words with the κορυφαῖος (268–72), and disappears from the play (589) long before they do. Here too, then, an actor who had played a 'non-Dionysiac' role in the tragedies which preceded reappeared in the closing satyr-drama in very obvious Dionysiac guise.

One piece of evidence for these (as for very many satyric) questions is particularly intriguing, namely the famous 'Pronomos Vase' (Plate 1), an Attic red-figure *kratēr* of *c.* 400 which was discovered in southern Italy and is preserved in the National Archaeological Museum in Naples;[79] the vase takes its name from the celebrated Theban aulos-player Pronomos who is shown on it. The Pronomos Vase depicts (on the so-called A-side) figures involved in a satyr play production; much remains disputed, but it is all but certain that these figures include 10 choreuts and a κορυφαῖος,[80] as well as Silenos, who is very clearly distinguished from the choreuts by position and dress.[81] This vase has been used to argue that at the end of the century the satyr-chorus numbered 12 (including Silenos); nevertheless on the vase at least, Silenos is separated from the choreuts, and therefore we must perhaps acknowledge that the vase cannot shed any precise light on the size of the satyr-chorus. There is, however, a scene of Dionysiac celebration in the wild on the so-called B-side of the vase; this shows four naked satyrs – not humans dressed as satyrs for a theatrical performance, but 'real' satyrs, such as are so common in vase-painting. Much has been written about the links between the two sides, but it is very tempting to take the four 'natural' satyrs as making the number of the depicted satyr-chorus up to 15; the Dionysiac scene in the wild will be a visualised satyric 'choral projection':[82] the depicted sides of Dionysiac energy, of music, dance, and erotics will be, as it were, what is always missing for the chorus of satyr-drama. This is what the satyrs of the chorus long to be doing, but never are. The 'Pronomos Vase' cannot prove that the satyr-chorus at the end of the fifth century consisted of 12 members, but it may well be thought to strengthen the case for 15 in very suggestive ways.

The 'Pronomos Vase' is also our most important piece of evidence for the costume of satyr-drama.[83] The choreuts on the vase, all apparently beardless young men, carry (or in one case wear) satyr-masks: the dark

[79] On the 'Pronomos Vase' see above all Taplin and Wyles 2010; there is a helpful brief account in Pickard-Cambridge 1968: 186–7, with Fig. 49.

[80] The *koryphaios* wears a short *chitōn* and not shorts like the other choreuts (cf. further below pp. 29–30), but he otherwise shares their physical attributes and is, like they, holding a satyr mask in his hand.

[81] Cf. below p. 30.

[82] For a full discussion cf. Laemmle 2019, picking up a suggestion of Seidensticker 2010: 213 n.; cf. also 679–80n. For choral self-consciousness in satyr-drama more generally cf. also Easterling 1997b: 42–3.

[83] Full bibliography in KPS 53–5 and Laemmle 2013: 57–61.

Plate 1a Attic red-figure volute-*kratēr*, c. 400 BC, the 'Pronomos Vase', 'A-side'. National Archaeological Museum of Naples H 3240

hair of the masks is pushed back, the hairline recedes, the ears are small and pointed, the snub nose is clearly marked in comparison with the noses of the choreuts themselves, as is the thick beard which adorns the mask. With two exceptions, the choreuts are portrayed as naked but for a pair of shorts,[84] which are covered with fur, presumably representing the shaggy hair of an animal (perhaps a goat),[85] and to which are attached a relatively short horse's tail and a (? leather) representation of human male genitalia of ordinary size with the penis erect; the contrast with the grotesque *phalloi* of Old Comedy is very clear.[86] One choreut wears smooth pants, which are decorated with geometric designs, as well as the tail and genitalia; other vase-paintings suggest that this was the earlier style which was gradually replaced by the shaggy pants in the course

[84] This is conventionally referred to as a περίζωμα on the basis of Dion. Hal. *AR* 7.72.10, a description of a Roman imitation of a Greek πομπή, where choruses of σατυρισταί danced the *sikin(n)is* (cf. 37n.) and wore 'περιζώματα and goatskins'; περίζωμα is the standard noun for any kind of shorts or apron worn around the waist, but there does not seem to be any other text in which it is used for the satyrs' pants. This passage of Dion. Hal. is also the only occurrence of the term σατυρισταί, 'men acting as satyrs'.

[85] On the associations of stage-satyrs with goats, despite their equine features, cf. 41–62n., Laemmle 2013: 440.

[86] In some other representations in vase-painting, men costumed as satyrs have larger and more conspicuous genitalia than do the choreuts on the 'Pronomos Vase'; different painters presumably gave different levels of attention to the matter. For a painting of an (otherwise naked) female wearing the satyric *perizōma* cf. Lissarrague 2013: 31 Fig. 8.

Plate 1b. 'Pronomos Vase', 'B-side'

of the fifth century. The other apparent exception is another beardless
figure carrying a satyr-mask, but otherwise dressed in a richly decorated
robe which reaches to his knees and a mantle thrown over his shoulder. It is very probable that he is to be identified as the κορυφαῖος. It
seems likely that the chorus of *Cyclops* looked very like the choreuts of
the 'Pronomos Vase', but for the fact that they wore goatskin cloaks on
top (cf. 8on.).

   An actor playing Silenos, the father of the satyrs, is also depicted on
the 'Pronomos Vase'. Unlike the choreuts, he is bearded and seems
to be older than the men dressed as satyrs. He carries a mask which is
clearly that of an old man, with straggly white beard and wrinkled forehead (cf. 227n.). He wears a tight-fitting, one-piece outfit which reaches
to his wrists and ankles and is covered all over with tufts of white, and he
carries a staff and a leopard-skin thrown over his shoulder;[87] the strange
tufted costume (now conventionally called a μαλλωτὸς χιτών)[88] is found in
other representations of *silēnoi* from a relatively early date. The Silenos of
Cyclops may well have looked like this; it is unclear whether he changed his
mask to indicate the alleged beating by Odysseus at vv. 226–30. As for the

----

[87] Silenos' costume seems also to be equipped with a phallos of 'lifelike' size, but –
in contrast with those of the satyr-choreuts – it is not erect, cf. 2n. On some other
representations of *silēnoi* wearing a tufted costume (cf. next n.) they are grossly
erect.
   [88] The term occurs only at Dion. Hal. *AR* 7.72.10, cf. above n. 84, Laemmle 2013:
61 n.39. In the procession described by Dion. Hal. this was worn by men dressed
as Silenoi, rather than as satyrs, and Dion. Hal. tells us that another name for this
outfit was χορταῖος, cf. Hesych. χ 649-51, Pollux 4.118.

other actors in *Cyclops*, vase-paintings suggest that the non-satyric characters of satyr-drama were costumed in the grand, highly decorated manner which was normal for tragic characters. This may well have been true for Odysseus, though the fact that he and his crew have been at sea for a long time and that he asks the Cyclops for πέπλοι (301) might suggest that he and his crew were in fact costumed rather less grandly than many tragic characters;[89] given that elsewhere in *Cyclops* Euripides seems to play with familiar themes of his tragedies, some of which had been mocked in comedy, it is tempting to think that he did not miss the chance in *Cyclops* to bring on an Odysseus whose costume (or lack of it) betrayed the long sea voyages he had endured and which gestured towards Euripides' comic reputation for characters in rags. As for the Cyclops, we must admit that we have no idea how he was costumed,[90] nor how his single eye was precisely represented on a mask; the effects of the blinding must have been represented on his mask from 663 until the end of the play, as presumably also with Oedipus in Sophocles, *Oedipus Tyrannus* and Polymestor in *Hecuba*, but the details can only be guessed.

Finally, one choreut on the 'Pronomos Vase' has put on his mask and is dancing (or practising dance-steps) (Plate 1a); the exaggerated movements of his left arm and leg and the fact that his right foot breaks the border of the depiction are all suggestive of the energy of choral satyric dancing (cf. 37n.); so, too, the fact that this one choreut is dancing while his colleagues chat and relax is indicative of the looseness and freedom of the satyric, as opposed to the tragic, chorus, in which choreuts often go their own way and there is no strict unity as in tragedy. What is also important, however, is that the dance-steps of the choreut are in part echoed by and in part quite distinct in their formality from the movements of the 'real' satyrs pursuing women on the other part of the vase, just as the pants worn by the choreuts proclaim them to be part of a theatrical performance, whereas the 'real' satyrs on the vase are naked – their erect penises are certainly their own. Satyr-drama is a very self-conscious and stylised theatrical form: the satyrs of the chorus are both like and unlike the satyrs of the mythic and iconographic *imaginaire*.

'What then was satyr play for?'[91] Pat Easterling's question has been answered in an extraordinary variety of ways,[92] in part because it is not

[89] On the Lucanian *kratēr* (below pp. 46–7) Odysseus is distinguished from his naked crew by a cloak around the neck and one arm, but this can tell us nothing about Euripides' production.
[90] On the apparent reference to a πέπλος in 327 cf. n. ad loc.
[91] Easterling 1997b: 38.
[92] For a summary of those answers cf. Laemmle 2013: 93–9.

just a historical question about the origins of the form, but also a question about what kept that form going as a central part of the Great Dionysia for (as far as we can tell) well over a century.[93] Particular attention has recently been paid both to the central importance of the satyr-play in ensuring a proper place for Dionysos at a dramatic festival in his honour (cf. above pp. 22–3), and also to how the Athenian mass (male) audience related to the satyrs they saw on stage year in and year out. In keeping with the dominant trends of dramatic criticism of the last few decades, answers have tended to concern how drama consolidated and represented Athenian identity and the relation between what was seen on the stage and Athenian social ideology.

François Lissarrague influentially argued that satyr-drama produced a distorted representation of Athenian cultural norms and behaviours (he used the image of a 'fun-house mirror'); the satyrs are 'antitypes of the Athenian male citizenry' and satyr-drama presents the spectators with a 'negative anthropology', which (so we are to infer) helps to define Athenian culture by marking out the boundaries beyond which only satyrs may go.[94] For Mark Griffith, satyr-drama co-operates with tragedy in offering the spectators a set of 'split and shifting subject positions', which amount to 'two kinds of male fantasy, one high, the other low' which 'create and reinforce' Athenian identity.[95] Alongside such approaches, many scholars have seen in satyr-drama a kind of release for the spectators from the psychological pressures and anxieties of watching tragedy. One version of this which has proved influential is Edith Hall's view that 'satyr play functioned to affirm a group identity founded in homosocial laughter and the libidinal awareness of its male, citizen audience';[96] the tragedies which preceded satyr-plays had encouraged the audience to 'identify with female characters and react with emotions often socially constructed as "feminine"', and the relentlessly male gender focus of satyr-play, a focus which (*inter alia*) espoused a particular brand of humour targeted at women and which encouraged sexual aggression, allowed the male citizens to leave the theatre once again comfortable with their own maleness. It has often been pointed out, however, that the satyrs of satyr-play seem singularly unsuccessful in their pursuit of sex and other satisfactions, and so are not obviously 'role models' for men who need to shed dangerous 'feminising' emotions.[97] All the more so, in fact, as the satyrs variously display character traits, perform activities

[93] Cf. below p. 34.
[94] Lissarrague 1990: 234–6.
[95] Griffith 2015: 90–2 (originally published in 2005).
[96] Hall 2006: 10; the following quotation comes from p. 143
[97] Cf., e.g., Griffith 2015: 94–5.

or assume roles which are marked, in more or less emphatic terms, as feminine.[98] In *Cyclops*, already in the very first lines of his prologue, Silenos reminisces about his role as the *paidotrophos* of young Dionysos (cf. 3–4n.) and he is, not long afterwards, recalling how he cradled the baby Maron in his arms (cf. 141–3n.);[99] his professed duty of keeping the master's cave clean is reminiscent of Electra's resolve to welcome her husband into a tidy home in the *Electra* (cf. 35n.). At the end of the prologue, Silenos comments on the satyrs' entry on the stage in words suggesting they are dancing with a female swagger in their hips (cf. 40n. on σαυλούμενοι); a feminised 'waggling of the buttocks' may in fact have been a characteristic movement of the *sikin(n)is*, the satyr-play dance *par excellence* (cf. 36–8n.).[100] Gender fluidity is another manifestation of the interstitial world which the satyrs inhabit.

There are, of course, also many examples in satyr-play of the satyrs and Silenos displaying virile if not hyper-virile energies, harassing women or fantasising about them: σοὶ μὲν γαμεῖσθαι μόρσιμον, γαμεῖν δ᾽ ἐμοί says someone in Aeschylus' *Amymone* fr. 13, no doubt Silenos or a satyr (if not the entire chorus) addressing Amymone; in Sophocles' *Ichneutai*, Silenos brags about his sexual exploits ('lying in caves with nymphs', 155), in Achaios' *Moirai* it is presumably again Silenos, who exclaims βαβαὶ βαβαί, βήσομαι γυναῖκας (*TrGF* 20 F 28),[101] and not even Danae's threat that she will hang herself should she be handed over to 'such beasts' (Aeschylus, *Diktyoulkoi* fr. 47.775) stops the satyrs from preparing their collective wedding with her. It is hardly to be doubted that females were routinely exposed to unwanted sexual advances in satyr-play, whether from the satyrs or from other males (under the satyrs' admiring eyes).[102] In *Cyclops*, too, we witness both Silenos (169–71) and the satyrs (179–81) fantasis-

---

[98] Cf., in particular, Voelke 2001: chapter 3.3 on the satyrs' intermediary status 'entre masculin et féminin'. Fragments in the tragic corpus have been denied to satyr-drama simply because they are attributed to plays with feminine plural titles (e.g., Aesch. *Phorkides*, Aristias *Keres*, Achaios *Moirai*); it is, however, likely that at least some of these plays were indeed satyr-plays and featured the chorus in feminine roles, cf. Laemmle 2013: 96–7 n. 21.

[99] In Aesch. *Diktyoulkoi* fr. 47a, Silenos, noting that Perseus is looking at him 'as at a venerable nanny', μαῖαν ὡς γερασμίαν, 770, invites the baby into his 'child-rearing hands' (… παιδοτρόφους ἐμάς / … χέρας, 807), before then envisaging himself as father (811) or 'papa' (πάπας, 812) for the boy.

[100] Cf. Bing 2014: 44.

[101] Silenos is presumably also the νυμφόβας of Achaios, *TrGF* 20 F 52.

[102] E.g. Cyllene in Soph. *Ichn.* 366–8, Xenodike in Eur. *Syleus* (cf. fr. 694 with KPS 472); Soph. *Inachos* fr. 269a has someone report in shock how a stranger 'put his arm around the girl' who subsequently metamorphosed into a cow. In Soph. *Achilleos Erastai* fr. 153 it is perhaps Achilles disguised as a girl who is the object of the satyrs' lust, cf. 583–4n.

ing about sex, but in contrast to what we know of other satyr-plays, there are no women in the *Cyclops*. Apart from mother sheep, the world of the Cyclops is monochromatically male. For the satyrs and Silenos, sex is a distant memory (cf. 38–40, 68–72) and it is unclear whether the Cyclops has ever even met a female: in contrast to the *Odyssey* (9.115), there is no mention of wives or children, just of 'brother-Cyclopes' (445–6, 531). So too, the silence of any reference to the satyrs' mother(s) is striking – not just in comparison with other satyr-plays,[103] but also in the light of the frequent references to the father–son relationship between Silenos and the satyrs. Wine in the *Cyclops*, as in real life, is a sexual stimulant and, for Silenos, prompts excited visions of male and female body-parts (169–71) and, for the Cyclops, hallucinations of flirtatious Graces (581), but this only highlights the absence of females in the play: the Cyclops finds the object of his desire in Silenos. When the satyrs wish for a world in which there are no women, except those reserved for satyrs (186–7n.), half at least of their wish has been fulfilled.

If *Cyclops* is indeed, then, a homosocial fantasy, it is one of a pointedly nuanced kind. The marked self-consciousness and almost paradoxical formality of satyr-drama work, in fact, against any simple model of 'identification' (even inverse identification) between the satyr-chorus and the male citizens. Neither chorus nor audience ever forget that this is, in Pat Easterling's words, 'a show for Dionysos', which is very differently constructed from the distance between performers and audience which tragedy imposes.[104] The fact that the satyrs are always placed in settings and stories (such as that of the Cyclops) where they do not 'naturally' belong, together with the sense of repetition and seriality which is built into satyr-drama more than into tragedy or comedy (cf., e.g., 1–10n.), increase our sense that it is indeed a 'show' that we are watching, a performance where repetitiveness and familiarity are, as with ritual, sources of power. In the case of *Cyclops*, the audience's knowingness, shared with the actors and chorus-members, of 'the script' of *Odyssey* 9 merely strengthens such self-conscious spectatorship. No doubt this familiarity and shared knowledge did encourage a sense of bonded communality in the audience, one based in the closural marking that the satyr-play brought to a set of tragedies, but there is no good reason to imagine that this communality was founded on audience identification (positive or negative) with the satyr-chorus, let alone that any particular aspect of the makeup of the audience, such as gender or political ideology, was paramount here.

[103] Contrast e.g. Aesch. *Theoroi* fr. 13–17; Soph. fr. 1130.7 ('We are the sons of nymphs').
[104] On this satyric distance cf. Lissarrague 1990: 236.

Scholars have tended to stress the changes in satyr-play which we can dimly perceive over the course of the fifth century; at least as important must have been the manner in which the repeated familiarity of satyr-play masked changes in the nature of tragedy in the course of the century: as long as 'the satyrs' danced, what we had just witnessed was indeed tragedy and it was in the god's honour. As for satyr-play itself, literary histories often point to its relatively rapid decline – at some point before 341 poets began to compete with just three tragedies and only one satyr-play for the whole festival was performed outside the competition[105] – but the longevity of the form also deserves notice. There is abundant literary and epigraphical evidence for the performance of satyr-play through the Hellenistic and imperial periods,[106] whatever weight one wants to give to Horace's interest in the genre in the *Ars Poetica* (vv. 229–31). Satyr-drama was closely tied to a particular social and cultural context, but its appreciation did not depend upon that context; here too, satyr-drama followed after tragedy.

5 LANGUAGE AND METRE

The language and metre of *Cyclops* and, as far as we can tell, of satyr-drama more generally, are essentially those of tragedy; the differences, which will be briefly outlined here, include features which satyr-play shares with Old Comedy, but the linguistic and metrical style of satyr-drama remain far closer to tragedy than to comedy, and this is very important for judging how satyr-drama resonated in performance.[107] The story that the language of *Cyclops* tells is thus essentially the same as that of the dramatic structure of the play: prologue, parodos, episodes and choral songs, framed by the entrance and exit of characters,[108] follow one another as in a Euripidean tragedy, but with enough difference to mark satyr-play as something special.[109] In stressing the general closeness of satyric style to that of tragedy, we must not forget that the overall effect and mood of satyr-drama must have been very different indeed.

[105] *IG* II² 2320, cf. Millis and Olson 2012: 61–9.

[106] Cf. Laemmle 2014: 929–31.

[107] For the links between satyr-play and comedy see Shaw 2014, citing earlier bibliography.

[108] An exception here is the anacreontic performance of the chorus and the Cyclops at 495–518.

[109] On the nature of the lyric verse in *Cyclops* cf. below p. 38. Some critics have seen the fact that the structure of *Cyclops* is, in broad terms, very similar to that of tragedy as a sign of the play's lateness, as there is some evidence that the structure of earlier satyr-play was rather looser, i.e. the separation between spoken parts and lyric performances of the chorus was not so neatly defined by the exits and entrances of the actors, cf. Taplin 1977a: 57–8, KPS 3,14-15. The difference may be correctly observed, but great caution is needed in seeking to draw chronological conclusions from it.

The principal difference between the language of *Cyclops* and that of the tragedies of Euripides lies in the admission of a more pronounced colloquial or conversational stratum than found in tragedy.[110] Such features include colloquial turns of phrase and words,[111] words describing physical processes which do not occur in tragedy,[112] exclamations and interjections,[113] and the use of diminutives[114] and deictic -ί.[115] There are, however, no basic obscenities (βινεῖν, etc.), with which, by contrast, Old Comedy is replete, and sexual matters are generally described through euphemism and innuendo;[116] τουτί τ’ ὀρθὸν ἐξανιστάναι (169, an erection) and αὐτὴν διεκροτήσατ’ (180, 'you gave her a thorough banging', with reference to the hated Helen) are to some extent exceptions. The picture is not fundamentally different in our remains of other satyr-play; satyrs are always interested in bodily processes and in sex, but the language to describe it tends towards the coy and/or allusive, even when the subject is perfectly clear.[117] So too, satyr-drama shows lively forms of discourse which are more closely paralleled in Old Comedy than in tragedy,

[110] The most helpful guide to the language and metre of Euripides' tragedies is Mastronarde 2002: 81–108; on the language of satyr-play see esp. Laemmle 2013: 64–76, Griffith 2015: 81–6.

[111] For the former cf., e.g., φέρ’ ἴδω (8), οὐ μὰ Δί’ (9, 555, 558, 560), εἰπέ μοι (138), κλαίειν κελεύειν and related forms (174, 340, 701), ἀπολεῖς (558); for the latter, cf., e.g., διαλαλεῖν (175, cf. λαλίστατος 315), διακροτεῖν (180), ἐσθίειν (233), πάνυ (646).

[112] Cf., e.g., ἐρυγγάνω (523), ἀπομακτέον/ἀπομυκτέον (561), σκαρδαμύσσειν (626), χρέμπτεσθαι (626); the last two are spoken by Odysseus as he lays down the law to the satyrs.

[113] Cf., e.g., ὤή (51), παπαῖ and related forms (110, 153, 503, 572), βαβαί (156), ἰοὺ ἰού (464, 576), ἰὼ ἰώ (656); ψύττα (49) is drawn from pastoral life.

[114] χρυσίον (161), ἀνθρώπιον (185), Κυκλώπιον (266, in an almost farcical context), δεσποτίσκος (267), ἀνθρωπίσκε (316), κράνιον (647, 683).

[115] τουτί (169, Silenos' penis).

[116] Cf. 171, 582–9; πείσομαι in 587 is euphemistic, though its physical sense is clear. On vv. 327–8 see n. ad loc. Lines 439–40 may contain a euphemistic reference to the penis, but the text is too corrupt for certainty.

[117] Aeschylus' *Diktyoulkoi* yields μιλτόπρεπτον φαλακρόν (fr. 47a.788, 'bright-red smoothness', perhaps a reference to Silenos' phallos) and ποσθοφιλής (fr. 47a.795, 'prick-loving' of a baby). Of particular interest is the relatively well-preserved fr. 47a.824–32 (anapaests) in which the satyrs celebrate the fact that Danae will be keen to have sex with all of them, because she has been without sex all the time she drifted on the sea. The meaning is very plain, but the language is euphemistic: τῆς ἡμετέρας/φιλότητος ἄδην κορέσασθαι (vv. 827–8, 'fill herself to repletion with our loving') is particularly telling (contrast *Cycl.* 180). In Sophocles' *Ichneutai* one may point to φάλητες (151) and perhaps a reference to masturbation in v. 368; other alleged instances in the remains of that play are textually uncertain. The fragments of Sophocles yield a few more instances of blunt language, such as ἀναστύψαι (fr. 421) and ἀποσκόλυπτε (fr. 423), and a few possible references to farting, etc., cf. Laemmle 2013: 72–4.

but these never predominate; in *Cyclops* one may, for example, point to self-correction (8) and surprise twists (*aprosdokēta*, cf. 186–7, 269, 272).[118]

In *Cyclops* the language of Odysseus is all but entirely free of the most colloquial features just listed; the most obvious exception (though a rather mild one) is his triumphant retort to the Cyclops at the very end of the play, κλαίειν σ' ἄνωγα (701, where see n. ad loc.). The language of Odysseus in *Cyclops* ranges from the familiar plain diction of Euripidean trimeters to rather grandiose passages where we may suspect a touch of knowing self-parody by the poet. Odysseus, a hero predominantly of epic and tragedy, has indeed landed in a new country, a 'city of Bromios' (99), where the inhabitants speak a recognisable, but also recognisably different language; the relationship of similarity and difference between satyr-play and tragedy appears to have been linguistically marked.

Very similar conclusions may be drawn from a consideration of metrical practice in the spoken trimeters of *Cyclops*.[119] Whereas the trimeters spoken by the Cyclops, Silenos and the chorus-leader exhibit certain mild differences from tragic trimeters, those of Odysseus, with a few disputed exceptions,[120] do not. The principal differences concern admitted forms and sequences of resolution and substitution and 'Porson's Law'. It is perhaps hardly surprising that tragedy offers no exact parallel to 203 and 210, two verses from the Cyclops' entrance speech which begin with three tribrachs, i.e. nine successive short syllables.[121] More significant is the role allowed to anapaests in the trimeter. Whereas tragedy normally allows only the first *anceps* of the verse to be substituted by two short syllables, with occasional exceptions to accommodate difficult proper names,[122] the *Cyclops* allows such substitution for any *anceps* or short syllable (except the last); the result is that anapaests ($\smile$ $\smile$ $-$) may appear in any foot except the last, though the great majority of cases beyond the first foot occur in the second foot.[123] Thus, for example, in 232 an anapaest replaces $\smile$ $-$ in the fourth foot:

---

[118] Sophocles, *Ichn.* 83–5 has been taken as a case of audience-address, cf. Zagagi 1999: 197–8. On satyric audience-address cf. Laemmle 2013: 39 n. 49.
[119] In addition to Mastronarde (above n. 110), see also Descroix 1931: 194–221, West 1982: 81–8.
[120] Cf. 260n.
[121] For a comic example cf. Ar. *Ach.* 1054. None of the few tragic verses which exhibit three resolutions have nine successive short syllables; for eight cf. Soph. *OT* 967 with Finglass' n.
[122] For such 'second-foot anapaests' in Euripides cf. *Ion* 21, *Or.* 1314, 1655, Diggle 1981: 47–8; for the fourth foot cf. *Or.* 65.
[123] Cf. Descroix 1931: 200, Ussher 1978: 208–9.

⏑ ⏑ ⏑ ⏑ – | ⏑ – ⏑ ⏑ – | ⏑ – ⏑ –
ἔλεγον ἐγὼ τάδ᾽· οἱ δ᾽ ἐφόρουν τὰ χρήματα

In this regard, however, Euripides' metrical practice in *Cyclops* falls far short of the freedom and extent of anapaestic substitution found in Old Comedy, though our very scanty evidence allows the suspicion that *Cyclops* is in fact somewhat freer than at least some earlier satyr-play.[124] As for Odysseus, the transmitted text has him using an anapaest in the second foot in 260, which may be easily emended, but otherwise his trimeters do not fall outside tragic practice in this regard.[125] It also seems clear that satyr-play does not generally follow comedy in permitting 'split anapaests', that is word division within the anapaest.[126] The three cases in *Cyclops* which seem certain all concern the formulaic oath μὰ Δί᾽ as the short syllables of a fourth-foot anapaest (154, 558, 560); all are spoken by Silenos. There are, however, four further possible examples (235, 265, 334, 343), the first two spoken by Silenos, the second two by the Cyclops, all of which could be removed by emendation, but which suggest that Euripides occasionally permitted this licence in satyr-drama.

'Porson's Law' refers to the shape of the end of the trimeter: 'the rhythm – – | – ⏑ – ‖, where the syllables – – belong to one word and the syllables – ⏑ to one word or word-group is avoided at the end of the trimeter';[127] this is sometimes referred to as 'the law of the final cretic', because 'if the final "cretic" (– ⏑ –) of the line is realized in a trisyllabic word, the preceding syllable must be short (unless it is a monosyllable)'.[128] Whereas the Law has no effect in comedy, tragedy admits very few apparent exceptions,[129] and *Cyclops* too, like what we can tell of satyr-drama more generally, seems very discreet in its breaches of the Law: in three cases, spoken by the Cyclops and the chorus-leader (210, 681, 682), the 'final cretic' is formed by the definite article and a disyllabic noun, and in 120 (cf. also 672) Silenos' οὐδὲν οὐδεὶς οὐδενός offers a breach which has parallels even in tragedy (cf. *Alc.* 671, with Parker's n.), and the amusing triple denial is a certain defence of the text. One transmitted case, however, concerns Odysseus. In 304 ἐχήρωσ᾽ Ἑλλάδα at the end of the trimeter would appear to breach the Law; emendation seems out of the question, but there are also a small number of apparent breaches in tragedy involving elision

---

[124] There appear to be fourth-foot anapaests in Aesch. fr. 205 and Soph. frr. 120 and 671 (both very uncertain), and in *Ichn.* 128; even from our limited evidence base, this is a very small haul.
[125] The second-foot anapaest in 590 accommodates the proper name Διονύσου.
[126] Cf. West 1982: 90, Hunter 1983: 92–3, 95.
[127] West 1982: 84–5.   [128] Mastronarde 2002: 102.   [129] Cf. West 1982: 85.

before the 'final cretic',[130] and this instance, particularly within Odysseus' patriotic rhetoric, hardly lowers the seriousness of his general mode of speech.

The overall picture seems very clear: in both verbal style and the metrical style of the trimeters *Cyclops* sits very close to Euripidean tragedy, but far enough away to make the small differences noticeable. 'Same, but different' seems in fact a reasonable characterisation of satyr-play's relation to tragedy in very many respects. More different than same, however, might be a better description of the structure of the relatively very short choral songs in *Cyclops*. The parodos consists of a single triad of strophe–antistrophe–epode, but the corresponding strophes are separated by a metrically distinct mesode, which may have been performed by a single choreut; the same structure, without the epode, informs the first choral song (356–74), whereas the last two songs (608–23, 656–62) are astrophic. The simplicity of these structures seems far removed from the elaborate high manner of the lyrics of Euripidean tragedy. The place of the third choral song is taken by an anacreontic exchange between the chorus and the Cyclops (495–518), introduced by a short anapaestic song; the exchange evokes the simple stanzas of sympotic lyrics exchanged between guests enjoying wine. What evidence we have, notably Aeschylus, *Diktyoulkoi* and Sophocles, *Ichneutai*, suggests that in earlier satyr-play choral songs may have been less structurally simple and more integrated into the principal dramatic action than they are in *Cyclops*; if so, this would be one aspect of earlier satyr-play which resembled Old Comedy more than tragedy. In *Cyclops* the metrical simplicity remains, but the structure of the play as a whole has been assimilated to that of Euripidean tragedy.

6 THE DATE OF *CYCLOPS*

In this edition it will be assumed that *Cyclops* is a late work of Euripides, very likely first produced in Athens in 408 BC. The reasons for this assumption are of very unequal weight, but the cumulative case seems very strong.

There is no external evidence, such as the ancient *hypotheseis* which survive for the 'non-alphabetic' plays (below p. 48), which sheds light on the date of the first performance of *Cyclops*. The principal method for the relative dating of Euripides' tragedies, in default of clear external evidence deriving ultimately from the official Athenian records, is the well-established fact that the freedom with which Euripides permitted and employed

---

[130] Cf. Soph. *Aj.* 1101 (with Finglass' n.), *Phil.* 22 (with Schein's n.).

resolutions in the iambic trimeter increased as his career progressed; to simplify considerably, the remarkable shift in his metrical practice can be seen from the fact that whereas in *Medea* (431 BC) and *Hippolytus* (428 BC) the ratio of resolutions to trimeters is (on average) some 6–7%, in *Bacchae* (*c.* 405 BC) it is about 44% and in *Orestes* (408 BC) nearly 50%.[131] These figures can, of course, only establish a loose relative chronology for plays or groups of plays, but the overall picture which emerges is clear and relatively consistent. Modern scholars disagree, however, as to whether this statistical method is applicable to satyr-drama, which otherwise shows some differences from tragedy in the treatment of the trimeter (cf. above pp. 36–7). Nevertheless, the language and metrical practice of Odysseus, clearly the least satyric character of *Cyclops* are, with a few minor exceptions,[132] in keeping with tragic practice, and the rate of resolution in the trimeters spoken by him (some 37%)[133] would, in a tragedy, strongly point to a date no earlier than the *Helen* of 412.[134] Whether or not chronological conclusions can be drawn from the metrical practice of particular characters in a satyr-play is likely always to remain a matter of contention, particularly as we have so few other trimeters which certainly derive from Euripidean satyr-drama. Nevertheless, the chronology suggested by this metrical criterion may be supported by arguments (of varying cogency) drawn from possible links between *Cyclops* and other dramas.

The Cyclops' exclamation on seeing the Greeks outside his cave (222)

ἔα· τίν' ὄχλον τόνδ' ὁρῶ πρὸς αὐλίοις;

is very like Aristophanes, *Thesmophoriazousai* 1105 ἔα· τίν' ὄχθον τόνδ' ὁρῶ καὶ παρθένον; from the parody of Euripides' *Andromeda*. The parodied verse spoken by Perseus ran ἔα· τίν' ὄχθον τόνδ' ὁρῶ περίρρυτον; (fr. 125.1). *Andromeda* was produced, along with *Helen*, in 412 and Aristophanes' comedy followed in 411.[135] The structure and rhythm of such an exclamation

---

[131] Cf. Cropp and Fick 1985: 5.   [132] Cf. 260, 304, 701nn.

[133] This is our calculation. Uncertainties arise from possible textual corruption and authenticity, questions of speaker distribution in stichomythia, trimeters divided between two speakers, etc. If vv. 480–2 are retained, the figure becomes some 36%.

[134] The standard study of metrical criteria for dating *Cyclops* is Seaford 1982, which should be consulted for a much more detailed analysis.

[135] Austin and Olson 2004: lxiv (and n. on Ar. *Thesm.* 1216–26, cf. also Ussher 1978: 204) also call attention to the similarity between the sport the satyrs have with the blinded Cyclops in vv. 675–88 and the fooling of the Scythian archer at the end of *Thesmophoriazousai*, while conceding that this similarity does not prove a connection between the plays.

are common enough to enjoin caution,[136] but some connection between these three verses seems very likely. Several scholars have suggested that *Cyclops* was staged in 412 with *Helen* and *Andromeda*,[137] in which case *Cyclops* 222 would be a kind of 'satyric' echo of what was obviously a prominent scene in one of the tragedies with which *Cyclops* was produced; it is not unlikely that such echoes occurred with some frequency between satyr-plays and the tragedies which preceded them, although we normally do not have the evidence to confirm (or dismiss) the suspicion. If this was the case with *Cyclops* 222, then Aristophanes' parody would perhaps not merely pick up the tragic verse, but also acknowledge that Euripides himself had used it as a kind of signature by repeating it in *Cyclops*. Nevertheless, another apparent echo of tragedy in *Cyclops* casts doubt upon the idea that it was first performed in 412.

In the *Philoctetes* of 409 BC Sophocles colours the picture of the solitary hero, abandoned for years on an island, with touches reminiscent of the wild solitariness of the Homeric Cyclops.[138] The similarities of situation and plot (both are visited, robbed and plotted against by Odysseus) make these evocations unsurprising, but also naturally give rise to consideration of whether there are any links between Sophocles' play and *Cyclops*.[139] One striking possibility is the Cyclops' final speech of the play, in which he says that he will go to higher ground δι' ἀμφιτρῆτος τῆσδε (707)[140] in order to hurl rocks down on the fleeing Greeks; it has long been noted that the only other occurrence of ἀμφιτρής is at Sophocles, *Philoctetes* 19 in Odysseus' description of Philoctetes' cave, δι' ἀμφιτρῆτος αὐλίου. As this is the only reference to the second entrance to the Cyclops' cave in *Cyclops*, and it has of course no counterpart in the Homeric tale,[141] whereas the idea is repeatedly noted in Sophocles' play (cf. 707n.), it is very tempting to see here a passing allusion by Euripides to Sophocles' play, and perhaps even to the apparent absence of any dramatic function for the motif in Sophocles. This would also make a production of *Cyclops* in 408 (with *Orestes*) very probable.[142]

---

[136] Cf., e.g., Battezzato 1995: 134–5.

[137] The suggestion seems to go back to Marquart 1912; cf. also Grégoire 1948 ('le plus probable'), Austin and Olson 2004: lxiii–iv. Wright 2005: 54–5 and 2006 argued that the four plays staged by Euripides in 412 were *Helen, Andromeda, Iphigeneia among the Taurians*, and *Cyclops*, but the *Iphigeneia* is almost certainly to be placed a few years earlier, cf. esp. Parker 2016: lxxvi–lxxx.

[138] Cf., e.g., Schein 2013: 17–18.

[139] It is striking that these are the only two plays of the tragic corpus without female characters.

[140] For the difficulties of this expression and the text of the verse cf. the n. ad loc.

[141] Cf. above pp. 13–14.

[142] Cf. Dale 1969: 129, Seaford 1982: 171. Müller 1997: 97–110, however, suggests that both *Philoctetes* and *Cyclops* are indebted to Euripides' *Philoctetes* and that therefore v. 707 does not show that *Cyclops* postdated *Philoctetes*.

If an allusion to Sophocles' *Philoctetes* be accepted, then the relationship between *Cyclops* and *Andromeda* cannot quite be as sketched above. Milman Parry suggested that in *Cyclops* Euripides responded to Aristophanes' parody of his earlier verse with a kind of defiant self-parody, and this view has been widely accepted.[143] Nevertheless, whereas the *Andromeda* is very clearly the object of Aristophanes' parody, we must remember that *Cyclops* 222 may have nothing to do with either play and that, some three years after Aristophanes' *Thesmophoriazousai*, the similarity would carry no great significance for the poet, let alone the audience. Here we are, as often, hindered by the fact that, since so much of fifth-century drama is lost, inferences about verbal and visual allusion between plays must always be expressed cautiously; we are, moreover, largely ignorant of how knowledge of earlier plays was preserved, whether through reperformances outside Athens, comic parody or the memory of the spectators and performers.[144] No doubt, also, playwrights sometimes (or indeed often) evoked earlier performances in ways which would not necessarily have been obvious to mass audiences. Some instances may be considered 'special cases', such as the apparent evocation of Agamemnon's death cries in Aeschylus' *Agamemnon* at *Cyclops* 663–5; the *Oresteia* (458 BC) seems to have been very well known in late fifth-century Athens. A more difficult, but perhaps more typical, case is Silenos' sweeping of the Cyclops' cave with an iron rake while he delivers the prologue of *Cyclops*.[145] It is perhaps here difficult for a modern reader not to be reminded of Ion's sweeping of the temple of Apollo while singing the monody to the god which immediately follows the prologue of *Ion*, and the similarities could easily be emphasised by stage action.[146] The young, pious and naïve devotee of Apollo and the salacious old follower of Dionysos in all his manifestations make no less an amusing contrast than do the riches and ornamental art of the Delphic shrine and a rustic cave surrounded by animal pens. The date of the *Ion* is, however, disputed; it is usually placed in the period 415–413 BC,[147] but one recent editor opts for a date after 412.[148] *If* the prologue of *Cyclops*

---

[143] Parry 1971: 319–20, cf. Seaford 1982: 170–1.
[144] For discussion and bibliography on the reperformance of tragedies in the fifth century cf. Lamari 2015, Hunter and Uhlig 2017.
[145] Cf. 33n. for the difficulties of ἁρπάγη in this context.
[146] One might even speculate that the same actor played both Ion and Silenos, which would give a dramaturgical joke probably appreciated by more than just the poet and actor.
[147] We are not aware that it has ever been suggested that *Cyclops* was the satyr-play produced together with *Ion*.
[148] Martin 2018: 24–32.

evokes the *Ion*, then we shall probably not want to date *Cyclops* too many years after that. But how many? Even to ask the question shows up the precariousness of debates of this kind: we simply do not know enough about Athenian dramatic culture (including the role of reperformances both in Athens and elsewhere) to rule out verbal and visual evocations across a considerable stretch of time. Aristophanes' parodies, though to some extent different in kind from evocations of tragedy in tragedy or of tragedy and satyr-play in satyr-play, nevertheless show that plays did not have to be 'recent' to be exploitable on the Athenian stage.

The situation is both complicated and made more intriguing by possible links between *Cyclops* and the (now fragmentary) *Hypsipyle*, which is dated to the period 411–408 BC by a scholium on Aristophanes (*Hypsipyle* T ii), a date which fits the metrical style of the extant trimeters. Hypsipyle is the grand-daughter of Dionysos, a queen who has become, like the satyrs, a slave in a distant land. The first word of her prologue-speech is Διόνυσος (fr. 752.1), whereas Silenos begins with an address ὦ Βρόμιε; in a monody Hypsipyle contrasts the lullabies she is now forced to sing to the baby she cares for with the worksongs of her previous life:

> οὐ τάδε πήνας, οὐ τάδε κερκίδος
> ἱστοτόνου παραμύθια Λήμνια
> Μοῦσα θέλει με κρέκειν, ὅ τι δ᾽ εἰς ὕπνον
> ἢ χάριν ἢ θεραπεύματα πρόσφορα
> π]αιδὶ πρέπει νεαρῶι
> τάδε μελωιδὸς αὐδῶ.
>
> Eur. *Hypsipyle* fr. 752f.9–14

These are not Lemnian songs, relieving the labour of weft-thread and web-stretching shuttle, that the Muse desires me to sing, but what serves for a tender young boy, to lull him or charm him or tend to his needs – this is the song I tunefully sing. (trans. Collard and Cropp)

The similarity to the complaints of the satyrs in the parodos of *Cyclops* is obvious:

> οὐ τάδε Βρόμιος, οὐ τάδε χοροὶ
> Βάκχαι τε θυρσοφόροι,
> οὐ τυμπάνων ἀλαλαγμοί,   65
> οὐκ οἴνου χλωραὶ σταγόνες   67
> κρήναις παρ᾽ ὑδροχύτοις.

The chorus of *Hypsipyle* then enter and ask Hypsipyle what she is doing outside the house:

τί σὺ παρὰ προθύροις, φίλα;
πότερα δώματος εἰσόδους
σαίρεις, ἢ δρόσον ἐπὶ πέδωι
βάλλεις οἷά τε δούλα;

Eur. Hypsipyle fr. 752f.15–18

Why are you here at the doorway, dear friend? Are you sweeping the house's entrance, or sprinkling water on the ground as a slave-woman will? (trans. Collard and Cropp)

Sweeping and washing the ground recall not just Ion's monody, but (again) Silenos and the prologue of *Cyclops*. What is to be done with these 'parallels'? If we knew that *Cyclops* was the satyr-play which followed a group of tragedies including *Hypsipyle*, then it would be attractive to see here further satyric 'echoes' of a preceding tragedy, but of course we do not know that. What must, however, be stressed is that there is no reason to assume that 'performative allusion' in a satyr-play must necessarily be to a tragedy of the same tetralogy.

One further set of apparently verbal and visual 'parallels' is even harder to judge. The *Hecuba* seems to have been produced in the period 424–418 BC, perhaps rather in the earlier part of that period.[149] In that tragedy, Polymestor is blinded in revenge by Hecuba, and his cries, which are verbally very like those of the Euripidean Cyclops, are heard, as are Polyphemos', from within the *skēnē* (vv. 1035–41); Polymestor is taunted by Hecuba and then appears, staggering on all fours and groping to find his tormentors. He even expresses a desire to eat his fill of their 'flesh and bones', thus exacting a cannibal revenge upon them (vv. 1070–4). The similarity of name, Polymestor ~ Polyphemos, has added to the sense that there must be a direct connection between these scenes, whether it be that *Cyclops* was performed with *Hecuba* or many years later.[150] If

---

[149] Cf. Battezzato 2018: 2–4.

[150] Sutton 1980: 114–20 argues for the former position. Seaford 1982: 169 suggests that this similarity between *Cyclops* and *Hecuba* in fact goes back to a dramatisation of the Cyclops story preceding *Hecuba*. It is typical of much discussion of dramatic 'intertextuality' that this suggestion is assumed to 'solve' the issue of the relation between *Hecuba* and *Cyclops*; of course it does not, as a 'common ancestor' does not stop poets from creating or audiences from constructing and appreciating a relationship between two descendants.

Cyclops was performed as the satyr-play following *Hecuba*, then the dramatic effect of the similarity would undoubtedly have been different than if the two plays were separated by, say, fifteen years, if we ignore the possible effects of reperformances of *Hecuba* in the intervening years. Given the other indications, however, it seems very unlikely that *Cyclops* could have been produced as early as *Hecuba*. The similarity between the two may have been recognised (and even discussed) by some 'theatrical experts' in Athens, but more important is the fact that the scene in *Hecuba* confirms, as do the apparent echoes of the death-cries of the Aeschylean Agamemnon, that the final scene of *Cyclops* mimics tragic structures, but plays them out in a 'lower', partly humorous mode appropriate to satyr-drama. Here, if anywhere, we can see what Demetrius, *On Style* 169 meant by suggesting that satyr-drama was 'tragedy at play' (τραγωιδία παίζουσα).[151]

Of the other arguments which have been adduced to date *Cyclops*, the most persistent in recent times has been a desire to associate the Sicilian setting in some way with the Athenian expedition to Sicily in 415–413 and/or its disastrous outcome.[152] Here again, however, no such connection is in fact necessary to explain the play or anything in it, though no doubt all things Sicilian carried a particularly grim resonance for some years after the expedition. Whether or not a performance of *Cyclops* after the failure of the expedition and to an audience familiar with stories of the terrible sufferings of the Greek prisoners in the stone-quarries at Syracuse (Thucyd. 7.87) would have been welcomed at Athens may be debated,[153] and here again we feel our ignorance of how Athenian dramatic culture actually 'worked' in its interaction with historical events. How many of a post-expedition audience would see *Cyclops* as a kind of dramatic allegory for what had happened to the Athenians in Sicily? 'Reminding the Athenians of misfortunes which were personal to them'

---

[151] The context in Demetrius (? late second century BC) is the difference between χάριτες and γέλως; comedy and satyr-play need both, whereas tragedy welcomes the former but is hostile to the latter. The game of 'blind man's buff' which the satyrs play with the Cyclops (cf. 679–90n.) presumably produced much laughter (cf. 687 οἴμοι γελῶμαι). In the third century AD, the Christian Origen of Alexandria knew that the satyr-dramas which tragedians wrote aimed at ἄσεμνοι γέλωτες (*Contra Celsum* 7.6); it is perhaps unlikely that his knowledge was based on first-hand evidence, and somewhere in the background may lie Aristotle, *Poetics* 1449a19–21.

[152] Cf., e.g., Grégoire 1948, Paganelli 1979, Worman 2008: 122–3, 136.

[153] Cf. Seaford 1982: 171–2, pointing out that the Athenians had taken revenge by imprisoning some Syracusans in quarries in Peiraeus (Xen. *Hell.* 1.2.14).

had done the tragedian Phrynichus no good many decades before (Hdt. 6.21.2), but Attic comedy shows that the boundaries of the permissible were capacious.

What is, however, not in doubt is that there is a significant body of evidence attesting to the connections between Euripides and Sicily and the popularity of the poet's plays with Sicilian audiences.[154] A passage of Aristotle's *Rhetoric* (2. 1384b11–16 = Euripides T 96) may even suggest that Euripides was at some time sent by the Athenians on an embassy to Syracuse; the passage has been emended or explained as referring to a different politician of that name,[155] but even if a reference to the tragedian were accepted, the date of this remarkable incident is entirely unclear,[156] and the temptation to assume that it was somehow connected with the aftermath of the Sicilian expedition should probably be resisted. Whatever the truth, it remains unclear whether and where *Cyclops* fits into this pattern of Euripidean relations with Sicily.

The similarities between *Cyclops* and *Bacchae* (posthumously produced, perhaps in 405 BC) are a fragile basis for chronological conclusions of any kind, but they are also very striking in several respects.[157] Both plays concern – as, of course, did other Athenian dramas – the introduction of Dionysiac rites and revelry to a land which had not embraced them before and the punishment of those who stood in the way, although the nature of those 'rites' differs in the two plays (ecstatic cult worship in *Bacchae*, wine-drinking and sympotic practice in *Cyclops*). In both plays the character who blocks the god is, through a kind of education, 'initiated' into the god's rites, but in such a way as to mark their earlier opposition: Pentheus becomes a 'male maenad' who spies on the rites rather than joining the *thiasos*, and the Cyclops' sympotic instincts are restrained so that he drinks alone; individual scenes or passages – the parodos of *Bacchae* and the *makarismos* of *Cyclops* 496–502, the visions of the drunken Cyclops and of Pentheus in the god's power – also seem strongly reminiscent of each other. Just how significant these similarities are may be debated, and they certainly do not demand that the plays were composed (or performed) within a short time of each other. Nevertheless, the similarity of the nar-

---

[154] Cf. Csapo and Wilson 2019: 369–75. The apparent passion for Euripides of Dionysius I of Syracuse is particularly worthy of note, cf. Eur. T 1 III 4, Wilson 2017: 11–14.

[155] Cf., e.g., Davies 1971: 202–4.

[156] Cf., e.g., Jameson 1971: 543–5, Wilson 2017: 5–6.

[157] Cf., e.g., Seaford 1981: 272–4, Hunter 2006: 74–6, 2009: 66–7.

rative pattern does seem to go beyond what might plausibly be explained by any shared debt to Dionysiac myth, and it would not, at the very least, be a surprise to learn that they were in fact composed relatively near to each other in time. If that were indeed the case, then the last decade of the century would have been marked by at least three plays, Euripides' *Cyclops* and *Bacchae* and Aristophanes' *Frogs*, all with Dionysos very much at their heart; in these perilous years the city perhaps felt a special need to emphasise the continuing and consequential presence of the god who presided over their greatest cultural achievement.

One final consideration, which is equally uncertain, cannot be left entirely out of account. A famous *kratēr* from southern Italy in the British Museum (inv. 1947.7–14.18, Plate 2) shows three of Odysseus' men lifting up a (? sharpened) tree-trunk in preparation for blinding the Cyclops who lies in a drunken stupor on the ground; Odysseus is apparently directing operations rather than physically helping with the blinding. Beside the Cyclops are a drinking-cup and a near-empty wineskin hanging from a small branch. The scene is framed on one side by two more of Odysseus' companions with torches and, on the other, by two satyrs apparently running or dancing in pleasure towards the scene; the action of one at least of the satyrs may easily be interpreted as showing the leg-movements of a dance such as the *siki(n)nis* (cf. 36–8n.). The *kratēr* must be dated within the last quarter of the fifth century, and expert opinion tends towards the penultimate decade of the century.[158] Although, if we disregard the dance-movements as inconclusive, there is no explicit indication, such as in the dress of the satyrs, that this scene is intended to evoke, or was inspired by, drama, most modern critics – with varying degrees of confidence – have associated this scene with Euripides' play, as the easiest explanation for the proximity of satyrs to the blinding;[159] that these satyrs are both excited at what is happening and keep themselves at a safe distance from the real action has been linked to the behaviour of the chorus in *Cyclops* 632–62.

[158] Cf. Trendall 1967: 25–7, Trendall and Webster 1971: 36 ('can hardly be … later than, if indeed as late as, 410 B.C.').
[159] The strongest claim of a link is probably that of Fellmann 1972: 32–3; most other scholars prefer a cautious 'probably', 'möglicherweise'. The principal exception is Taplin 2007: 272–3 who notes that the *kratēr* 'may well be earlier than Euripides' play' and concludes that 'only a dedicated philodramatist would put money on this one', i.e. as being a representation of the satyr-drama. It is perhaps worth mentioning the possibility that the extraordinary size of the tree-trunk with which the Cyclops is to be blinded on the *kratēr* has something to do with the 'spell of Orpheus' which the satyrs promise at *Cycl.* 646; Orpheus was notorious for persuading trees, as well as other parts of nature, to follow his music.

Plate 2 Lucanian red-figure calyx-*kratēr*, late fifth century BC. British
Museum inv. 1947.7-14.18

If this vase was inspired by a satyric version of the Cyclops-story, then
Aristias' play (above p. 4) must also be taken into account; Euripides
is not the only possible source of that inspiration. Secondly, however,
it may be questioned just how precisely the vase can be dated: is the
period 410–400 BC really impossible? It would be very dangerous to
reject a late date for *Cyclops* on the basis of this vase alone. On balance,
therefore, we favour a date for *Cyclops* in the latter part of Euripides'
career and consider 408 BC the most likely absolute date to have been
proposed.

7 TEXT AND TRANSMISSION

Cyclops is one of nine extant plays of Euripides for the complete text of which we have only one independent witness, a manuscript written in the early fourteenth century at Thessaloniki and preserved in the Laurentian library in Florence, hence its standard designation as L (Laurentianus plut. 32.2).[160] The titles of all these nine plays begin with E, H, I or K and the group is thus regularly referred to as the 'alphabetic' plays,[161] to distinguish them from the other ten extant plays (including the spurious *Rhesos*) which survive in a richer manuscript tradition and which emerged gradually during antiquity as the corpus of Euripides most familiar to both scholars and performers; that there are no scholia in L to the alphabetic plays is another sign of how these plays were for centuries essentially 'unknown' to the grammatical tradition. There is also to date only one known ancient papyrus containing verses of *Cyclops*; this is *POxy* 4545 (fourth century AD) preserving parts of vv. 455–71, 479–81, 484–96.

The survival of the 'alphabetic plays', and hence, in *Cyclops*, of our only complete ancient satyr-drama, was a very close-run thing.[162] The evidence for first-hand knowledge of these plays becomes increasingly sparse in later antiquity, and we simply do not have enough evidence to try to write the history of how and why they all but disappeared. It has been argued that a sixth-century AD chronicler, John Malalas from Antioch, still had direct knowledge of some of the alphabetic plays, but the matter is far from certain.[163]

The alphabetic principle of arrangement goes back to the Alexandrian edition of Euripides' plays which was probably prepared by Aristophanes of Byzantium, who was Head of the Alexandrian Library in the early second century BC.[164] The nine 'alphabetic plays' do not present a contin-

---

[160] L is best accessible at http://mss.bmlonline.it/catalogo.aspx?Collection=Plutei&Shelfmark=Plut.32.2. The Euripidean part of L is reproduced in facsimile in Spranger 1921.
[161] The others are *Helen, Electra, Heraclidae, Heracles, Supplices* (in Greek '*Hiketides*'), *Iphigeneia at Aulis, Iphigeneia in Tauris, Ion*.
[162] The brief account which follows is very heavily indebted to Turyn 1957, Zuntz 1955: 146–52 and Zuntz 1965; it should be stressed that a very great deal still remains controversial, and the present account is intended merely as an introduction to the subject. All information about textual readings which appears in the apparatus is based on Diggle's edition.
[163] Cf. Hunter 2020, citing earlier bibliography.
[164] For initial guidance on the history of the text of Euripides in antiquity cf. Zuntz 1965: chapter 6, Mastronarde 2017. The evidence for alphabetical arrangement is based both upon knowledge of the use of this principle elsewhere in Alex-

uous alphabetic sequence (there are known plays missing) and so the origin of this grouping must to some extent remain guesswork,[165] but it is clear that the papyrus rolls on which they survived must have been copied in late antiquity or the early Byzantine period into a single codex which survived by lucky chance, very likely in Constantinople. The rhetorician and theologian Eustathius, best known to classicists for his commentaries on Homer, worked in Constantinople in the twelfth century and cites at least from the *Ion*, apparently from first-hand knowledge. In his note on *Odyssey* 18.355 Eustathius (*Hom.* 1850.35) discusses the nature of satyr-drama and refers to ὁ μέχρι νῦν εὑρισκόμενος Εὑριπίδειος Κύκλωψ; this is the earliest certain reference to the play since antiquity,[166] and suggests both that *Cyclops* was the only satyr-play known to Eustathius and perhaps that it had only recently been rediscovered.[167]

In 1175 Eustathius left Constantinople to become Archbishop of Thessaloniki. It is (another) reasonable speculation that it was Eustathius who brought the text of the alphabetic plays to Thessaloniki where it was copied into miniscule, unless Eustathius himself had already seen to that in Constantinople, and then became, some two centuries later, the ancestor of L. L itself, which contains, as well as Hesiod's *Works and Days* and plays of Aeschylus and Sophocles, all the extant plays of Euripides except *Troades* and the second half of *Bacchae*, was produced in the circle of the scholar Demetrius Triclinius, quite probably indeed under Triclinius' supervision.[168] What is certain is that, very soon after L had been produced, Triclinius corrected and revised it, very probably using

andrian scholarship and on surviving papyri of Euripidean *hypotheseis* and lists of titles (cf. *POxy* 2455–6, Eur. T 6–8).

[165] Snell 1935 ingeniously argued that the choice of nine plays goes back to the fact that papyrus rolls were held in boxes each containing five rolls and that *Hecuba* was omitted when the 'alphabetic plays' were copied, as it was already known from elsewhere.

[166] Magnelli 2003 has argued for a reworking of *Cycl.* 683–4 in Eustathius' older Constantinopolitan contemporary Theodoros Prodromos; the case is attractive but uncertain.

[167] Eustathius' older contemporary John Tzetzes claims to have read 'many satyr-plays of Euripides' (cf. Kaibel 1899: 30, *Prolegomena de comoedia* XIa 152–6 Koster), which, if there is any substance to this claim, may be a reference to the *Cyclops* in the same copy which Eustathius knew. For the evidence cf. Eur. T 221a–c, *Autolykos* T iv, *Syleus* T iiia; for discussion cf. Wilson 1966: 338, Masciadri 1987, Luppe 1996: 219–21, Pechstein 1998: 51–5, Kannicht on Eur. T 221a–c.

[168] On Triclinius' Euripidean activities cf., in addition to Turyn 1957 and Zuntz 1965, Wilson 1983: 249–56 and Reynolds and Wilson 2013: 76–7; Meriani 1999 discusses his treatment of two lyric passages of *Cycl.*

not just his scholarly knowledge but also the manuscript from which L
had been copied.

After Triclinius' first round of corrections, the alphabetic plays were
copied from L into another early fourteenth-century manuscript, standardly designated P. This manuscript is now divided into two; the part containing *Cyclops* is Palatinus gr. 287, preserved in the Vatican Library; a
folio containing vv. 244–351 has dropped out.[169] The value of P lies in
the fact that, after it was produced, Triclinius subsequently corrected and
emended L again (with particular attention to the colometry of the lyrics),
but in a much more radical way which has in many places left the original reading of L unclear and turned what was already a difficult manuscript to read into a very challenging one; in those places, therefore, P is
a crucial witness to what was originally in L or at least in L after Triclinius'
first revision. P also sometimes offers obvious corrections of minor slips in
L. There are three further later copies of all or part of L which are sometimes helpful in establishing L's reading or a subsequent emendation; one
of these is cited in the apparatus, following Diggle, as apogr. Par.[170] The
first printed edition ('Aldina') of the 'alphabetic plays' was produced by
Aldus Manutius at Venice in 1503.[171]

The 'indirect tradition' of *Cyclops*, i.e. quotations in ancient authors,
anthologists and grammarians, is relatively meagre, but may help to track
knowledge of the play in later antiquity, although citations in grammarians and compilatory authors such as Athenaeus do not necessarily imply
first-hand knowledge of the play, rather than the use of earlier compila-
tions and anthologies. The following is a list of ancient citations (unless
otherwise indicated, all citations are explicitly ascribed to Euripides,
Cyclops):

98   Photius, *Lexicon* ο 31 Theodoridis glosses ὀδῆσαι as ὠνήσασθαι
        and gives two illustrations from Euripides, fr. 113 (*Alopē*) and
        Cycl. 98.

102–4   Cited by Schol. Sophocles, *Ajax* 190 for the identification of
        Sisyphos as Odysseus' father, cf. 104 n.

104   According to Eustathius (*Hom.* 1455.34), Aristophanes of
        Byzantium (fr. 31 Slater) noted that Euripides used δριμύ with
        the meaning συνετόν; the reference is probably to *Cyclops* 104, cf.
        n. ad loc.

136   Cited by Athenaeus 14.658c for the cheese called ὀπίας.

---

[169] P is best accessed at: https://digi.vatlib.it/view/MSS_Pal.gr.287. P is also reproduced in facsimile in Spranger 1939–46.
[170] See 'Sigla' p. 53 for details of this manuscript.   [171] Cf. Sicherl 1975.

154–5   The use of γεύεσθαι of smell (ἐπὶ τοῦ ὀσφραίνεσθαι) is ascribed to
        Euripides' *Cyclops* in *Antiatticist* γ 30 Valente, cf. 153–4n.

213   Cited from Euripides without play-title by Choeroboscus I
        272.33–4 Hilgard (= *GG* IV 1.272.33–4) and *Anecdota Par.* IV
        194.8-10 Cramer (= Cramer 1841: 194) for the short iota in
        Ὠρίωνα.

332–5   332–3 are cited by Plutarch, *Mor.* 435b for the dangers of replac-
        ing explanations for prophecy based on the divine by appeals to
        natural phenomena, and by Athenagoras, *Legatio* 25.2 (without
        ascription to poet or play) for God's care for mankind.[172] 334–5
        are then in part paraphrased and in part quoted in the same
        passage of Plutarch.

394   παλιούρου κλάδωι is cited by Athenaeus 14.650a for παλίουρος.

410   Cited by Athenaeus 1.23e for the verb ἀναπίπτειν.

514   λύχνα as a neuter noun is illustrated from Euripides' *Cyclops* by
        Antiatticist λ 6 Valente. This is the only citation from a passage of
        lyric verse.

534   Cited from Euripides without play-title by Athenaeus 2.36d on
        the effects of drink, cf. n. ad loc.

654   Cited by Schol. Plato, *Laches* 187b and Schol. Plato, *Euthydemus*
        285c for the proverb ἐν τῶι Καρὶ κινδυνεύειν.

With the exceptions of 332–5 and 534, all these quotations may be
described as grammatical or lexicographical. The citation of 332–5 in
two different imperial authors and the possibility that this speech of the
Cyclops is also echoed in Roman poetry[173] suggest that this speech may
have been anthologised and/or raided in various citational traditions,
thus making it better known than much of the play; both the subject-matter of the speech and the fact that it is delivered by the supposedly ἀμαθής
Cyclops must have made it a prime candidate for anthologising.[174]

---

[172] Athenagoras was a Christian apologist of the later second century AD. Immediately before the citation of *Cycl.* 332-3, Euripides fr. 901 and *Trag. Adesp.* 99 K–S
are cited.
[173] Cf. Catullus 32.10–11 ~ *Cycl.* 326–8 and Ovid, *Met.* 13.857–8 ~ *Cycl.* 320–1.
In the former case, this would suggest that Catullus read πέπλον/κρούω in the
Cycl. passage, which should almost certainly be emended (see n. ad loc.), but the
corruption may well have occurred before Catullus; *satur supinus* would be a very
pointed marker of the allusion. The Ovidian Cyclops' speech is replete with echoes of both Homer and Theocritus, and the Euripidean Cyclops would be a plausible further literary predecessor in the mix.
[174] The context of the citation in Athenagoras at least allows the question of
whether Aristotle might already have cited these verses (cf. Arist. fr. 796 Gigon);
the matter is, however, very uncertain.

In seeking to move beyond these explicit citations to less specific allusions to *Cyclops*, we must always bear in mind that allusions to, or evocations of, the story of Odysseus and the Cyclops in ancient authors will almost inevitably refer in the first instance to the Homeric account, or be taken as so referring; the paucity of specific references to Euripides' play does not, by itself, therefore necessarily mean that it was all but ignored from a relatively early date.[175]

---

[175] For possible allusions to or borrowings from *Cyclops* at an early date cf. 283–4, 475, 503–10nn.

SIGLA

ΕΥΡΙΠΙΔΟΥ ΚΥΚΛΩΨ

ΥΠΟΘΕΣΙΣ ΚΥΚΛΩΠΟΣ

Ὀδυσσεὺς ἀναχθεὶς ἐξ Ἰλίου εἰς Σικελίαν ἀπερρίφη, ἔνθα ὁ Πολύφημος· εὑρὼν δὲ δουλεύοντας ἐκεῖ τοὺς Σατύρους οἶνον δοὺς ἄρνας ἤμελλε λαμβάνειν καὶ γάλα παρ' αὐτῶν. ἐπιφανεὶς δ' ὁ Πολύφημος ζητεῖ τὴν αἰτίαν τῆς τῶν ἰδίων ἐκφορήσεως. ὁ Σιληνὸς δὲ τὸν ξένον λῃστεύοντα καταλαβεῖν φησιν...
τὰ τοῦ δράματος πρόσωπα· Σιληνός, χορὸς Σατύρων, Ὀδυσσεύς, Κύκλωψ.

ΣΙΛΗΝΟΣ

Ὦ Βρόμιε, διὰ σὲ μυρίους ἔχω πόνους   1
νῦν χὦτ' ἐν ἥβηι τοὐμὸν ηὐσθένει δέμας·
πρῶτον μὲν ἡνίκ' ἐμμανὴς Ἥρας ὕπο
Νύμφας ὀρείας ἐκλιπὼν ὤιχου τροφούς·
ἔπειτά γ' ἀμφὶ γηγενῆ μάχην δορὸς   5
ἐνδέξιος σῶι ποδὶ παρασπιστὴς βεβὼς
Ἐγκέλαδον ἰτέαν ἐς μέσην θενὼν δορὶ
ἔκτεινα—φέρ' ἴδω, τοῦτ' ἰδὼν ὄναρ λέγω;
οὐ μὰ Δί', ἐπεὶ καὶ σκῦλ' ἔδειξα Βακχίωι.
καὶ νῦν ἐκείνων μεῖζον' ἐξαντλῶ πόνον.   10
ἐπεὶ γὰρ Ἥρα σοι γένος Τυρσηνικὸν
λῃστῶν ἐπῶρσεν, ὡς ὁδηθείης μακράν,
⟨ἐγὼ⟩ πυθόμενος σὺν τέκνοισι ναυστολῶ
σέθεν κατὰ ζήτησιν. ἐν πρύμνηι δ' ἄκραι
αὐτὸς βεβὼς ηὔθυνον ἀμφῆρες δόρυ,   15
παῖδες δ' ⟨ἐπ'⟩ ἐρετμοῖς ἥμενοι γλαυκὴν ἅλα
ῥοθίοισι λευκαίνοντες ἐζήτουν σ', ἄναξ.

Hypothesis

personarum indicem add. Tr¹ : om. L

Text

2 ηὐσθένει Heath: εὐσθένει L   5 δ' Heath   6 βεβὼς Kassel: γεγὼς L   13 ⟨ἐγὼ⟩ Tr²
15 βεβὼς Diggle: λαβὼν L: σταθεὶς Napolitano   ηὔθυνον Heath: εὔθ- L   16 παῖδες
δ' Tr¹: παῖδες L   ⟨ἐπ'⟩ Seidler

ἤδη δὲ Μαλέας πλησίον πεπλευκότας
ἀπηλιώτης ἄνεμος ἐμπνεύσας δορὶ
ἐξέβαλεν ἡμᾶς τήνδ' ἐς Αἰτναίαν πέτραν,   20
ἵν' οἱ μονῶπες ποντίου παῖδες θεοῦ
Κύκλωπες οἰκοῦσ' ἄντρ' ἔρημ' ἀνδροκτόνοι.
τούτων ἑνὸς ληφθέντες ἐσμὲν ἐν δόμοις
δοῦλοι· καλοῦσι δ' αὐτὸν ὧι λατρεύομεν
Πολύφημον· ἀντὶ δ' εὐίων βακχευμάτων   25
ποίμνας Κύκλωπος ἀνοσίου ποιμαίνομεν.
παῖδες μὲν οὖν μοι κλειτύων ἐν ἐσχάτοις
νέμουσι μῆλα νέα νέοι πεφυκότες,
ἐγὼ δὲ πληροῦν πίστρα καὶ σαίρειν στέγας
μένων τέταγμαι τάσδε, τῶιδε δυσσεβεῖ   30
Κύκλωπι δείπνων ἀνοσίων διάκονος.
καὶ νῦν, τὰ προσταχθέντ', ἀναγκαίως ἔχει
σαίρειν σιδηρᾶι τῆιδέ μ' ἁρπάγηι δόμους,
ὡς τόν τ' ἀπόντα δεσπότην Κύκλωπ' ἐμὸν
καθαροῖσιν ἄντροις μῆλά τ' ἐσδεχώμεθα.   35
ἤδη δὲ παῖδας προσνέμοντας εἰσορῶ
ποίμνας. τί ταῦτα; μῶν κρότος σικινίδων
ὁμοῖος ὑμῖν νῦν τε χὦτε Βακχίωι
κῶμος συνασπίζοντες Ἀλθαίας δόμους
προσῆιτ' ἀοιδαῖς βαρβίτων σαυλούμενοι;   40

ΧΟΡΟΣ ΣΑΤΥΡΩΝ
       παῖ γενναίων μὲν πατέρων   [στρ.
       γενναίων δ' ἐκ τοκάδων,
       πᾶι δή μοι νίσηι σκοπέλους;
       οὐ τᾶιδ' ὑπήνεμος αὔ-
          ρα καὶ ποιηρὰ βοτάνα,   45
       δινᾶέν θ' ὕδωρ ποταμῶν
       ἐν πίστραις κεῖται πέλας ἄν-
          τρων, οὗ σοι βλαχαὶ τεκέων;

32 ἔχει TrP: ἔχοι L^{uv}P^s   39 κῶμος Diggle: κῶμοι L: κώμωι Porson   41 παῖ
Dindorf: πᾶ δή μοι L   42 δ' Ludwig Dindorf: τ' L   44 αὔρα L: αὐλὰ Musgrave
48 οὗ Casaubon: οὔ Tr¹: * * L

ψύττ'· οὐ τᾶιδ', οὔ;   [μεσωιδ.
οὐ τᾶιδε νεμῆι κλειτὺν δροσεράν;   50
ὠή, ῥίψω πέτρον τάχα σου·
ὕπαγ' ὦ ὕπαγ' ὦ κεράστα
†μηλοβότα στασιωρὸν†
Κύκλωπος ἀγροβάτα.

σπαργῶντας μαστοὺς χάλασον·   [ἀντ.
δέξαι θηλαῖσι τροφὰς   56
ἃς λείπεις ἀρνῶν θαλάμοις.
ποθοῦσί σ' ἀμερόκοι-
    τοι βλαχαὶ σμικρῶν τεκέων.
εἰς αὐλὰν πότ' †ἀμφιβαίνεις†   60
ποιηροὺς λιποῦσα νομοὺς
Αἰτναίων εἴσω σκοπέλων;

οὐ τάδε Βρόμιος, οὐ τάδε χοροὶ   [ἐπωιδ.
Βάκχαι τε θυρσοφόροι,
οὐ τυμπάνων ἀλαλαγμοί,   65
οὐκ οἴνου χλωραὶ σταγόνες   67
κρήναις παρ' ὑδροχύτοις·   66
οὐδ' ἐν Νύσαι μετὰ Νυμ-   68
    φᾶν Ἴακχον Ἴακχον ὠι-
δᾶι μέλπω πρὸς τὰν Ἀφροδί-   70
ταν, ἃν θηρεύων πετόμαν
Βάκχαις σὺν λευκόποσιν.
†ὦ φίλος ὦ φίλε Βακχεῖε
ποῖ οἰοπολεῖς
ξανθὰν χαίταν σείεις;†   75
ἐγὼ δ' ὁ σὸς πρόπολος
Κύκλωπι θητεύω

50 νεμῆι Matthiae: νέμη L   52 ὕπαγ' ὦ ὕπαγ' ὦ apogr. Par.: ὑπάγω ὑπάγω L
53 <πρὸς> μηλοβότα Wecklein στασιωρὲ post Stephanum Wilamowitz
54 ἀγροβάτα Tr²: -βότα L   56 τροφὰς Wieseler: σποράς L   63 τάδε ... τάδε
Aldina: τᾶδε ... τᾶδε L   66 post 67 trai. Hermann   68 Νύσαι Musgrave: νύσσα
<L>P   69 ὠιδᾶι Kassel: ὠιδὰν L: ὠιδαῖς Seaford   70 πρὸς del. Wecklein   73
Βακχεῖε Tr²: aut -εῖε aut -ῖε L   74 ποῦ οἰο- Wecklein   75 <ποῦ> ξανθὰν
Conradt   77 Κύκλωπι θητεύω Fritzsche: θητεύω Κύκλωπι L

　　　　τῶι μονοδέρκται δοῦλος ἀλαίνων
　　　　σὺν τᾶιδε τράγου χλαῖναι μελέαι   80
　　　　σᾶς χωρὶς φιλίας.

Σι.　σιγήσατ', ὦ τέκν', ἄντρα δ' ἐς πετρηρεφῆ
　　　　ποίμνας ἀθροῖσαι προσπόλους κελεύσατε.
Χο.　χωρεῖτ'· ἀτὰρ δὴ τίνα, πάτερ, σπουδὴν ἔχεις;
Σι.　ὁρῶ πρὸς ἀκταῖς ναὸς Ἑλλάδος σκάφος   85
　　　　κώπης τ' ἄνακτας σὺν στρατηλάτηι τινὶ
　　　　στείχοντας ἐς τόδ' ἄντρον· ἀμφὶ δ' αὐχέσιν
　　　　τεύχη φέρονται κενά, βορᾶς κεχρημένοι,
　　　　κρωσσούς θ' ὑδρηλούς. ὦ ταλαίπωροι ξένοι·
　　　　τίνες ποτ' εἰσίν; οὐκ ἴσασι δεσπότην   90
　　　　Πολύφημον οἷός ἐστιν ἄξενόν τε γῆν
　　　　τήνδ' ἐμβεβῶτες καὶ Κυκλωπίαν γνάθον
　　　　τὴν ἀνδροβρῶτα δυστυχῶς ἀφιγμένοι.
　　　　ἀλλ' ἥσυχοι γίγνεσθ', ἵν' ἐκπυθώμεθα
　　　　πόθεν πάρεισι Σικελὸν Αἰτναῖον πάγον.   95

ΟΔΥΣΣΕΥΣ
　　　　ξένοι, φράσαιτ' ἂν νᾶμα ποτάμιον πόθεν
　　　　δίψης ἄκος λάβοιμεν εἴ τέ τις θέλει
　　　　βορὰν ὀδῆσαι ναυτίλοις κεχρημένοις;
　　　　⟨ἔα·⟩
　　　　τί χρῆμα; Βρομίου πόλιν ἔοιγμεν ἐσβαλεῖν·
　　　　Σατύρων πρὸς ἄντροις τόνδ' ὅμιλον εἰσορῶ.   100
　　　　χαίρειν προσεῖπα πρῶτα τὸν γεραίτατον.
Σι.　χαῖρ', ὦ ξέν', ὅστις δ' εἶ φράσον πάτραν τε σήν.
Οδ.　Ἴθακος Ὀδυσσεύς, γῆς Κεφαλλήνων ἄναξ.
Σι.　οἶδ' ἄνδρα, κρόταλον δριμύ, Σισύφου γένος.
Οδ.　ἐκεῖνος αὐτός εἰμι· λοιδόρει δὲ μή.   105
Σι.　πόθεν Σικελίαν τήνδε ναυστολῶν πάρει;
Οδ.　ἐξ Ἰλίου γε κἀπὸ Τρωϊκῶν πόνων.

---

86 ἄνακτας Tr²: -τα L　　91 τε γῆν Jacobs: στέγην L　　93 τὴν apogr. Par.: τήνδ' L
ἀνδροβρῶτα P²: -βῶτα L　post hunc uersum notam interrogationis posuit F. J.
Williams　99 ⟨ἔα·⟩ Wecklein　101 προσεῖπον Fix　104 γένος L: γόνον Schol.
Soph. *Aj.* 190　　105 αὐτός Ludwig Dindorf: οὗτος L

Σι. πῶς; πορθμὸν οὐκ ἤιδησθα πατρώιας χθονός;
Οδ. ἀνέμων θύελλαι δεῦρό μ' ἥρπασαν βίαι.
Σι. παπαῖ· τὸν αὐτὸν δαίμον' ἐξαντλεῖς ἐμοί. 110
Οδ. ἦ καὶ σὺ δεῦρο πρὸς βίαν ἀπεστάλης;
Σι. ληιστὰς διώκων οἳ Βρόμιον ἀνήρπασαν.
Οδ. τίς δ' ἥδε χώρα καὶ τίνες ναίουσί νιν;
Σι. Αἰτναῖος ὄχθος Σικελίας ὑπέρτατος.
Οδ. τείχη δὲ ποῦ 'στι καὶ πόλεως πυργώματα; 115
Σι. οὐκ ἔστ'· ἔρημοι πρῶνες ἀνθρώπων, ξένε.
Οδ. τίνες δ' ἔχουσι γαῖαν; ἦ θηρῶν γένος;
Σι. Κύκλωπες, ἄντρ' ἔχοντες, οὐ στέγας δόμων.
Οδ. τίνος κλύοντες; ἢ δεδήμευται κράτος;
Σι. μονάδες· ἀκούει δ' οὐδὲν οὐδεὶς οὐδενός. 120
Οδ. σπείρουσι δ'—ἢ τῶι ζῶσι;—Δήμητρος στάχυν;
Σι. γάλακτι καὶ τυροῖσι καὶ μήλων βορᾶι.
Οδ. Βρομίου δὲ πῶμ' ἔχουσιν, ἀμπέλου ῥοάς;
Σι. ἥκιστα· τοιγὰρ ἄχορον οἰκοῦσι χθόνα.
Οδ. φιλόξενοι δὲ χὤσιοι περὶ ξένους; 125
Σι. γλυκύτατά φασι τὰ κρέα τοὺς ξένους φορεῖν.
Οδ. τί φήις; βορᾶι χαίρουσιν ἀνθρωποκτόνωι;
Σι. οὐδεὶς μολὼν δεῦρ' ὅστις οὐ κατεσφάγη.
Οδ. αὐτὸς δὲ Κύκλωψ ποῦ 'στιν; ἦ δόμων ἔσω;
Σι. φροῦδος, πρὸς Αἴτνηι θῆρας ἰχνεύων κυσίν. 130
Οδ. οἶσθ' οὖν ὃ δρᾶσον, ὡς ἀπαίρωμεν χθονός;
Σι. οὐκ οἶδ', Ὀδυσσεῦ· πᾶν δέ σοι δρώιημεν ἄν.
Οδ. ὄδησον ἡμῖν σῖτον, οὗ σπανίζομεν.
Σι. οὐκ ἔστιν, ὥσπερ εἶπον, ἄλλο πλὴν κρέας.
Οδ. ἀλλ' ἡδὺ λιμοῦ καὶ τόδε σχετήριον. 135
Σι. καὶ τυρὸς ὀπίας ἔστι καὶ βοὸς γάλα.
Οδ. ἐκφέρετε· φῶς γὰρ ἐμπολήμασιν πρέπει.
Σι. σὺ δ' ἀντιδώσεις, εἰπέ μοι, χρυσὸν πόσον;
Οδ. οὐ χρυσὸν ἀλλὰ πῶμα Διονύσου φέρω.
Σι. ὦ φίλτατ' εἰπών, οὗ σπανίζομεν πάλαι. 140
Οδ. καὶ μὴν Μάρων μοι πῶμ' ἔδωκε, παῖς θεοῦ.
Σι. ὃν ἐξέθρεψα ταῖσδ' ἐγώ ποτ' ἀγκάλαις;

108 ἤιδησθα Matthiae: ἤδεισθα L   112 διώκων <γ' > Wecklein   116 ἔστ'
Schenk: εἶσ' L   120 μονάδες V. Schmidt: νομάδες L   123 ῥοάς Reiske: ῥοαῖς
L   131 δρᾶσον Canter: δράσεις L   136 βοὸς L: Διὸς Ath. 14.658c

Οδ. ὁ Βακχίου παῖς, ὡς σαφέστερον μάθηις.
Σι. ἐν σέλμασιν νεώς ἐστιν ἢ φέρεις σύ νιν;
Οδ. ὅδ' ἀσκὸς ὃς κεύθει νιν, ὡς ὁρᾶις, γέρον.   145
Σι. οὗτος μὲν οὐδ' ἂν τὴν γνάθον πλήσειέ μου.
⟨Οδ.   ⟩
⟨Σι.   ⟩
Οδ. ναί· δὶς τόσον πῶμ' ὅσον ἂν ἐξ ἀσκοῦ ῥυῆι.
Σι. καλήν γε κρήνην εἶπας ἡδεῖάν τ' ἐμοί.
Οδ. βούληι σε γεύσω πρῶτον ἄκρατον μέθυ;
Σι. δίκαιον· ἦ γὰρ γεῦμα τὴν ὠνὴν καλεῖ.   150
Οδ. καὶ μὴν ἐφέλκω καὶ ποτῆρ' ἀσκοῦ μέτα.
Σι. φέρ' ἐκπάταξον, ὡς ἀναμνησθῶ πιών.
Οδ. ἰδού.   Σι. παπαιάξ, ὡς καλὴν ὀσμὴν ἔχει.
Οδ. εἶδες γὰρ αὐτήν;   Σι. οὐ μὰ Δί', ἀλλ' ὀσφραίνομαι.
Οδ. γεῦσαί νυν, ὡς ἂν μὴ λόγωι 'παινῆις μόνον.   155
Σι. βαβαί· χορεῦσαι παρακαλεῖ μ' ὁ Βάκχιος.
     ἆ ἆ ἆ.
Οδ. μῶν τὸν λάρυγγα διεκάναξέ σου καλῶς;
Σι. ὥστ' εἰς ἄκρους γε τοὺς ὄνυχας ἀφίκετο.
Οδ. πρὸς τῶιδε μέντοι καὶ νόμισμα δώσομεν.   160
Σι. χάλα τὸν ἀσκὸν μόνον· ἔα τὸ χρυσίον.
Οδ. ἐκφέρετέ νυν τυρεύματ' ἢ μήλων τόκον.
Σι. δράσω τάδ', ὀλίγον φροντίσας γε δεσποτῶν.
     ὡς ἐκπιεῖν κἂν κύλικα †μαινοίμην† μίαν
     πάντων Κυκλώπων ἀντιδοὺς βοσκήματα   165
     ῥῖψαι τ' ἐς ἅλμην Λευκάδος πέτρας ἄπο
     ἅπαξ μεθυσθεὶς καταβαλών τε τὰς ὀφρῦς.
     ὡς ὅς γε πίνων μὴ γέγηθε μαίνεται·
     ἵν' ἔστι τουτί τ' ὀρθὸν ἐξανιστάναι
     μαστοῦ τε δραγμὸς καὶ †παρεσκευασμένου†   170
     ψαῦσαι χεροῖν λειμῶνος ὀρχηστύς θ' ἅμα
     κακῶν τε λῆστις. εἶτ' ἐγὼ ⟨οὐ⟩ κυνήσομαι

---

144 σέλμασιν Aldina: σέλμασι L   145 ἀσκὸς Radermacher: ἀσκὸς L   146 post
hunc uersum lacunam statuerunt Nauck, Kirchhoff   148 τ' Reiske: γ' L
152 ἐγκάναξον Valckenaer, Pierson   164 ἐκπιὼν Kirchhoff κἂν Paley: γ' ἂν
L μαιοίμην F.W. Schmidt   166 ῥῖψαι (sic) L: ῥῖψας Kirchhoff   169 τ' ὀρθὸν
Seidler: τοὐρθὸν L   171 ὀρχηστύς Canter: ὀρχηστύος L   172 ⟨οὐ⟩ κυνήσομαι
Matthiae: κυνήσομαι L: ⟨οὐ⟩κ ὠνήσομαι Tyrwhitt

toióvδε πῶμα, τὴν Κύκλωπος ἀμαθίαν
κλαίειν κελεύων καὶ τὸν ὀφθαλμὸν μέσον;

Χο. ἄκου', Ὀδυσσεῦ· διαλαλήσωμέν τί σοι.   175
Οδ. καὶ μὴν φίλοι γε προσφέρεσθε πρὸς φίλον.
Χο. ἐλάβετε Τροίαν τὴν Ἑλένην τε χειρίαν;
Οδ. καὶ πάντα γ' οἶκον Πριαμιδῶν ἐπέρσαμεν.
Χο. οὔκουν, ἐπειδὴ τὴν νεᾶνιν εἵλετε,
     ἅπαντες αὐτὴν διεκροτήσατ' ἐν μέρει,   180
     ἐπεί γε πολλοῖς ἥδεται γαμουμένη,
     τὴν προδότιν, ἣ τοὺς θυλάκους τοὺς ποικίλους
     περὶ τοῖν σκελοῖν ἰδοῦσα καὶ τὸν χρύσεον
     κλωιὸν φοροῦντα περὶ μέσον τὸν αὐχένα
     ἐξεπτοήθη, Μενέλεων ἀνθρώπιον   185
     λῶιστον λιποῦσα; μηδαμοῦ γένος ποτὲ
     φῦναι γυναικῶν ὤφελ', εἰ μὴ 'μοὶ μόνωι.
Σι. ἰδού· τάδ' ὑμῖν ποιμένων βοσκήματα,
     ἄναξ Ὀδυσσεῦ, μηκάδων ἀρνῶν τροφαί,
     πηκτοῦ γάλακτός τ' οὐ σπάνια τυρεύματα.   190
     φέρεσθε· χωρεῖθ' ὡς τάχιστ' ἄντρων ἄπο,
     βότρυος ἐμοὶ πῶμ' ἀντιδόντες εὐίου.
     οἴμοι· Κύκλωψ ὅδ' ἔρχεται· τί δράσομεν;
Οδ. ἀπολώλαμέν γ' ἄρ', ὦ γέρον· ποῖ χρὴ φυγεῖν;
Σι. ἔσω πέτρας τῆσδ', οὗπερ ἂν λάθοιτέ γε.   195
Οδ. δεινὸν τόδ' εἶπας, ἀρκύων μολεῖν ἔσω.
Σι. οὐ δεινόν· εἰσὶ καταφυγαὶ πολλαὶ πέτρας.
Οδ. οὐ δῆτ'· ἐπεί τἂν μεγάλα γ' ἡ Τροία στένοι,
     εἰ φευξόμεσθ' ἕν' ἄνδρα, μυρίον δ' ὄχλον
     Φρυγῶν ὑπέστην πολλάκις σὺν ἀσπίδι.   200
     ἀλλ', εἰ θανεῖν δεῖ, κατθανούμεθ' εὐγενῶς
     ἢ ζῶντες αἶνον τὸν πάρος συσσώσομεν.

181 ἥδεται P²: ἥδετε L   184 κλωιὸν Dindorf: κλοιὸν L   187 'μοὶ Bothe: μοι L
188 ποιμνίων Scaliger   193 Sileno contin. Ludwig Dindorf: Vlixi trib. L: οἴμοι
... ἔρχεται Sileno, τί δράσομεν; Vlixi trib. Hermann   194 γ' ἄρ' nos: γὰρ L: τἄρ'
Hartung   198 στένοι P²: στένει L   202 πάρος συσσώσομεν Schenk: πάρος εὖ
σώσομεν L: πάροιθε σώσομεν Hartung: παρόντ' εὖ σώσομεν Wieseler

64 ΕΥΡΙΠΙΔΟΥ

ΚΥΚΛΩΨ
ἄνεχε πάρεχε· τί τάδε; τίς ἡ ῥαιθυμία;
τί βακχιάζετ'; οὐχὶ Διόνυσος τάδε,
οὐ κρόταλα χαλκοῦ τυμπάνων τ' ἀράγματα.　205
πῶς μοι κατ' ἄντρα νεόγονα βλαστήματα;
ἦ πρός τε μαστοῖς εἰσι χὐπὸ μητέρων
πλευρὰς τρέχουσι, σχοινίνοις τ' ἐν τεύχεσιν
πλήρωμα τυρῶν ἐστιν ἐξημελγμένον;
τί φατέ, τί λέγετε; τάχα τις ὑμῶν τῶι ξύλωι　210
δάκρυα μεθήσει. βλέπετ' ἄνω καὶ μὴ κάτω.
Χο. ἰδού· πρὸς αὐτὸν τὸν Δί' ἀνακεκύφαμεν
καὶ τἄστρα καὶ τὸν Ὠρίωνα δέρκομαι.
Κυ. ἄριστόν ἐστιν εὖ παρεσκευασμένον;
Χο. πάρεστιν· ὁ φάρυγξ εὐτρεπὴς ἔστω μόνον.　215
Κυ. ἦ καὶ γάλακτός εἰσι κρατῆρες πλέωι;
Χο. ὥστ' ἐκπιεῖν γέ σ', ἢν θέληις, ὅλον πίθον.
Κυ. μήλειον ἢ βόειον ἢ μεμειγμένον;
Χο. ὃν ἂν θέληις σύ· μὴ 'μὲ καταπίηις μόνον.
Κυ. ἥκιστ'· ἐπεί μ' ἂν ἐν μέσηι τῆι γαστέρι　220
πηδῶντες ἀπολέσαιτ' ἂν ὑπὸ τῶν σχημάτων.
ἔα· τίν' ὄχλον τόνδ' ὁρῶ πρὸς αὐλίοις;
ληισταί τινες κατέσχον ἢ κλῶπες χθόνα;
ὁρῶ γέ τοι τούσδ' ἄρνας ἐξ ἄντρων ἐμῶν
στρεπταῖς λύγοισι σῶμα συμπεπλεγμένους　225
τεύχη τε τυρῶν συμμιγῆ γέροντά τε
πληγαῖς μέτωπον φαλακρὸν ἐξωιδηκότα.
Σι. ὤμοι, πυρέσσω συγκεκομμένος τάλας.
Κυ. ὑπὸ τοῦ; τίς ἐς σὸν κρᾶτ' ἐπύκτευσεν, γέρον;
Σι. ὑπὸ τῶνδε, Κύκλωψ, ὅτι τὰ σ' οὐκ εἴων φέρειν.　230
Κυ. οὐκ ἦισαν ὄντα θεόν με καὶ θεῶν ἄπο;
Σι. ἔλεγον ἐγὼ τάδ'· οἱ δ' ἐφόρουν τὰ χρήματα,
καὶ τόν γε τυρὸν οὐκ ἐῶντος ἤσθιον

---

203 uersum Cyclopi trib. Tyrwhitt, Sileno L　204 οὐχὶ Διόνυσος Musgrave: οὐ διώνυσος L　207 ἦ Hermann: ἢ L　τε Ludwig Dindorf: γε L　212, 215, 217, 219 chori duci trib. Tyrwhitt, Sileno L　213 καὶ τἄστρα L: τά τ' ἄστρα Choerob. *In Theod.* 1.272　216 ἢ Tr¹: ἦ L　219 ὃν L: ὧν Kaibel　'μὲ Matthiae: με L　220 μ' Seidler: γ' L　227 μέτωπον Tyrwhitt: πρόσωπον L　233 τῶν γε τυρῶν Markland　ἐῶντος P²: ἐόντος L

τούς τ' ἄρνας ἐξεφοροῦντο· δήσαντες δὲ σὲ 235
κλωιῶι τριπήχει κατὰ τὸν ὀφθαλμὸν μέσον
τὰ σπλάγχν' ἔφασκον ἐξαμήσεσθαι βίαι,
μάστιγί τ' εὖ τὸ νῶτον ἀπολέψειν σέθεν,
κἄπειτα συνδήσαντες ἐς θἀδώλια
τῆς ναὸς ἐμβαλόντες ἀποδώσειν τινὶ
πέτρους μοχλεύειν, ἢ 'ς μυλῶνα καταβαλεῖν. 240
Κυ. ἄληθες; οὔκουν κοπίδας ὡς τάχιστ' ἰὼν
θήξεις μαχαίρας καὶ μέγαν φάκελον ξύλων
ἐπιθεὶς ἀνάψεις; ὡς σφαγέντες αὐτίκα
πλήσουσι νηδὺν τὴν ἐμὴν ἀπ' ἄνθρακος
θερμὴν διδόντες δαῖτα τῶι κρεανόμωι, 245
τὰ δ' ἐκ λέβητος ἑφθὰ καὶ τετηκότα.
ὡς ἔκπλεώς γε δαιτός εἰμ' ὀρεσκόου·
ἅλις λεόντων ἐστί μοι θοινωμένωι
ἐλάφων τε, χρόνιος δ' εἴμ' ἀπ' ἀνθρώπων βορᾶς.
Σι. τὰ καινά γ' ἐκ τῶν ἠθάδων, ὦ δέσποτα, 250
ἡδίον' ἐστίν. οὐ γὰρ οὖν νεωστί γε
ἄλλοι πρὸς ἄντρα σοὐσαφίκοντο ξένοι.
Οδ. Κύκλωψ, ἄκουσον ἐν μέρει καὶ τῶν ξένων.
ἡμεῖς βορᾶς χρῄζοντες ἐμπολὴν λαβεῖν
σῶν ἆσσον ἄντρων ἤλθομεν νεὼς ἄπο. 255
τοὺς δ' ἄρνας ἡμῖν οὗτος ἀντ' οἴνου σκύφου
ἀπημπόλα τε κἀδίδου πιεῖν λαβὼν
ἑκὼν ἑκοῦσι, κοὐδὲν ἦν τούτων βίαι.
ἀλλ' οὗτος ὑγιὲς οὐδὲν ὧν φησιν λέγει,
ἐπεὶ γ' ἐλήφθη σοῦ λάθραι πωλῶν τὰ σά. 260
Σι. ἐγώ; κακῶς γ' ἄρ' ἐξόλοι'. Οδ. εἰ ψεύδομαι.
Σι. μὰ τὸν Ποσειδῶ τὸν τεκόντα σ', ὦ Κύκλωψ,
μὰ τὸν μέγαν Τρίτωνα καὶ τὸν Νηρέα,
μὰ τὴν Καλυψώ τάς τε Νηρέως κόρας,

234 ἐξεφροῦντο Musgrave σὲ Nauck: σε L   235 κατὰ Canter: κᾶτα L   236 ἐξαμήσεσθαι Duport: ἐξαμήσασθαι L   237 ἀπολέψειν Ruhnken: ἀποθλίψειν L   238 θἀδώλια Seidler: τἀδώλια L   239 ναὸς Blaydes: νηὸς L   240 ἢ 'ς μυλῶνα Ruhnken: ἢ πυλῶνα L   243 ὡς apogr. Par.: ὦ L   245 διδόντες Heath: ἔδοντος L   247 εἴμ' ὀρεσκόου Stephanus: ἱμεροσκόου L   251 ἡδίον' Tr¹: ἥδιον L   οὖν Reiske: αὖ L   252 σοὐσαφίκοντο Murray: τὰ σ' ἀφίκοντο L   258 τούτων Barnes: τούτω L   260 γ' ἐλήφθη Heath: κατελήφθη L   261 γ' ἄρ' Kirchhoff: γάρ L

μὰ θαίερὰ κύματ᾽ ἰχθύων τε πᾶν γένος,   265
ἀπώμοσ᾽, ὦ κάλλιστον ὦ Κυκλώπιον,
ὦ δεσποτίσκε, μὴ τὰ σ᾽ ἐξοδᾶν ἐγὼ
ξένοισι χρήματ᾽. ἢ κακῶς οὗτοι κακοὶ
οἱ παῖδες ἀπόλοινθ᾽, οὓς μάλιστ᾽ ἐγὼ φιλῶ.

Χο. αὐτὸς ἔχ᾽. ἔγωγε τοῖς ξένοις τὰ χρήματα   270
περνάντα σ᾽ εἶδον· εἰ δ᾽ ἐγὼ ψευδῆ λέγω,
ἀπόλοιθ᾽ ὁ πατήρ μου· τοὺς ξένους δὲ μὴ ἀδίκει.

Κυ. ψεύδεσθ᾽· ἔγωγε τῶιδε τοῦ Ῥαδαμάνθυος
μᾶλλον πέποιθα καὶ δικαιότερον λέγω.
θέλω δ᾽ ἐρέσθαι· πόθεν ἐπλεύσατ᾽, ὦ ξένοι;   275
ποδαποί; τίς ὑμᾶς ἐξεπαίδευσεν πόλις;

Οδ. Ἰθακήσιοι μὲν τὸ γένος, Ἰλίου δ᾽ ἄπο,
πέρσαντες ἄστυ, πνεύμασιν θαλασσίοις
σὴν γαῖαν ἐξωσθέντες ἥκομεν, Κύκλωψ.

Κυ. ἦ τῆς κακίστης οἳ μετήλθεθ᾽ ἁρπαγὰς   280
Ἑλένης Σκαμάνδρου γείτον᾽ Ἰλίου πόλιν;

Οδ. οὗτοι, πόνον τὸν δεινὸν ἐξηντληκότες.

Κυ. αἰσχρὸν στράτευμά γ᾽, οἵτινες μιᾶς χάριν
γυναικὸς ἐξεπλεύσατ᾽ ἐς γαῖαν Φρυγῶν.

Οδ. θεοῦ τὸ πρᾶγμα· μηδέν᾽ αἰτιῶ βροτῶν.   285
ἡμεῖς δέ σ᾽, ὦ θεοῦ ποντίου γενναῖε παῖ,
ἱκετεύομέν τε καὶ λέγομεν ἐλευθέρως·
μὴ τλῆις πρὸς ἄντρα σοὺσαφιγμένους φίλους
κτανεῖν βοράν τε δυσσεβῆ θέσθαι γνάθοις·
οἳ τὸν σόν, ὦναξ, πατέρ᾽ ἔχειν ναῶν ἕδρας   290
ἐρρυσάμεσθα γῆς ἐν Ἑλλάδος μυχοῖς·
ἱερᾶς τ᾽ ἄθραυστος Ταινάρου μένει λιμὴν
Μαλέας τ᾽ ἄκρας κευθμῶνες ἥ τε Σουνίου
δίας Ἀθάνας σῶς ὑπάργυρος πέτρα
Γεραίστιοί τε καταφυγαί· τά θ᾽ Ἑλλάδος   295
†δύσφρον᾽ ὀνείδη† Φρυξὶν οὐκ ἐδώκαμεν.

265 μὰ θαίερὰ Franke: μά θ᾽ ἱερὰ L: τά θ᾽ ἱερὰ Hermann   273 τῶιδε Canter: τοῦδε L   274 μᾶλλον Kirchhoff: πολλὰ L   288 σοὺσαφιγμένους Radermacher: σοὺς ἀφιγμένους L   290 ναῶν Canter: νεῶν L   291 ἐρρυσάμεσθα Matthiae: εἰρυσάμεσθα L   292 ἱερᾶς Barrett, Kassel: ἱερεύς L: ἱερός apogr. Par.   ἄθραυστος Tr¹: ἄθαυστος L   293 ἄκρας Seaford: ἄκροι L   ἥ apogr. Par.: οἵ L   295 post hunc uersum lacunam indicauit Hermann   296 δύσφορά γ᾽ ὀνείδη apogr. Par.

ὧν καὶ σὺ κοινοῖ· γῆς γὰρ Ἑλλάδος μυχοὺς
οἰκεῖς ὑπ' Αἴτνηι, τῆι πυριστάκτωι πέτραι.
νόμος δὲ θνητοῖς, εἰ λόγους ἀποστρέφηι,
ἱκέτας δέχεσθαι ποντίους ἐφθαρμένους   300
ξένιά τε δοῦναι καὶ πέπλους ἐπαρκέσαι,
οὐκ ἀμφὶ βουπόροισι πηχθέντας μέλη
ὀβελοῖσι νηδὺν καὶ γνάθον πλῆσαι σέθεν.
ἅλις δὲ Πριάμου γαῖ' ἐχήρωσ' Ἑλλάδα
πολλῶν νεκρῶν πιοῦσα δοριπετῆ φόνον   305
ἀλόχους τ' ἀνάνδρους γραῦς τ' ἄπαιδας ὤλεσεν
πολιούς τε πατέρας. εἰ δὲ τοὺς λελειμμένους
σὺ συμπυρώσας δαῖτ' ἀναλώσεις πικράν,
ποῖ τρέψεταί τις; ἀλλ' ἐμοὶ πιθοῦ, Κύκλωψ·
πάρες τὸ μάργον σῆς γνάθου, τὸ δ' εὐσεβὲς   310
τῆς δυσσεβείας ἀνθελοῦ· πολλοῖσι γὰρ
κέρδη πονηρὰ ζημίαν ἠμείψατο.
Σι. παραινέσαι σοι βούλομαι· τῶν γὰρ κρεῶν
μηδὲν λίπηις τοῦδ'· ἢν δὲ τὴν γλῶσσαν δάκηις,
κομψὸς γενήσηι καὶ λαλίστατος, Κύκλωψ.   315
Κυ. ὁ πλοῦτος, ἀνθρωπίσκε, τοῖς σοφοῖς θεός,
τὰ δ' ἄλλα κόμποι καὶ λόγων εὐμορφία.
ἄκρας δ' ἐναλίας αἷς καθίδρυται πατὴρ
χαίρειν κελεύω· τί τάδε προυστήσω λόγου;
Ζηνὸς δ' ἐγὼ κεραυνὸν οὐ φρίσσω, ξένε,   320
οὐδ' οἶδ' ὅτι Ζεύς ἐστ' ἐμοῦ κρείσσων θεός.
οὔ μοι μέλει τὸ λοιπόν· ὡς δ' οὔ μοι μέλει
ἄκουσον· ὅταν ἄνωθεν ὄμβρον ἐκχέηι,
ἐν τῆιδε πέτραι στέγν' ἔχων σκηνώματα,
ἢ μόσχον ὀπτὸν ἤ τι θήρειον δάκος   325
δαινύμενος, †ἐν στέγοντι† γαστέρ' ὑπτίαν,
ἐπεκπιὼν γάλακτος ἀμφορέα, πέδον
κρούω, Διὸς βρονταῖσιν εἰς ἔριν κτυπῶν.

297 κοινοῖ Seidler: κοινοῦ L   298 Αἴτνης Hermann   299 νόμος Musgrave:
νόμοις L εἰ Reiske: εἰς L   301 πέπλους Blaydes: πέπλοις L   305 δοριπετῆ
Nauck: δορυπετῆ L   314 δὲ Lenting: τε L 316 τοῖς Tr²: τοῖ L   317 εὐμορφία
Nauck: εὐμορφίαι L   318 αἷς Paley: ἃς L   319 λόγου Barrett: λόγω L 324 ἔχων
Reiske: ἔχω L   325 ἢ L: καὶ Boissonade   326 εὖ τέγγων τε Reiske   327
πέδον Musgrave: πέπλον L

ὅταν δὲ βορέας χιόνα Θρήικιος χέηι,
δοραῖσι θηρῶν σῶμα περιβαλὼν ἐμὸν   330
καὶ πῦρ ἀναίθων, χιόνος οὐδέν μοι μέλει.
ἡ γῆ δ' ἀνάγκηι, κἂν θέληι κἂν μὴ θέληι,
τίκτουσα ποίαν τἀμὰ πιαίνει βοτά.
ἀγὼ οὔτινι θύω πλὴν ἐμοί, θεοῖσι δ' οὔ,
καὶ τῆι μεγίστηι, γαστρὶ τῆιδε, δαιμόνων.   335
ὡς τοὔμπιεῖν γε καὶ φαγεῖν τοὐφ' ἡμέραν,
Ζεὺς οὗτος ἀνθρώποισι τοῖσι σώφροσιν,
λυπεῖν δὲ μηδὲν αὑτόν. οἳ δὲ τοὺς νόμους
ἔθεντο ποικίλλοντες ἀνθρώπων βίον,
κλαίειν ἄνωγα· τὴν ⟨δ'⟩ ἐμὴν ψυχὴν ἐγὼ   340
οὐ παύσομαι δρῶν εὖ, κατεσθίων γε σέ.
ξένια δὲ λήψηι τοιάδ', ὡς ἄμεμπτος ὦ,
πῦρ καὶ πατρῶιον τόνδε χαλκόν, ὃς ζέσας
σὴν σάρκα †δυσφόρητον† ἀμφέξει καλῶς.
ἀλλ' ἕρπετ' εἴσω, τοῦ κατ' αὔλιον θεοῦ   345
ἵν' ἀμφὶ βωμὸν στάντες εὐωχῆτέ με.

Οδ. αἰαῖ, πόνους μὲν Τρωϊκοὺς ὑπεξέδυν
θαλασσίους τε, νῦν δ' ἐς ἀνδρὸς ἀνοσίου
ὠμὴν κατέσχον ἀλίμενόν τε καρδίαν.
ὦ Παλλάς, ὦ δέσποινα Διογενὲς θεά,   350
νῦν νῦν ἄρηξον· κρείσσονας γὰρ Ἰλίου
πόνους ἀφῖγμαι κἀπὶ κινδύνου βάθρα.
σύ τ', ὦ φαεννὰς ἀστέρων οἰκῶν ἕδρας
Ζεῦ ξένι', ὅρα τάδ'· εἰ γὰρ αὐτὰ μὴ βλέπεις,
ἄλλως νομίζηι, Ζεῦ, τὸ μηδὲν ὢν θεός.   355

Χο. εὐρείας φάρυγος, ὦ Κύκλωψ,   [στρ.
ἀναστόμου τὸ χεῖλος· ὡς ἕτοιμά σοι
ἐφθὰ καὶ ὀπτὰ καὶ ἀνθρακιᾶς ἄπο ⟨θερμὰ⟩
χναύειν βρύκειν   358

330 περιβαλὼν Tr¹ : περιλαβὼν L   333 τίκτουσα L: φύουσα Athenagoras,
Suppl. 25.2   336 τοὔμπιεῖν Reiske: τοῦ πιεῖν L   338 λυπεῖν Tr² : λιπεῖν
L   340 ⟨δ'⟩ Barnes   341 γε Hermann: τέ L   σέ Fix: σε L   342 δὲ Fix: τε L
ἄμεμπτος Aldina: ἄμεπτος L   343 χαλκόν Jackson: λέβητά γ' L   345 τοῦ ... θεοῦ
Blaydes: τῶ ... θεῶ L   346 βωμὸν Stephanus: κῶμον L   349 ὠμὴν Reiske: γνώμην
L   353 φαεννὰς Kassel: φαεννῶν L   354 Ζεῦ Tr¹ : ζεῦς Lᵘᵛ   355 Ζεῦ Seaford:
Ζεὺς L   356 φάρυγος Hermann: φάρυγγος L   358 ἄπο ⟨θερμὰ⟩ χναύειν Hermann:
ἀποχναύειν L   βρύκειν Casaubon: βρύχειν L

κρεοκοπεῖν μέλη ξένων
δασυμάλλωι ἐν αἰγίδι κλινομένωι.   360

μὴ 'μοὶ μὴ προσδίδου·   [μεσωιδ.
μόνος μόνωι γέμιζε πορθμίδος σκάφος.
χαιρέτω μὲν αὖλις ἅδε,
χαιρέτω δὲ θυμάτων
ἀποβώμιος †ἃν ἔχει θυσίαν†   365
Κύκλωψ Αἰτναῖος ξενικῶν
κρεῶν κεχαρμένος βορᾶι.

†νηλὴς ὢ τλᾶμον ὅστις δωμάτων†   [ἀντ.
ἐφεστίους ἱκτῆρας ἐκθύει ξένους,   371
ἐφθά τε δαινύμενος μυσαροῖσί τ᾽ ὀδοῦσιν 373
κόπτων βρύκων   372
θέρμ᾽ ἀπ᾽ ἀνθράκων κρέα   374
⟨   ⟩.

Οδ. ὢ Ζεῦ, τί λέξω, δείν᾽ ἰδὼν ἄντρων ἔσω   375
      κοὐ πιστά, μύθοις εἰκότ᾽ οὐδ᾽ ἔργοις βροτῶν;
Χο. τί δ᾽ ἔστ᾽, Ὀδυσσεῦ; μῶν τεθοίναται σέθεν
      φίλους ἑταίρους ἀνοσιώτατος Κύκλωψ;
Οδ. δισσούς γ᾽ ἀθρήσας κἀπιβαστάσας χεροῖν,
      οἳ σαρκὸς εἶχον εὐτραφέστατον πάχος.   380
Χο. πῶς, ὢ ταλαίπωρ᾽, ἦτε πάσχοντες τάδε;
Οδ. ἐπεὶ πετραίαν τήνδ᾽ ἐσήλθομεν †χθόνα†,
      ἀνέκαυσε μὲν πῦρ πρῶτον, ὑψηλῆς δρυὸς
      κορμοὺς πλατείας ἐσχάρας βαλὼν ἔπι,
      τρισσῶν ἁμαξῶν ὡς ἀγώγιμον βάρος,   385
      καὶ χάλκεον λέβητ᾽ ἐπέζεσεν πυρί.   392
      ἔπειτα φύλλων ἐλατίνων χαμαιπετῆ   386
      ἔστρωσεν εὐνὴν πλησίον πυρὸς φλογί.

359 κρεοκοπεῖν apogr. Par. : κρεω- L   360 κλινομένωι Reiske: καινόμενα L   361 'μοὶ Conradt: μοι L   362 γέμιζε Wecklein: κόμιζε L   363 ἅδε Dindorf: ἥδε L   371 ἐφεστίους Bothe: ἐφεστίους ξενικοὺς L   ξένους Kirchhoff: δόμων L   373 ante 372 trai. Hermann   μυσαροῖσί τ᾽ Kirchhoff: μυσαροῖσιν L   372 βρύκων Casaubon: βρύχων L   374 θέρμ᾽ Hermann: ἀνθρώπων θέρμ᾽ L   post h.u. <δασυμάλλωι ἐν αἰγίδι κλινόμενος> Haupt   377 τεθοίναται Reiske: γε θοινᾶται L   380 εὐτραφέστατον Scaliger: ἐντρεφ- L: εὐτρεφ- P²   382 στέγην Musgrave   392 huc traiecit Paley   387 ἔστρωσεν Pierson: ἔστησεν L

κρατῆρα δ' ἐξέπλησεν ὡς δεκάμφορον,
μόσχους ἀμέλξας, λευκὸν ἐσχέας γάλα,
σκύφος τε κισσοῦ παρέθετ' εἰς εὖρος τριῶν   390
πήχεων, βάθος δὲ τεσσάρων ἐφαίνετο,   391
ὀβελούς τ', ἄκρους μὲν ἐγκεκαυμένους πυρί,   393
ξεστοὺς δὲ δρεπάνωι τἄλλα, παλιούρου κλάδων,
†Αἰτναῖά τε σφαγεῖα πελέκεων γνάθοις†.   395
ὡς δ' ἦν ἕτοιμα πάντα τῶι θεοστυγεῖ
Ἅιδου μαγείρωι, φῶτε συμμάρψας δύο
ἔσφαζ' ἑταίρων τῶν ἐμῶν †ῥυθμῶι τινι†
τὸν μὲν λέβητος ἐς κύτος χαλκήλατον
⟨   ⟩
τὸν δ' αὖ, τένοντος ἁρπάσας ἄκρου ποδός,   400
παίων πρὸς ὀξὺν στόνυχα πετραίου λίθου
ἐγκέφαλον ἐξέρρανε· καὶ †καθαρπάσας†
λάβρωι μαχαίραι σάρκας ἐξώπτα πυρί,
τὰ δ' ἐς λέβητ' ἐφῆκεν ἕψεσθαι μέλη.
ἐγὼ δ' ὁ τλήμων δάκρυ' ἀπ' ὀφθαλμῶν χέων   405
ἐχριμπτόμην Κύκλωπι κἀδιακόνουν·
ἄλλοι δ' ὅπως ὄρνιθες ἐν μυχοῖς πέτρας
πτήξαντες εἶχον, αἷμα δ' οὐκ ἐνῆν χροΐ.
ἐπεὶ δ' ἑταίρων τῶν ἐμῶν πλησθεὶς βορᾶς
ἀνέπεσε, φάρυγος αἰθέρ' ἐξανεὶς βαρύν,   410
ἐσῆλθέ μοί τι θεῖον· ἐμπλήσας σκύφος
Μάρωνος αὐτῶι τοῦδε προσφέρω πιεῖν,
λέγων τάδ'· Ὢ τοῦ ποντίου θεοῦ Κύκλωψ,
σκέψαι τόδ' οἷον Ἑλλὰς ἀμπέλων ἄπο
θεῖον κομίζει πῶμα, Διονύσου γάνος.   415
ὁ δ' ἔκπλεως ὢν τῆς ἀναισχύντου βορᾶς
ἐδέξατ' ἔσπασέν ⟨τ'⟩ ἄμυστιν ἑλκύσας
κἀπήινεσ' ἄρας χεῖρα· Φίλτατε ξένων,

389 ἐγχέας Herwerden   394 τἄλλα Scaliger: γ' ἀλλὰ L   κλάδων Scaliger: κλάδω L et Ath. 14.650a: κλάδους Kirchhoff   397 Ἅιδου Stephanus: δίδου L   δύο apogr. Par.: δύω L   398 ῥυθμῶι θ' ἐνὶ Wilamowitz   399 κύτος Aldina: σκύτος L   post h. u. lac. indic. Diggle   401 στόνυχα Scaliger: γ' ὄνυχα L   404 τὰ δ' Heath: τάδ' L   406 κἀδιακόνουν Dindorf: καὶ διηκόνουν L   407 ἄλλοι Kirchhoff: ἄλλοι L   410 φάρυγος Scaliger: φάρυγγος L   ἐξανεὶς Porson: ἐξιεὶς L: ἐξανιεὶς Ath. 1.23e   412 αὐτῶι τοῦδε Ludwig Dindorf: αὐτοῦ τῶδε L   417 ⟨τ'⟩ Barnes

καλὸν τὸ πῶμα δαιτὶ πρὸς καλῆι δίδως.
ἡσθέντα δ' αὐτὸν ὡς ἐπηισθόμην ἐγώ,   420
ἄλλην ἔδωκα κύλικα, γιγνώσκων ὅτι
τρώσει νιν οἶνος καὶ δίκην δώσει τάχα.
καὶ δὴ πρὸς ὠιδὰς εἶρπ'· ἐγὼ δ' ἐπεγχέων
ἄλλην ἐπ' ἄλληι σπλάγχν' ἐθέρμαινον ποτῶι.
ἄιδει δὲ παρὰ κλαίουσι συνναύταις ἐμοῖς   425
ἄμουσ', ἐπηχεῖ δ' ἄντρον. ἐξελθὼν δ' ἐγὼ
σιγῆι σὲ σῶσαι κἄμ', ἐὰν βούληι, θέλω.
ἀλλ' εἴπατ' εἴτε χρήιζετ' εἴτ' οὐ χρήιζετε
φεύγειν ἄμεικτον ἄνδρα καὶ τὰ Βακχίου
ναίειν μέλαθρα Ναΐδων νυμφῶν μέτα.   430
ὁ μὲν γὰρ ἔνδον σὸς πατὴρ τάδ' ἤινεσεν·
ἀλλ' ἀσθενὴς γὰρ κἀποκερδαίνων ποτοῦ
ὥσπερ πρὸς ἰξῶι τῆι κύλικι λελημμένος
πτέρυγας ἀλύει· σὺ δέ (νεανίας γὰρ εἶ)
σώθητι μετ' ἐμοῦ καὶ τὸν ἀρχαῖον φίλον   435
Διόνυσον ἀνάλαβ', οὐ Κύκλωπι προσφερῆ.
Χο. ὦ φίλτατ', εἰ γὰρ τήνδ' ἴδοιμεν ἡμέραν
Κύκλωπος ἐκφυγόντες ἀνόσιον κάρα.
ὡς διὰ μακροῦ γε †τὸν σίφωνα τὸν φίλον
χηρεύομεν τόνδ' οὐκ ἔχομεν καταφαγεῖν.†   440
Οδ. ἄκουε δή νυν ἣν ἔχω τιμωρίαν
θηρὸς πανούργου σῆς τε δουλείας φυγήν.
Χο. λέγ', ὡς Ἀσιάδος οὐκ ἂν ἥδιον ψόφον
κιθάρας κλύοιμεν ἢ Κύκλωπ' ὀλωλότα.
Οδ. ἐπὶ κῶμον ἕρπειν πρὸς κασιγνήτους θέλει   445
Κύκλωπας ἡσθεὶς τῶιδε Βακχίου ποτῶι.
Χο. ξυνῆκ'· ἔρημον ξυλλαβὼν δρυμοῖσί νιν
σφάξαι μενοινᾶις ἢ πετρῶν ὦσαι κάτα.
Οδ. οὐδὲν τοιοῦτον· δόλιος ἡ προθυμία.
Χο. πῶς δαί; σοφόν τοί σ' ὄντ' ἀκούομεν πάλαι.   450
Οδ. κώμου μὲν αὐτὸν τοῦδ' ἀπαλλάξαι, λέγων

419 καλῆ Tr²: καλὸν L: καλὴ Lˢ uel Tr¹   422 οἶνος Murray: οἶνος L   425 συνναύταις Aldina: σὺν ναύταις L   426 ἐπηχεῖ Barnes: ἐπήχει L   430 Ναΐδων Casaubon: δαναΐδων L   436 ἀνάλαβ', οὐ apogr. Par., ἀναλαβοῦ L   440 οὐκ Tr¹: *κ L καταφυγεῖν apogr. Par.: καταφυγὴν Hermann   447 δρυμοῖσί Tyrwhitt: ῥυθμοῖσί L 448 κάτα apogr. Par.: κάτω L   449 ἡ προθυμία Musgrave: ἡ 'πιθυμία L

ὡς οὐ Κύκλωψι πῶμα χρὴ δοῦναι τόδε,
μόνον δ' ἔχοντα βίοτον ἡδέως ἄγειν.
ὅταν δ' ὑπνώσσηι Βακχίου νικώμενος,
ἀκρεμὼν ἐλαίας ἔστιν ἐν δόμοισί τις,
ὃν φασγάνωι τῶιδ' ἐξαποξύνας ἄκρον   455
ἐς πῦρ καθήσω· κἆιθ' ὅταν κεκαυμένον
ἴδω νιν, ἄρας θερμὸν ἐς μέσην βαλῶ
Κύκλωπος ὄψιν ὄμμα τ' ἐκτήξω πυρί.
ναυπηγίαν δ' ὡσεί τις ἁρμόζων ἀνὴρ   460
διπλοῖν χαλινοῖν τρύπανον κωπηλατεῖ,
οὕτω κυκλώσω δαλὸν ἐν φαεσφόρωι
Κύκλωπος ὄψει καὶ συναυανῶ κόρας.
Χο. ἰοὺ ἰού·
γέγηθα μαινόμεσθα τοῖς εὑρήμασιν.   465
Οδ. κἄπειτα καὶ σὲ καὶ φίλους γέροντά τε
νεὼς μελαίνης κοῖλον ἐμβήσας σκάφος
διπλαῖσι κώπαις τῆσδ' ἀποστελῶ χθονός.
Χο. ἔστ' οὖν ὅπως ἂν ὡσπερεὶ σπονδῆς θεοῦ
κἀγὼ λαβοίμην τοῦ τυφλοῦντος ὄμματα   470
δαλοῦ; φόνου γὰρ τοῦδε κοινωνεῖν θέλω.
Οδ. δεῖ γοῦν· μέγας γὰρ δαλός, οὗ ξυλληπτέον.
Χο. ὡς κἂν ἁμαξῶν ἑκατὸν ἀραίμην βάρος,
εἰ τοῦ Κύκλωπος τοῦ κακῶς ὀλουμένου
ὀφθαλμὸν ὥσπερ σφηκιὰν ἐκθύψομεν.   475
Οδ. σιγᾶτέ νυν· δόλον γὰρ ἐξεπίστασαι·
χὤταν κελεύω, τοῖσιν ἀρχιτέκτοσιν
πείθεσθ'. ἐγὼ γὰρ ἄνδρας ἀπολιπὼν φίλους
τοὺς ἔνδον ὄντας οὐ μόνος σωθήσομαι.
[καίτοι φύγοιμ' ἂν κἀκβέβηκ' ἄντρου μυχῶν·   480
ἀλλ' οὐ δίκαιον ἀπολιπόντ' ἐμοὺς φίλους
ξὺν οἷσπερ ἦλθον δεῦρο σωθῆναι μόνον.]

453 βίοτον Tr¹: βίοντον L   454 ὑπνώσσηι Hermann: ὑπνώση L   456 ἐξαποξύνας Tr¹: ἀποξύνας L   458 βαλῶ Pierson: βαλὼν Π¹L   459 ὄμμα τ' Pierson: ὄμματ' L   461 κωπηλατεῖ L: τ]ροχηλατει Π¹   468 ἀποστελῶ Tr¹: ἀποστέλλω L   469 ὡσπερεὶ Reiske: ὥσπερ ἐκ L   471 φόνου L: πόνου Nauck   472 οὗ Reiske: ὃν L   473 ἀραίμην Matthiae: ἀροίμην L   475 ἐκθύψομεν Hertlein: ἐκθρύψομεν L   480–2 del. nescioquis   481 ἐμοὺς apogr. Par.: ἐμοῦ L

Χο. ἄγε, τίς πρῶτος, τίς δ᾽ ἐπὶ πρώτωι
ταχθεὶς δαλοῦ κώπην ὀχμάσαι
Κύκλωπος ἔσω βλεφάρων ὤσας   485
λαμπρὰν ὄψιν διακναίσει;
[ὠιδὴ ἔνδοθεν.]
σίγα σίγα. καὶ δὴ μεθύων
ἄχαριν κέλαδον μουσιζόμενος
σκαιὸς ἀπωιδὸς καὶ κλαυσόμενος   490
χωρεῖ πετρίνων ἔξω μελάθρων.
φέρε νυν κώμοις παιδεύσωμεν
τὸν ἀπαίδευτον·
πάντως μέλλει τυφλὸς εἶναι.

μάκαρ ὅστις εὐιάζει   [στρ.α
βοτρύων φίλαισι παγαῖς   496
ἐπὶ κῶμον ἐκπετασθεὶς
φίλον ἄνδρ᾽ ὑπαγκαλίζων,
ἐπὶ δεμνίοις τε †ξανθὸν†
χλιδανᾶς ἔχων ἑταίρας   500
μυρόχριστον λιπαρὸς βό-
στρυχον, αὐδᾶι δέ· Θύραν τίς οἴξει μοι;

Κυ. παπαπαῖ· πλέως μὲν οἴνου,
γάνυμαι ⟨δὲ⟩ δαιτὸς ἥβαι,   [στρ.β
σκάφος ὁλκὰς ὣς γεμισθεὶς   505
ποτὶ σέλμα γαστρὸς ἄκρας.
ὑπάγει μ᾽ ὁ φόρτος εὔφρων
ἐπὶ κῶμον ἦρος ὥραις
ἐπὶ Κύκλωπας ἀδελφούς.
φέρε μοι, ξεῖνε, φέρ᾽, ἀσκὸν ἔνδος μοι.   510

484 δαλοῦ Stephanus: δαλῶ L ὀχμάσαι Musgrave: ὀχμάσας L   487 ὠιδὴ
ἔνδοθεν habent Π¹L   491 χωρει Π¹: χωρεῖ Tr²: χωρεῖ γε L   492 νυν Diggle:
νιν Π¹L   495 μάκαρ Π¹ (Hermann): μακάριος L   496 παγαῖς Willink: πηγαῖς
L   500 χλιδανᾶς Diggle: -ης L   501 μυρόχριστον Musgrave: -χριστος L   502 τίς
Aldina: τις L   503 παπαπαῖ Hermann: πα πα πᾶ L   504 ⟨δὲ⟩ Tr² ἥβαι Diggle
(ἥβηι Lobeck): ἥβης L   507 φόρτος Seymour: χόρτος L   510 ξεῖνε φέρ᾽ Tr²: φέρε
ξέν᾽ ⟨L⟩P

Χο. καλὸν ὄμμασιν δεδορκὼς   [στρ.γ
   καλὸς ἐκπερᾶι μελάθρων.
   ⟨   ⟩ φιλεῖ τίς ἡμᾶς;
   λύχνα δ᾽ †ἀμμένει δαῖα σὸν
   χρόα χώς† τέρεινα νύμφα   515
   δροσερῶν ἔσωθεν ἄντρων.
   στεφάνων δ᾽ οὐ μία χροιά
   περὶ σὸν κρᾶτα τάχ᾽ ἐξομιλήσει.

Οδ. Κύκλωψ, ἄκουσον· ὡς ἐγὼ τοῦ Βακχίου
   τούτου τρίβων εἴμ᾽, ὃν πιεῖν ἔδωκά σοι.   520
Κυ. ὁ Βάκχιος δὲ τίς; θεὸς νομίζεται;
Οδ. μέγιστος ἀνθρώποισιν ἐς τέρψιν βίου.
Κυ. ἐρυγγάνω γοῦν αὐτὸν ἡδέως ἐγώ.
Οδ. τοιόσδ᾽ ὁ δαίμων· οὐδένα βλάπτει βροτῶν.
Κυ. θεὸς δ᾽ ἐν ἀσκῶι πῶς γέγηθ᾽ οἴκους ἔχων;   525
Οδ. ὅπου τιθῆι τις, ἐνθάδ᾽ ἐστὶν εὐπετής.
Κυ. οὐ τοὺς θεοὺς χρὴ σῶμ᾽ ἔχειν ἐν δέρμασιν.
Οδ. τί δ᾽, εἴ σε τέρπει γ᾽; ἢ τὸ δέρμα σοι πικρόν;
Κυ. μισῶ τὸν ἀσκόν· τὸ δὲ ποτὸν φιλῶ τόδε.
Οδ. μένων νυν αὐτοῦ πῖνε κεὐθύμει, Κύκλωψ.   530
Κυ. οὐ χρή μ᾽ ἀδελφοῖς τοῦδε προσδοῦναι ποτοῦ;
Οδ. ἔχων γὰρ αὐτὸς τιμιώτερος φανῆι.
Κυ. διδοὺς δὲ τοῖς φίλοισι χρησιμώτερος.
Οδ. πυγμὰς ὁ κῶμος λοίδορόν τ᾽ ἔριν φιλεῖ.
Κυ. μεθύω μέν, ἔμπας δ᾽ οὔτις ἂν ψαύσειέ μου.   535
Οδ. ὦ τᾶν, πεπωκότ᾽ ἐν δόμοισι χρὴ μένειν.
Κυ. ἠλίθιος ὅστις μὴ πιὼν κῶμον φιλεῖ.
Οδ. ὃς δ᾽ ἂν μεθυσθείς γ᾽ ἐν δόμοις μείνηι σοφός.
Κυ. τί δρῶμεν, ὦ Σιληνέ; σοὶ μένειν δοκεῖ;
Σι. δοκεῖ· τί γὰρ δεῖ συμποτῶν ἄλλων, Κύκλωψ;   540
Οδ. καὶ μὴν λαχνῶδες τοῦδας ἀνθηρᾶς χλόης.
Σι. καὶ πρός γε θάλπος ἡλίου πίνειν καλόν.

---

512 καλὸς Scaliger: καλὸν L   513 τις Aldina   514 ἀμμένει Tr¹ uel Tr² et P:
ἀμμέν**L (probabiliter ἀμμένει)   517 χροιὰ Barnes: χρόα L   520 πιεῖν apogr.
Par.: πιὼν L   525 οἴκους Canter: οἴνους L   526 τιθῆι Porson: τιθεῖ L   534
sic L: πληγὰς ὁ κῶμος λοίδορόν θ᾽ ὕβριν φέρει Ath. 2.36d   535 μεθύω μέν Reiske:
μεθύωμεν L   541 uersum Vlixi trib. Mancini, Cyclopi L   γ᾽ οὖδας Porson

κλίθητί νύν μοι πλευρὰ θεὶς ἐπὶ χθονός.
Κυ. ἰδού.
τί δῆτα τὸν κρατῆρ' ὄπισθ' ἐμοῦ τίθης; 545
Σι. ὡς μὴ παριών τις καταβάλῃι. Κυ. πίνειν μὲν οὖν
κλέπτων σὺ βούληι· κάτθες αὐτὸν ἐς μέσον.
σὺ δ', ὦ ξέν', εἰπὲ τοὔνομ' ὅτι σε χρὴ καλεῖν.
Οδ. Οὖτιν· χάριν δὲ τίνα λαβών σ' ἐπαινέσω;
Κυ. πάντων σ' ἑταίρων ὕστερον θοινάσομαι. 550
Σι. καλόν γε τὸ γέρας τῶι ξένωι δίδως, Κύκλωψ.
Κυ. οὗτος, τί δρᾶις; τὸν οἶνον ἐκπίνεις λάθραι;
Σι. οὔκ, ἀλλ' ἔμ' οὗτος ἔκυσεν ὅτι καλὸν βλέπω.
Κυ. κλαύσηι, φιλῶν τὸν οἶνον οὐ φιλοῦντα σέ.
Σι. οὐ μὰ Δί', ἐπεί μού φησ' ἐρᾶν ὄντος καλοῦ. 555
Κυ. ἔγχει, πλέων δὲ τὸν σκύφον δίδου μόνον.
Σι. πῶς οὖν κέκραται; φέρε διασκεψώμεθα.
Κυ. ἀπολεῖς· δὸς οὕτως. Σι. οὐ μὰ Δί', οὐ πρὶν ἄν γέ σε
στέφανον ἴδω λαβόντα γεύσωμαί τέ τι.
Κυ. οἰνοχόος ἄδικος. Σι. <οὐ> μὰ Δί', ἀλλ' οἶνος
γλυκύς. 560
ἀπομακτέον δέ σοὐστὶν ὡς λήψηι πιεῖν.
Κυ. ἰδού, καθαρὸν τὸ χεῖλος αἱ τρίχες τέ μου.
Σι. θές νυν τὸν ἀγκῶν' εὐρύθμως κᾆτ' ἔκπιε,
ὥσπερ μ' ὁρᾶις πίνοντα χὦσπερ †οὐκ ἐμέ.
Κυ. ἆ ἆ, τί δράσεις; Σι. ἡδέως ἡμύστισα. 565
Κυ. λάβ', ὦ ξέν', αὐτὸς οἰνοχόος τέ μοι γενοῦ.
Οδ. γιγνώσκεται γοῦν ἄμπελος τῆμῆι χερί.
Κυ. φέρ' ἔγχεόν νυν. Οδ. ἐγχέω, σίγα μόνον.
Κυ. χαλεπὸν τόδ' εἶπας, ὅστις ἂν πίνηι πολύν.
Οδ. ἰδού, λαβὼν ἔκπιθι καὶ μηδὲν λίπηις· 570
συνεκθανεῖν δὲ σπῶντα χρὴ τῶι πώματι.

544 ἰδού add. Tr¹: om. L   545 ὄπισθ' ἐμοῦ Diggle: ὄπισθέ μου L   τίθης Tr²: τιθεῖς L
546 παριών Reiske: παρών L   καταβάλῃ P²: καταλάβῃ L   550 ὕστατον
Hermann   551 uersum Sileno trib. Lenting, Vlixi L   553 uersum Sileno trib.
L¹ᶜ uel Tr¹, Ulixi L   554 σέ Diggle: σε L   555 οὐ Diggle: ναὶ L   φησ' Florens
Christianus: φὴς L   558 οὐ μὰ Wecklein: ναὶ μὰ L   559 τέ τι Nauck: τ' ἔτι L
560 οἰνοχόος Canter: ὦ οἰνο- L   <οὐ> Hermann: rasura in L: <ναὶ > Aldina   οἶνος
Canter: ὦνος L   561 ἀπομακτέον Cobet: ἀπομυκτέον L   σοὐστὶν ὡς Wilamowitz:
σοι ὡς L: σοί γ' ὅπως Tr¹   564 οὐκ ἐμέ L: οὐκέτι Nauck   566 λάβ', ὦ ... τέ μοι
Dobree: λαβὼν ... γέ μου L   569 πίηι Fix   571 σπῶντα Casaubon: σιγῶντα L

Κυ. παπαῖ, σοφόν γε τὸ ξύλον τῆς ἀμπέλου.

Οδ. κἂν μὲν σπάσηις γε δαιτὶ πρὸς πολλῆι πολύν,
τέγξας ἄδιψον νηδύν, εἰς ὕπνον βαλεῖ,
ἢν δ᾽ ἐλλίπηις τι, ξηρανεῖ σ᾽ ὁ Βάκχιος.   575

Κυ. ἰοὺ ἰού·
ὡς ἐξένευσα μόγις· ἄκρατος ἡ χάρις.
ὁ δ᾽ οὐρανός μοι συμμεμειγμένος δοκεῖ
τῆι γῆι φέρεσθαι, τοῦ Διός τε τὸν θρόνον
λεύσσω τὸ πᾶν τε δαιμόνων ἁγνὸν σέβας.   580
οὐκ ἂν φιλήσαιμ᾽· αἱ Χάριτες πειρῶσί με.
ἅλις· Γανυμήδη τόνδ᾽ ἔχων ἀναπαύσομαι
κάλλιον ἢ τὰς Χάριτας. ἥδομαι δέ πως
τοῖς παιδικοῖσι μᾶλλον ἢ τοῖς θήλεσιν.

Σι. ἐγὼ γὰρ ὁ Διός εἰμι Γανυμήδης, Κύκλωψ;   585

Κυ. ναὶ μὰ Δί᾽, ὃν ἁρπάζω γ᾽ ἐγὼ 'κ τῆς Δαρδάνου.

Σι. ἀπόλωλα, παῖδες· σχέτλια πείσομαι κακά.

Κυ. μέμφηι τὸν ἐραστὴν κἀντρυφᾶις πεπωκότι;

Σι. οἴμοι· πικρότατον οἶνον ὄψομαι τάχα.

Οδ. ἄγε δή, Διονύσου παῖδες, εὐγενῆ τέκνα,   590
ἔνδον μὲν ἀνήρ· τῶι δ᾽ ὕπνωι παρειμένος
τάχ᾽ ἐξ ἀναιδοῦς φάρυγος ὠθήσει κρέα.
δαλὸς δ᾽ ἔσωθεν αὐλίων †ὠθεῖ† καπνὸν
παρηυτρέπισται, κοὐδὲν ἄλλο πλὴν πυροῦν
Κύκλωπος ὄψιν· ἀλλ᾽ ὅπως ἀνὴρ ἔσηι.   595

Χο. πέτρας τὸ λῆμα κἀδάμαντος ἕξομεν.
χώρει δ᾽ ἐς οἴκους πρίν τι τὸν πατέρα παθεῖν
ἀπάλαμνον· ὥς σοι τἀνθάδ᾽ ἐστὶν εὐτρεπῆ.

Οδ. Ἥφαιστ᾽, ἄναξ Αἰτναῖε, γείτονος κακοῦ
λαμπρὸν πυρώσας ὄμμ᾽ ἀπαλλάχθηθ᾽ ἅπαξ,   600
σύ τ᾽, ὦ μελαίνης Νυκτὸς ἐκπαίδευμ᾽, Ὕπνε,

---

573 σπάσηις Dobree: σπάση L   574 βαλεῖ Musgrave: βαλεῖς L   575 ἐλλίπηις
Herwerden: ἐκλίπης L   582 Γανυμήδη Elmsley: -μήδην L   583 κάλλιον ἢ
Spengel: κάλλιστα νὴ L   586 τῆς Hermann: τοῦ L   588 κἀντρυφᾶις Casaubon:
κἀντρυφαῖς L πεπωκότι Scaliger: πεπωκότα L   589 uersum Sileno trib.
apogr. Par., Cyclopi L   590 διονύσου P: διωνύσου L   591 ἀνήρ Matthiae:
ἀνὴρ L   592 φάρυγος Barnes: φάρυγγος L   594 κοὐδὲν Kirchhoff: δ᾽ οὐδὲν L
598 ἀπάλαμνον Canter: ἀπαλλαγμὸν L

ἄκρατος ἐλθὲ θηρὶ τῶι θεοστυγεῖ,
καὶ μὴ 'πὶ καλλίστοισι Τρωϊκοῖς πόνοις
αὐτόν τε ναύτας τ' ἀπολέσητ' Ὀδυσσέα
ὑπ' ἀνδρὸς ὧι θεῶν οὐδὲν ἢ βροτῶν μέλει.   605
ἢ τὴν τύχην μὲν δαίμον' ἡγεῖσθαι χρεών,
τὰ δαιμόνων δὲ τῆς τύχης ἐλάσσονα.

Χο. λήψεται τὸν τράχηλον
ἐντόνως ὁ καρκίνος
τοῦ ξενοδαιτυμόνος· πυρὶ γὰρ τάχα   610
φωσφόρους ὀλεῖ κόρας.
ἤδη δαλὸς ἠνθρακωμένος
κρύπτεται ἐς σποδιάν, δρυὸς ἄσπετον   615
ἔρνος. ἀλλ' ἴτω Μάρων, πρασσέτω,
μαινομένου 'ξελέτω βλέφαρον
Κύκλωπος, ὡς πίηι κακῶς.
κἀγὼ τὸν φιλοκισσοφόρον Βρόμιον   620
ποθεινὸν εἰσιδεῖν θέλω,
Κύκλωπος λιπὼν ἐρημίαν·
ἆρ' ἐς τοσόνδ' ἀφίξομαι;

Οδ. σιγᾶτε πρὸς θεῶν, θῆρες, ἡσυχάζετε,
συνθέντες ἄρθρα στόματος· οὐδὲ πνεῖν ἐῶ,   625
οὐ σκαρδαμύσσειν οὐδὲ χρέμπτεσθαί τινα,
ὡς μὴ 'ξεγερθῆι τὸ κακόν, ἔστ' ἂν ὄμματος
ὄψις Κύκλωπος ἐξαμιλληθῆι πυρί.
Χο. σιγῶμεν ἐγκάψαντες αἰθέρα γνάθοις.
Οδ. ἄγε νυν ὅπως ἅψεσθε τοῦ δαλοῦ χεροῖν   630
ἔσω μολόντες· διάπυρος δ' ἐστὶν καλῶς.
Χο. οὔκουν σὺ τάξεις οὕστινας πρώτους χρεών
καυτὸν μοχλὸν λαβόντας ἐκκαίειν τὸ φῶς
Κύκλωπος, ὡς ἂν τῆς τύχης κοινώμεθα;
Χο.ᵃ ἡμεῖς μέν ἐσμεν μακροτέρω πρὸ τῶν θυρῶν   635

---

604 ναύτας Trᵃ: ναῦς <L>P   610 ξενοδαιτυμόνος Hermann: ξένων δαιτυμόνος L
617 μαινομένου 'ξελέτω Hermann: μαινόμενος ἐξελέτω L   626 χρέμπτεσθαι Trᵃ:
χριμπτ- L   633 καυτὸν Hermann: καὶ τὸν L   ἐκκαίειν Aldina: ἐκκάειν L   635-41
de distributione uersuum non constat   635 Χο.ᵃ] χο. L   μακροτέρω Matthiae:
-ότεροι L

ἑστῶτες ὠθεῖν ἐς τὸν ὀφθαλμὸν τὸ πῦρ.
Χο.β ἡμεῖς δὲ χωλοί γ' ἀρτίως γεγενήμεθα.
Χο.α ταὐτὸν πεπόνθατ' ἄρ' ἐμοί· τοὺς γὰρ πόδας
ἑστῶτες ἐσπάσθημεν οὐκ οἶδ' ἐξ ὅτου.
Οδ. ἑστῶτες ἐσπάσθητε; Χο.α καὶ τά γ' ὄμματα   640
μέστ' ἐστὶν ἡμῖν κόνεος ἢ τέφρας ποθέν.
Οδ. ἄνδρες πονηροὶ κοὐδὲν οἵδε σύμμαχοι.
Χο. ὁτιὴ τὸ νῶτον τὴν ῥάχιν τ' οἰκτίρομεν
καὶ τοὺς ὀδόντας ἐκβαλεῖν οὐ βούλομαι
τυπτόμενος, αὕτη γίγνεται πονηρία;   645
ἀλλ' οἶδ' ἐπωιδὴν Ὀρφέως ἀγαθὴν πάνυ,
ὥστ' αὐτόματον τὸν δαλὸν ἐς τὸ κρανίον
στείχονθ' ὑφάπτειν τὸν μονῶπα παῖδα γῆς.
Οδ. πάλαι μὲν ἤιδη σ' ὄντα τοιοῦτον φύσει,
νῦν δ' οἶδ' ἄμεινον. τοῖσι δ' οἰκείοις φίλοις   650
χρῆσθαί μ' ἀνάγκη. χειρὶ δ' εἰ μηδὲν σθένεις,
ἀλλ' οὖν ἐπεγκέλευέ γ', ὡς εὐψυχίαν
φίλων κελευσμοῖς τοῖσι σοῖς κτησώμεθα.
Χο. δράσω τάδ'· ἐν τῶι Καρὶ κινδυνεύσομεν.
κελευσμάτων δ' ἕκατι τυφέσθω Κύκλωψ.   655

ἰὼ ἰώ·
ὠθεῖτε γενναιότατα,
σπεύδετ', ἐκκαίετ' ὀφρὺν
θηρὸς τοῦ ξενοδαίτα.
τύφετ' ὦ, καίετ' ὦ
τὸν Αἴτνας μηλονόμον.   660
τόρνευ' ἕλκε, μή σ' ἐξοδυνηθεὶς
δράσηι τι μάταιον.

---

637 Χο.β] ἡμιχ. L   χωλοί Tr²: χολοί <L>P   638 Χο.α] ταὐτὸν ... ἐμοί Vlixi trib. L
ἄρ' Tr²: ἄρ' L   638–9 τοὺς ... ὅτου choro trib. L   640 ἑστῶτες ἐσπάσθητε;
Vlixi trib. L: choreutae B uel C etiam possis   Χο.α] χο. Tr¹ et fort. L   641 μέστ'
ἐστὶν Scaliger: μέτεστιν L   ἡμῖν Barnes: ἡμῶν L   κόνεος Musgrave: κόνεως L   647
ὥστ' Blaydes: ὡς L   649 ἤιδη Heath: ἤδειν L   654 κινδυνευτέον Schol. Pl.
Laches 187b   656–7 ὠθεῖτε γενναιότατα Diggle: γενν- ὠθ- L   ὀφρὺν Hermann:
τὴν ὀφρὺν L   659 τύφετ' ὦ, καίετ' ὦ Musgrave: τύφετω καιέτω L   661 numeri
incerti   ἕλκε τόρνευε Hunter   μὴ 'ξοδυνη- /θεὶς apogr. Par.

Κυ. ὤμοι, κατηνθρακώμεθ' ὀφθαλμοῦ σέλας.
Χο. καλός γ' ὁ παιάν· μέλπε μοι τόνδ' αὖ, Κύκλωψ.
Κυ. ὤμοι μάλ', ὡς ὑβρίσμεθ', ὡς ὀλώλαμεν.   665
   ἀλλ' οὔτι μὴ φύγητε τῆσδ' ἔξω πέτρας
   χαίροντες, οὐδὲν ὄντες· ἐν πύλαισι γὰρ
   σταθεὶς φάραγγος τῆσδ' ἐναρμόσω χέρας.
Χο. τί χρῆμ' αὐτεῖς, ὦ Κύκλωψ; Κυ. ἀπωλόμην.
Χο. αἰσχρός γε φαίνηι. Κυ. κἀπὶ τοῖσδέ γ' ἄθλιος.   670
Χο. μεθύων κατέπεσες ἐς μέσους τοὺς ἄνθρακας;
Κυ. Οὖτίς μ' ἀπώλεσ'. Χο. οὐκ ἄρ' οὐδείς ⟨σ'⟩ ἠδίκει.
Κυ. Οὖτίς με τυφλοῖ βλέφαρον. Χο. οὐκ ἄρ' εἶ τυφλός.
Κυ. †ὣς δὴ σύ†. Χο. καὶ πῶς σ' οὖτις ἂν θείη τυφλόν;
Κυ. σκώπτεις. ὁ δ' Οὖτις ποῦ 'στιν; Χο. οὐδαμοῦ,   675
   Κύκλωψ.
Κυ. ὁ ξένος ἵν' ὀρθῶς ἐκμάθηις μ' ἀπώλεσεν,
   ὁ μιαρός, ὅς μοι δοὺς τὸ πῶμα κατέκλυσεν.
Χο. δεινὸς γὰρ οἶνος καὶ παλαίεσθαι βαρύς.
Κυ. πρὸς θεῶν, πεφεύγασ' ἢ μένουσ' ἔσω δόμων;
Χο. οὔτοι σιωπῆι τὴν πέτραν ἐπήλυγα   680
   λαβόντες ἑστήκασι. Κυ. ποτέρας τῆς χερός;
Χο. ἐν δεξιᾶι σου. Κυ. ποῦ; Χο. πρὸς αὐτῆι τῆι πέτραι.
   ἔχεις; Κυ. κακόν γε πρὸς κακῶι· τὸ κρανίον
   παίσας κατέαγα. Χο. καί σε διαφεύγουσί γε.
Κυ. οὐ τῆιδέ πηι, τῆιδ' εἶπας; Χο. οὔ· ταύτηι λέγω.   685
Κυ. πῆι γάρ; Χο. περιάγου κεῖσε, πρὸς τἀριστερά.
Κυ. οἴμοι γελῶμαι· κερτομεῖτέ μ' ἐν κακοῖς.
Χο. ἀλλ' οὐκέτ', ἀλλὰ πρόσθεν οὗτός ἐστι σοῦ.
Κυ. ὦ παγκάκιστε, ποῦ ποτ' εἶ; Οδ. τηλοῦ σέθεν
   φυλακαῖσι φρουρῶ σῶμ' Ὀδυσσέως τόδε.   690
Κυ. πῶς εἶπας; ὄνομα μεταβαλὼν καινὸν λέγεις.
Οδ. ὅπερ μ' ὁ φύσας ὠνόμαζ' Ὀδυσσέα.
   δώσειν δ' ἔμελλες ἀνοσίου δαιτὸς δίκας·

664 αὖ Markland: ὦ L   668 τῆσδ' Nauck: τάσδ' L   672 ἀπώλεσ' Matthiae: ἀπώλεσεν L ⟨σ'⟩ Battierius   674 σ' οὖτις Canter: σύ· τίς σ' L   677 κατέκλυσεν Canter: κατέκαυσε L   678 uersum choro trib. Reiske, Cyclopi L   οἶνος Camper: οἶνος L   685 τῆιδέ πηι Blaydes: τῆδ' ἐπεὶ L   686 περιάγου κεῖσε Nauck: περιάγουσί σε L   688 σοῦ Diggle: σου L   690 σῶμ' Canter: δῶμ' L   692 μ' Nauck: γ' L: μ' post φύσας apogr. Par.

κακῶς γὰρ ἂν Τροίαν γε διεπυρώσαμεν
εἰ μή σ' ἑταίρων φόνον ἐτιμωρησάμην.   695
Κυ. αἰαῖ· παλαιὸς χρησμὸς ἐκπεραίνεται·
τυφλὴν γὰρ ὄψιν ἐκ σέθεν σχήσειν μ' ἔφη
Τροίας ἀφορμηθέντος. ἀλλὰ καὶ σέ τοι
δίκας ὑφέξειν ἀντὶ τῶνδ' ἐθέσπισεν,
πολὺν θαλάσσηι χρόνον ἐναιωρούμενον.   700
Οδ. κλαίειν σ' ἄνωγα· καὶ δέδραχ' ὅπερ λέγεις.
ἐγὼ δ' ἐπ' ἀκτὰς εἶμι καὶ νεὼς σκάφος
ἥσω 'πὶ πόντον Σικελὸν ἔς τ' ἐμὴν πάτραν.
Κυ. οὐ δῆτ', ἐπεί σε τῆσδ' ἀπορρήξας πέτρας
αὐτοῖσι συνναύταισι συντρίψω βαλών.   705
ἄνω δ' ἐπ' ὄχθον εἶμι, καίπερ ὢν τυφλός,
δι' ἀμφιτρῆτος τῆσδε προσβαίνων ποδί.
Χο. ἡμεῖς δὲ συνναῦταί γε τοῦδ' Ὀδυσσέως
ὄντες τὸ λοιπὸν Βακχίωι δουλεύσομεν.

694 καλῶς Dobree   διεπυρώσαμεν Fix: διεπυρωσάμην L   701 λέγεις Paley: λέγω L
704 σε Tr¹: γε L   705 συνναύταισι Barnes: σὺν ναύταισι L   707 de lacuna post
hunc uersum cogitauit Diggle

COMMENTARY

HYPOTHESIS

As also for *Her.*, L preserves only the first part of a *hypothesis* ('plot summary') to *Cycl.* which goes back eventually to a collection of such 'tales from Euripides' probably composed in the first or second century AD; they were not for those who intended to read the plays, but rather offered easy and simple access to Euripidean myths. Nevertheless, it is clear that the author of the *hypothesis* knew *Cycl.* well. The geography, which elides all of the Homeric Odysseus' travels before reaching the land of the Cyclopes, is that of Euripides, not Homer, and may derive from 106–7 (cf. 109n.). The Sicilian setting is assumed, and what remains of the plot summary is clearly indebted to the opening scenes between Silenos, Odysseus and the Cyclops, notably the idea that Odysseus and his men were going to steal lambs (cf. 223n.); the late word ἐκφόρησις was very likely suggested by τούς τ' ἄρνας ἐξεφοροῦντο in 234 (cf. also 137, 162, 232).

The *hypothesis* refers to ὁ Πολύφημος, as though the Homeric story were well known, which is indeed an important assumption of Euripides' play (cf. 24–5n., above p. 19); in the list of *dramatis personae* which he added in L, Triclinius refers instead to Κύκλωψ, as the title-figure of the play. For further discussion of Euripidean *hypotheseis* cf. Zuntz 1955: 134–46, Rusten 1982, Rossum-Steenbeek 1998: 1–32, Diggle 2005.

1–40 PROLOGUE

Silenos probably enters from the central door of the *skēnē*, which represents the cave of the Cyclops, Polyphemos; he is holding some kind of metal rake (33n.), and the actor may have gone through a 'raking' routine before he begins to speak; Silenos explains how it is that he and the satyrs have come to be the slaves of the Cyclops. On the similarities to Ion's monody cf. above pp. 41–2 and 1, 33nn., and on the possible links to the *Hypsipyle* above pp. 42–3. For Silenos' appearance and costume cf. above p. 29.

1–10 Euripidean prologues often begin with an exclamatory address or prayer, cf. *Alc.*, *Andr.*, *Ph.* (with Mastronarde on vv. 3–4), *Suppl.*, Schadewaldt 1926: 99–101; earlier stages of the form are visible in the openings of Aesch. *Suppl.* and *Ch.* Comedy parodied the form (cf. esp. Ar. *Eccl.* 1–18), and Silenos' complaints have more than a tinge of the 'mock-tragic' (or 'mock-epic'). Euripides' satyric *Skiron*, another play in which the satyrs were enslaved to a monster, began with a prayer-style address by (very probably) Silenos to Hermes (fr. 674a), and the satyric *Bousiris* may have begun ὦ δαῖμον (fr. 312b). Here Silenos recalls past labours on the god's behalf which pale beside the trouble he is now facing. Such a paratactic structure, the so-called 'priamel', which leads up to and gives particular emphasis to the final item in the series, i.e. the immediate situation, finds a close parallel in the opening monologue of Ar. *Ach.*, in which Dicaeopolis contrasts his past experiences with his current distress, cf. Davies 1999, Compton-Engle 2001. Some, if not all, of Dicaeopolis' past experiences are drawn from the world of theatre and musical performance, and it is tempting to think that Silenos' past πόνοι also had been the subject of satyr-dramas familiar to the audience (so Waltz 1931, cf. further 3–4n.).

Although the narratives of vv. 3–4 and 5–9 are very elliptical, the implicit 'message' seems clear: Silenos has helped Dionysos in the past, and now the god should repay and rescue him (cf. Pulleyn 1997: 17–38 on this rhetoric of prayer); the point will have come with greater force if the actor directly addressed the statue of the god in the theatre (Pickard-Cambridge 1968: 60).

1 ὦ Βρόμιε: Bromios, later at least understood as the 'Thunderer' or 'Roarer' from βρέμειν (cf. Diod. Sic. 4.5.1), is one of the most common titles by which Dionysos is addressed in *Ba.* and *Cycl.* (99, 112, etc.); in the *Homeric Hymn* (7) the god introduces himself at the end as Διόνυσος ἐρίβρο-μος (v. 56). The name evokes the noise with which Dionysiac cult was filled, cf. Pratinas, *PMG* 708.3 ἐμὸς ἐμὸς ὁ Βρόμιος, ἐμὲ δεῖ κελαδεῖν, ἐμὲ δεῖ παταγεῖν, *Ba.* 156 βαρυβρόμων ὑπὸ τυμπάνων, Cat. 64.251–64, 8n. on Ἐγκέλαδον. For Silenos, however, that raucous noise is now a distant memory. It is almost impossible to identify rules for the difference in tone between vocative addresses to gods with and without ὦ; here, the interjection may either mark Silenos' proximity to the god, or it may be a touch of high prayer-style, like διὰ σέ which follows, cf. *Ba.* 584 ὦ Βρόμιε Βρόμιε (an impassioned plea from the chorus), *Ion* 125–7 (Ion to Apollo), Ar. *Eccl.* 1 ὦ λαμπρὸν ὄμμα τοῦ τροχηλάτου λύχνου κτλ., Scott 1905: 34–9, McClure 1995: 50–5, Dickey 1996: 199–206.

διὰ σέ evokes the style of prayers of gratitude to and praise of a god, both serious and parodic, cf. Ar. *Birds* 1546 (with Dunbar's n.), *Pl.* 145–83, *Eccl.* 975 διὰ τοι σὲ πόνους ἔχω (a young man appealing to his beloved), Timocreon, *PMG* 731.3. Here the language of gratitude, which is immediately undercut by μυρίους ἔχω πόνους, carries an implicit reproof of the god. Gods themselves have no πόνοι, because they accomplish everything 'with ease', cf. Ar. *Frogs* 402 (Iakkhos), *Ba.* 194, 614

(Dionysos). *Ba.* 618–22 powerfully illustrates the gap between human πόνοι and divine ἡσυχία.

μυρίους … πόνους: Silenos presents himself as a great hero such as Heracles, cf. *Her.* 1275–6, 1353 πόνων δὴ μυρίων ἐγευσάμην, Laemmle 2013: 165 n.35. In view, however, of the self-fashioning to follow, we may also hear a claim to the πολλὰ ἄλγεα of Odysseus (*Od.* 1.4), appropriately placed at the very beginning of Silenos' 'epic', cf. Hunter 2009: 60, above p. 19. πόνος in the service of a god should be a pleasure (cf. e.g. *Ba.* 66 Βρομίωι πόνον ἡδὺν/κάματόν τ' εὐκάματον, Soph. *Ichn.* 223–8, where Cyllene describes the satyrs' ecstatic revelry with Dionysos as πόνοι), but Silenos now sees things differently. The pleasure of labour (πόνοι, μόχθοι) for the god is a persistent motif in the young Ion's monody while sweeping the temple of Apollo at Delphi, cf. *Ion* 102–3, 128, 131, 133, 181, and the old Silenos' sweeping may perhaps evoke that scene, cf. above pp. 41–2; if so, we may have here a Dionysiac 'subversion' of a very Apolline scene.

2 χὤτ' ἐν ἥβηι τοὐμὸν ηὐσθένει δέμας 'and when in my prime my body had its full strength'. Like Nestor (cf., e.g., *Il.* 7.157, 11.670) or Aristophanic choruses of old men (*Ach.* 210–18, *Wasps* 230–41, *Lys.* 271–85), Silenos likes to reminisce about the exploits of his youth, but it is likely that, for the audience, the Silenos of satyr-drama had no youth; he is in fact eternally old. Aristotle says of old men that 'they live in their memories' and 'take pleasure in remembering' (*Rhet.* 2.1390a6, 10), and Horace might almost have had Silenos in mind in his description of the old man, *difficilis, querulus, laudator temporis acti/se puero, castigator censorque minorum* (*AP* 173–4), even if Silenos is certainly not the only old man whose account of his youth is a wishful fiction. Silenos perhaps here gestures (or looks sadly) towards his genitals (cf. 169), as sex is one area where he claims former prowess, cf. Soph. *Ichn.* 154–5 οὗ πόλλ' ἐφ' ἥβης μνήματ' ἀνδρείας ὕπο κτλ. (apparently of past sexual 'conquests'), Ar. *Wasps* 1062–3 (the chorus of old men lament that once they were κατ' αὐτὸ τοῦτο μόνον/ ἄνδρες ἀλκιμώτατοι). δέμας euphemistically suggests 'penis' at Plato Com. fr. 189.10, in a high-style hexameter parody of Philoxenus, and could no doubt, like ἥβη itself (Aesch. *Dikt.* fr. 47a.830, Ar. *Clouds* 976, Theopomp. Com. 37.2), take on that resonance from the context; Silenos' use of the term 'body' is similarly suggestive, rather than explicit, as he has (*inter alia*) military exploits in mind.

ηὐσθένει: there is no inscriptional evidence to indicate whether verbs compounded with εὖ took the augment at this period, and ευ- and ηυ- would not have been distinguished in the old Attic alphabet; the evidence of ancient grammarians and MSS is divided, and on balance there is no good reason to deny the augment, cf. Mastronarde 1989, Rijksbaron 1991: 133–5. εὐσθενεῖν and εὐθενεῖν, 'flourish', are standardly confused in

MSS; L. Dindorf proposed ηὐθένει here, but the existence of εὐσθενεῖν seems sufficiently established.

3–4 Silenos recalls an episode in which Dionysos had been sent mad by Hera, presumably (as with Heracles) because he was one of Zeus's bastard children. In the *Iliad*, Diomedes alludes to a story in which Lycurgus 'chased off the nurses of maddened Dionysos down holy Nysa' and the god himself 'dived in fright into the waves of the sea, and Thetis received the terrified god in her bosom' (6.130–7). This seems to be an episode from the god's childhood, and it would make rhetorical sense for Silenos to begin with a memory which showed that he had been serving the god 'from the beginning' or, at least, since his earliest appearance in epic poetry. Silenos is often depicted with the divine baby in both satyr-drama (cf., e.g., Soph. *Dionysiskos* fr. 171) and art, cf. *LIMC* s.v. Dionysos no. 686. Apollodorus 3.5.1, however, seems to place this story later in the god's life (cf. Nonnus, *Dion.* 32.98–150), but also has Lycurgus taking prisoner 'the Bacchants and the crowd of satyrs who followed the god'; this evokes a familiar 'enslavement' narrative of satyr-drama, of which *Cyclops* itself is an example. Aeschylus wrote a satyric *Lycurgus* (frr. 124–6, Laemmle 2013: 129–32), but very little can be said with certainty of its plot. *Cycl.* 3–4 is the earliest testimony to Hera's role in the madness, but at Pl. *Laws* 2.642b the Athenian reports a story that in revenge for Hera 'destroying his soul's judgement' the god introduced Bacchic rites and frenzied (μανική) dancing. Much later sources report a story that, sent mad by Hera, Dionysos fled west, hoping to consult the oracle at Dodona, and was helped across a flooded marsh by an ass which was subsequently placed among the stars out of gratitude (cf. Hyginus, *Astr.* 2.23, Robert 1878: 90–1); one source attributes this story to Philiscus, perhaps the Alexandrian tragedian and priest of Dionysos (cf. *TrGF* 104 T1). It is intriguing that this story is found in connection with another 'ass-story' about the Gigantomachy (cf. 5–9n.), but there is no necessary link to vv. 3–4. If vv. 3–4 do refer to a satyr-drama, then we can only speculate as to its identity: Aesch. *Lycurgus* (cf. O'Sullivan 2005: 130), Aesch. *Trophoi* (cf. Laemmle 2013: 132–40) and Soph. *Dionysiskos* (cf. Sutton 1974) have all been suggested. For possible iconographic depictions of the god's madness cf. Carpenter 1997: 36–8.

ὕπο: when a disyllabic preposition follows its noun ('anastrophe'), the accent is recessive, i.e. moves to the first syllable, cf. Smyth §175.

Νύμφας ... τροφούς 'you went off (ᾤχου, 2nd pers. sing. imperfect οἴχομαι), leaving behind the mountain Nymphs, your nurses'. At *HHymn* 26.3–5 Dionysos' nurses are 'fair-tressed nymphs in the glades of Nysa' (cf. *Il.* 6.133, Diod. Sic. 4.2.3–5, Hedreen 1994: 49–50), and Hes. fr. 10a.17–18 makes the satyrs siblings of 'the goddess Nymphs of the mountains'. Vase-painting often depicts the baby god being handed over to or reared by nymphs, cf. *LIMC* s.v. Dionysos nos. 682–5, 696–700, Heydemann 1885: 18–25. The 'nurses' (τιθῆναι) of *Il.* 6.132 seem to correspond to what would later be called Maenads, and at Soph. *OC* 680 the god is accompanied by his 'divine nurses'. In another version the god was raised by nymphs on Naxos, cf. Diod. Sic. 5.52, Hunter on Ap. Rhod. *Arg.* 4.425. A later rationalising account explained that the nymphs were said to be Dionysos' 'nurses' because they make the god (i.e. wine) expand and cause him to be healthful, cf. Phanodemus, *FGrHist* 325 F12, Philochorus, *FGrHist* 328 F5a; νύμφη is a common term for water (LSJ s.v. II 2).

5–9 Silenos' second memory is of the Gigantomachy, in which the Olympians put down a revolt of the Giants; Dionysos' role in the battle is very frequently recorded in literature and art, including on the east metope of the Parthenon and the north frieze of the Siphnian Treasury at Delphi, cf. *Ion* 216–18 (probably evoking the Siphnian Treasury, cf. Simon 1984), Mayer 1887: 319–28, *LIMC* s.v. Dionysos nos. 609–63, Carpenter 1997: chapter 2. Vase-painting of the later fifth century shows Dionysos attended or 'assisted' at the Gigantomachy by Maenads and satyrs, including satyrs of the theatrical type (cf. *LIMC* s.v. Silenoi nos. 129–40), and it has often been guessed that art has here been influenced by a satyr-drama; unsurprisingly, however, nothing as heroic as Silenos' memory here is depicted. Eratosthenes, *Catasterismoi* 11 (cf. Hyginus, *Astr.* 2.23.3, Pàmias i Massana and Zucker 2013: 35, Robert 1878: 92–3) tells how the braying of the asses (very Dionysiac-satyric animals) on which Dionysos, Hephaistos and the satyrs rode to the Gigantomachy put the Giants to flight, and this was the origin of the star group of Asses; the story has excellent potential to be a satyr-drama (cf. Laemmle 2013: 184–5, Pàmias i Massana and Zucker 2013: 183), but, as with the story of the god's nurses, there is no clear testimony for such a fifth-century play.

5 ἔπειτά γ': γε emphasises ἔπειτα and draws attention to the grandeur and importance of this memory: the Gigantomachy gets five verses, whereas Dionysos' nurses had only two. ἔπειτα δ' would be the more common form of connective (Davies 1999: 428 n.4), and several editors adopt Heath's emendation.

ἀμφὶ γηγενῆ μάχην δορός: lit. 'at the earthborn spear-battle', i.e. 'at the battle with the Earthborn Giants'; Silenos' style rises with his epic pretensions. The exact nuance of ἀμφί is uncertain: temporal, 'at the time of' (cf. LSJ s.v. C II), or spatial 'on the fringes of' (LSJ s.v. C I 1–2), with a vagueness which suits Silenos' imaginative reconstruction? The Giants were the children of Earth and Ouranos, and γίγας and γηγενής were linked from an early date, cf. *Ph.* 1131 (with Mastronarde's n.), Soph. *Tr.* 1058–9, *Orphica* fr. 188 Bernabé. For μάχη δορός cf. fr. 360.24, Soph. fr. 1130.9–10, Fraenkel on Aesch. *Ag.* 439.

6 lit. '… taking my stand as a shield-bearer on the right side of your foot'. Silenos imagines himself (anachronistically) as a hoplite, standing in the line with Dionysos; the gods and the Giants are both armed as hoplites in some representations of the battle, such as the Siphnian frieze at Delphi. Hoplites held their shields on their left arm and so the relatively unprotected right side was defended by the left side of the shield of the man on the right (cf. Thucyd. 5.71.1, with the caution of Van Wees 2004: 185–6). Silenos, a *miles* truly *gloriosus* (cf. Soph. *Ichn.* 158 for his alleged feats with the spear), thus arrogates to himself a position of crucial importance as the god's 'right-hand man', cf. *El.* 886 (Pylades to Orestes); later, Plautus' Pyrgopolinices perhaps claims to have saved Mars himself in battle (Plaut. *MG* 13–15). In Lucian's comic account of the god's Indian wars, Silenos commands the prestigious right wing (*Bacch.* 4). Satyrs are often depicted on vases as light-armed peltasts (cf. Heinemann 2016: 367–73), but for a hoplite satyr cf., e.g., Lissarrague 2013: fig. 153, and below 38–9n.; on a red-figure vase of the early fifth century Dionysos arms himself while a satyr stands beside him holding the armour (*LIMC* s.v. Dionysos n. 609).

παρασπιστὴς βεβώς: the noun is found only in Eur. For βεβώς cf. *Ph.* 1073–4 οὗ παρ' ἀσπίδα/βέβηκας αἰεὶ πολεμίων εἴργων βέλη, *Suppl.* 885 ἐν μάχηι βεβώς; the participle also suggests the brave soldier 'standing firm', cf. Archil. fr. 114.4 W ἀσφαλέως βεβηκὼς ποσσί, LSJ s.v. βαίνω A2. The transmitted γεγώς, defended by Biehl 1986: 5–8, gives the much less colourful 'being your shield-neighbour …'

7 As he relives his (imagined) *aristeia*, Silenos probably makes thrusting gestures with his rake to illustrate his achievement. His mime may remind the audience of armed dances such as the *pyrrhichē* (cf. further 36–8n., Laemmle 2013: 186–8); vase-paintings from c. 500 show armed satyrs dancing with spears at the ready, cf. Ceccarelli 2004: 108–11, Heinemann 2016: 370.

Ἐγκέλαδον: one of the best known Giants, usually said to have been killed by Athena (*Her.* 908, *Ion* 209–11, *LIMC* s.v.). Silenos chooses to claim Enkelados as his victim for various reasons. First, simply because of this Giant's prominence in the Athenian version of the Gigantomachy – Silenos amusingly takes the place of the city's patron goddess; secondly, the name, 'he who has the κέλαδος', suggests the loud noise often found in contexts of Dionysiac cult, cf. Pratinas, *PMG* 708.3 (cited in 1n.), Melero 1984, Laemmle 2013: 180–1; we should perhaps here recall the story of the braying asses at the Gigantomachy (5–9n.). That this etymology of Ἐγκέλαδος was felt is supported by the fact that another Giant-victim of Athena on the frieze of the Siphnian Treasury was Ἐρίκτυπος, cf. *LIMC* s.v. Thirdly, some later versions name Enkelados, rather than Typhoeus (Pind. *Pyth.* 1.16, etc.), as the Giant trapped beneath Mt Etna, cf. Call. fr. 1.35–6 (with Hunter and Laemmle 2019), Virg. *Aen.* 3.578–82, Laemmle 2013: 186 n.144; Apollodorus 1.6.2 reports that, as Enkelados fled from the battle, Athena threw Sicily on top of him. How early this version arose we do not know, but it is tempting to think that Silenos here takes pleasure in prancing quite literally 'on top of' his alleged victim, cf. further 9n.

ἰτέαν ἐς μέσην: ἰτέαν is scanned as two long syllables with synizesis, cf. Diggle 1994: 314. To strike the middle of an opponent's shield or body is a further mark of the epic hero, cf. e.g. *Il.* 7.258, 13.438, 646, 22.290, etc. As some of these epic examples show, however, striking the middle of the shield can be very different from actually 'killing'; Silenos' expression 'striking Enkelados on the middle of his shield' is again teasingly ambiguous: Silenos may simply have made a racket by banging on the shield, cf. Call. *HDelos* 136–7.

θενών: strong aor. participle of θείνω, cf. *Hcld.* 271 θενεῖν.

8 ἔκτεινα is in emphatic enjambment, so emphatic in fact that the improbability even brings Silenos up short.

φέρ᾽ ἴδω, 'ah, let me see …', a colloquialism common in comedy, but found in this form only here in Eur., cf. Collard 2018: 95–6 (~ Stevens 1976: 42); there are a few instances of φέρε or φέρε δή with the subjunctive, cf. 492, 557, *Her.* 529, *Ion* 544, and φέρ᾽… ἴδω at *Hipp.* 864–5 more closely resembles them than it does the expression here. The contrast with the epic grandeur which has preceded is bathetic. The repetition φέρ᾽ ἴδω, τοῦτ᾽ ἰδών shows the 'formulaic' character of φέρ᾽ ἴδω, in which ἴδω carries no necessary sense of vision.

τοῦτ᾽ ἰδών ὄναρ λέγω; 'Am I recounting this after seeing it in a dream?'; for adverbial ὄναρ cf. *IT* 518, *Her.* 495, LSJ s.v. II. For similar 'did I dream it?' by-play at the expense of Dionysos himself, also in a context of military exploits, cf. Ar. *Frogs* 49–51.

9 The switch to the third person Βακχίωι (contrast σῶι ποδί in 6 and the second persons of the following narrative) shows that Silenos' musings are half addressed to himself. What precisely he means by 'I showed Dionysos the spoils' is unclear. Homeric warriors regularly strip the armour from their dead opponents, and its display can bring the victor μέγα κλέος (cf. *Il.* 17.130–1); Silenos might even mean that he put on Enkelados' armour (after Athena had killed the Giant?), as Hector put on Patroclus'. 'I showed' can hardly mean 'I dedicated'; Silenos' action is more that of a proud child. Laemmle 2013: 182 suggests that Silenos' 'showing' was in fact a Dionysiac dance full of κέλαδος (cf. 7n.), once Ἐγ-κέλαδος was vanquished.

οὐ μὰ Δί': a comic and colloquial oath, not found in Euripides outside *Cycl.*, cf. 154, 560 (always spoken by Silenos).

καί: probably 'in fact' (*GP²* 297), rather than 'also'.

10 ἐξαντλῶ: lit. 'I drain to the full', i.e. 'I endure, suffer', cf. 110, 282, fr. 454.2–3 (Merope) μυρίαι / τὸν αὐτὸν ἐξήντλησαν ὡς ἐγὼ βίον.

11–17 This is the only evidence for a role for Hera in the story of Dionysos' abduction by pirates, most familiar to us (and perhaps also the audience) from the *Homeric Hymn to Dionysos* (7), and the only textual evidence for the satyrs searching for him after that incident, though iconography often depicts them sharing the god's adventure; on the frieze of the Monument of Lysicrates in Athens (dated to 334), satyrs fight the pirates while the god watches from a distance (*LIMC* VIII s.v. Silenoi, no. 205), and in some later versions they were with Dionysos when the pirates struck, cf. Philostr. *Imag.* 1.19. There is no evidence for a satyr-play on this subject, although the narrative almost calls out for satyric treatment, and it is often guessed that Silenos is here (again) referring to an earlier play (Waltz 1931: 289–92). There is also no evidence that the satyric *Cyclops* of Aristias, son of Pratinas, involved the pirate-story, cf. Introduction p. 4. Iconography suggests that at this date there was in fact no 'canonical' version of Dionysos' encounter with the pirates, cf. Csapo 2003.

11 γένος suggests that all 'Tyrrhenians' are pirates; there is no need to explain the present expression as involving a transferred epithet ('*enallage*') for τὸ τῶν Τυρσηνικῶν ληιστῶν γένος.

Τυρσηνικόν: cf. *HHDion.* 7–8. Τυρρηνοί referred either to an early people of the northern Aegean, sometimes connected or identified with the Pelasgians and particularly associated with Lemnos (Hdt. 5.26, 6.137–40, Thucyd. 4.109.4, Soph. fr. 270.4), or to a people of the west, later identified as the Etruscans (*Hcld.* 830, *Ph.* 1377–8 of the 'Etruscan trumpet'), who became notorious for piracy (Strabo 5.2.2, etc.). It has been argued that the setting of the play on Sicily points towards these latter 'western Τυρρηνοί', and that identification for the pirates who abducted Dionysos, which became explicit in later antiquity (e.g. Hyg. *Fab.* 134), is assumed in much modern scholarship, but the case is far from conclusive. (i) Silenos may simply be recalling the story of the *Homeric Hymn*; (ii) although at 112 he tells Odysseus that they were 'pursuing' (διώκειν) the pirates, the narrative of the prologue strongly suggests that they went off in 'search' (14, 17) of the god, without any idea of where he had gone; (iii) they were blown off course by an east wind (19–20), which suggests that they were not deliberately heading west after the pirates. Cf. further 18n. Euripides' audience are likely first to have associated 'Tyrrhenian' with the traditional story represented for us by the *Homeric Hymn* and to have interpreted the term here in whatever way they understood it in the *Hymn*. In Apollod. 3.5.3 (cf. Ov. *Met.* 3.636–7, Hyg. *Astr.* 2.17, *Fab.* 134) the god hires a 'Tyrrhenian pirate trireme' to take him from Ikaria to Naxos, and the pirates plan to sell him 'in Asia'.

12 ἐπῶρσεν 'roused up' (ἐπόρνυμι). The verb occurs nowhere else in Euripides, but is used in *Od.* of divinely sent obstacles placed in the way of the hero's travels (5.109, 7.271, 9.67); Silenos thus emphasises the epic nature of the events. Hera's role is analogous to that of Poseidon in *Od.*

ὡς ὁδηθείης μακράν 'so that you would be sold far away'; ὁδᾶν, lit. 'put on the road (ὁδός)', is a very rare verb (cf. fr. 113) which occurs four times in *Cycl.* (98, 133, and in the compound ἐξοδᾶν at 267), cf. 98n., Konstan 1990: 213–14. Adverbial μακράν without a noun to be supplied is a common idiom (*IT* 629, Fraenkel on Aesch. *Ag.* 916), but here, with ὁδηθείης, ὁδός itself may well resonate. In *HHDion.* the god is threatened with a journey 'to Egypt or Cyprus or the Hyperboreans or further' (vv. 28–9).

13 ⟨ἐγώ⟩ suits Silenos' self-aggrandisement and his claims of extraordinary services to the god. Diggle proposed ⟨εὐθύς⟩, which would also stress Silenos' devotion.

τέκνοισι: one of Silenos' standard designations for the satyrs, cf. 16 (παῖδες), above p. 33.

ναυστολῶ 'I set sail'; the present tense is intended to impress the god with its urgency.

14–15 ζήτησιν: the noun does not otherwise occur in Euripides and perhaps sounds rather self-important, cf. the -σις nouns in the satyrs' boasts at Soph. fr. **1133.15–16 (with Laemmle 2018: 55).

ἐν πρύμνηι δ' ἄκραι/αὐτὸς βεβὼς ηὔθυνον ἀμφῆρες δόρυ 'I stood myself on the high point of the stern and steered the double-sided ship'. Silenos sees himself (again) as an epic hero, or rather as Odysseus himself; in both texts and images the steersman normally *sits* at the stern, at a level higher than the seated rowers, but Silenos misses no opportunity for self-importance, cf. Virg. *Aen.* 8.680 (Augustus) *stans celsa in puppi*, Lucian, *Bis acc.* 2 (Zeus) ὑψηλὸς ... ἐπὶ τῆς πρύμνης ἔστηκα. The transmitted λαβών is very difficult to construe, as δόρυ must be the ship, not the rudder (cf., e.g., *Hel.* 1610–11, Aesch. *Pers.* 411). When λαβών is very weak or almost 'pleonastic', the object is standardly either expressed or easily understood (Stinton 1975: 84, K–G II 87), but Silenos did not 'take' the ship 'on the high point of the stern'; contrast *Od.* 15.269 ἑτάρους τε λαβὼν καὶ νῆα μέλαιναν (Telemachos reporting his search for Od.). βεβώς or σταθείς both mend the sense and give a suitable contrast between Silenos and the seated satyrs (16), to whom he assigns a 'lower' role in every sense. Cf. further Diggle 1994: 5–6, Napolitano 1992.

ἀμφήρες was, at least later, understood as 'rowed (ἐρέσσειν) on both sides' (Hesych. α 3936), i.e. rowers sat on both sides of the boat; Thucyd. 4.67.3 uses the form ἀμφηρικόν of a small boat which is 'sculled'. Here the audience may have heard an epic-sounding compound (cf. the Homeric νῆας ... ἀμφιελίσσας, e.g. *Il.* 2.165) without giving a very specific meaning to the second element.

16–17 ⟨ἐπ'⟩ ἐρετμοῖς ἥμενοι 'sitting at the oars'. The corresponding expression in Homer is ἐπ' ἐρετμά (*Od.* 12.171, with the comic by-play of Ar. *Frogs* 197–200), whereas Homer standardly uses the dative for the action of the oars in the water, as in the formulaic verses *Od.* 9.179–80 ἐπὶ κληῖσι καθῖζον,/ἑξῆς δ' ἑζόμενοι πολιὴν ἅλα τύπτον ἐρετμοῖς; these verses occur four times in *Od.* 9 (also 103–4, 471–2, 563–4) and the echo here strengthens Silenos' epic claims. The Homeric construction, however, leads some to understand ἐρετμοῖς ... ῥοθίοισι without a preposition as '(whitening the grey sea) with their splashing oars', but this leaves ἥμενοι awkwardly unqualified, and a pointed contrast between 'standing on the high point of the stern' and 'sitting at the oars' suits Silenos' sense of the order of things. ἐρετμοῖς ἥμενοι without a preposition can hardly give the required sense 'sitting at the oars'.

γλαυκήν is already an epithet of the sea at *Il.* 16.34 (where see Janko's n.), and here adds to the epic colour of Silenos' report, cf. *Hel.* 400–1 (Menelaos' 'Odyssean' monologue) ἐγὼ δ' ἐπ' οἶδμα πόντιον γλαυκῆς ἁλός / τλήμων ἁλῶμαι. The meaning of the term has been much debated (cf. Maxwell-Stuart 1981, Pötscher 1998, *LfgrE* s.v.), but here, set against λευκαίνοντες, it is probably 'blueish/grey', pointing to the apparent gleam that the sea contains within itself, cf. *Hel.* 1501–3 (where there is some doubt about the text) γλαυκὸν ἐπ' οἶδμ' ἅλιον/κυανόχροά τε κυμάτων/ῥόθια πολιὰ θαλάσσας. At Pl. *Tim.* 68c6–7 γλαυκόν is described as κυανοῦ ... λευκῶι κεραννυμένου.

ῥοθίοισι λευκαίνοντες 'whitening (the grey sea) with their splashing'. The noise of oars in water is usually ῥόθος, but τὰ ῥόθια seems also to have been used in this sense, cf. *IT* 407, LSJ s.v. II, Diggle on *Phaethon* 80. For the 'epic' nature of the scene cf. *Od.* 12.171–2 (Odysseus' crew) οἱ δ' ἐπ' ἐρετμὰ/ἑζόμενοι λεύκαινον ὕδωρ ξεστῆισ' ἐλάτηισιν.

18 Cape Malea at the south-eastern tip of the Peloponnese was notorious for dangerous winds, cf. *Od.* 3.287, 4.514, 19.187, Hdt. 4.179.2, 7.168.4, and Strabo 8.6.20 cites the proverb 'when you have rounded Malea, forget what is at home'; most famously of all, it was where the Homeric Odysseus' real adventures began, ἀλλά με κῦμα ῥόος τε περιγνάμπτοντα Μάλειαν/καὶ βορέης ἀπέωσε κτλ. (*Od.* 9.80–1), cf. 109n. Silenos' 'Odyssean' pretensions here reach their height, cf. Hunter 2009: 60–1. Odysseus was rounding

Malea from east to west when he was blown south, but Silenos merely says that he and the satyrs 'had already sailed near Malea'; this studied vagueness both allows the crucial name of Malea to resonate and also leaves quite unclear where the satyrs were and in what direction they were sailing, cf. 11n. It is not impossible that we are to understand that they were making for the southern Peloponnese, with which various traditions associated Silenos himself (Paus. 3.25.2–3, citing Pind. fr. 156 M); ἤδη δέ, suggesting a sense of safety, would fit such a scenario, cf. Od. 10.29 τῆι δεκάτηι δ᾽ ἤδη ἀνεφαίνετο πατρὶς ἄρουρα (followed by a disastrous release of the winds), Ap. Rhod. Arg. 4.1228–9. Cf. further 109n.

19 ἀπηλιώτης: an Ionic term for the east wind, the wind 'from the sun'; Attic retains the Ionic form without aspirate (ἀπ- rather than ἀφ-), cf. Thucyd. 3.23.5, Gomme 1948: 12. This is the term's only occurrence in poetry: Silenos is perhaps showing off his nautical knowledge.

ἐμπνεύσας: perhaps a touch borrowed from HHDion. 33 ἔμπνευσεν δ᾽ ἄνεμος μέσον ἱστίον.

20 The localisation of the Cyclopes in Sicily was not Euripides' invention, cf. Thucyd. 6.2.1, where the Cyclopes and the Laistrygonians 'are said to have lived in a certain part [of Sicily] in very ancient times' (cf. Hornblower ad loc.); Epicharmus' Cyclops was presumably set on Sicily (cf. PCG I 49, above p. 5). Cycl. is the earliest surviving attestation for the localisation around Mount Etna, but it seems very likely also for Philoxenus' dithyrambic Cyclops or Galateia (cf. PMG 817), and Etna may well have been the setting for Epicharmus' comedy; it is later assumed in Theocritus 11.

τήνδ᾽: such deictics are very common at the start of plays. One wonders whether the actor gestured jokingly towards the Acropolis towering over the theatre, as Etna towers over that part of Sicily.

21 μονῶπες: that the Cyclopes are one-eyed (cf. 79, 174) is implied by the Homeric story and made explicit already at Hes. Theog. 144–5 (see next note); Cratinus seems to have used μονόμματος of the Cyclops (fr. 156). The Cyclops often, however, seems to have two eyes in archaic iconography, cf. LIMC s.v. Kyklops, Kyklopes, Snodgrass 1998: 90–8, although the artist's conception of the Cyclops may be uncertain when the monster is portrayed in profile.

22 Κύκλωπες: closeness to μονῶπες perhaps evokes the same etymology as at Hes. Theog. 144–5, 'because a circular (κυκλοτερής) single eye (ὀφθαλμός) is set in their forehead'.

ἄντρ᾽ ἔρημ᾽ does not just suggest Silenos' disgust at his current surroundings, but evokes the whole 'Cyclopean' ethnography of Od. 9.112–15, 'they have neither assemblies where decisions are made nor ordinances, but they dwell in hollow caves on the tops of lofty mountains, and each one governs his own children and wives, and they take no thought for one another', cf. *Od.* 9.399–400 and 122n. below.

ἀνδροκτόνοι foreshadows the plot of the play.

23–4 'We live in captivity in the house of one of them as slaves'.

τούτων ἑνός colours both δόμοις and δοῦλοι and is moved to emphatic 'topical' position at the head of the sentence: this 'one' is now where our attention is directed.

ληφθέντες ἐσμέν: lit. 'we are in a state of having been captured', i.e. we were captured and remain so, cf. 381n., K–G I 38–9.

δόμοις has a wry tinge after 'deserted caves', cf. 33, 118, Buxton 1994: 104–8 on the *imaginaire* of caves which are 'both like and not like a house'.

δοῦλοι is placed in emphatic enjambment at the head of the trimeter. There is no sign in Homer that the 'self-sufficient' Cyclopes have slaves, and Euripides' Polyphemos entirely elides the issue in his boasts at 320–41; the slavery of the satyrs is a very common dramatic motif, cf., e.g., Voelke 2001: 72–83, Griffith 2015: chapter 1, above p. 13 n.44, Laemmle 2017.

24–5 αὐτόν is often thought to suggest 'the master', as in the Pythagorean αὐτὸς ἔφα (cf. Dover on Ar. *Clouds* 219, Diggle on Theophr. *Char.* 2.5), as τοῦτον might otherwise have been expected; αὐτός in that sense is, however, not normally followed by a relative clause, and αὐτόν is better here taken as emphatic, 'this very one' (K–G I 654).

λατρεύομεν: for Ion this verb denoted a very positive activity (*Ion* 124, 129, 152), for Silenos it is hateful; as 25–6 make clear, Polyphemos has replaced Dionysos as 'the one whom Silenos and the satyrs serve', cf. 76–81. δεσπότης of the Cyclops at 34 and 90 makes the same point. LSJ distinguish the 'religious' sense of λατρεύειν, 'serve', from the secular, 'be enslaved to', but usage defies such simple dichotomies.

καλοῦσι ... Πολύφημον suggests an etymology of the Cyclops' name, 'much famed'; he is 'much famed' precisely because of the *Od.*, which Silenos almost invites the audience to remember, cf. 89–93n. Silenos again uses the name Polyphemos in the third person at 91, but otherwise the monster is always '(the) Cyclops'; in Odysseus' narrative in *Od.* 9 he always calls him '(the) Cyclops' until he has heard the other Cyclopes use the name 'Polyphemos' (cf. Schol. on *Od.* 9.403). The name first appears in *Od.* at 1.69–72, where Zeus reports Poseidon's continued anger about 'the Cyclops, whose eye [Odysseus] blinded, godlike Polyphemos, whose strength is the greatest of all the Cyclopes'. Κύκλωψ might there have momentarily been understood as a name. Memory of that passage shows how serious Silenos' plight really is. Cf. further Hunter on Theocritus 11.72.

25–6 ἀντὶ δ' εὐίων βακχευμάτων 'instead of (performing) ecstatic Bacchic rites …'; for this somewhat loose use of ἀντί cf. *Andr.* 164–6, Soph. *OT* 1490–1. εὔιος is derived from the ritual cry εὐοῖ and is not limited to Dionysiac cult (cf. *Tr.* 451), though usually found in such contexts, cf. 495, Soph. *Ichn.* 227; in *Ba.* it is used as a cult name for Dionysos (566, 579) and at 157 he is ὁ εὔιος θεός, cf. *PMG* 1003, Bremmer 2006: 37–8. The fact of 'no more Dionysos' is expressed in different modes by Silenos here and then subsequently by the chorus (63–5) and the Cyclops (203–5).

ἀνοσίου points to the Cyclops' eating of human flesh, cf. 31.

ποίμνας … ποιμαίνομεν might be thought particularly 'degrading', as shepherding has nothing to do with more violent maenadic and Dionysiac activities. There is perhaps a pun (or an actor could make one) in ποιμαίνομεν: this is (alas) the only 'madness' now on offer. The *Cyclops* was almost certainly not the only play in which the satyrs appeared in a pastoral role, cf. Laemmle 2013: 172.

27 μὲν οὖν introduces a self-correction (*GP*² 478–9): the satyrs are doing the shepherding, whereas Silenos himself has different tasks. Others, however, understand that Silenos now turns from the general situation to the immediate present, with μὲν οὖν marking the transition (*GP*² 470–4).

κλειτύων ἐν ἐσχάτοις 'on the furthest parts of the hills'. The phrase evokes ἐσχατιαί, marginal land far from farm buildings where flocks graze, often under the control of young boys (28), cf. *Od.* 14.104, Theocr. 13.25–6 (with Gow's n.). Such marginal spaces are often the setting of satyr-drama, cf. Voelke 2001: 37–44. In *Od.* Polyphemos' cave itself is ἐπ' ἐσχατιῆι (9.182), though he does not see it in that way (9.280).

28 νέα νέοι need not imply that the satyrs are only looking after lambs, presumably in spring/early summer, cf. 57–8; the emphatic doubling of νέος emphasises the satyrs' youth (from Silenos' perspective). Such juxtapositions of different forms of the same adjective are a common Euripidean mannerism (Denniston on *El.* 337, Diggle on *Phaethon* 94); for examples with νέος cf. *Alc.* 471, *Her.* 128. The relevance of the repeated adjective to the two nouns with which it is associated may vary considerably.

29 Two alliterative phrases express Silenos' disgust at the tasks he must perform; Silenos almost spits out his distaste for what he is doing. This emphatic alliteration is continued in vv. 30–1 with τ and δ sounds.

πίστρα 'drinking-troughs'; a feminine form is used in 47. Later, the form ποτίστρα occurs (Call. *h.* 3.50). Drawing water for animals seems even more 'degrading' than doing it for humans (cf. Electra's explanation at *El.* 55–6).

σαίρειν στέγας: sweeping can be represented as a very 'low' activity, particularly for those used to higher things, cf. *Andr.* 166, *Hec.* 363, and 35n.; for possible visual allusion here to *Ion* and *Hypsipyle* cf. above pp. 41–3. στέγαι is very common in Euripides for 'dwelling, palace', but here too there is probably a touch of distaste, cf. 118. In tragedy the term need not denote grandeur and is used, in both singular and plural, for Philoctetes' cave, cf. Soph. *Phil.* 286 (with Schein's n.), 298, 1262, above p. 40.

30–1 μένων 'remaining behind'.

τῶιδε: for ὅδε used of someone not visible but 'present to the mind' cf. *Hel.* 100, Soph. *El.* 540, Hunter 1983: 106, K–G I 644. For the juxtaposition of two forms of ὅδε, here separated by a break in the syntax, cf. Soph. *Tr.* 716 ἐκ δὲ τοῦδ' ὅδε.

δυσσεβεῖ ... ἀνοσίων: there is here no real difference of meaning: both the Cyclops and his meals offend the gods, cf. Dover 1974: 247–8, Mikalson 1991: 157–8.

διάκονος can be a pejorative term, 'lackey' (cf. [Aesch.] *PV* 942), and Silenos clearly finds not just the Cyclops' meals but also his own subordinate position distasteful, cf. 406. A papyrus hypothesis to the satyric *Skiron* (*TrGF* 5.2, 660) apparently describes Silenos as that monster's διάκονος τῆς ὕβρεως.

32 τὰ προσταχθέντ' 'with respect to the orders I have been given', a 'programmatic' appositional accusative phrase which gives the subject of the utterance to follow, cf. Aesch. *Ag.* 550 τὸ σὸν δή, 830 τὰ δ' ἐς τὸ σὸν φρόνημα, K–G I 285; the phrase picks up τέταγμαι in 30. ἀναγκαίως ἔχει, lit. 'there is a situation of necessity', is regularly followed by the infinitive (*Her.* 502, *Hel.* 1399–1401, etc.).

33 σιδηρᾶι: the feminine dat. sing. of the contracted Attic form σιδηροῦς -ᾶ -οῦν.

ἁρπάγηι is here apparently used of some kind of rake, whereas it most naturally means a 'hook', whether a meat-hook or a hook for drawing a water-bucket up from a well, as the later lexicographers claim is its meaning, cf. Gomme and Sandbach on Men. *Dysk.* 599–600, Kassel and Austin on Men. fr. 421. It is puzzling that Silenos should use this word in an apparently unexampled sense, when he would indeed need a 'hook' to help him draw water for the drinking-troughs (29), but there seems no obvious way of postulating a textual lacuna to explain this difficulty.

δόμους: cf. 23–4n.

34 δεσπότην: cf. 24–5n.; at Soph. *Ichn.* 224 the satyrs' δεσπότης is most likely Dionysos; 'my absent master' here almost cries out for the supplement 'Dionysos', but Κύκλωπ' shows the harsh new reality, cf. 76–7, 435–6, 708–9. δεσπότης is the standard word both for a slave's master and the 'master of the house'.

35 Silenos has to 'receive' both the Cyclops and the flocks, which presumably are the cause of most of what needs sweeping up (cf. *Od.* 9.329–30 for the dung in the cave), in a clean (lit. 'pure') cave; the phrase is tinged with bitter sarcasm. It is again tempting to think of the very different καθαρειότης, both literal and metaphorical, which is prominent in Ion's monody (*Ion* 96, 105). Silenos is here forced to behave like a 'model wife', cf. *El.* 73–6 (Electra to her farmer husband) 'You have enough to do outside. I must look after things inside the house. It is pleasant for a workman when he returns home to find things inside neat and tidy', above p. 32.

36–40 Silenos announces the arrival of the chorus in a structure which eventually led to the 'formulaic' announcement of the chorus at the end of the first act of Menander's comedies, cf. *Hipp.* 51–7, *Ph.* 193–201 (with Mastronarde's n.), Arnott on Alexis fr. 112. The choruses of New Comedy often seem to have been comastic revellers, cf. Alexis fr. 112 where there is also a reference to very vigorous dancing, and excessive intake of alcohol is often imputed to them (Men. *Aspis* 247–8, *Epitrep.* 169–70, *Perik.* 191–2); here the satyrs enter dancing (37n.), but alcohol has – alas – nothing to do with it. The chorus of κωμωιδία always remained both a κῶμος and a χορός, such as we also have here.

The satyrs enter probably dancing the *sikinis* (36–8n.) and Silenos expresses his surprise that they still dance 'as in the old days', despite their current joyless situation. The satyr-chorus' habitual noisy dancing to some extent works amusingly against Silenos' complaints, and 37–40 remind us, as also does the end of the play, of the repetitiveness of satyric performance: they may be captives of the Cyclops, but this is still the same satyr-chorus which we know and love. Silenos' strong reactions to the movements of the satyrs seem to be a recurrent motif of satyr-play, cf. Soph. *Ichn.* 124–52 (Silenos' failure to understand the chorus' 'tracking' and subsequent abuse of them, with τί ταῦτα; in v. 129).

36–8 The sequence of thought will be 'I have to get the house ready – here come the flocks already, which means that the Cyclops too will soon be returning'. For the time-scheme of the play cf. 213, 353–5nn.

παῖδας προσνέμοντας εἰσορῶ / ποίμνας 'I see my children driving the flocks in this direction', cf. *Od.* 9.233 (the Cyclops) ἐπῆλθε νέμων.

τί ταῦτα; is not restricted to satyr-play and comedy, cf. *Andr.* 548, *Ph.* 362, Collard 2018: 75 (~ Stevens 1976: 31).

μῶν κρότος σικινίδων/ὁμοῖος ὑμῖν νῦν τε χὤτε κτλ. 'the thumping of your *sikinis*-dances is not, is it, the same now as when …?' μῶν here expresses surprise (cf. K–G II 525, Barrett on *Hipp.* 794), but without apparent irony (contrast 158, 377). In the freedom with which characters comment upon the mode of choral performance, satyr-drama is clearly distinguished from tragedy. An alternative scenario would be that the satyrs do not in fact here dance as they normally do (cf. 63–5, Easterling 1997b: 43), but merely drive flocks, and Silenos' comment is a wry observation about their current plight, with μῶν, as regularly, expecting a negative answer: there are in fact no *sikinis*-dances. However, the surprise expressed in τί ταῦτα; favours the first explanation, as also does the parallel reaction of the Cyclops at 203–5.

κρότος most naturally refers to the thumping of feet in a vigorous dance, cf. *Hcld.* 783, *Tr.* 546, Soph. *Ichn.* 217–20, 237.

σικινίδων: ancient scholars identified the *sikinis* as the satyric dance *par excellence*, cf. Aristoxenos fr. 104 W², Aristocles in Ath. 14.630b–c; both σίκινις and the more common σίκιννις are attested – and both spellings are found as names for satyrs on vases (Kossatz-Deissmann 1991: 168) – but as the length of the second vowel is unknown, we have retained the spelling with single ν. This is the earliest attestation of the term, although σίκιννι]ν is plausibly restored at Soph. fr. 772. Ancient (and fanciful) etymologies connecting the term with σείεσθαι and κίνησις (Ath. loc. cit.) point to lively movement as a hallmark of the dance, and fifth-century vase-painting shows actors in satyr costume performing σχήματα (cf. 221) involving kicks and exaggerated arm movements, cf. above pp. 27–30 (the 'Pronomos Vase'), Seidensticker 2010; the chorus of Soph. *Ichn.* 218–19 announce that they will make the ground ring πηδήμασιν κραιπνοῖσι καὶ λακτίσμα-σιν, and this is almost certainly a reference to the *sikinis*, cf. also Pratinas, *PMG* 708.14 ἅδε σοι δεξιᾶς καὶ ποδὸς διαρριφά. There seem to have been similarities between the *sikinis* and the armed *pyrrhichē*, cf. 7n., Pl. *Laws* 7.815b–c, Ath. 14.630d, Ceccarelli 1998: 213–15, Voelke 2001: 149–51, Laemmle 2013: 193–201, D'Alessio 2020. It is probable that, unlike the choral dancing of tragedy, the *sikinis* was not reliant on choral uniformity and syncopated movement: individual satyrs could 'do their own thing'; our evidence suggests that the satyr-chorus often did break up into indi-viduals or factions, cf. below p. 233.

38–9 νῦν τε χὤτε: the echo and repetition from v. 2 marks Silenos' recurrent obsession with the past.

Βακχίωι/κῶμος συνασπίζοντες: lit. 'bearing your shields side-by-side as a κῶμος with the Bacchic one …', i.e. escorting Dionysos as a band of revel-lers. κῶμος is a collective singular, here expressed with a plural verb, cf. *Tr.* 614, *Ba.* 56, Smyth §950; the transmitted κῶμοι is impossible, as the satyrs form a single κῶμος, and the singular could easily have been corrupted to the plural. Several editors adopt κώμωι συνασπίζοντες, 'escorted (the Bacchic one) in a revel', but the juxtaposed datives are unconvincing. As they revel to Althaia's house, the satyrs form a κῶμος which is both the Dionysiac cultic revel and also the 'secular' erotic κῶμος familiar from Hellenistic and Roman poetry (Headlam on Hds. 2.34–7), which is to play such a significant role later in the play. Silenos is thus made to foreshadow important elements of the play to come. The satyrs here play the role of the friends who regularly accompany the lover in later literary κῶμοι, cf., e.g., Theocr. 2.119. The imagined scene is thus very close to Cat. 64.251–65 where the god, *cum thiaso Satyrorum et Nysigenis Silenis*, appears in revel to find his new bride Ariadne. Κῶμος is a well-attested satyr-name on vases, cf. *RE* 11.1298–9, Kossatz-Deissmann 1991: 157–9, Curbera 2019: 121–2, and it has often been guessed that the chorus of Epicharmus' Κωμασταὶ ἢ Ἅφαιστος were satyrs.

συνασπίζοντες: the verb occurs only here before Hellenistic prose; Xenophon uses συνασπιδοῦν (*Hell.* 3.5.11, 7.4.23). In suggesting that the erotic κῶμος was like a hoplite formation, Silenos transfers military language to the erotic and sympotic sphere, as was to become very familiar in Roman poetry, cf. Spies 1930, McKeown on Ov. *Am.* 1.9 (*militat omnis amans ...*). Other early foreshadowings of this metaphorical system include *Hipp.* 527, Sappho fr.1.28 σύμμαχος ἔσσο (addressed to Aphrodite), Pratinas, *PMG* 708.8–9 (also a comastic context), Soph. *Ant.* 781; at *Ph.* 790 a destructive army is a κῶμος ἀναυλότατος. As, however, certain types of drinking-bowl could resemble or even be called 'shields' (Arist. *Poet.* 1457b20–2, *Rhet.* 3.1407a6, Anaxandrides fr. 110, Aristophon fr. 13.2, Paus. 5.10.4, Gagné 2016: 228–9), συνασπίζοντες, 'those who bear the shield together', might be a sympotic term applied by groups of drinking-partners to one another, or at least suggestive of such terms. We may perhaps compare the use of θωρηχθείς and related terms to mean 'drunk', cf. Soph. fr. 173 (*Dionysiskos*), Diphilus fr. 45.2, LSJ s.v. θωρήσσω II, and at Antipater Thess., *APl* 184.1 (= *GP* 239) Dionysos is a συνασπιστής of 'Italian Piso'. There is also here an echo of the very rare παρασπιστής in 6.

Ἀλθαίας δόμους is the 'accusative of motion towards' with προσῆιτ'. According to later sources (Satyros, F 28 fr. 1 col. II Schorn, Apollod. 1.8.1, Hyginus, *Fab.* 129), Dionysos slept with Althaia, the wife of Oineus ('Mr Wine'), when the latter entertained the god in his house. The result of the union was Deianeira, Heracles' later wife, and Oineus was taught the art of viticulture in return. The story seems perfect for satyr-drama (Waltz 1931: 292–3), but no such play can be identified. *Oineus* tragedies were written by Philocles, Eur. (frr. 558–70) and Chaeremon, and cf. also *Adesp. Trag.* 625; none may, however, have dealt with the story of Dionysos and Althaia (Eur.'s tragedy certainly did not). Soph. fr. 1130 may come from a satyric *Oineus* (cf. Laemmle 2018), but this too will not be the story of Althaia.

40 ἀοιδαῖς βαρβίτων σαυλούμενοι 'waggling your buttocks to songs to the accompaniment of lyres'. For ἀοιδαῖς βαρβίτων cf. *Med.* 424–5 λύρας ... ἀοιδάν; the genitive is hard to characterise, but easy to understand, and

ἀοιδή is almost never used of purely instrumental music (Bacchyl. 18.4 uses it of the sound of a σάλπιγξ). βάρβιτοι were lyres which were narrower and longer than λύραι, and thus had a lower pitch; they were particularly associated with Dionysiac and comastic revelry (cf. *Alc.* 343–7, Alcaeus fr. 70.3–5) and with poets such as Anacreon (cf. 495–518n.), and they were believed to have come to Athens from the (effeminate) east. Satyrs with βάρβιτοι are often depicted on vases, cf. Maas and Snyder 1989: chapter 5, Voelke 2001: 97–103, Lissarrague 2013: Figures 53, 116, Austin and Olson on Ar. *Thesm.* 137–8. Dionysos might have carried a βάρβιτος in Aeschylus' *Edonoi* (cf. fr. 61). Cf. further 443–4n.

σαυλούμενοι suggests exaggerated movements of the buttocks which, depending on context, may be self-conscious or effeminate or lewd or some combination of these, cf. Anacreon, *PMG* 458, 411 (Διονύσου σαῦλαι Βασσαρίδες), Ar. *Wasps* 1173 (σαυλοπρωκτιᾶν), Voelke 2001: 66–8, 176–7, Bing 2014: 44, Thomas 2015. Here the word presumably indicates one feature of the *sikin(n)is*, cf. 36–8n.

41–81 PARODOS

The chorus of satyrs enters driving a flock of sheep, perhaps in scattered groups, or even singly, rather than in closely knit choral formation, cf. 36–8n., Seidensticker 2010: 227–8. Whether in the original production the sheep were real or human extras dressed as sheep or both or whether the entire matter was left to the audience's imagination we shall never know. The song falls into two parts. Lines 41–62 consist of two corresponding strophes separated by a metrically distinct mesode (cf. the structure of 356–74); these verses seek by enticements and threats to make the sheep return to the fold. Lines 63–81 form an epode in which the satyrs pick up Silenos' laments for their current situation and their separation from Dionysos. The suggestion that the mesode (49–54), which interrupts the sequence of cajoling blandishments in the surrounding strophes, was sung by a single chorus-member (so Wilamowitz 1921: 224), who, like the errant sheep, breaks off from the main group, is very attractive, but cannot be regarded as proven.

Metre. The strophe and antistrophe are formed from two simple aeolic lengths, one of which may be seen as an 'acephalous' version of the other:

o o – × – ◡ ◡ –
× – × – ◡ ◡ –

The longer form is given various names in modern scholarship, 'choriambic dimeter', 'anaclastic glyconic', 'wilamowitzian' (*wil*); this last is adopted here. The shorter form will be referred to as an 'aeolic heptasyllable' (*hept*). On these forms, of which Euripides makes great use, see Wilamowitz 1921: 210–44, Itsumi 1982, Lourenço 2011: 108–11. § indicates that a word runs into the next colon by one syllable ('dovetailing').

Some of the resonance of these choriambic forms is with simple and popular song, and that is certainly appropriate to the present case; the parodos of the *Phaethon*, for example, begins with two responding strophes composed in this length and describing the coming of daylight and the impetus it gives to shepherds and hunters (vv. 63–78 Diggle). The pattern of the strophe and antistrophe is as follows:

‒ ‒ ‒ ‒ ‿ ‿ ‒	wil	
παῖ γενναίων μὲν πατέρων		41
‒ ‒ ‒ ‒ ‿ ‿ ‒	hept	
γενναίων δ' ἐκ τοκάδων,		
‒ ‒ ‒ ‒ ‒ ‿ ‿ ‒	wil	
πᾶι δή μοι νίσηι σκοπέλους;		
‒ ‒ ‿ ‒ ‿ ‿ ‒	hept§	
οὐ τᾶιδ' ὑπήνεμος αὔ-		
‒ ‒ ‒ ‒ ‿ ‿ ‒	wil	
ρα καὶ ποιηρὰ βοτάνα,		45
‒ ‒ ‒ ‒ ‒ ‿ ‿ ‒	wil	
δινᾶέν θ' ὕδωρ ποταμῶν		
‒ ‒ ‒ ‒ ‒ ‿ ‿ ‒	wil§	
ἐν πίστραις κεῖται πέλας ἄν-		
‒ ‒ ‒ ‒ ‿ ‿‒	wil	
τρων, οὔ σοι βλαχαὶ τεκέων;		48
‒ ‒ ‒ ‒ ‒ ‿ ‿ ‒	wil	
σπαργῶντας μαστοὺς χάλασον·		
‒ ‒ ‒ ‒ ‿ ‿ ‒	hept	
δέξαι θηλαῖσι τροφὰς		56
‒ ‒ ‒ ‒ ‒ ‿ ‿ ‒	wil	
οὓς λείπεις ἀρνῶν θαλάμοις.		
‿ ‒ ‿ ‒ ‿ ‿ ‒	hept§	
ποθοῦσί σ' ἁμερόκοι-		
‒ ‒ ‒ ‒ ‿ ‿‒	wil	
τοι βλαχαὶ σμικρῶν τεκέων.		
‒ ‒ ‒ ‿	wil (presumably)	
εἰς αὐλὰν πότ' †ἀμφιβαίνεις†		60
‒ ‒ ‿ ‿ ‿ ‒	wil	
ποιηροὺς λιποῦσα νομοὺς		
‒ ‒ ‒ ‒ ‿ ‿ ‒	wil	
Αἰτναίων εἴσω σκοπέλων;		

The strong preference for long syllables, suggestive of deliberate movement, in the first part of the verse perhaps suggests a contrast between the
satyrs' movments with the sheep and the lively movements of the *sikinis*,
cf. 36–8n.

Analysis of the mesode is complicated in the second half by textual and
colometric uncertainty; the details are discussed in the appropriate place
in the commentary. The anapaestic rhythm of the first half is, however,
unmistakeable. In the uncertain second half, Diggle's text (reproduced
below) gives a length, 'diomedean' (cf. Lourenço 2011: 75), which fits
easily into anapaestic and dactylic contexts; the pattern of 'diomedean'
followed by paroemiac (catalectic anapaestic dimeter) is also found at
Alc. 457–8.

— — — —	anap	
ψύττ'· οὐ τᾶιδ', οὔ;		
— — ◡ ◡ — — — ◡ ◡ —	2 anap	
οὐ τᾶιδε νεμῆι κλειτὺν δροσεράν;		50
— — — — — — ◡ ◡ —	2 anap	
ὠή, ῥίψω πέτρον τάχα σου·		
◡ ◡ — ◡ ◡ — ◡ — —	diom	
ὕπαγ' ὢ ὕπαγ' ὢ κεράστα		
— — ◡ ◡ — ◡ ◡— —	paroemiac	
<πρὸς> μηλοβότα στασιωρὸν		
◡ — ◡ — ◡ ◡ —	hept	
Κύκλωπος ἀγροβάτα.		

Textual problems also affect part of the epode, but it is nevertheless clear
that this to some extent continued the rhythms of the earlier part of the
song. 65 is a relatively rare, though well attested, choriambic length which
Lourenço 2011: 102 calls a 'pendent aeolic octosyllable' (*oct*); it may also
be thought of as an anaclastic version of the hagesichorean (× – ◡ ◡ – ◡
– –).

Diggle's colometry is reproduced below:

— ◡ ◡ ◡ ◡ ◡ — ◡ ◡ ◡ —	2 ia	
οὐ τάδε Βρόμιος, οὐ τάδε χοροὶ		
— — ◡ — ◡ ◡ —	hept	
Βάκχαι τε θυρσοφόροι,		
— — ◡ — ◡ ◡ — —	oct	
οὐ τυμπάνων ἀλαλαγμοί,		65
— — — — — ◡ ◡ —	wil	
οὐκ οἴνου χλωραὶ σταγόνες		67
— — ◡ — ◡ ◡ —	hept	
κρήναις παρ' ὑδροχύτοις·		66

− − − − ‿ ‿ −	hept§	
οὐδ' ἐν Νύσαι μετὰ Νυμ-		68
− ‿ − ‿ ‿− ‿ −	glyconic§	
φᾶν ἴακχον ἴακχον ὠι-		
− − − − − ‿ ‿ −	wil§	
δᾶι μέλπω πρὸς τὰν Ἀφροδί-		70
− − − −− ‿ ‿ −	wil	
ταν, ἃν θηρεύων πετόμαν		
− − − − ‿ ‿ −	hept	
Βάκχαις σὺν λευκόποσιν.		
†ὦ φίλος ὦ φίλε Βακχεῖε		
ποῖ οἰοπολεῖς		
ξανθὰν χαίταν σείεις;†		75
‿ − ‿ − ‿ ‿ −	hept	
ἐγὼ δ' ὁ σὸς πρόπολος		
‿ − ‿ − − −	ia sp	
Κύκλωπι θητεύω		
− ‿ ‿ − − − ‿ ‿ − −	2 anap	
τῶι μονοδέρκται δοῦλος ἀλαίνων		
− − ‿ ‿ − − − ‿ ‿−	2 anap	
σὺν τᾶιδε τράγου χλαίναι μελέαι		80
− − − ‿ ‿ −	? anap -	
σᾶς χωρὶς φιλίας.		

Labelling of the closural final verse is uncertain, cf. Lourenço 2011: 48, 111. An aeolic analysis, perhaps as a 'reversed' form of dodrans (−‿‿−‿−), is possible; Willink 2001: 523 suggested that it may be a 'doubly acephalous' wil.

41–62 These verses form 'the earliest extant pastoral song' (Seaford 1984: 106). Euripides here transposes into choral dramatic action the strong pastoral flavour of *Od.* 9; the Homeric Cyclops was a fearsome monster, but he was also a skilled pastoralist who cared for his animals and felt closely attached to at least one of them (*Od.* 9.183–8, 219–23, 237–49, 447–60, below p. 103). It can hardly be a coincidence that this song occurs in a play set on Sicily. Later, Theocritus of Syracuse was to evoke traditions of popular 'bucolic' singing in Sicily and southern Italy and to fashion the young Sicilian Cyclops as a bucolic singer and lover *avant la lettre*; Sicily is always central to accounts of the invention of bucolic and to the story of the bucolic 'hero' Daphnis (cf. Hunter 1999: 63–7, 217–19). Some striking similarities of technique and motif between the parodos of *Cycl.* and Theocritean bucolic (cf. 44–8, 49–54nn.) suggest that both

draw upon pre-existing forms of song. Theocritus makes rich use of the
Sicilian poetic heritage (Stesichorus, Sophron, Epicharmus, cf., e.g., Willi
2012a: 285–8), and it is likely enough that his 'bucolic' poems as a group
are highly sophisticated 're-imaginings' of (real or believed) traditions
of work-songs and song-exchanges, such as have been identified from
rural communities all over the Mediterranean. Athenaeus reports that a
Sicilian cowherd called Diomos was the 'first inventor' of βουκολιασμός,
a song for 'those leading flocks', and that Epicharmus mentioned him
in two plays (Ath. 14.619a–b, Epicharmus frr. 4, 104, cf. Hunter 1999:
9–10); it is quite possible that Epicharmus' *Cyclops* (cf. above pp. 4–5) also
contained a bucolic element. The parody at Ar. *Wealth* 290–315 strongly
suggests that Philoxenus too exploited Sicilian traditions of bucolic or
pastoral song in his *Cyclops or Galateia* (above pp. 8–9). The generic and
local resonances of the parodos will thus probably have been strongly felt
by at least some of Euripides' audience.

A striking feature of these verses is the verbal repetition between strophe and antistrophe, which goes well beyond the echoing which is often
found between corresponding stanzas: σκοπέλους ~ σκοπέλων, ποιηρὰ
βοτάνα ~ ποιηρούς … νομούς, βλαχαὶ τεκέων ~ βλαχαὶ σμικρῶν τεκέων (and
cf. also 44n.). This may be imitative of a real or believed feature of such
popular 'work songs'; it is not, however, the verbal poverty of such songs
which is here the poet's target, so much as the paradoxical humour to be
derived from the satyrs' new occupation.

In his account of Dionysos, Diodorus Siculus reports that the satyrs in
the god's retinue 'afforded him delight and great pleasure through their
dances and their τραγωιδίαι' (4.5.3). This claim may be a product of a
period when satyrs had become more closely associated with, and were
imagined to resemble, goats than they were in the classical period, but it
does serve as a reminder that satyr-play was a part of 'tragic' performance
and that, at least later, τραγωιδία (first attested in Ar. *Ach.*) was understood to mean 'goat-song' (cf., e.g., Pickard-Cambridge 1962: 112–24).
The only explicit reference to goats in *Cycl.* is the satyrs' complaint about
the 'wretched goatskin cloak' which they have to wear (80n.); whereas
the Homeric Cyclops is said explicitly to keep goats as well as sheep (*Od.*
9.220, 239), in Euripides it is the satyrs who are the closest thing to goats
on Sicily. An entry of the satyrs with a pastoral song of 'popular' generic
affiliations and a striking mixture of 'low' subject-matter and high style
may suggest one view of the relation between and historical development
of satyr-plays and the tragedies which preceded them; the parodos may
thus gesture not just to Sicilian song-traditions, but also to the generic
place of the dramatic form we are currently witnessing. For further discussion cf. Hunter 2009: 58–9, Laemmle 2013: 242–3. It is not unlikely that

the satyrs had performed similar tasks in earlier plays, but we can point to no certain case; it is often thought that they looked after cattle in Soph. *Inachos*, and if Soph. *Poimenes* were satyric, then this might be a case of pastoralist satyrs. In the third century, Sositheus' *Daphnis or Lityerses* had an agricultural context, and Euripides may have dramatised the same story in the satyric *Theristai* ('Harvesters').

A further question of structure concerns the animals addressed in these verses. The antistrophe is certainly addressed to one or more ewes and the mesode to a ram (though Willink 2001: 517–18 emends to make it too addressed to a ewe). The indications for the strophe are mixed. It is now normally assumed that the grand opening address of 41–2 must, particularly for an audience whose minds have been directed to *Od.* 9, evoke the famous ram of *Od.* 9.447–60, which will then be the subject of attention right through to the end of the mesode, cf. Kassel 1991: 192–4, 53n. on στασιωρόν; there will be a wry humour in the fact that the ram which in Homer was always 'first out and first back', perhaps as the κτίλος or sheep that led the flock (so Eustath. *Hom.* 1638.60, Thompson 1932), here proves disobedient and reluctant to return. Others doubt that a reference to the bleating lambs (48) would carry much weight with a ram, and thus the strophe, like the antistrophe, must be addressed to a maternal ewe (cf., e.g. Serrao 1969: 58–60, Voelke 2001: 176). It is perhaps the noble address of 41–2 (where see n.) which makes the strongest argument: the ram which was always first out to graze the τέρεν' ἄνθεα ποίης (*Od.* 9.449) must here be lured by the ποιηρὰ βοτάνα rather nearer home.

41–2 A high-style, almost paratragic address to a sheep, cf. 286, *Ion* 262–3, Soph. *El.* 129, *Phil.* 96. Theocritus 5 similarly begins with an address by Komatas to his goats, telling them to avoid a nearby shepherd.

γενναίων, 'noble', is standardly used of excellent 'pedigree' animals, as well as of high-born or virtuous human beings (cf. Xen. *Oec.* 15.4, LSJ s.v. I 1, Arnott 1972: 27), and as such draws attention to the amusing 'humanisation' of the sheep, particularly in the mouth of the satyrs. It is less important that (ancient and modern) shepherds may, like dog-owners, talk to their animals in 'human' terms than that this perhaps recalls the shared feeling which the Homeric Cyclops imputes to his ram, whom he also addresses incongruously as ὦ κριὲ πέπον (*Od.* 9.447).

πατέρων 'male ancestors'.

δ': the transmitted τ' would give an unparalleled case of μὲν … τε linking two instances of a word repeated in anaphora.

ἐκ may govern both nouns, cf. *Hec.* 144, *IT* 886–7, K–G I 550, or γενναίων … πατέρων depends upon παῖ.

τοκάδων 'female ancestors'. This word is standardly used of animals which have recently given birth (*Med.* 187, *Od.* 14.16 (Eumaeus' pigs)), but here it is a poeticism for 'mothers' (cf. *Hipp.* 560), thus creating a similar mixed effect to γενναίων.

43 πᾶι δή μοι νίσηι σκοπέλους; 'by what route, may I ask, are you heading for the boulders?'

δή is common in surprised questions, cf. *Med.* 516, *Hec.* 113, *GP²* 210–11.

μοι: the so-called 'ethic' dative, in which a pronoun conveys the speaker's involvement in what is said; it is often best translated as 'tell me, please', cf. 206, 543, *CGCG* 30.53. The usage is notably polite (or ironic) when addressed to an animal.

νίσηι is here present (followed by a simple accusative of motion, Smyth §1588), but probably future at *Ph.* 1234 (cf. Mastronarde on *Ph.* 1233–5).

44–8 The chorus try to lure the sheep home by describing the steading in terms of a *locus amoenus* (cf. Nisbet and Hubbard 1978: 52–3, Hunter 1999: 12–17): lush grass and running water are standard elements of such descriptions. In Theocritus too such descriptions are regularly used to entice a (human) character to choose one place over another, cf. 1.106–7, 5.31–4, 45–9, 11.45–8 (the Cyclops to Galateia). Eur. may here have borrowed (and mildly parodied) a convention known to him from Sicilian traditions.

44–5 οὐ τᾶιδ' ... 'Are there not this way ...?'

ὑπήνεμος αὔρα: breezes are a regular part of the *locus amoenus* (*Med.* 837–9, Pl. *Phdr.* 230c1 (τὸ εὔπνουν), Hor. *C.* 3.4.8, etc.), and it is amusing that the satyrs try to lure a sheep with something that humans might enjoy but which is unlikely to matter much to a woolly quadruped. Moreover, it is a little strained (even for the satyrs) to claim that there is a breeze in one spot but not in another which cannot be that far away from the first. The epithet, however, is very difficult. ὑπήνεμος normally means 'sheltered from the wind', and this seems a very awkward way to describe a 'gentle breeze' (the now standard interpretation); no good parallel has been adduced (ἀνεμόεσσα ... αὔρα at Soph. *Trach.* 954 does not help). εὐήνεμος might perhaps offer an easier combination; ἡδύπνοος would be perfect, but the corruption very hard to explain. An alternative approach is offered by Musgrave's conjecture αὐλά: the satyrs offer the sheep a 'fold out of the wind'. If correct, this would then give another case of verbal repetition between strophe and antistrophe (cf. 60, above p. 102). That the antistrophe seems to place the αὐλά and the availability of grass in separate realms is not a decisive argument against placing them together here; at 541 Odysseus claims, perhaps untruthfully, that there is lush growth in front of the cave.

ποιηρὰ βοτάνα: the lushness of the *locus amoenus* is amusingly here not an invitation to lie upon it but rather (as at [Theocr.] 8.67–8) to eat it, cf. Pl. *Phdr.* 230c3–5 (Socrates showing that he can do a rhetorical *locus amoenus*) 'the best thing of all is the grass (τὸ τῆς πόας) – you can lay your head on the gentle slope and it's wonderful'. The Homeric model is *Od.* 9.449 (cf. 41–62n.).

46–8 Some editors place a question mark after 45 and, with Wecklein's δ' for θ', make 46–8 a statement rather than part of the question; it seems better, however, to keep all the delights which the chorus offer to the sheep as part of one syntactical unit. Cool, often running, water is another standard element of the *locus amoenus*, but here the water is in drinking-troughs; so, too, caves often feature in such descriptions or themselves can be the subject of them (cf. Theocr. 11.44–8 (the Cyclops' cave), Hor. *C.* 1.5.3), but the delights on offer in the Cyclops' cave are at least mixed, even for sheep. *Od.* 13.103–12 describes the marvellous 'cave of the nymphs' which has two entrances, as does – so we shall learn at 707 – the Cyclops' cave, cf. above p. 40.

δινᾶεν is a common epithet of rivers in Homer, but here the water swirls (if it does) because it has been emptied into the troughs (cf. 29); to understand the epithet solely with ποταμῶν by transference ('*enallagē*') is to miss the humour of this satyric (and satiric) *locus amoenus*. Somewhere behind these verses may lie *Od.* 6.89–90, where Nausicaa and her attendants allow their mules ποταμὸν πάρα δινήεντα / τρώγειν ἄγρωστιν μελιηδέα.

πίστραις: cf. 29n.

οὗ, 'where', seems far more natural than οὕ, which offers a reversion to the question-style of 44.

49–54 The satyrs, or perhaps one satyr (cf. above p. 98), turn from enticements to threat, or – if these verses refer to a different sheep than the strophe – break off to deal with a particularly recalcitrant ram. There is a somewhat similar sequence at Theocr. 4.45–9, also marked by σίττα, where Komatas breaks off his conversation with Battos to threaten his cows if they do not move in the desired direction, cf. Serrao 1969: 59–60.

49–50 Cf. Theocr. 5.100–1 'Hey (σίττ')! Away from the olive, you kids! Graze here where the ground slopes down and there are tamarisks'.

ψύττ', and elsewhere σίττα, represents a whistling noise to attract the animals' attention, cf. Theocr. 4.45 (with Gow's n.), 5.3, 100, 8.69, Rossi 1971b: 7–9; ψό is attested perhaps as a shepherd's call from Soph. *Poimenes* (fr. 521, cf. above p. 35).

οὐ τᾶιδ', οὔ; 'Won't you <come> this way, won't you?' For such a verbless command to grazing animals cf. Theocr. 5.3 οὐκ ἀπὸ τᾶς κράνας; σίττ', ἀμνίδες.

οὐ τᾶιδε νεμῆι κλειτὺν δροσεράν; 'Will you not graze the dewy slope over here?' Such questions expressed with the future tense amount to commands; K–G I 176 describe the form as 'polite', but there is no need to take it as such here. Cf. *Ion* 174 οὐ πείσηι; (Ion to one of the birds nesting in the temple).

κλειτύν: this epigraphically attested spelling is, as here, standardly replaced in MSS by κλιτύς, cf. Wackernagel 1916: 74–5.

51 σου: the genitive marks the direction or target aimed at, cf. *Ba.* 1096, 1099–1100, Smyth §1349, K–G I 351; the usage may be compared to the genitive following verbs of desire and striving.

52 ὕπαγ' 'move along'; for this intransitive use cf. Ar. *Wasps* 290 ὕπαγ', ὦ παῖ, ὕπαγε, *Clouds* 1298, LSJ s.v. B II 1.

κεράστα: cf. Theocr. 5.145 αἶγες ἐμαὶ ... κερουχίδες, 8.51 ἴθ', ὦ κόλε. It is possible that Κεράστης, 'Mr Horns', is to be understood as the ram's name; Arist. *HA* 6.573b27 reports that the animals which lead the flock are trained to answer to their name. Thompson 1932 suggested that this word lived on in the Sicilian *crastu* for a leading sheep, but that word is much more likely to be a dialect form of *castrone*.

53–4 στασιωρόν: this noun should mean 'guardian of the steading'; for στάσις in this sense cf. fr. 442, Serrao 1969: 53–7. The standard term in Homer for 'homestead', whether of the Cyclops or Eumaeus, is σταθμός. The 'guardian of the Cyclops' steading' could be either Silenos (cf. 29–35) or, given the Homeric background, the ram; the latter would be a flattering half-untruth, but hardly an impossible one: the presence of a large, horned ram can still be a deterrent to trespassers. If Silenos is understood as the guardian (so, e.g., Serrao 1969: 61–2, Diggle 1994: 36–7), then a preposition such as <πρός> must be added. It is, however, at least unexpected for the satyrs to tell the ram to return 'to Silenos': 'it gives him a prominence ... he does not clearly deserve' (Kovacs 1994: 145). A vocative addressed to the ram is an attractive alternative. This problem cannot, however be divorced from the apparent accumulation of epithets for the Cyclops: μηλοβότα ... ἀγροβάτα. This is not impossible, cf. *El.* 169–70 γαλακτοπότας ἀνὴρ/ Μυκηναῖος οὐριβάτας, *Tr.* 436–7 (without asyndeton) ὠμοβρώς τ' ὀρειβά-της/Κύκλωψ, but the proximity of two adjectives close in both meaning and sound is at least awkward. Some have tried deleting one or other of the epithets (Wilamowitz 1921: 224, Willink 2001: 518–19), or we might read μηλοβάτα, 'flock-mounting', as a vocative addressed to the ram; at [Theocr.] 8.49 a goatherd addresses a he-goat as τᾶν λευκᾶν αἰγῶν ἄνερ. The mating drive of animals is one motif very familiar from later bucolic which is otherwise missing from the parodos and might be thought dear to the satyrs' interests; in a satyr-play of Achaios, Silenos was called νυμφόβας (fr. 52). Pan is αἰγιβάτης, and ps.-Oppian, *Cyn.* 1.388 uses μηλοβατεῖν of rams; μηλοβάτα στασιωρέ would be a suitably honorific form of address for the noble ram. If this is correct, the two epithets in -βάτης with different implications would play off amusingly against each other.

μηλοβότα: if sound, this will be a Doric genitive of μηλοβότης, 'shepherd'; at 660 the Cyclops is called τὸν Αἴτνας μηλονόμον.

ἀγροβάτα 'who treads the open spaces', seems a certain correction, cf. *Tr.* 436 (cited above), Soph. *Phil.* 214 ποιμὴν ἀγροβάτας (where ἀγροβότας is in a minority of MSS).

55–7 The description of the Maenads suckling animals at *Ba.* 699–702 seems to rework these verses, 'Some held a young deer or wild wolf-cubs in their arms and gave them white milk – those who had recently given birth and left their babies with their breasts still full' (αἱ δ' ἀγκάλαισι δορκάδ' ἢ σκύμνους λύκων/ἀγρίους ἔχουσαι λευκὸν ἐδίδοσαν γάλα,/ὅσαις νεοτόκοις μαστὸς ἦν σπαργῶν ἔτι/ βρέφη λιπούσαις), cf. above pp. 45–6. The Homeric model is *Od.* 9.438–9, where the blinded Cyclops' ewes have not been milked and so are bleating, οὔθατα γὰρ σφαραγεῦντο.

μαστούς: μαστός is found elsewhere of an animal's teat, but here it is part of the 'personification' of the ewes, as the satyrs appeal to their maternal instincts: θαλάμοις, ποθοῦσι and σμικρῶν τεκέων all belong to the same discourse.

56–7 'Receive with your teats the young lambs (lit. the nurslings of lambs) which you leave behind in their chambers'.

τροφάς ... ἀρνῶν: cf. 189n. The transmitted θηλαῖσι σπορᾶς would mean very much the same, but is metrically faulty (– – – ⏑ – for – – ⏑⏑ –); the corruption is hard to explain, but τροφάς keeps the preciosity of expression which is part of the satyrs' wheedling tone. Diggle accepts Broadhead's θηλὰς πορίσασ' ... 'receive those of the lambs (partitive gen., cf. *Suppl.* 201–2, *Her.* 283, *IT* 736) which [οὓς Diggle: ἃς] you leave behind in their chambers, providing your teats'.

θαλάμοις continues the appeal to the ewe's maternal instinct, cf. 55–7n.; in Homer the lambs have σηκοί (*Od.* 9.219, 439).

58–9 ἀμερόκοι-/τοι βλαχαὶ σμικρῶν τεκέων 'day-sleeping bleatings of the little children', i.e. 'your bleating little children who sleep during the day', another precious, amusingly silly phrase: the lambs will be bleating now, because they are hungry, but will not have been during the day, when asleep. Some of the preciosity may be removed by invoking '*enallage*' again (cf. 46n.), so that ἀμερόκοιτοι 'really' belongs with τεκέων, but here style is what matters most. Among the terrible sounds of the city at war at Aesch. *Sept.* 348–51 are βλαχαὶ δ' αἱματόεσσαι/τῶν ἐπιμαστιδίων/ἀρτιτρεφεῖς; the phrasing is perhaps not close enough to make a convincing case for parody here (Bers 1974: 40, 67).

ἀμερόκοι-/τοι: cf. Hes. *WD* 605 where 'day-sleeping' is a 'kenning' for a thief.

60–2 †ἀμφιβαίνεις† is both unmetrical (a choriamb is required) and without meaning, but no conjectured verb (including Triclinius' ἀμφιβαλεῖς) has any plausibility; for various attempts cf. Jackson 1955: 134–5, Willink 2001: 520. A common alternative is to seek an appropriate epithet for αὐλάν: ἀμφιλαφῆ (Hartung), ἀμφίθυρον (Seaford), ἀμφίβολον (Eden 1990: 26–7). With such an approach, it is then assumed either that there will be a further ellipse of a verb (cf. 49, though the present case would be much more difficult) or that εἴσω should be replaced by Seidler's εἴσει 'will you enter?'

Αἰτναίων εἴσω σκοπέλων: if, as seems likely, the sheep are imagined to graze on the foothills of Etna (cf. 27), then their pastures are not unreasonably described as 'within the boulders of Etna'.

63–81 The satyrs regret the lost pleasures of the Dionysiac life; such wishful projection to an imagined world of choral freedom was very probably a common motif in satyr-play. Cyllene offers a similar account of the satyrs' habitual activities at Soph. *Ichn.* 225–8. The epode begins with an iambic dimeter with three resolutions; the short syllables and asyndetic parataxis produce an effect analogous to the opening of Pratinas, *PMG* 708 (almost certainly satyric) τίς ὁ θόρυβος ὅδε; τί τάδε τὰ χορεύματα;/τίς ὕβρις ἔμολεν ἐπὶ Διονυσιάδα πολυπάταγα θυμέλαν;/ἐμὸς ἐμὸς ὁ Βρόμιος, ἐμὲ δεῖ κελαδεῖν, ἐμὲ δεῖ παταγεῖν κτλ. For further discussion cf. Laemmle 2019a, above p. 25.

63 τάδε ... τάδε: cf. 204, *Hypsipyle* fr. 752f.9–10 οὐ τάδε πήνας, οὐ τάδε κερκίδος/ἱστοτόνου κτλ. (discussed above pp. 42–3). The use of plural pronouns such as ταῦτα or τάδε to refer to single situations in their entirety is common, cf. K–G I 67–8.

Βρόμιος: cf. 1n.

χοροί: cf. 124. The constant moving and dancing of the satyr-chorus which represents the perpetual movement of the Dionysiac κῶμος is opposed to the pastoral (and relatively sedentary) drudgery to which the chorus finds itself bound, cf. 36–8n., Laemmle 2013: 234. The chorus' complaint may also be understood as 'there are no choruses here'; this is not just wrily self-referential, but makes the point that, without Dionysos, there is no theatre, even as we are watching a play set in a land without the god, cf. further 204n.

64 Wilamowitz proposed βακχεῖαι, 'Bacchic rites', as following more naturally upon χοροί, but 'Bacchants' belong to any satyric imagining, and the repetition in 72 is not at all awkward; Βάκχαι is also a more natural noun for θυρσοφόροι.

θυρσοφόροι: in the classical period the thyrsus is normally depicted as a long, thin fennel rod, with ivy leaves at the tip, cf. Dodds on *Ba.* 113; θυρσοφορεῖν is used of the god at *Ba.* 557, and cf. *Hypsipyle* fr. 752 Διόνυσος, ὃς θύρσοισι καὶ νεβρῶν δοραῖς/καθαπτὸς κτλ.

65 τυμπάνων: cf. 205n.

ἀλαλαγμοί 'loud soundings', cf. *Hel.* 1352 (of the αὐλός, also in a context of ecstatic rites), *Ba.* 592 Βρόμιος … ἀλα-/λάζεται, Aesch. fr. 57.7 (ecstatic rites) ψαλμὸς δ᾿ ἀλαλάζει. At *Ba.* 156 such drums are called βαρύβρομα.

67–6 Retention of the transmitted order and the carrying of the final syllable of ἀλαλαγμοί into the following verse would produce a very regular pattern of *hept wil wil* (so Wilamowitz 1921: 224), but Hermann's transposition is very attractive. The combination of wine and water evokes a rural and uncontrolled version of the symposium, an institution which will become very important later in the play; the wine is still being crushed, just as the water is still flowing in springs. There seems, however, no reason to accept the suggestion of Biehl 1986: 177–82 that the verses refer to the Athenian Pithoigia festival and the cult of Dionysos 'in the Marshes'. So, too, the transposition creates an effective crescendo as the satyrs' vision of the life they have lost verges on the dithyrambic ('by streams gushing with water'). For σταγόνες in such a context cf. Timotheus, *PMG* 780.1–2 (from *Cyclops*), Antiphanes fr. 172.3 describing a drinking-cup full τῆς τρυφερᾶς ἀπὸ Λέσβου σεμνογόνου σταγόνος.

χλωραί suggests the fresh power and vital life within the grape, just as the god himself is in the wine (519–20n.), cf. Clarke 2004. χλωρός, which is standardly translated 'fresh, green, vigorous', is commonly used of liquids; Plutarch reports that Greeks considered Dionysos to be responsible for and the source of 'all which is naturally moist' (πᾶσα ὑγρὰ φύσις, *Mor.* 365a).

ὑδροχύτοις occurs only here in Greek literature.

68–70 The colometry adopted here, with three successive overruns, evokes the breathless speed of the satyrs' pursuit in the open spaces (71). Willink 2001: 522 n.17 prefers to remove the glyconic of 69, a length not otherwise found in *Cycl.*

68 Νύσαι: Nysa was very early associated with Dionysos, but there was no agreement as to where this place was, cf. *Il.* 6.132, *HHDion.* (1) fr. A 9–10 West, Dodds on Eur. *Ba.* 556–9. Hesych. ν 742 notes that it is 'a mountain, not in any one place' and enumerates 15 Nysas in various locations; Dionysiac cults all over the Greek world presumably tended to identify a 'Mount Nysa' in their own local area.

Νυμ-/φᾶν: cf. 4n. Although the differences between nymphs and Bacchant women may be blurred in both literature (cf. Soph. *Ant.* 1129 νύμφαι βακχίδες) and iconography, here the audience very likely felt a distinction between these nymphs and the βάκχαι of 72, cf. Hedreen 1994.

69–70 'Nor … do I celebrate in song Iacchos Iacchos to Aphrodite …' The text is not secure. The transmitted ἴακχον ᾠδάν is very hard to parallel

in the sense 'song for Iacchos' or 'Iacchic song'; Ἴακχος is the name either
of the god (see below) or of the song in his honour (Hdt. 8.65.1, Ar. *Frogs*
320, etc.). Moreover, the repetition must evoke the ritual cry in honour of
the god (cf. Ar. *Frogs* 316–17, 325, etc.). ὠιδᾶι, which is palaeographically
easier than ὠιδαῖς, would in this context very easily have become ὠιδάν;
cf. *Antiope* fr. 223.121 μέλπειν θεοὺς ὠιδαῖσιν, Ar. *Thesm.* 988–9, *Delphic
Paean* (*CA* p. 141) 3 ἵνα Φοῖβον ὠιδαῖσι μέλψητε. Textual disturbance may,
however, go deeper than this. The satyrs sing 'to Aphrodite' whom they
pursue; there is no difficulty with Aphrodite's link to Dionysiac celebration (see below), but it is awkward that they should sing the Iacchos-song
'to her' and also pursue her. Wecklein deleted πρός, with the result that
the satyrs celebrate Aphrodite, and celebrating and pursuing Aphrodite
would give a clear metonymic description of the satyrs' sexual activities;
retention of πρός produces a possibly awkward mixture of metonymy and
the 'real' goddess. If something along these lines is correct, Ἴακχον Ἴακχον
perhaps conceals a version of the ritual cry Ἴακχ' ὦ Ἴακχε inserted paren-
thetically; ὠιδάν might then easily have entered the text from a marginal
note explaining the cry.

Ἴακχον: Iacchos, whose name derives from the ecstatic shout ἴακχε, was
a god connected with the Eleusinian Mysteries, and his image was carried
in the Eleusinian procession; well before *Cycl.*, however, he had been associated and/or identified with Dionysos, cf. Soph. *Ant.* 1152–4, Ar. *Frogs*
316–20, Dodds on *Ba.* 725, Graf 1974: 51–66, Ford 2011.

τὰν Ἀφροδί-/ταν: Aphrodite is often celebrated alongside Dionysos, cf.,
e.g., *Ba.* 402–8 (with Dodds on 402–16), Anacreon, *PMG* 357 (Dionysos
accompanied by Eros, the nymphs and Aphrodite in the mountains), Pl.
Crat. 406b7–d2; the two are also often conjoined in sympotic contexts
(cf., e.g., Panyassis fr. 17.2–4 Bernabé). For Aphrodite in satyr-play more
generally cf. Griffith 2015: 146–69. More banally, it is a common idea that
wine is a sexual stimulant (Pl. *Laws* 1.645d6–8, etc.).

71 θηρεύων: the satyrs 'hunt/chase' Aphrodite, i.e. they try (usually
unsuccessfully) to catch nymphs or maenads for sex, cf. *Ba.* 459, 688.
Hunting-imagery is very common in erotic contexts.

πετόμαν: the imperfect (here without augment) poignantly expresses
the satyrs' nostalgia for their past life; for the speed of Dionysiac movement
cf. *Ba.* 166, 748–50, 1090 (with Dodds's n.). As many modern languages
do, Greek uses 'fly' to depict rapid movement, cf., e.g., Ar. *Lys.* 55, 321.

72 λευκόποσιν: the Bacchants are barefoot (cf. *Ba.* 863), thus revealing
the desirable whiteness of female flesh, cf. Irwin 1974: 123–6.

73–5 The metre is apparently anapaestic, but ὦ φίλος ὦ φίλε seems
impossible and Βακχεῖος, as opposed to Βάκχιος, is never used by itself to

refer to the god, only as an adjective with an appropriate noun (cf. Ar. *Thesm.* 988–9, Soph. *OT* 1105, etc.). ὦ φίλε is very likely a gloss on ὦ φίλος (cf. *Andr.* 510, 530, etc.), a form of address with the nominative which perhaps conveys the deep emotional attachment of the satyrs to their god, cf. West 1966: 140. The second problem is usually solved by the addition of a noun: Kovacs proposed ὦ φίλος ὦναξ Βακχεῖε and Willink (after Diggle) φίλος ὦ Βακχεῖε ... ὦναξ; for other proposals cf. Diggle 1971: 44–5. One of the two transmitted verbs should probably be a participle (οἰοπολῶν Nauck, σείων Tr²), unless ποῖ (or ποῦ, Conradt) be repeated, thus creating two emotional questions addressed to the god: 'Where do you wander? <Where> do you shake your hair?', a perfectly believable sequence. <ποῦ> ξανθὰν χαίταν σείεις; would give an excellent paroemiac closure to the address to the god. At *Ba.* 556–75 the chorus wonder where their god is and imagine the places where he might currently be celebrating his rites. Paley's < δ'> after ποῖ in 74 avoids correption of the monosyllable (cf. 358, 360); for postponed δέ in questions cf. *GP²* 174.

οἰοπολεῖς 'wander alone'; the corresponding adjective is used in Homer of lonely, isolated places (e.g. *Il.* 13.473, *Od.* 11.574). The satyrs project their loneliness on to the god: without them, he is alone. οἰοπολεῖν is found elsewhere only at Leonidas, *AP* 7.657.1 (= *HE* 2062) οἳ ταύτην ὄρεος ῥάχιν οἰοπολεῖτε, and perhaps the satyrs here fantasise not only that their god is alone, but that, like them, he is forced to herd animals; οἰοπόλος seems later to have been understood as both 'alone' and 'sheep-tending', cf. Hunter on Ap. Rhod. *Arg.* 4.1322, 1412–14.

ξανθὰν χαίταν σείεις: the throwing back of the head and shaking of the hair are standard features of the fifth-century iconography of Bacchants, and cf. *Ba.* 184–5 ποῖ δεῖ ... κρᾶτα σεῖσαι πολιόν;, Ar. *Lys.* 1312–13, Dodds on *Ba.* 862–5. In the *Homeric Hymn* the young god's hair shakes around him as he appears, but the hair is κυάνεαι, 'dark' (*HHDion.* 4–5); here the god is given the heroic hair-colour which, as at *Ba.* 235, carries an erotic charge.

76–81 It is not unusual for choruses to close with reflection of their own situation or emotions, cf. 620–3, Kranz 1933: 120–3, 298.

76 ἐγὼ δ' ὁ σὸς πρόπολος: cf. Soph. fr. 1130.7, the satyrs' self-presentation as Βακχίου ... ὑπηρέται. πρόπολος is regular for the servants or ministers of a god, cf. *Hel.* 570, LSJ s.v. I 2. Such 'glorious' service (cf. 23–4n.) is here contrasted with the menial drudgery of θητεύειν (*Alc.* 6, *Od.* 11.489). Strabo 10.3.7 numbers satyrs and silens among δαίμονες ἢ πρόπολοι θεῶν.

77 Κύκλωπι θητεύω: for *ia sp* in Euripidean lyrics cf. *Alc.* 401~413, *Suppl.* 781 ~ 789, Diggle 1994: 38. Stinton 1977: 137–8 proposed the deletion of Κύκλωπι and Willink 2001: 523 θητεύω Κύκλωπι <πικρῶς>, another *wil.*

78 μονοδέρκται appears only here (cf. 21n.), a strange word for a strange condition.

ἀλαίνων suggests the wandering of the exile, cf. Denniston on *El.* 204–5.

80 The satyrs are wearing the goatskin cloak of shepherds and impoverished peasants, cf. Ar. *Clouds* 72, Men. *Dysk.* 415, *Epitr.* 229, Theocr. 7.15–16. Despite τράγου (contrast αἰγίδι at 360), there is no strong reason to see a reference to the default costume (or lack of it) of the chorus, if at least the depiction on the 'Pronomos Vase' (above pp. 27–9) is not entirely misleading, cf. Wilamowitz 1920: 19. Rather, in view of what has preceded, there is probably an implicit contrast with the fawnskins worn in ecstatic rites, cf. fr. 752 (above 64n.), Soph. *Ichn.* 225–6. Cf. further above p. 102 on the relation between the parodos and τραγωιδία.

81 The satyrs view their relationship with Dionysos as φιλία, cf. Soph. *Ichn.* 76 θεὸς ὁ φίλος. The sentiment that nothing is possible or successful and no one happy without (χωρίς) the gods is very common (cf., e.g., frr. 391.1, 617a.1, *PMG* 813.10, Norden 1913: 157–9), but the satyrs' lament is a pathetic complaint, not a theological claim.

82–355 FIRST EPISODE

Silenos sees some Greeks approaching who are clearly in need of supplies. Odysseus engages him in conversation, identifies himself, and is instructed by Silenos about Cyclopean society. Odysseus and Silenos agree to an exchange of food for wine, and Silenos goes into the cave to get supplies for his visitors. While he is away, the satyrs question Odysseus about Helen. No sooner has Silenos returned than the approach of the Cyclops is spotted with alarm. When the Cyclops sees some of his lambs assembled outside the cave, Silenos pretends that Odysseus beat him up while he was trying to stop the Greeks stealing the lambs and claims that the Greeks made outrageous threats against the Cyclops. Odysseus and Silenos compete in trying to persuade the Cyclops of 'what really happened' before Odysseus and the Cyclops exchange long speeches, the former claiming that the service which they performed for Greece at Troy deserves a better fate than being eaten, whereas the Cyclops explains why he is entirely self-sufficient and has no need of νόμοι or other moral constraints. He drives the Greeks into the cave to prepare his cannibal feast.

82–95 Silenos sees Odysseus and his men approaching; he assumes from what they are carrying that they are seeking food and water and expresses pity for them in their ignorance of the Cyclops' love for human flesh. The audience will not need to be told who the visitors are. Such lengthy entry-announcements as new characters proceed into the acting area, whether essentially monologic (as here) or in dialogue (cf., e.g., *El.*

962–87) or even in lyric (Soph. *Phil.* 201–18), are familiar from tragedy of all periods (cf. Taplin 1977a: 297–9), and can serve to create dramatic tension; here the fact that the audience know who these Greek sailors are builds expectation as to how the meeting of Odysseus with Silenos and the satyrs is to be played out.

82 σιγήσατ': cf. 476n.

πετρηρεφῆ 'rock-roofed', cf. *Ion* 1400 (the cave where Ion was exposed), [Aesch.] *PV* 300–1 (the caves of Okeanos). πέτρα is used for the cave at 195, 197, as also for Philoctetes' cave (Soph. *Phil.* 16).

83 ἀθροῖσαι with ἐς suggests 'collect the sheep and drive them into the cave'.

προσπόλους: it is common in tragedy for characters to give orders to 'attendants', whether visible to the audience or hidden behind the *skēnē*, to carry objects 'inside' (e.g. *El.* 393–4, *Hel.* 1169–70), open doors, etc.; these mute attendants are the ancient equivalent of 'silent extras' or stage-hands, cf. Stanley-Porter 1973, Bain 1981, Mastronarde 1979: 105–13 and 2002: 42–4. It is usually assumed that here the 'attendants', who are never mentioned again (but see 241–3n.), entered with the satyrs during the parodos, 'to look after the sheep while the chorus dance' (Seaford); if correct, this would lessen the sense of a breaking of the dramatic illusion (cf., e.g., Ar. *Peace* 729–31), but in fact unusual attention is called to the 'attendants' (whenever they in fact entered) by Silenos telling the satyrs to tell them what to do, rather than just doing it himself. The effect of this by-play is to direct attention to the conditions of theatrical performance in a way which we would not expect in tragedy.

84 τίνα … σπουδὴν ἔχεις; 'What <cause for> haste do you have?' Others understand 'What <cause for> anxiety do you have?' (cf. *Alc.* 778, 1014); σπουδή allows both senses to resonate, but the satyrs are most surprised at the need for urgency.

85 πρὸς ἀκταῖς may be 'on the beach' or 'beside the shore'. In Homer ships could be run ashore bow first (as at 'Goat Island', *Od.* 9.147–50) or moored stern first with cables (πρυμνήσια) attaching the ship to land (e.g. *Od.* 10.126–7); 'beaching', usually stern first, was still very common with classical triremes, cf. Morrison and Williams 1968: 311, Casson 1971: 89–90.

ναὸς Ἑλλάδος σκάφος 'hull of a Greek ship', cf. 362, 467, 702, *Tr.* 686. The Doric form ναός, equivalent to epic νηός, is a metrically convenient alternative to Attic νεώς (144, 255, 467); νηός is transmitted at 239 and *IT* 1385, but epic forms are not usually found in dramatic dialogue. Ἑλλάδος in such phrases (cf. *IT* 1292, Soph. *Phil.* 223) is usually taken adjectivally, 'Greek' (cf. LSJ s.v. II, K–G II 272), rather than as the noun 'of Greece', though if and how strongly speakers felt this distinction may be doubted.

Silenos, like Philoctetes, is likely to be more interested in Greek visitors than in those of any other nationality, but we should not ask too closely how he knows that the ship is Greek (contrast Philoctetes' recognition of Greek clothing at Soph. *Phil.* 223–4).

86 κώπης ... ἄνακτας 'lords of the oar', cf. Aesch. *Pers.* 378. Arist. *Rhet.* 3.1405a29–31 criticises κώπης ἀνάσσων from Eur. *Telephos* (fr. 705.1) as ἀπρεπές, because the verb is 'too great' (μεῖζον) for what is described and the metaphor is therefore 'not concealed', i.e. obvious; for related expressions cf. *Alc.* 498, *IA* 1260, *Hel.* 1039–40 (with Allan's n.), West 1997: 545–6. Silenos' slightly portentous periphrases (cf. ἄντρα ... πετρηρεφῆ, ναὸς Ἑλλάδος σκάφος) add to the suspenseful theatricality of Odysseus' entrance. In Homer Odysseus took 12 crew-members with him to the Cyclops' cave (9.195); we need not assume that that number enters here, but the Cyclops' relatively empty space is about to get very crowded – satyrs, sheep, stage attendants, Greek sailors.

στρατηλάτηι τινί teases the audience with their knowledge of Homer; the noun is a touch grand for someone in charge of one ship (cf. previous n.), but we all know who this really is.

87 In *Od.* Odysseus and his men do indeed head purposefully for the cave which they had noted even before landing (9.181–3); Silenos' claim that the Greeks are 'heading towards this cave' is 'natural' from his point of view, but also betrays the Homeric background.

ἀμφὶ δ' αὐχέσιν: presumably by means of some kind of yoke or carrying-pole, such as are still very common in rural societies. Silenos' words act as a stage-direction for the benefit of the audience.

88 τεύχη ... κενά could be a natural inference from the way the pots are being carried, but (again) we should not press the source of Silenos' knowledge too closely.

φέρονται: the middle voice suggests 'they are carrying (for their own use)', cf. 191, *Ba.* 1280 (with Dodds's n.), Men. *Dysk.* 448, K–G I 109.

βορᾶς κεχρημένοι: βορά can, as here, 99, and 254, be used neutrally for 'food' (cf. Aesch. *Pers.* 490), but often denotes animal food or food which is tainted, like the Cyclops' cannibal diet, cf. 249, 367, 409, 416. In *Od.*, the visit to the Cyclops is prompted by Odysseus' curiosity (9.174–6, 229), as 'Goat Island' offers the Greeks an abundant supply of water (9.140–1) and food (9.152–65); when his men urge Odysseus to steal some cheeses and animals, this is opportunistic (sailors restock where they can), not driven by need. Here, Odysseus is just like any other traveller, and his intellectual curiosity and μῆτις are both downplayed, cf. Hunter 2009: 63–4, above p. 14.

89 κρωσσοὺς ... ὑδρηλούς 'pitchers for water', another rather overblown phrase. ὑδρηλός, like ὑδρηρός (Sophron fr. 4.46, Diogenes, *TrGF* 88

F7.6), otherwise means 'moist, composed of water'; its only occurrence in Homer is *Od.* 9.133 (the meadows on 'Goat Island'), and that passage is perhaps lurking in the background here. In Aesch. fr. 96 the citing sources differ between κρωσσούς … ὑδηρούς and κρωσσούς … ὑδατηρούς.

89–93 'They do not know the character of my master Polyphemos, and that this land on which they tread is inhospitable and that, to their cost, they have arrived at the man-eating Cyclopean jaw'. Silenos' apparent pity is very close to Iphigeneia's expression of sympathy (*IT* 479–81) for the Greek strangers who, like Odysseus and his men, seem destined to die in an inhospitable land, 'Where on earth have you come from, wretched strangers? You have sailed a very long way to this land, and you will be away from your homes for a long time beneath the earth'. Cf. further below on ἄξενόν τε γῆν. The contrast between Silenos' apparent regret and his teasing of (and later betrayal of) Odysseus is not simply the inconsistency appropriate to this character; it also recalls how, in the prologue, Silenos posed as an Odysseus-figure: the real hero will now appear to steal his thunder. F.J. Williams suggested that 90–3 should be a question 'Do they not know …?'; this is attractive, but in fact only someone who did not know about the Cyclops would indeed approach his cave, and cf. *Hipp.* 56–7 (Aphrodite announcing Hippolytus' approach) οὐ γὰρ οἶδ' ἀνεωιγμένας πύλας/Ἅιδου, φάος δὲ λοίσθιον βλέπων τόδε. Silenos is here given some of the foreshadowing function often performed by divine prologists.

οὐκ ἴσασι δεσπότην/Πολύφημον κτλ.: whether as a statement or a question (see previous n.), Silenos' words are tantamount to 'do they not know the *Odyssey*?', and allow an etymology of Πολύφημος as 'very famous, much renowned' to resonate again, cf. 24–5n. In *Od.*, the Cyclops observes that Odysseus must either be a fool or have come from far away not to know that the Cyclopes take no notice of gods (9.273–6); the monster's sense of self-importance has, by Euripides' time, been confirmed: everyone does know about the Cyclopes.

δεσπότην: cf. 34n.

ἄξενόν τε γῆν: the adj. is predicative (see translation above). The Greeks' ignorance evokes the concern of the Homeric Odysseus with the φιλοξενία of the lands he visits, cf. 125n., *Od.* 6.120–1, 175–6 (the Cyclops). Eight of the 15 occurrences of ἄξενος in Eur. are in *IT*, set on the shores of the '(In)hospitable Sea'; like Odysseus, Orestes arrives ἄγνωστον ἐς γῆν ἄξενον (*IT* 94), cf. Wright 2006: 32. The transmitted ἄξενον στέγην weakens the force of Silenos' forebodings as there would only be one thing which the Greeks 'do not know', namely the character of the Cyclops, and ἐμβεβῶτες normally means 'stepping on to', not 'entering'; the parallels with *IT* help to confirm Jacobs' conjecture. For a survey of the inhospitable environments in which the satyrs often find themselves cf. Voelke 2001: 301–13.

Κυκλωπίαν γνάθον: elsewhere in Euripides 'Cyclopean' refers to the monumental architecture of Mycenae (e.g. *Her.* 15, *Tr.* 1088), cf. our 'Cyclopean walls', and so here we must envisage a jaw which really is huge; Silenos' pity is tinged with verbal humour as he re-literalises the metaphor latent in the epithet. Any mention of the Cyclops' jaw will recall the horrific Homeric description of his eating (*Od.* 9.292–3).

τὴν ἀνδροβρῶτα is preferable to τήνδ' ἀνδρ-, as in this case the 'jaw' is not really already 'present to the mind' (cf. 30–1n.). For the adj. cf. Moschion, *TrGF* 97 F 6.14–15 (the life of early man) βοραὶ δὲ σαρκοβρῶτες ἀλληλοκτόνους/παρεῖχον αὐτοῖς δαῖτας.

94–5 The instruction to keep quiet is entirely 'natural', but ἡσυχία is not the satyrs' natural mode: they are always dancing around (cf. 220–1), and the prospect of the arrival of strangers has presumably led to renewed excitement and dancing, cf. 204–5, 476n.

πάρεισι with an accusative implies '(arrive at and then) be present at', cf. 106, *Ba.* 5, *El.* 1278.

Αἰτναῖον πάγον serves as an emphatic announcement of where the newcomers have reached, cf. fr. 960.9 Αἴτνας … πάγον and 114n.

96–100 are an example of a common Euripidean technique by which an entering character at first sees some, but not all, of the scene which confronts him on stage, cf., e.g., *Hel.* 68–74, Bain 1977: 61–6, Mastronarde 1979: 22–6. Odysseus sees a group of people in front of him and addresses them (96–8), but only when he gets closer does he realise that they are satyrs, cf. 99n. The entry of the Cyclops at 203–23 uses this technique of 'partial vision' somewhat differently.

96 ξένοι picks up ἄξενόν τε γῆν (91): Odysseus is in for a surprise.

φράσαιτ' ἄν: the optative with ἄν expresses a polite request, cf. *IT* 513, Smyth §1830, K–G I 233–4.

νᾶμα ποτάμιον: Odysseus' politeness leads him to adopt an amusingly high style, marked also by the postponement of πόθεν, cf. the parodic Βακχίου τε νάματος at Ar. *Eccl.* 14 and νᾶμα Νυμφῶν at Men. *Dysk.* 947. The connection between νᾶμα and νάω is probably felt here, as drinking-water is normally drawn from a flowing spring, but elsewhere the link is weak or apparently non-existent (*Ph.* 126, Wilamowitz on *Her.* 625).

97 δίψης ἄκος is in apposition to νᾶμα ποτάμιον; such an apposition is itself a feature of high style. For the 'remedying' of thirst cf. *Il.* 22.2 (literal), Pind. *Pyth.* 9.103–4 (metaphorical).

98 βορὰν … κεχρημένοις: cf. 88n. Odysseus confirms Silenos' surmise, in appealing to a universal recognition of shared human need.

ὀδῆσαι: Photios, *Lex.* ο 31 cites this form from *Cycl.* and *Alope* (fr. 113). Of the four occurrences of the verb in *Cycl.* (cf. 12n.), two (98, 133) are spoken by Odysseus. At *Od.* 8.163–4 Euryalos had taunted Odysseus as ἐπίσκοπος ... ὁδαίων/κερδέων θ᾽ ἁρπαλέων. The meaning of ὁδαῖα has been much debated (cf. Garvie on *Od.* 8.163, *LfgrE* s.v.), but the word associates Odysseus with unheroic mercantile trade and thus foreshadows an important aspect of his representation in *Cycl.*, cf. above pp. 14–15. The repeated verb perhaps evokes a current (comic?) etymology of Odysseus' name.

99 ἔα, often but not always *extra metrum*, is a standard feature of such Euripidean entrances (96–100n.), as the entrant realises something that he had not at first seen, cf. *Suppl.* 87–92, *Hel.* 68–77, 1165–79. Its reasonable insertion here makes the current scene conform to this pattern. τί χρῆμα; is also standard in such scenes (Kassel 1991: 201). Such a sequence from Eur. *Andromeda* (frr. 124–5) is parodied at Ar. *Thesm.* 1098–1106, cf. 222n., above pp. 39–41. When Odysseus catches sight of the satyrs, the style of his language drops appropriately, and a verse with two resolutions (the first since his opening verse) marks his surprise. Odysseus enters as though he were in a tragedy, but suddenly realises he is in a different dramatic genre.

Βρομίου πόλιν: cf. 1n. The name Βρόμιος is not found in Homer (cf. above p. 17), but the god and Odysseus' knowledge of him have moved on since then; *Cycl.* puts Dionysos back into Homer, as satyr-drama puts Dionysos back into tragedy, cf. above pp. 22–3, Hunter 2009: 64. Later at least, there were eastern cities called Dionysopolis (*RE* 5.1008–10), but there is no obvious fifth-century 'Bromiopolis' to which Odysseus may be alluding.

ἔοιγμεν is an Attic syncopated form of ἐοίκαμεν, cf. *Hcld.* 681, Soph. *Ichn.* 101.

ἐσβαλεῖν 'to have fallen upon/entered', here constructed with a simple accusative, cf. *Hipp.* 1198, *Andr.* 968, LSJ s.v. II 1.

100 τόνδ᾽ ὅμιλον is not necessarily impolite (as in 'this rabble'); ὅμιλος occurs only twice in Old Comedy, both in polite contexts (Ar. *Peace* 920, Crat. fr. 360.1). The deictic is standard in such utterances cf. *Alc.* 24, *Andr.* 494–5, Diggle 1994: 171–3.

101 χαίρειν...γεραίτατον: lit. 'I first bid the most reverend one to fare well', i.e. 'I bid good day to ...' The greeting itself would be τὸν γεραίτατον χαίρειν, with an imperative infinitive in which the sense of ellipse of a verb of speaking was no longer felt, cf. Pl. *Ion* 530a1 τὸν Ἴωνα χαίρειν (with Rijksbaron 2007: 98), Theocr. 14.1 χαίρειν πολλὰ τὸν ἄνδρα Θυώνιχον. The so-called instantaneous aorist (cf. 266), here a performative marker of politeness, does not differ in meaning from the present tenses at, e.g., *El.* 552, Soph. *Tr.* 227–8, cf. Smyth §1937, Lloyd 1999: 34, Bary 2012. Ar. seems to have recognised this aorist as a tragic idiom, cf. *Ach.* 266–7, 485, *Peace* 528 (all paratragic). First-person εἶπα does not certainly occur in Attic texts before the fourth century, though second-person εἶπας is common (e.g. 148), and many editors adopt προσεῖπον here.

τὸν γεραίτατον 'oldest', but also 'most revered', a comically formal and ingratiating mode of address, particularly given what is to come, cf. Ar. *Ach.* 286 (Dicaiopolis' first encounter with the hostile chorus) ὠχαρνέων γεραίτατοι; for the definite article in such situations cf. passages cited in n. on χαίρειν προσεῖπα.

102 Silenos wastes no time on the niceties of epic hospitality, but gets straight down to asking the question familiar from Homer, cf. *Od.* 1.170, 9.252–5 (the Cyclops to Odysseus). Odysseus is the epic ξένος *par excellence*, cf. 510, 548, *Od.* 8.461 (Nausicaa to Odysseus) χαῖρε, ξεῖν' κτλ.

103 Odysseus announces himself in a manner similar to his self-presentation to the Phaeacians at *Od.* 9.19–21, cf. Hunter 2009: 60. Whereas, however, in *Od.* Odysseus does everything to conceal his name and identity both on Scherie and then on Ithaca, in *Cycl.* he immediately reveals the truth to Silenos and the satyrs; they use his name freely in the scene which follows (cf. 132, 175, 189), but never once the Cyclops has entered. As in Homer, then, the Cyclops does not hear the name of Odysseus until it is too late (690–2). Silenos' silence about the stranger's name in his confrontation with Odysseus in 228–72 is particularly notable; the Homeric motif is there given a new spin.

Ἴθακος: for the form cf. Ar. *Wasps* 185 (with the n. of Biles and Olson). Homer uses Ἰθακήσιος, as does Odysseus at 277. *Tr.* 277 begins Ἰθάκης Ὀδυσσεύς, and in the citation of the present verse at Schol. Soph. *Aj.* 190d the transmission is split between Ἴθακος and Ἰθάκης, but there are no grounds for change here.

γῆς Κεφαλλήνων ἄναξ: in the *Iliad* (e.g. 2.631–7) and the Ithacan books of the *Odyssey* (e.g. 20.210, 24.355), Homer uses 'Cephallenians' to refer to those from Ithaca and nearby islands who were under Odysseus' command. Odysseus speaks with a certain pride, but at Soph. *Phil.* 264, 791 Philoctetes mocks him as 'Cephallenian', and Silenos too certainly remains unimpressed. Paganelli 1979: 128–31 suggests that Cephallenia is here evoked because of that island's loyalty to Athens during the Sicilian campaign, but that seems very unlikely. Like Silenos, the Sophoclean Philoctetes also speaks scornfully of Odysseus as 'son of Sisyphos' (v. 417), cf. 104n. For links between *Cycl.* and Soph. *Phil.* see Introduction pp. 40–1.

104 οἶδ' ἄνδρα suggests that Silenos knows *Od.* 1.1 (ἄνδρα μοι ἔννεπε, Μοῦσα, πολύτροπον κτλ.), but he instantly shows his command of another representation of Odysseus; the satyric version (104) replaces the epic (103). A rather similar play with *Od.* 1.1 may have occurred in Cratinus' *Odysseis* in which the Cyclops seems (the text is uncertain) to have asked Odysseus ποῦ ποτ' εἶδές μοι τὸν ἄνδρα, παῖδα Λαέρτα φίλον; (fr. 147.1), cf.

above p. 6. At Ar. *Ach.* 430, however, Euripides tells Dicaeopolis οἶδ᾽ ἄνδρα, Μυσὸν Τήλεφον; the second phrase is drawn from Eur. *Telephos* (fr. 704), but it is unclear whether the first is paratragic.

κρόταλον δριμύ 'a clever chatterer'. κρόταλον, lit. 'castanet/clapper' (an instrument of Dionysiac cult and thus very familiar to Silenos, cf. 205n.), is twice used in Ar. *Clouds* (260, 448) of the kind of speciously clever and deceitful talker who is the typical product of Socrates' school. Words derived from κροτεῖν seem early to have acquired the resonance 'wily, cunning'; at Hes. fr. 198.22 (= 154c.22 Most) Odysseus is πολύκροτα μήδεα εἰδώς, and at some point πολύκροτον replaced πολύτροπον in *Od.* 1.1, cf. Harder 2012: 2.550–1. κρότημα, lit. 'something hammered together', is also applied to Odysseus at *Rhes.* 498–9 and Soph. fr. 913 πάνσοφον κρότημα, Λαέρτου γόνος (where see the notes of Pearson and Radt). δριμύς, lit. 'sharp, bitter, pungent', occurs only here in Eur.; it was used of people to mean 'shrewd, clever' (LSJ s.v. III), usually with a negative resonance, cf. Pl. *Tht.* 173a1–3 (describing the 'Odyssean' lawyer/politician) 'they are keen and shrewd (ἔντονοι καὶ δριμεῖς) and know how to flatter their master with their words and worm their way into his favour with their deeds', Arist. *Top.* 8.156b36–7, Clements 2013: 78. Aristophanes of Byzantium (fr. 31 Slater) noted that Euripides used δριμύ to mean συνετόν, very likely with reference to *Cycl.* 104, and Dio Chrysostom describes the Odysseus of Aeschylus' *Philoctetes* as δριμὺν καὶ δόλιον and ascribes τὸ ἀκριβὲς καὶ δριμὺ καὶ πολιτικόν to the same figure in Euripides' version of that story (52.15). In a letter of Synesius (late fourth century AD), the Cyclops tells Odysseus that he seems to be a δριμύτατον ἀνθρώπιον (cf. 316), but even so he will not escape; this passage (*PMG* 818) is normally thought to paraphrase Philoxenus' *Cyclops or Galateia* (cf. above pp. 8–9, Fongoni 2014: 106, LeVen 2014: 235–7).

Σισύφου γένος 'son of Sisyphos'. For γένος in this sense cf., e.g., Soph. *Ant.* 1117, LSJ s.v. II; γόνον in the scholium on Soph. *Aj.* 190 (cf. *IA* 1362) is a common form of simplification. The story that Odysseus was the son of Sisyphos, because his mother Antikleia was already pregnant by Sisyphos when she married Laertes, is first attested in Aesch. fr. 175 and Soph. *Aj.* 189 and from the fifth century on is commonly used to mock the hero. Sisyphos was a paradigm of the cunning, untrustworthy trickster who even talked his way out of the Underworld where, however, he finally met his eternal punishment, cf. *Il.* 6.153, *Od.* 11.593–600, Theognis 701–12, Olson on Ar. *Ach.* 391–2. Hes fr. 10a.26 calls Sisyphos αἰολομήτης, and such an epithet might easily be applied to Odysseus. Sisyphos was a familiar figure in satyr-play (cf. Critias, *TrGF* 43 F 19, Laemmle 2013: 306); Aeschylus, Euripides and perhaps Sophocles (fr. 545) all wrote *Sisyphos* satyr-plays, and Sisyphos also played an important role in at least one of Euripides' satyr-dramas entitled *Autolycus*. Silenos' view of Odysseus is thus appropriately satyric.

105 ἐκεῖνος αὐτός εἰμι 'I am that very man'. ἐκεῖνος αὐτός and the more common αὐτὸς ἐκεῖνος are found with both first- and third-person reference, whereas the transmitted ἐκεῖνος οὗτος is third-person, cf. Headlam on Herodas 1.3, K–G I 650, Janko 1985. The first-person is also expressed by ὅδε … ἐκεῖνος, cf. Soph. *Phil.* 261, *OC* 138.

λοιδόρει δὲ μή, 'but do not abuse me', amounts to 'no need for the jokes'; this Odysseus knows how others see him.

106 Σικελίαν τήνδε 'Sicily here', cf. 20n.

πάρει: cf. 94–5n.

107 ἐξ Ἰλίου picks up the first word of Odysseus' narrative to the Phaeacians, Ἰλιόθεν, *Od.* 9.39.

γε is commonly found in answers to open questions, cf. *GP*² 133.

Τρωϊκῶν πόνων: cf. 282, 347, 603, Soph. *Phil.* 247–8, Hunter 2020. Odysseus here clearly uses the phrase with pride, and Hdt. 9.27.4 suggests that it might have had some currency in the rhetorical memorialisation of the Greek past, cf. Paganelli 1979: 65–6.

108 πορθμὸν … πατρώιας χθονός 'the passage/route to your native land'; for the genitive cf. *IT* 1066 γῆς πατρώιας νόστος. Silenos' incredulous (and mocking) question and his choice of πορθμός ('strait') are perhaps influenced by his knowledge of the relatively short distance between the east coast of Sicily and Ithaca.

109 Odysseus cannot mention Cape Malea (18n.), because – in the real geography now assumed by the play – adverse winds there would not have blown him off course to Sicily; he is therefore made to recall *Od.* 10.48–9 (the bag of the winds) instead, τοὺς δ' αἶψ' ἁρπάξασα φέρεν πόντονδε θύελλα/ κλαίοντας. Apart from possible hints in 264, 348 and 700 (where see nn.), *Cycl.* passes in silence over all Odysseus' adventures except the meeting with the Cyclops.

110 παπαῖ here expresses ironic surprise, cf. 18n.; Odysseus is of course here the model for Silenos' *daimon*, so surprise is hardly in place.

τὸν αὐτὸν δαίμον': the pattern of our lives can be our δαίμων, and so here 'the same set of events, the same fate', cf. *Or.* 504, Soph. *OC* 1337, Men. *Dysk.* 281–2. There seems no reason to sense Dionysos behind the phrase (*pace* Griffith 2015: 26 n.39, who suggests that we are to realise that Dionysos is responsible for Odysseus' 'fortuitous' arrival).

ἐξαντλεῖς: cf. 10n.

111 ἀπεστάλης 'were driven, sent off course'; ἀποστέλλεσθαι is more commonly used of a deliberate 'sending away' (e.g. *IT* 1409), but cf. *Hel.* 660 (Menelaos to Helen) δόμων πῶς τῶν ἐμῶν ἀπεστάλης;

112 Silenos now offers a more heroic version than that of the prologue, cf. 11n. διώκων <γ᾽> would add a welcome 'yes' to Silenos' reply and may well be correct.

113 Odysseus' first question might seem already to have been answered (106); χώρα might mean 'region', rather than '(large) country' (cf. 114), but having established how the satyrs got to Sicily, Odysseus now goes directly into a version of the questions he always ponders in the *Odyssey*: where am I and what are the people like? τίς δ᾽ ἥδε χώρα; is the beginning of the 'ethnographical excursus', which translates Odysseus' Homeric account of the Cyclopes (*Od.* 9.106–15) into a 'modern' idiom and form (stichomythia).

114 ὄχθος, 'hill', might seem to understate the manner in which Etna looms over the eastern Sicilian landscape (cf. 95 πάγον), but it is elsewhere used of the Athenian Acropolis (*Ion* 12), and so does in fact emphasise the visibility of the mountain. Silenos seems comically proud of what has become 'his' mountain, in the manner of a tourist guide; how he knows that it is the highest mountain in Sicily is something we should probably not ask, and his pomposity may be an attempt to conceal his failure to answer Odysseus' second question. Etna is considerably higher and more prominent than Mount Olympus.

115 The Homeric Odysseus may ask after πόλεις (cf. *Od.* 6.175–9 to Nausicaa), but here in his Euripidean incarnation he seems surprised: like many in the Athenian audience, he knows that eastern Sicily is inhabited and fortified. In response to 114, there may be an allusion to the city of Aitna, founded by Hieron I, cf. Hunter 2009: 63. τείχη and πυργώματα can be virtually synonymous (*Tr.* 1174, *IT* 133–4), so Odysseus' question responds in kind to Silenos' pomposity.

116 ἔστ᾽: cf. 207–9n.; walls and towers are thought of as a single feature of a landscape, and the singular verb is expected with the neuter plural subject.

πρῶνες here probably refers to the land between Etna and the sea, rather than strictly to 'headlands'.

117 This may seem an odd question after 116; Odysseus may infer from what he sees around him that the land is indeed inhabited by some living creatures – if not ἄνθρωποι, then θῆρες – but when in 'ethnographical investigation' mode, Odysseus ploughs through his questions in sequence: after the location, the nature of the inhabitants. Cf. further 119n.

θηρῶν γένος may be an ironic hit back at Silenos and the satyrs, cf. 624; Cyllene calls the satyrs θῆρες at Soph. *Ichn.* 221, cf. Laemmle 2013: 437–40. For the Cyclops as a θήρ cf. 602, 658.

118 Cyclopes are neither man nor beast, cf. Konstan 1990: 212; as sons of Poseidon (21), they are as close to gods as to either of these other categories. Previously the Cyclops' cave has been both a cave (22, 82, 87) and his στέγαι or δόμοι (23, 29, 33); as this verse makes clear, the former is Silenos' view of the matter, the latter has the Cyclops himself as 'implied focaliser' – he does indeed regard the cave as 'home'. That, before the crucial step of the development of *poleis* (cf. Pl. *Prt.* 322a–c), mankind lived in 'sunless caves' is a familiar idea of Greek anthropology (cf. [Aesch.] *PV* 453, Moschion, *TrGF* 97 F5).

119 We might have expected Odysseus to ask after the nature of Cyclopes, if they are not men, but after the identity of the inhabitants comes their political system, as Odysseus goes through the sequence of his questioning. Odysseus' alternatives amount to 'monarchy or democracy?', cf. Oedipus' question about the inhabitants of Kolonos in somewhat similar circumstances, Soph. *OC* 66 ἄρχει τις αὐτῶν, ἢ 'πὶ τῶι πλήθει λόγος; The noun δημοκρατία and the associated verb first appear in Hdt., but Euripides not infrequently makes his characters speak anachronistically of contemporary political systems and ideas (most notoriously *Suppl.* 429–55); here Odysseus knows about democracy, as he knows about satyrs and the city of Aitna (cf. 115n.). For the general issues involved cf. Easterling 1985, esp. 2–3.

δεδήμευται κράτος 'Is the power divided among the *demos*?' δημεύειν is normally 'to confiscate, make public property', but cf. Pl. *Phlb.* 14d4–5 τὰ δεδημευμένα τῶν θαυμαστῶν, 'wonders which belong to everyone'.

120 A strong rewriting of *Od.* 9.114–15 θεμιστεύει δὲ ἕκαστος/παίδων ἠδ' ἀλόχων, οὐδ' ἀλλήλων ἀλέγουσι, cf. above pp. 15–16.

μονάδες '(they are) solitary'; the abruptness suggests Silenos' disgust for such non-sociability, which reflects both the Homeric model and more recent speculation about 'primitive' man, cf. Pl. *Prt.* 322b1, 'in the beginning men lived σποράδην', *Laws* 3.680d7–8 early man lived 'scattered in single households and clans'. The transmitted νομάδες (from νέμειν) poses two problems: it is not an answer to Odysseus' question, and the Cyclopes are not 'nomads', but pastoralists. Accounts of pastoral and/or nomadic life do indeed contain much that recalls Cyclopean society, and 'nomads' tended towards the same anarchic political structure as the Cyclopes, cf. Hdt. 4.46, 106 (Scythian nomads called Ἀνδροφάγοι), Paganelli 1978/9: 197–200, Shaw 1982/3: 21–3. In the fourth century Dicaearchus theorised ὁ νομαδικὸς βίος as the second stage of human development, between the Golden Age and the settled agricultural life (fr. 56A Fortenbaugh and Schütrumpf), but this shows how absurd Odysseus' question in 121 would be if he had just been told that the Cyclopes were νομάδες. The error may have arisen from a mixture of 'anagrammatism' and the fact that this exchange might indeed make anyone think of accounts of νομάδες, cf. Schmidt 1975.

ἀκούει δ’ οὐδὲν οὐδεὶς οὐδενός 'no one obeys anyone in any respect'; Silenos' bitter experience of the Cyclops leads to a humorously emphatic triple negative; for such collocations cf. Smyth §2761, K–G II 204. The end of the verse appears to infringe Porson's Law, but οὐδείς in this position is involved in other apparent breaches in tragedy, cf. *Ph.* 747, West 1982: 85, above p. 37.

121–2 After the (absence of) power structure comes 'How do the inhabitants feed themselves?' In Homer, the Cyclopes had no agriculture as such, but nature itself bore 'wheat and barley and vines' for them (*Od.* 9.107–11, 357–8); here, however, the Cyclopean diet is entirely meat and dairy products, and again Euripides will reflect fifth-century speculation about the place of agriculture in the development of human culture, cf. *Suppl.* 205–6. In some accounts, the coming of agriculture, whether 'invented' by mankind or a gift from the gods, was the first step forward towards human survival and civilisation, cf. Pl. *Prt.* 322a7–8, *Plt.* 274d1, Isocr. *Paneg.* 28a (Demeter's gift of καρποί is responsible for the fact that Athenians do not live θηριωδῶς), *SGO* 01/19/05, Guthrie 1969: 60–84. Pl. *Laws* 3.680e–1a links the coming of agriculture to the building of walls and common dwellings (and cf. Moschion, *TrGF* 97 F 6.23–9).

ἤ τῶι ζῶσι; 'or by what means (τῶι = τίνι) do they live?'; for the parenthetic question cf. *Tr.* 299, *Hel.* 1579, Diggle 1981: 115–16. The effect is somewhat softened here as σπείρουσι does not in fact require an object (Hes. *WD* 391, etc.).

Δήμητρος στάχυν is a common type of locution in high poetry, cf. the epic Δημήτερος ἀκτή; the manner of Odysseus' question, however, allows the godlessness of the Cyclopes to resonate in the background. Prodicus of Ceos argued that early man considered grain and wine as gods because of the benefit they brought to human life and therefore identified them with Demeter and Dionysos (fr. 5 D-K = 74 Mayhew), cf. *Ba.* 274–85, 123n. below. The absence of the 'grain of Demeter' from Sicily would be, for Euripides' audience, particularly notable as Demeter was one of the island's principal deities (Hinz 1998), and Sicily was also believed to be a very rich source of grain; at Thucyd. 6.20.4 Nicias tells the Athenians that the Sicilians are self-sufficient in grain. That the Cyclopes do not apparently eat bread is a striking indication that Demeter, too, like Dionysos, is absent from their island, cf. 123n. Dionysos and Demeter may have worked together in the satyric *Aithon* of Achaios, cf. Laemmle 2013: 143–4.

γάλακτι: Greeks associated milk-drinking with shepherds and barbarians, cf. *Il.* 13.5–6, Hdt. 1.216.4, etc.

τυροῖσι: Sicily was a noted source of excellent cheese in Athens, cf. Ar. *Wasps* 838, Hermippos fr. 63.9, Antiphanes fr. 233.4. At Theocr. 11.36–7 the Cyclops tells Galateia that his cheese-racks are laden all year round, and at Antiphanes fr. 131 his wedding-feast will include six different types of cheese.

μήλων βορᾶι: it was normally assumed that pastoralists on occasion enjoyed the meat of their animals, as well as the dairy products, cf. 325, *Od.* 4.86–9, Hdt. 4.186.1. In Pl. *Laws* 3, the earliest men (after recovery from cosmic catastrophe) were pastoralists and 'were in no way lacking in milk and meat, and hunting also provided them with food which was both excellent and plentiful' (679a2–4); Euripides' Cyclops is in some respects a version of such 'primitives', and Plato explicitly compares his vision of a just form of early man to the Homeric Cyclopes (680b–c citing *Od.* 9.112–15, cf. Schöpsdau 1994: 354–71, Prauscello 2017). In Homer, there is no sign that the Cyclopes eat their flocks, but it is not explicitly excluded, and the pile of wood which he brings with him 'to use for dinner' (*Od.* 9.233–4) might even suggest this; both ancient (cf. scholia ad loc., Eustath. *Hom.* 1626.51) and modern scholars have had to invent other explanations. The view that the normal diet of the Cyclops in Homer was 'strictly vegetarian' (Bakker 2013: 57) requires caution; in Euripides there is no doubt that the Cyclops is a carnivore.

123 A question about wine follows naturally upon the enquiry into food, cf. Moschion, *TrGF* 97 F 6.9–13. Demeter and Dionysos (Bromios) standardly 'travel together' in accounts of cultural development, cf. esp. *Ba.* 275–80 (279 βότρυος ὑγρὸν πῶμ', 280 ἀμπέλου ῥοῆς), and are very often paired in various contexts (cf. Call. *h.* 6.70–1).

ἀμπέλου ῥοάς 'streams of the vine', a rather grandiloquent apposition to Βρομίου … πῶμ', cf. 415.

124 For Silenos, wine means dancing; for the ironic relation between the complaints of Silenos and the chorus and the dancing within the play, cf. above p. 25. It is tempting to understand ἄχορον as both 'without dancing' and 'without choruses', cf. 63n.

ἥκιστα, 'not at all', has a colloquial flavour (cf. 220, Collard 2018: 46 (~ Stevens 1976: 14)), but is not uncommon in Soph. and Eur.

τοιγάρ 'as a consequence'.

125 From the internal arrangements of Cyclopean society, Odysseus moves to relationships with outsiders, always a matter of the greatest interest for Odysseus, cf. *Od.* 6.119–21, 9.174–6, verses which echo in Odysseus' question here.

περὶ ξένους 'towards/in the matter of strangers', cf. *Alc.* 1148 εὐσέβει περὶ ξένους, *Suppl.* 367, LSJ s.v. περί C I 5.

126 Silenos evokes a society of hunters who discuss the relative merits of the meat of their prey: for these 'connoisseur' hunters it is (human) ξένοι who are really the rare catch.

τὰ κρέα: κρέας appears six times in *Cycl.* (and κρεανόμος in 245), but otherwise in Eur. only in fr. 907 describing Heracles eating (play unknown, but probably satyric). In Aeschylus the simple noun appears only three times, all in *Ag.* to describe Thyestes eating his children: *Ag.* 1220 χεῖρας κρεῶν πλήθοντες, οἰκείας βορᾶς catches the horror (cf. 88n., Fraenkel on *Ag.* 1592); whether or not κρέας appears at all in Sophocles is unclear. The word is brutal, simple and un-poetic.

φορεῖν may just mean 'have, possess' (LSJ s.v. I 3), but there is perhaps a suggestion that men 'wear' (LSJ s.v. I 2) flesh, which can be stripped off them, like clothes.

127 βορᾶι ... ἀνθρωποκτόνωι 'food derived from the killing of men', cf. Moschion, *TrGF* 97 F 6.14–15 (cited in 89–93n.). ἀνθρωπόκτονος, the adjective used here, is to be distinguished from ἀνθρωποκτόνος, 'murderous, man-killing' (*IT* 389).

128 '(There is) no one who has not been slaughtered after coming here'. At this stage the audience will not be concerned with the fact that the satyrs have not been eaten (cf. 220–1).

129 Silenos has not explicitly mentioned 'his' Cyclops, 'the Cyclops himself', and though Odysseus may be able to infer the exact situation from what he has seen and heard, he here draws on his 'knowledge' of *Od.*, cf. above p. 19, Laemmle 2013: 340. So, too, in 131 Odysseus assumes that the satyrs will want to escape with him. Odysseus' question, 'Where is the Cyclops himself?', is also our question, as we sit in the theatre waiting to see how Euripides will portray the monster.

130 Cf. *Hel.* 153–4 (another murderous ruler whom Greek visitors should avoid) ἄπεστι δὲ / κυσὶν πεποιθὼς ἐν φοναῖς θηροκτόνοις.

πρὸς Αἴτνηι 'near Etna', presumably in the foothills, but Reiske's πρὸς Αἴτνην is attractive.

κυσίν 'with his dogs', a dative of accompaniment or perhaps of the 'forces' with which he is hunting (Smyth §1524, 1526). For hunting with dogs as a pastime of the leisured rich cf. Solon fr. 23 West, Xen. *Cyn. passim*, Men. *Sam.* 14 (with Sommerstein's n.). Philip Thess., *AP* 11.321.6 (= *GP* 3038) cites 'whether the Cyclops had dogs' as a typically pointless question pursued by pedantic grammarians; this seems more likely to derive from Homer's silence on the subject, which is what makes the 'problem' so completely absurd, than from other texts where he does have a dog or dogs, cf. Hunter on Theocr. 6.9.

131 οἶσθ' οὖν ὃ δρᾶσον 'Do you know what you have to do ...?', an idiomatic combination of a question and an imperative, cf. *Hec.* 225, *Ion* 1029, Collard 2018: 84 (~ Stevens 1976: 36), Diggle 1994: 500, Kannicht on *Hel.* 315. Corruption to δράσεις occurs elsewhere also (*Hec.* 225, Ar. *Birds* 80). Odysseus now switches from the inquisitive mode of his early questions to much more rapid and lively planning, cf. Mureddu 1993: 596–7; he wants to make the most of the Cyclops' absence.

ἀπαίρωμεν 'we may depart from, sail off from'; the original ellipse of ναῦν 'launch a boat from', is no longer felt, cf. *Med.* 938, *IA* 664, LSJ s.v. ἀπαίρω II 2.

132 δρώιημεν: the plural very probably includes the satyrs.

133 ὄδησον: cf. 12n.

134–6 play with stichomythic form: Silenos requires two verses to repeat the substance of 122, but the form demands that the 'menu' be interrupted by an observation from Odysseus. Silenos also teases Odysseus: the latter asks for σῖτος, probably in the general sense 'food' (LSJ s.v. 3), but Silenos answers as if he has been asked for 'bread', an impossibility as there is no grain. Already in Homer the Cyclops 'did not resemble a grain-eating (σιτοφάγωι) man' (*Od.* 9.190–1), and Silenos here pushes the Homeric epithet to its literal extreme.

καὶ τόδε 'this also', rather than 'even this'.

ἡδὺ λιμοῦ ... σχετήριον '(is) a pleasant remedy against hunger'. σχετήριον appears otherwise only in the medical writer Oribasios (fourth century AD), but does not seem to have a particular technical nuance here, cf. δίψης ἄκος in 97.

τυρὸς ὀπίας 'cheese made with milk curdled with ὀπός (vegetable juice)'; the setting-agent in question was usually fig-juice, cf. Ath. 14.658e, *Il.* 5.902–3, Empedocles fr. 33 D–K (= D72 Laks–Most), Arist. *HA* 3.522b2–5. Ath. describes such cheese as δριμύς, 'sharp'. ὀπίας could also be used on its own, without τυρός, cf. Ar. *Wasps* 353.

βοὸς γάλα: for the Cyclops' cattle cf. 218, 325, 389; the possession of cattle herds, which was generally rare in classical antiquity, is a mark of the Euripidean Cyclops' wealth, cf. Pl. *Tht.* 174d5–6, Bakker 2013: 48–9. For the milking of cows in various parts of the ancient world cf. Arist. *HA* 3.522b12–25.

137 ἐκφέρετε is addressed to Silenos and the satyrs, cf. Odysseus' opening words at 96–101 and above p. 113; members of the chorus would not normally enter the *skēnē* (cf. 635–41n.), but Odysseus' instruction is natural, given that it is clear from 96–101 that Silenos and the satyrs are standing very close together. If the instruction was addressed to otherwise mute stage-attendants (83n.), we would expect it to be carried out at once (cf. Bain 1981), but this plainly does not happen, cf. 162.

φῶς γὰρ ἐμπολήμασιν πρέπει 'daylight is appropriate for (viewing) goods for sale'; Odysseus' 'nose for business', here expressed in what sounds like a piece of proverbial wisdom, is part of his κερδαλέος (in both senses) nature, cf. 98n. For the thought cf. Eubulus fr. 67.3 (in a brothel you can observe the girls πρὸς τὸν ἥλιον), Hor. *Sat.* 1.2.83–93.

138 εἰπέ μοι: a colloquial parenthesis, very common in Aristophanes but found only here in the tragedians (Soph. *OT* 157 is very different); Silenos is now getting down to serious bargaining. His interest in gold is also on show in Soph. *Ichn.* (51, 78, 208), where he and Apollo settle a deal for the return of the god's lost cattle (cf. Zagagi 1999: 181–8), and in the satyric *Skiron* he appears to set variable prices for different prostitutes (fr. 675).

139 In *Od.* Maron had given Odysseus not only the wonderful wine, but also a large amount of gold (9.202), which he had presumably left on his ship when he set out for the Cyclops' cave (cf. 144); if we remember this, we may suspect that Odysseus does indeed have gold to offer, but he is too good a tradesman to reveal that. φέρω may be strictly true, 'I am not *at this moment* carrying gold', but it allows Silenos to understand 'I have no gold on my ship', as in the English 'we are not carrying ...' Cf. further 160n.

140 ὦ φίλτατ' εἰπών 'Ah! You have spoken music to my ears (lit. "the dearest things")', cf. *Ion* 1488, Soph. *Phil.* 1290.

οὗ: i.e. πῶμα.

σπανίζομεν: the repetition of Odysseus' verb (133) shows that both sides badly need this deal.

141–3 In *Od.* Maron was a priest of Apollo at Ismaros in Thrace (9.197–201); his father's name was Euanthes, 'Mr Fair Flower', which could easily be given a Dionysiac resonance (cf. οἶνος ἀνθοσμίας). Already Hesiod, however, made him grandson of Oinopion, 'Mr Wine', and great-grandson of Dionysos himself (fr. 238 = 180 Most), and the Homeric scholia reveal that some ancient scholars were puzzled by the fact that Homer connected him with Apollo, rather than with Dionysos. Maron later had a cult with Zeus and Dionysos at Thracian 'Maroneia' and Samothrace (*RE* 14.1911–12), and various later traditions made him the child or grandchild of Dionysos and Ariadne (cf. Alexis fr. 113, Satyrus, *FGrHist* 631 F1 = fr. 29.25 Schorn, Schol. Ap. Rhod. *Arg.* 3.997–1004); Nonnus makes him a son of Silenos (*Dion.* 14.99), perhaps following these verses of *Cycl.*, and Maron is attested as a satyr-name on two late mosaics (Kossatz-Deissmann 1991: 160–1) and as an attendant of the god (e.g. Philostratus, *Imag.* 1.192). At 412 and 616 'Maron' is used, as 'Dionysos' could be, as a metonymy for wine, cf. Cratinus fr. 146. Whether or not Odysseus here improvises with the claim that Maron was the god's son, the claim is clearly designed to strike home with Silenos, just as the Homeric Odysseus' account of Maron pointedly suggests to the listening Phaeacians both Odysseus' piety and the need for proper hospitality and gift-giving.

καὶ μήν 'and moreover', an emphatic progression, cf. 151, *GP²* 351–2.

ὅν must be Maron, not Dionysos; it is often thought that, if he too is not just matching Odysseus' improvisation, Silenos is again evoking here an earlier satyr-drama involving Maron. The motif of παιδοτροφία is very familiar in satyr-drama (Soph. *Dionysiskos*, etc.), though no evidence for such a play involving Maron can be adduced. De Falco 1935/6 takes ὅν to refer to the god and argues that Silenos is here trying to understand Odysseus' claim against the background of his own (and the audience's) knowledge of Homer, and that confusion over the reference of ὅν is the source of later traditions about Maron. Line 143, in which ὁ Βακχίου παῖς spells out παῖς θεοῦ more clearly, would, however, then be a very odd continuation, and there are good reasons for thinking (see above) that the Dionysiac traditions for Maron go back long before *Cycl.*

ταῖσδ' ... ἀγκάλαις: Silenos presumably accompanies this with a suitable cradling gesture. Hypsipyle describes her care for the baby Opheltes in very similar terms at fr. 757.841–3, cf. above p. 42.

144 σέλμασιν νεώς 'the planking of the ship', i.e. the deck, cf. 506, rather than a mere periphrasis for 'the ship' (*Or.* 242). νεώς is scanned as a single syllable with synizesis, cf. Diggle 1981: 93. The transmitted σέλμασι creates a tribrach with word-division after the second syllable, a comic licence found nowhere else in tragedy or satyr-play.

145 ὅδ' ἀσκὸς ὃς κεύθει νιν 'This is the skin which contains/conceals it ...' Odysseus now holds up the wineskin, presumably dangling it seductively in front of Silenos.

146 In Homer the skin is 'large' (*Od.* 9.212), but Silenos is too good a bargainer to be impressed by the first offer he is made. Satyrs were associated with drinking prodigious amounts of wine, cf. Soph. *Ichn.* 225 and the images in Lissarrague 2013: Figures 118–22; in Figure 120 a satyr dives head first into a jar of wine.

μέν implies an unstated comparison with a larger skin, cf. *Suppl.* 939, *GP*² 381.

147 As transmitted, this cannot be an answer to 146 (at the very least there would need to be a γάρ, which Murray in fact suggested). Most likely, two verses have accidentally dropped out; in the lacuna Odysseus may have claimed (another improvisation?) that the skin magically re-fills itself with double the amount, like a spring (cf. 148); such a motif would be appropriate to satyr-play and would suggest to Silenos that he will never again run out of wine. Others emend ναί to νᾶι, 'flows', which is either a claim that one gets twice as much wine as comes out of the skin or (so Cerri 1976) a reference to the need to mix the wine with water (in the very strong proportion of 1:1, if δὶς τόσον is taken literally), in which case there will be twice as much to drink as there is wine in the skin. In Homer this wine required 20 parts of water (*Od.* 9.209–10, cf. 557n.). It is, however, absurd to think that Silenos needs any instruction in the protocols of wine-drinking, whereas a self-refilling skin might well draw forth the admiration of 148. On balance, we think that positing a lacuna is the best solution to a difficult passage.

δὶς τόσον … ὅσον ἄν … 'twice as much as whatever …', cf. *Hec.* 392, *Med.* 1134–5, 1047.

ῥυῆι: aorist subjunctive, passive in form (ἐρρύην), of ῥέω, cf. *Hipp.* 443.

148 εἶπας 'you have described', cf. 101n.

149 'Do you want me to give you first a taste of the wine unmixed?' The paratactic construction of the aorist subjunctive following directly on a verb of wishing *uel sim.*, is colloquial, but not uncommon in Euripides (*Hel.* 1427, *Or.* 218, etc.) and Sophocles (*Phil.* 761, etc.), cf. Collard 2018: 128 (~ Stevens 1976: 60–1), K–G I 221–2. For γεύειν with a double accusative, 'give someone a taste of something', cf. Eubulus fr. 136, Theopomp. Com. fr. 66.

ἄκρατον μέθυ: it was no doubt normal 'business practice' for a potential buyer to taste wine 'unmixed' before purchase; otherwise, unmixed wine was only normally used for libations, though satyrs had their own rules, cf. Achaios fr. 9, Voelke 2001: 194–6, Laemmle 2013: 441–3. There is no reason to think that the specification 'unmixed' relates to whatever was said in the missing verses after 146.

150 ἦ γάρ introduces the explanation of why Odysseus' offer is 'fair', cf. *GP²* 284; 'a taste invites a sale' again sounds proverbial, cf. 137n. Silenos here reflects that Odysseus' offer is not purely altruistic.

151 καὶ μήν: cf. 151n.

ἐφέλκω: lit. 'I drag along', like one boat towing another, cf. *Her.* 631–2; the cup may be attached to the skin or to Odysseus' belt. At Leonidas, *AP* 7.67.5 (= *HE* 2335) the Cynic Diogenes describes his flask and staff as his ἐφόλκια, 'what he brings with him'.

ποτῆρ᾽: ποτήρ, rather than the standard diminutive ποτήριον, is found only here and *Alc.* 756 (Heracles), but there is no good reason to think that it indicates an unusually large cup.

152 ἐκπάταξον: lit. 'knock it out', apparently a vivid synonym of ἐκχεῖν. The frequently accepted emendation ἐγκάναξον (cf. 158) derives from Ar. *Knights* 105–6 ἴθι νυν, ἄκρατον ἐγκάναξόν μοι πολύν/σπονδήν, where the scholia gloss the term as ἔκχεον and explain that it refers to the noise (καναχή) made by the poured wine. All things Dionysiac and satyric are full of words denoting loud sounds, and although ἐκπάταξον is from ἐκπατάσσω, it might suggest also the πάταγος of pouring wine, cf. 7n., Laemmle 2013: 183–4.

ὡς ἀναμνησθῶ πιών suggests both 'so that I can remember what drinking is like' and 'so that while I am drinking my memories will come back'. For the 'coincident' use of the aorist participle cf. Barrett on *Hipp.* 289–92.

153–5 present problems of interpretation and perhaps text, but the division of both verses ('*antilabē*', cf. 546, 669–90nn.) makes clear Silenos'

impatient anticipation of getting a taste of the wine. The standard interpretation is that Odysseus pours a drop into the cup, but in such a way
that Silenos cannot see the wine, or that at least Silenos reacts before he
can possibly have seen the 'taster' (cf. 154); when Odysseus then asks in
apparent surprise 'Did you see it?', he is reacting to Silenos' use of the
word καλή to refer to an aroma, whereas ἡδεῖα is the standard term, as
in the model passage at *Od.* 9.210–11. Although 'smell' is occasionally
described as 'seen' (Ar. *Birds* 1715–16, Alexis fr. 224.3–4, Theocr. 1.149,
Arnott 1996: 642), this seems a very lame exchange. Alternatively, some
understand εἶδες … ; as 'Did you notice it?', with Silenos then taking εἶδες
more literally as 'see'; this too is not particularly witty. The verses have not
yet been satisfactorily explained. Kovacs replaced ὀσμήν by χροιάν, 'com-
plexion, colour' (1994: 147–8), explaining that the error may have arisen
from an anticipation of the following verse. This would certainly account
for Odysseus' surprised question, if he knows that Silenos cannot yet have
seen the wine; wine-tasting may have been (as today) a synaesthetic activity in which colour and aroma were often discussed together, and cf. the
exchange at Ar. *Pl.* 1020–1 in which an old woman is reminiscing about
her young lover, Γρ. ὄζειν τε τῆς χροιᾶς ἔφασκεν ἡδύ μου./Χρ. εἰ Θάσιον ἐνέχεις,
εἰκότως γε νὴ Δία. The *Antiatticist Lexicon* (γ 30 Valente, cf. above p. 51)
explains that γεύεσθαι (155) is used ἐπὶ τοῦ ὀσφραίνεσθαι; this seems to be
a misunderstanding, but it is a pity that we do not know more of what lies
behind this note.

ἰδού: a colloquial indicator, very common in Euripides and Aristophanes,
that a request has been carried out, cf. 188, 544, Collard 2018: 82 (~
Stevens 1976: 35).

παπαιάξ, only here in Euripides, expresses a mixture of pleasure and
surprise, cf. Ar. *Lys.* 924, Kinesias' reaction to Myrrhine's grant of a kiss
(delivered with an ἰδού).

γάρ marks a surprised question, cf. 585, 686, Soph. *Phil.* 248, *GP*² 78–9.

οὐ μὰ Δί': cf. 9n. μὰ Δί', ἀλλ' forms a 'split anapaest' (above p. 37) at a
very comic moment.

γεῦσαι: aor. mid. imperative.

'παινῆις: i.e. ἐπαινῆις, an instance of 'prodelision', which may occur
when a word ending in a long vowel or diphthong is followed by a word
beginning with a short vowel and which is very common in drama. Cf.
187, K–B I 241, Platnauer 1960.

156 A drop of wine brings the spring back into Silenos' step and sets
him dancing, cf. 123–4, 171, Theocr. 7.151–3, *Od.* 14.463–6, Ar. *Wasps*
1476–9 (Philocleon dances all night long after, like Silenos, first tasting
wine 'after a long break').

βαβαί ... ἄ ἄ ἄ: like comedy, satyr-drama was probably full of such representations of expressive noise, cf. παπαιάξ in 153, Soph. *Ichn.* 66–7, 176, Laemmle 2013: 67.

158 'Did it gurgle pleasantly through your throat?' or perhaps 'Did it make your throat gurgle pleasantly?'. The compound διακανάσσω occurs only here, though the noun καναχή is not uncommon, cf. 152n.

μῶν here indicates feigned surprise, cf. 377, K–G II 525.

159 'Yes, it reached my very extremities!', cf. Rhianus, *AP* 12.93.10 κἀς νεάτους ἐκ κορυφῆς ὄνυχας.

160 μέντοι introduces a further item in a sequence, cf. *GP²* 407.

νόμισμα: Odysseus' offer of 'coinage' is perhaps to be understood as a 'step down' from Silenos' request for gold (138n.); the 'anachronism' (Easterling 1985: 6–7) is in part softened by the context of bargaining which has preceded. The deal between Odysseus and Silenos is set both in the distant world of story and the more familiar world of fifth-century commercial exchange, cf. von Reden 1995: 138, Dougherty 1999: 329.

161 χάλα probably means 'loosen', i.e. 'make slack', by emptying wine out of the now full, and therefore 'tight', skin, cf. 55, LSJ s.v. I 1 and the late sixth-century depiction of a satyr emptying wine from a skin into a mixing-bowl, Osborne 1998: 17–18, Figure 5. The standard term for 'opening' a wineskin is λύειν.

μόνον: cf. 219, 568.

ἔα τὸ χρυσίον 'Forget the money!', cf. the equally impatient Kinesias at Ar. *Lys.* 945 ἔα αὖτ', ὦ δαιμονία. The diminutive χρυσίον is not uncommon, even in formal contexts, but here it expresses Silenos' scorn: money is no substitute for wine. Silenos expresses a lack of interest in gold also at Soph. *Ichn.* 208, though there not because his mind is on wine.

162 Odysseus requests 'cheese or meat', although one might have expected 'cheese *and* meat' (Wilamowitz suggested τύρευμα καί); the point, however, is presumably 'I've shown you what I have (wine), now you show me (some of) what you have to offer'.

ἐκφέρετε: cf. 137n.

μήλων τόκον is a slightly absurd periphrasis in the circumstances.

163 γε gives emphasis, as frequently in such a participial clause.

δεσποτῶν may just be plural for singular (cf. 477, *Hec.* 1237), but it is difficult not to feel some resonance of 'my masters', i.e. the Cyclopes as a group (cf. 165), with *the* Cyclops then specified in 173–4.

164–7 '[? My desire would be] to drain just one cup, in return for the flocks of all the Cyclopes, and <then> to throw myself into the sea from the Leucadian rock, when I had once got drunk and let my hair [lit. brows] down'; a difficult passage with considerable textual uncertainty, cf. Di Marco 2013: 239–51. Silenos appears to be saying 'After just one drink of this wine I would die happy' (cf. Kassel 1991: 203–4), and Paley's κἄν, 'even', which is frequently found with 'one' (Soph. *OT* 615, Eubulus fr. 92.1, LSJ s.v. κἄν I 3), is very attractive. The transmitted μαινοίμην can hardly be followed by an infinitive (despite the corrupt Aelian fr. 122 Hercher); Schmidt's μαιοίμην, 'I would long to, search to', would have been very easily corrupted to μαινοίμην in this Dionysiac context, but μαινοίμην might conceal another verb altogether (the Aldine edition cut the knot by replacing μαινοίμην with βουλοίμην), and μαίεσθαι is not otherwise found in Euripides. If μαινοίμην (no longer with ἄν) is retained (and μαίνεται in 168 suggests as much), perhaps as a wish 'May I go crazy (by drinking)', cf. *PMG* 902 θέλω μαίνεσθαι, etc. for the pleasures of sympotic 'madness', then the infinitives must be replaced by Kirchhoff's participles, with the aorists 'coincident' (cf. 152n.); the resultant text seems, however, over-burdened with participles. At Theocr. 5.15–16 a shepherd declares that, if he is not telling the truth, 'May I go crazy and leap into the Krathis from that rock', but that seems to be a different kind of madness. Other editors follow Hartung in reading ἐκπιὼν γ' ἄν … μαινοίμην … <μὴ> ἀντιδούς, 'After drinking just one cup, I would be crazy if I did not offer in return …'

ὡς … γ' explains the statement of 163, cf. 247, 336, *GP*² 143.

μίαν / πάντων: a pointed juxtaposition.

ῥῖψαι: for this intransitive use cf. *Alc.* 897, *Hel.* 1325, Theognis 175–6 (a similar context), Men. fr. 258.3 K–T (Sappho's leap from the Leucadian rock), LSJ s.v. VII.

Λευκάδος πέτρας 'rock of Leukas'. Strabo reports that criminals were thrown from the beetling cliffs of Leukas in a kind of scapegoat ritual (10.2.9), but the leap from the 'Leukadian rock' is found from an early date as a metaphor for various states of supreme happiness. Of particular interest is Anacreon, *PMG* 376 ἀρθεὶς δηὖτ' ἀπὸ Λευκάδος/πέτρης ἐς πολιὸν κῦμα κολυμβῶ μεθύων ἔρωτι: Anacreon is very important to a later scene (cf. 495–518n.), and here Silenos echoes these anacreontic verses and makes the metaphor of drunkenness completely literal, cf. 495–518n., Bing 2014: 42 n.45. When the first hope for a real drink is raised, Silenos' language naturally reaches for the sympotic poet *par excellence*, Anacreon. Later, the 'rock of Leukas' was particularly associated with Sappho's leap to cure herself of her love for Phaon.

μεθυσθείς: cf. 538n.

καταβαλών τε τὰς ὀφρῦς 'and letting down my brows', i.e. relaxing and having a good time, cf. LSJ s.v. καταβάλλω II 1. Raised or 'knitted' brows can be a sign of worry (Ar. *Ach.* 1069, *Lys.* 8) or of a sense of arrogant self-importance, such as philosophers can have, cf. Arnott 1996: 99, 101. The standard verbs for 'raising' the brows are ἀνασπᾶν, ἐπαίρειν and ἀνέλκειν, and for 'relaxing' them λύειν (*Hipp.* 290) and μεθιέναι (*IA* 648). Giving in to such ordinary pleasures as enjoying a party is an important element of the Dionysiac spirit, cf. *Ba.* 399–402, 427–33; at *Alc.* 800–2 Heracles accompanies his instruction to the servant to drink and enjoy himself with the observation 'all those who are haughty and whose brows are knitted (τοῖς γε σεμνοῖς καὶ συνωφρυωμένοις) have a life which is not a life, but a disaster'. It is tempting to think that there may here also be a metatheatrical reference to Silenos' mask; on the 'Pronomos Vase' (above pp. 27–30), the mask is characterised by prominent brows and wrinkles suggestive of old age and serious worries, cf. Di Marco 2013: 246–51.

168 Real 'madness' consists in not taking pleasure in drinking, i.e. in not giving in to the proper 'madness' of Dionysos. For such statements condemning the 'madness' of a class of people cf. Amphis fr. 26; the form of expression is quite likely colloquial.

169–73 Silenos now explains the pleasures which accompany drinking; ἵν', 'where', means 'when there is drinking going on', virtually 'at symposia'.

ἔστι might at first seem to mean 'it is possible', with the following infinitive, but unless there is textual disturbance, such as a lacuna, it must be 'there is …' with ἐξανιστάναι and ψαῦσαι as nominal infinitives without the article, cf. *Tr.* 637, Fraenkel on Aesch. *Ag.* 584, K–G II 3–4. Alternatively, Silenos' mounting excitement at the prospect of alcohol perhaps reveals itself in broken syntax.

τουτί τ' ὀρθὸν ἐξανιστάναι 'raising this up straight'; the affective deictic in -ί is not found in tragedy, cf. Soph. *Ichn.* 120. Silenos gestures towards his (currently flaccid) phallus, cf. Ar. *Lys.* 937 ἐπῆρται τουτογί, *Wasps* 1062 αὐτὸ τοῦτο.

μαστοῦ τε δραγμός 'fondling of a breast'; this is virtually the only occurrence of δραγμός (< δράσσομαι) in Greek literature. μαστός is more common in the context of breast-feeding than of erotic play (where τιτθίον is regular). One might think of reading μαστῶν, though vase-painting normally shows men touching or reaching for one of a woman's breasts, and as women's tunics were normally pinned at the shoulder, one breast would be revealed before the other when the tunic was unclasped; at *Andr.* 629 Menelaos is said to have dropped his sword when he saw Helen's breast (singular).

†παρεσκευασμένου† ... λειμῶνος: 'meadow' is obviously a reference to the female pubic hair and genitalia; κῆπος is more common in this sense, cf. Archilochus fr. 196a.23–4 West, Archippos fr. 50.2–3, Henderson 1991:

135–6. The comparison of a woman to a meadow became a common *topos* of later sophistic prose, cf. Aristaen. 2.1.44–52 Mazal, Drago 2007: 433–4. The transmitted 'prepared, made ready' is often understood as 'groomed' i.e. depilated, cf. Ar. *Thesm.* 590–1, *Lys.* 89, Herodas 2.69–70, Kilmer 1993: 133–59, but this seems a remarkably coy way for Silenos to express himself; OSC suggest a reference to 'lubrication, natural or otherwise', cf. 516, but that seems even less easy to understand from the text.

ὀρχηστύς 'dancing', an Ionic form occurring only here between early epic and later prose (Lucian, *Timon* 55). There may be a pun, perhaps made clear by a gesture, with ὄρχεις, 'testicles', cf. Hdt. 6.129.4, Soph. fr. 1130.15, Laemmle 2018: 55. For dancing as the natural reaction to drinking cf. 156n.

κακῶν τε λῆστις: cf. *Ba.* 278–83, 381, 423, Ar. *Frogs* 346, etc. Death, as well as drinking or Dionysiac revel, can of course be a 'forgetfulness of troubles', cf. Astydamas, *TrGF* 60 F 5.

172–4 The rehearsal of the pleasures of drinking leads Silenos to only one possible conclusion as to what he should do. The verses may be addressed to no one in particular – almost certainly not the chorus who would be very keen to share Silenos' good fortune – but the audience will feel themselves addressed, cf. above p. 36 n.118.

εἶτ' introduces a 'logical' conclusion to what has gone before, cf. *Alc.* 957, *Andr.* 666, LSJ s.v. II.

ἐγώ ⟨οὐ⟩ is scanned as two syllables with 'synaloephe', cf. 272, 334; this was perhaps a factor in the omission of the negative.

⟨οὐ⟩ κυνήσομαι 'Will I not kiss ...?' In many depictions of satyrs drinking from wine-jars, it might seem as though they were 'kissing' the jar or the wine, cf. Lissarrague 2013: 144, Figure 119; even copulation with a wine-jar is not uncommon, cf. Kilmer 1993: Figures R126, R148, Voelke 2001: 204–6; in 553 Silenos claims that the wine kissed him, and the analogy between drinking and kissing later became a commonplace, cf. Gow on Theocr. 7.70. Nevertheless, ⟨οὐ⟩κ ὠνήσομαι deserves to be taken very seriously, even though it would be contextually more obvious (and perhaps less amusing) than ⟨οὐ⟩ κυνήσομαι.

ἀμαθίαν, like σκαιότης (cf. 490n.), covers behaviour and attitudes which are considered 'unlearned, uncultured, boorish, stupid'; here there is a particular stress on 'uncultured' or indeed 'uninitiated' because 'un-Dionysiac', and the same charge is brought against Pentheus, cf. *Ba.* 480, 490. In *Epigr.* 46.2 Callimachus, principally in reaction to Theocr. 11, declares that the Cyclops was οὐκ ἀμαθής because he found a way to lessen the effects of love. Elsewhere, ἀμαθία can denote lack of delicacy or human sympathy (*El.* 294–5) or an arrogant complacency: 'when one who is neither fine and good (καλὸν κἀγαθόν) nor intelligent thinks himself sufficient (ἱκανόν)', Pl. *Symp.* 204a4–5, certainly suits the Cyclops. Cf. further Dover 1974: 122–3, Bond on *Her.* 347. The phrase τὴν Κύκλωπος ἀμαθίαν has something of the flavour of periphrases such as the epic 'the might of Heracles' for 'mighty Heracles' (cf. *Ph.* 56, *Od.*11.601, etc.), but Silenos really is bidding farewell to the 'uncultured lifestyle' which the Cyclops represents.

κλαίειν κελεύων: lit. 'telling X to weep', i.e. 'saying good riddance to X', cf. 319, 340, 701; such expressions are very common in comedy (Olson on Ar. *Ach.* 1131), but never found in tragedy. The second object for the expression, 'the eye in the middle', comes as a surprise, as it almost literalises the standard colloquialism: eyes really can weep. The κ alliteration, with Κύκλωπος in the previous verse, lends vehemence to the utterance.

175–87 While Silenos is in the cave getting provisions to exchange for the wine, the satyrs, speaking through the chorus-leader, take the opportunity to question Odysseus on a subject which interests them greatly.

175 διαλαλήσωμέν τί σοι 'let us talk something over with you', 'let's have a natter ...', a polite request expressed through the 'hortatory' aorist subjunctive; διαλαλεῖν, which occurs only here in the classical period, is probably a comic–satyric equivalent of διαλέγεσθαι. λαλεῖν is not certainly found in tragedy (λακεῖν is probably correct at Soph. *Phil.* 110); Eur. elsewhere has λάλος (*Suppl.* 462, fr. 1032) and perhaps λάλημα (*Andr.* 937, del. Nauck) and Soph. λάλημα (*Ant.* 320) and in satyr-drama perhaps λαλίστατος (*Ichn.* 135) and λάλησις (fr. 1130.16). In Ar. *Frogs* Euripides is associated with λαλεῖν, cf. vv. 954, 1069, Laemmle 2018: 51–6.

176 καὶ μήν expresses polite consent, cf. *El.* 669–70, *GP²* 353–4, and γε gives emphasis to the declaration of φιλία (*GP²* 120).

προσφέρεσθε 'you are approaching', cf. Pl. *Phdr.* 252d5, Xen. *Anab.* 5.5.19 οὐ γὰρ ὡς φίλοι προσεφέροντο, LSJ s.v. Β I 4.

177–8 Cf. the exchange between Helen herself and Teucer at *Helen* 105–6: ἦλθες γάρ, ὦ ξέν᾽, Ἰλίου κλεινὴν πόλιν;/ καὶ ξύν γε πέρσας αὐτὸς ἀνταπωλόμην.

177 'Did you seize Troy and get your hands on Helen?' Cf. Peleus' accusations against Menelaos at *Andr.* 627–31: when he had captured Troy, he did not kill his wife, χειρίαν λαβών, but allowed himself to be won over by her erotic charms, προδότιν αἰκάλλων κύνα, cf. 182.

178 Cf. 278. Odysseus' self-satisfaction echoes *Od.* 1.2; πτολίπορθος and πτολιπόρθιος are standard epithets of Odysseus (and of no other figure) in *Od.*, including the boastful 9.504.

καὶ ... γ᾽ 'Yes, and ...', cf. 640.

179 οὔκουν here introduces what is not a real question, but rather a statement of the satyrs' belief or fantasy, cf. Barrett on *Hipp.* 331–2, *GP²* 431.

τὴν νεᾶνιν εἵλετε: Helen was hardly a νεᾶνις when Troy fell, but the satyrs' sexual fantasy needs her to be as attractive and arousing as possible. εἵλετε alludes to an etymology of Helen's name most familiar from Aesch. *Ag.* 687–90, ἑλέναυς ἕλανδρος ἑλέπτολις, cf. *Hec.* 442–3 (del. Dindorf), *Tr.* 891–2, 1214, *Hel.* 115. The allusion to the etymology is in keeping with the play with tragic motifs in this speech, cf. 181–6n.

180 The satyrs fantasise that Helen was punished by being raped by each of the Greek commanders in turn; for such a pattern of 'group sex' among the satyrs cf. Aesch. *Dikt.* fr. 47a. 821–32, Hall 2006: 148, Griffith 2015: 107, Laemmle forthcoming. [Heraclitus], Περὶ ἀπίστων 25 associates such behaviour with 'Pans and satyrs'. Helen may have appeared with a satyric chorus in various fifth-century plays, such as Soph., *Marriage of Helen*, and certainly did so in Cratinus' comic *Dionysalexandros*. According to Stesichorus (fr. 106 Finglass), Helen was saved by her beauty from being stoned, and in the *Little Iliad* (fr. 18 Bernabé) it was the sight of her breasts which caused Menelaos to drop his sword (cf. *Andr.* 627–31, Ibycus, *PMG* 296, Ar. *Lys.* 155–6, Davies and Finglass 2014: 436–8).

αὐτὴν διεκροτήσατ' 'gave her a thorough banging'; κρούω and its compounds are more common than κροτέω in this sense, cf. Ar. *Eccl.* 990, 1017–21, Henderson 1991: 171.

181–6 Euripidean characters often attack Helen's morals and the damage she did to Greece, cf. *El.* 213–14, *IT* 525, Wright 2005: 117. Closest to the present passage is *Tr.* 991–7 (Hecuba claims that Helen was excited by fancy-pants Paris' barbarian clothes and luxury), and there is an amusingly Euripidean flavour to Euripides' satyrs here. The theme of Helen's attraction to Paris' gorgeous clothes may ultimately go back to the *Cypria* (and cf. *Il.* 3.392), and it is common in vase-paintings of the meeting of Paris and Helen, at least from the fourth century on, for Paris to be represented in richly decorated Phrygian costume, cf. Ghali-Kahil 1955: 168–7, with Plates xix–xxx. Similar, highly decorated clothes are commonly worn by Paris in depictions of the Judgement, cf. *LIMC* s.v. Paridis iudicium.

181 Myth told of 'marriages' of Helen to Menelaos, Paris and (after Paris' death) Deiphobos (cf. *Tr.* 959–60), but when young she had also been carried off by Theseus; it is possible that the *Cypria* related an erotic encounter between Achilles and Helen, cf. *Arg. Cypr.* 11. Stesichorus (fr. 85 Finglass = *PMG* 223) told how Aphrodite punished Tyndareos for forgetting her at a sacrifice by making his daughters διγάμους τε καὶ τριγάμους .../ καὶ λιπεσάνορας, and at *Andr.* 229 Andromache sarcastically refers to Helen's φιλανδρία, cf. Laemmle 2019b. The middle γαμεῖσθαι is standard of a woman, with the man she marries, as here, in the dative, but the satyr-leader also exploits (and perhaps illustrates with gestures) γαμεῖν/γαμεῖσθαι in the less formal sense, 'have sex with' (cf. Aesch. fr. 13): Helen both had many marriages and took pleasure in 'sex with many men', hence the sarcastic fantasy of gang-rape.

182–5 '... the traitor, who, when she saw <him> wearing the deco-rated sacks around his legs and the golden collar around the middle of his neck, lost her mind ...'; θυλάκους τοὺς ποικίλους, which depends upon φοροῦντα, is moved to the head of the clause for emphasis. Alternatively, ἰδοῦσα governs both θυλάκους and <νιν understood> φοροῦντα, 'seeing the sacks ... and him wearing ...', but the parallel (and no doubt contemp-tuous) details of 'around his legs' (cf. Hdt. 2.81.1, 7.61.1) and 'around his neck' favour the former interpretation. Some (e.g. Henderson 1991: 27, Hall 2006: 148–9) posit an elaborate sexual pun in 182–4, on the basis of αὐχήν suggesting 'penis' at Ar. *Lys.* 681 (which itself is very far from even probable) and θύλακος suggesting θυλάκη 'scrotum'; κλωιόν is not explained in this reading. This seems unproved and unnecessary.

τὴν προδότιν: the satyrs speak as Greeks, cf. *Tr.* 630 and Helen's own account at *Hel.* 926–31; calling women 'traitors' is one of the charges brought against Euripides at Ar. *Thesm.* 393.

θυλάκους 'sacks', a contemptuous (Ar. *Wasps* 1087 with Biles and Olson's n.) term for ἀναξυρίδες, 'trousers', which fifth-century Greeks imagined to be standard dress for contemporary Persians of high stock, cf. Hdt. 5.49.3–4, 7.61.1, Miller 1997: 184–5, with Figures 110–11. Xen. *Anab.* 1.5.8 combines these trousers (τοὺς ποικίλας ἀναξυρίδας) with necklaces, as here. To Greek male taste, these trousers were feminising, but it was assumed that women found them sexy, just as in *Ba.* Pentheus assumes that women are attracted to the stranger from the east who has arrived in Thebes.

τοῖν σκελοῖν: the dual is common in comedy, but absent from tragedy, and may have a colloquial flavour. σκέλος itself is a 'low' word (Janko on *Il.* 16.313–15, Laemmle forthcoming) expressive of the chorus' distaste; the only other occurrence in Euripides is *Ph.* 1400 (a special military phrase).

κλωιόν: a pejorative term (it is used for collars for dogs, criminals, etc.) for στρεπτοί, cf. Hdt. 3.20.1 (gifts from Cambyses include χρύσεον στρε-πτὸν περιαυχένιον), 9.80, Pl. *Rep.* 7.553c7, Xen. *Cyr.* 1.3.2 (regarded as typically Median).

ἐξεπτοήθη 'went all aflutter', cf. *Tr.* 992 ἐξεμαργώθης φρένας, *IA* 585–6 (the chorus apostrophise Paris about Helen, ἔρωτι ... ἐπτοήθης), Sappho fr. 22.13–14, Alcaeus fr. 283.3. See further next n. The satyrs present Helen as the reverse image of a model Athenian wife, cf. a husband's praise for his dead wife on *CEG* 573 (fourth century) 'She did not admire (ἐθαύμασεν) clothes or gold while alive, but [loved] her husband and chas-tity (σωφροσύνην)'.

185–6 The sight of Paris set Helen aflutter, and she left Menelaos after this; ἐξεπτοήθη does not then refer merely to her first emotional reaction, but to the whole state of excitement in which she followed Paris to Troy.

The verses inevitably suggest Sappho fr. 16.7–9 'Helen left behind the very best of husbands (τὸν ἄνδρα τὸν [... ἄρ]ιστον) and sailed off to Troy', and cf. also Alcaeus fr. 283.7–8. An echo of Sappho is here not improbable, cf. Paganelli 1978/9: 200–1, Di Marco 1980a [= 2013: 231–7]; this satyr amusingly knows his lyric poetry, as well as his Euripides, cf. 164–7n.

ἀνθρώπιον: the diminutive is often derogatory (cf. fr. 282a (ἀνδρίον), Xen. *Mem.* 2.3.16, *Cyr.* 5.1.14, Dem. 18.242), like ἀνθρωπίσκε at 316, but here it is rather pitying or affectionate, cf. Ar. *Peace* 263; the effect, which in part confirms and in part undercuts the description of Menelaos as 'the best', is humorously paradoxical, as Menelaos very rarely gets a good press in drama.

186–7 are a kind of parody of a familiar Euripidean *topos*, the denunciation of women, cf. *Med.* 573–5, *Hipp.* 616–68; the cursing of the whole γένος is typical of this mode, cf. fr. 498 πλὴν τῆς τεκούσης θῆλυ πᾶν μισῶ γένος. Irrespective of the date of *Cycl.* (cf. above pp. 38–47), Euripides may here be playing with his comic persona as a misogynist. At *Od.* 14.68–9 Eumaeus curses the whole Ἑλένης φῦλον, but the principal impetus for the theme is Hesiodic, cf. esp. *Theog.* 585–612: the γένος γυναικῶν is a καλὸν κακόν (585) and a πῆμα μέγα (592), but without a good wife a man endures a horrible old age. The present verses express a satyric version of that ambivalence; the comic twist at the end of 187 was perhaps accompanied by gestures appropriate to how satyrs think women should be treated. The language of μηδαμοῦ ... φῦναι suggests also that there may here be a further satyric and gendered twist on the 'wisdom of Silenos' that the best thing is never to have been born, cf. Theognis 425–8, Soph. *OC* 1224, Arist. fr. 65 Gigon, Easterling 2013.

εἰ μὴ 'μοὶ μόνωι expresses a fundamental paradox of satyr-drama: the *koryphaios* speaks for the satyrs as a group, but that group can present itself as a single individual, cf. Soph. fr. 1130 with Laemmle forthcoming.

188 Silenos returns from the cave with (probably) lambs and cheese. In *Od.* Odysseus is urged by his men to carry off cheeses, kids and lambs (9.224–7), but instead they eat some cheeses and wait (9.232).

ἰδού: cf. 153–4n.

ποιμένων βοσκήματα 'animals reared by shepherds', an absurd periphrasis, but one matched by the grandiosity of 189–90. Silenos is putting the best possible face on his side of the bargain. Scaliger's ποιμνίων, 'creatures from the flocks', would give a slightly more regular phrasing, cf. *El.* 494–5 ἥκω φέρων σοι τῶν ἐμῶν βοσκημάτων/ποίμνης νεογνὸν θρέμμ' ὑποσπάσας τόδε, *Ba.* 677–8 ἀγελαῖα ... βοσκήματ' ... μόσχων, and would be more closely parallel to 189; in this repetitive style, however, sense cannot be the only consideration. Silenos' language is reminiscent of the 'dithyrambic' style in which food is often described in Middle Comedy, cf. Hunter 1983: 19–20, Nesselrath 1990: 241–66.

189 ἄναξ Ὀδυσσεῦ: Silenos is very polite, now that possession of the wine is very close; ἄναξ is the title he also gave to Dionysos (17).

μηκάδων ἀρνῶν τροφαί is usually understood as 'nurslings/objects of rearing of the bleating sheep', a very strained phrase; for τροφή in this sense cf. (probably) Soph. *OT* 1. If this is correct, then ἄρνες will here be 'sheep' rather than 'lambs' (224, 234, 256), although Euripides seems elsewhere to reserve that usage for the sheep/lamb with the golden fleece (*El.* 705, 719, 196). Alternatively, 'rearings (consisting in) bleating lambs' would not be out of place in this style and would allow ἄρνες its regular sense, cf. 56 (with Wieseler's τροφάς), Pl. *Laws* 7.790d1 τὰ νεογενῆ παίδων θρέμματα, Smyth §§1323–4. Jebb on Soph. *OT* 1 understands ἀρνῶν τροφαί as a periphrasis for ἄρνες ἐκτεθραμμέναι. Homer uses μηκάς only of goats (three times in *Od.* 9 and nowhere else in *Od.*), but μηχᾶσθαι for both sheep and goats (*Il.* 4.435, *Od.* 9.439).

190 πηκτοῦ 'curdled' (< πήγνυμι), cf. 134–6n., Gow on Theocr. 11.20.

τ' in third position is well attested for tragedy also, cf. *GP²* 517, Fraenkel on Aesch. *Ag.* 229f.

οὐ σπάνια: the emphatic litotes, 'not few' i.e. many, is again the patter of a salesman.

191 φέρεσθε 'Take them (away)', cf. 88n. The following asyndeton points to the urgency of the situation.

192 εὐίου: cf. 25–6n.

193 L gives this verse to Odysseus, which is not impossible, particularly if γάρ is retained in 194, but it seems to make for a better scene if Silenos sees his master coming. Hermann's division of the verse has its attractions (cf. 153–4n.), but on balance the question seems to be a further sign of Silenos' panic.

194 Odysseus' initial reaction is very different from the heroic pose he strikes when he has had time to pull himself together (198–202), cf. 198n.

γ' ἄρ': if all of 193 is spoken by Silenos, then γάρ is much less likely than γ' ἄρ', marking an emphatic inference from information just learned, cf. Lowe 1973. τἄρ', i.e. τοι ἄρα, would make much the same point, cf. *GP²* 555. An alternative (proposed by Desrousseaux, cf. Paganelli 1980: 426–7), regardless of the attribution of 193, would be to give ἀπολώλαμεν γάρ to Silenos and the rest of the verse to Odysseus; ὦ γέρον seems however to come better after, than before, the relevant utterance.

195–7 play with our, and the characters', knowledge of the Homeric story, cf. Laemmle 2013: 348; Silenos is doubtless as uncertain as anyone

that the Greeks will be able 'to escape notice' in the cave, and his γε has
a certain malicious irony about it. In *Od.* Odysseus and his men rush ἐς
μυχὸν ἄντρου at the Cyclops' appearance, from where they watch him milking the animals; as soon as he has lit a fire, however, he catches sight of
them (9.236–51). It is very likely that Silenos fled into the cave at 197
(which would make a splendid exit-verse), to reappear only at some point
before 228; more than one staging can be imagined here.

τόδ' looks forward, cf. *IT* 1201.

ἀρκύων μολεῖν ἔσω has a proverbial ring, though there is no very close
parallel in surviving collections of proverbs, cf. *El.* 965 ἄρκυν ἐς μέσην, *Ba.*
451–2 (part of a long sequence of hunting-imagery), 848, etc.

καταφυγαί 'places to hide'.

198–202 The pompous change from 194 (where see n.) is comical –
there is no reason to insist on perfect 'consistency' in Odysseus' character; Odysseus suddenly realises (again) 'who he is' and in what story he
finds himself (201–2n.) and thus he strikes a suitably epic pose. In *Od.*
also, it was his decision to face the Cyclops rather than fleeing with some
booty (9.224–9).

198 οὐ δῆτ' expresses strong denial or refusal 'to obey a command or
follow a suggestion' (*GP²* 275), in this case, despite 194, the idea of hiding, cf. 704. For the idea that a subsequent act of cowardice will besmirch
the glory of victory at Troy cf. *El.* 336–8, *Hel.* 948–9, Denniston on *El.*
184–9.

τἄν ... στένοι: i.e. τοι ἄν ... στένοι, 'would indeed groan'. At Hdt. 7.159
the Spartan envoy reacts to Gelon's claim to command of the force resist-
ing Persia in similar terms: 'Greatly indeed would Agamemnon son of
Pelops groan (ἦ κε μέγ' οἰμώξειε), were he to learn that the Spartiates had
been deprived of the command by Gelon and Syracusans'.

199–200 In *Od.* the Cyclops is an ἀνὴρ πελώριος (9.187), who in no
way resembles a 'grain-eating man' (9.190–1), but Odysseus is here very
much in heroic mode: his meeting with the Cyclops is to be a kind of epic
duel or *aristeia*. The 'teeming hordes' of the 'Phrygians' assimilates the
Trojans to the 'Persian hordes' which were so central to Athenian cultural
memory after the Persian Wars, cf. Hall 1988, 1989: 38–9. Odysseus here
carves for himself a role not just as epic hero (cf. next n.) but also as the
embodiment and champion of Greek values.

πολλάκις brings Odysseus uncomfortably close to the fantasies of Silenos
in the prologue (cf. Voelke 2001: 345–7), despite *Il.* 11.401–75, in which
he is cut off and does indeed fight 'alone' against the Trojans. His words
here seem to evoke vv. 404–10 of that scene: 'Alas, what is to become
of me? It is a great disgrace to flee the multitude (πληθύν) in fear, but it
would be worse if I taken alone. The son of Kronos has put the rest

of the Danaans to flight. But why does my own heart speak to me like this? I know that cowards (κακοί) avoid warfare, but he who would be finest in battle (ὃς δέ κ' ἀριστεύηισι μάχηι ἔνι) must boldly stand his ground and either be struck or strike another'.

201–2 For such resolutions cf. *Or.* 1151–2, *Il.* 11.404–10 (previous n.), *Il.* 22.304–5 (Hector) μὴ μὰν ἀσπουδεί γε καὶ ἀκλείως ἀπολοίμην, / ἀλλὰ μέγα ῥέξας τι καὶ ἐσσομένοισι πυθέσθαι, Soph. *Ajax* 479–80 ἀλλ' ἢ καλῶς ζῆν ἢ καλῶς τεθνηκέναι / τὸν εὐγενῆ χρή.

αἶνον τὸν πάρος συσσώσομεν '...we shall preserve (together with our life) the glorious story/reputation we had before'. The text must be regarded as uncertain. The transmitted πάρος εὖ σώσομεν is unmetrical, and may be mended in various ways (see apparatus, and Nauck suggested πάρος γε σώσομεν). Wieseler's παρόντ(α), 'the one I have/present with me' (cf. *Od.* 9.19–20, etc.) would, if correct, bring out the ambivalence of αἶνον: not just 'reputation' (LSJ s.v. II), but also 'tale, story': were Odysseus to flee, we would not have the 'story' of the confrontation with the Cyclops so familiar from Homer, cf. Wright 2006: 34, Hunter 2009: 59.

203 begins with three successive tribrachs (i.e. nine short syllables) expressive of the Cyclops' imperious urgency, cf. 210; this licence is not found in the ordinary trimeters of tragedy, cf. Descroix 1931: 152–5, above p. 36.

ἄνεχε πάρεχε: the meaning and origin of the phrase are unclear. The same words are shouted by the drunken Philocleon at his entrance at Ar. *Wasps* 1326 and are often taken to mean 'Get out of the way!', cf. *Wasps* 949 πάρεχ' ἐκποδών. *Tr.* 308, *IA* 732–3 and Ar. *Birds* 1720 (where see Dunbar's n.) perhaps suggest an origin in a wedding-procession passing through the streets. ἀνέχειν may have an intransitive sense 'stop' (LSJ s.v. B 4–5). It seems clear that the Cyclops (not Silenos, as L) shouts the words as he enters and realises that something unusual is happening; it is less clear whether the words are addressed to the satyrs or to otherwise silent 'extras', representing other slaves of the Cyclops (cf. 23–4n.), who return from the hunt with their master (cf. 83n.) and are told to 'get out of the way'.

ῥαιθυμία 'relaxation', 'levity' i.e. the satyrs are not paying due attention to their tasks, as 206–9 make clear. The word can imply 'partying' (cf. Theopompus, *FGrHist* 115 F 139) and there is some of that resonance in the Cyclops' use here. Clement of Alexandria (*Paed.* 1.7.55.1–2) reports that the slave of Themistocles called Sikinnos, who carried the treacherous message to the Persians (Hdt. 8.75, Garvie on Aesch. *Pers.* 355–6) and was later credited with the invention of the satyric *sikin(n)is* dance (cf. 36–8n.), was an οἰκέτης ῥάιθυμος: 'they say that he used to dance and invented the *sikinnis*'.

204 τί βακχιάζετ'; 'What's all this Bacchic nonsense?' Cf. 63–6, where the tone is very different, *Ba.* 931 (Pentheus in the grip of Dionysos), Soph. *Ichn.* 133 τί ποτε βακχεύεις ἔχων;, 'Why are you in a Bacchic frenzy?' The Cyclops' approach very probably led the chorus to nervous and agitated dancing (cf. 36–8n., 94n., Seidensticker 2010: 215), but his question, like the claim which immediately follows, points to a central paradox of satyr-play: Dionysos is always both absent and very much present, cf. Laemmle 2019a, above pp. 25–6. On the Cyclops' knowledge of Dionysiac cult and use of Dionysiac terminology cf. above p. 18.

οὐχὶ Διόνυσος τάδε: lit. 'this situation is not Dionysos ...', cf. *Andr.* 168–9 (Hermione to Andromache) οὐ γάρ ἐσθ' Ἕκτωρ τάδε κτλ. From another point of view, the satyr-play we are watching is very much 'Dionysos', cf. 63n. The transmitted Διώνυσος is an epic form (also in L contrary to metre in 590), and the peremptory οὐχὶ Διόνυσος is more forceful than Porson's οὐχ ὁ Διόνυσος.

205 '... nor clappers of bronze and beatings on drums'. The chiastic shape of the verse emphasises κρόταλα as a word of sound (< κροτέω) parallel to ἀράγματα (< ἀράσσω); it is almost as though κρόταλα is κρότος, and the sense is 'rattlings of bronze ...', cf. Theocr. 2.36 with Gow's n.

κρόταλα are small percussion instruments, 'cymbals', of metal or shell, said by Schol. Ar. *Clouds* 260 to be mounted on split reeds, cf. Michaelides 1978: 179, West 1992: 125; vase-painting frequently depicts satyrs or maenads with κρόταλα, cf. *LIMC* VIII. 1.107, 107a, Osborne 1998: Figure 81, Voelke 2001: 103–7. Like drums, they are associated with the cult of the Great Mother, as well as with Dionysos, cf. 17n., *Hel.* 1308, *HHymn* 14.3, Pind. fr. 70b.9–10 M, Laemmle 2013: 191–3. For bronze κρόταλα cf. Call. fr. 761, Antipater of Sidon, *AP* 9.603.6 (= *HE* 597), *PMG* 955 κρέμβαλα χαλκοπάραια.

τυμπάνων: cf. 65, *Ba.* 59, 124–5, etc. These 'drums' consisted of skin stretched over a small circular frame (*Hel.* 1347 τύπανα ... βυρσοτενῆ); the drums were usually held in the left hand and 'beaten' with the right, cf. West 1992: 124. Maenads and satyrs are often depicted with these instruments, cf. Boardman 1989: Figures 177, 229, Voelke 2001: 107–11.

206 μοι is the so-called 'ethic' dative, expressing the Cyclops' concern in the matter, cf. 43n. There is an ellipse of ἔχουσι, 'How are my lambs ... ?'

νεόγονα βλαστήματα: an absurdly grandiose description of lambs, cf. *Hcld.* 1006 ἐχθροῦ λέοντος δυσμενῆ βλαστήματα.

207–9 The Cyclops asks whether the milking, which happens before the lambs are allowed to feed, has been completed and whether the milk has been set aside for cheese-making, cf. *Od.* 9.244–9. In Homer, the Cyclops did all these tasks himself. Whether the lambs are feeding is the important question and so is placed first, before the chronologically prior 'running under their mothers' flanks'.

ἤ introduces a 'follow-up' question, as often (*GP*² 283). The transmitted γε lacks point, whereas τε introduces a series of demands.

εἰσι ... τρέχουσι: when a plural verb is used with a neuter plural subject, the effect is usually (as here) to stress the plurality of individual (animate) items which make up the subject, cf. K–G I 65–6; the lambs are thought of as living beings, not as an undifferentiated group.

σχοινίνοις τ' ἐν τεύχεσιν 'in wicker containers'. The Homeric Cyclops has ταρσοί, which are also called πλεκτοὶ τάλαροι, 'plaited baskets', where curdled milk was placed to set into cheese (*Od.* 9.219, 247, cf. Theocr. 11.35–7, Gow on Theocr. 5.86); Euripides' phrase varies the πλεκτοὶ τάλαροι.

πλήρωμα ... ἐξημελγμένον: lit. 'the milked complement of cheeses'; the Cyclops asks whether the cheese-making is completed. ἐξ- reinforces πλήρωμα: he is concerned that *all* the milk for cheese has been extracted.

210 For the rhythm cf. 203n.; there is an infringement of Porson's Law, cf. 681–2, West 1982: 85, above p. 37.

τῶι ξύλωι presumably refers to a club or staff the Cyclops is carrying and evokes the great ῥόπαλον with which he is blinded (455–63, *Od.* 9.319); for depictions of Polyphemos with a club cf. *LIMC* VIII.1 s.v. Polyphemos I, 40–3, 46. Threats of physical violence were probably very common in satyr-play, as they are in comedy, and were perhaps particularly associated with Heracles, the most famous 'club-wielding' hero (cf. *Her.* 568–70), cf. following n.; at Soph. *Ichn.* 168 Silenos threatens the satyrs, κλαίοντες αὐτῆι δειλίαι ψοφήσετε.

211 βλέπετ' ἄνω καὶ μὴ κάτω: the satyrs are looking down out of embarrassment and fear and perhaps also protecting their faces from the swishing club. The gesture may convey a wide range of nuance in both epic and drama, cf. Muecke 1984, Diggle 2004: 448–9. This scene perhaps evokes another satyric scene involving Heracles and his club or even a repeated scene of satyr-drama, cf. Ael. Arist. 3.672 'Once one of the stage satyrs cursed Heracles and then looked down (ἔκυψεν ... κάτω) when Heracles approached', Radt on Soph. fr. 756.

212–19 L makes Silenos the interlocutor of the Cyclops, but he is very likely no longer on stage (cf. 195–7n.), and certainly he does not speak again until 228; it is the chorus-leader who must answer the Cyclops' questions, cf. Introduction pp. 26–7.

ἰδού: cf. 153–4n.

πρὸς αὐτὸν τὸν Δί' ἀνακεκύφαμεν: the perfect indicates that the satyrs have already done as commanded and are now 'looking up'. κύπτειν and its compounds are not found in tragedy; such body-movements belong rather to satyr-play and comedy. 'Zeus himself' refers both to the sky and (flatteringly) to the Cyclops, who certainly considers himself the equal of Zeus (320–41).

213 The satyrs claim that they are looking fixedly ἄνω towards heaven and the stars (cf. Thales at Pl. *Tht.* 174a4–5). This need not necessarily mean that night has now arrived (cf. 214, 353–4nn.): the satyrs' claim to be looking at Orion is an improvised piece of flattery in an attempt to avoid punishment; the variant τά τ' ἄστρα, if construed with πρός, would weaken the force of their gambit. οὐρανοῦ/μέτρησις is one of the skills claimed by the satyrs at Soph. fr. 1130.14–15. The constellation of the 'mighty' Orion (e.g. *Il.* 18.486) was, like Polyphemos, a hunter, the carrier of a club and a son of Poseidon; in various versions he was also blinded and/or suffered eternal punishment in the Underworld, cf. Hes. fr. 148a = 244 Most, *Od.* 11.572–5, Erat. *Catast.* 32, Pàmias i Massana 2013: 98–9, 284–8, *LIMC* s.v. The satyrs flatter Polyphemos with the comparison – this is the Orion they are looking at, but some at least of the audience will have understood the implicit warning in their words, cf. O'Sullivan 2005: 129. Sophocles' satyric *Kedalion* may have dealt with parts of the Orion story, but the matter is very uncertain, cf. KPS 344–8.

214 ἄριστον: like a good hunter (cf. Xen. *Cyr.* 1.6.39–40, Ap. Rhod. *Arg.* 4.109–13, with Hunter's n. on vv. 112–13), the Cyclops will have made an early start and now has a sharp appetite. His meal is in fact standing in front of him, though he has not seen them yet. In classical literature, ἄριστον normally indicates any meal taken before the break in the day, so in other contexts 'breakfast' is often a more appropriate translation; the evening meal was normally δεῖπνον. Here, it has been thought that Euripides' time-scheme for *Cycl.* is incoherent as the flock has already returned from grazing, and so it should be the end of the working day, or at least afternoon (cf. Arnott 1961: 168–9); the sense of the ending of the day also suits the late, fourth position in which satyr-plays were performed (above p. 24). It may be that Euripides did not worry over-much about the chronology within the rapid action and short narrative space of *Cycl.* (cf. previous n.), but it seems very unlikely that he would write as carelessly as has been supposed. As was observed by Aristarchus (Schol. *Il.* 24.124), ἄριστον appears only once in each of the Homeric poems (*Il.* 24.124, *Od.* 16.2); in Homer, δεῖπνον is the standard term for any meal taken before the end of the day, with δόρπον as the term for the evening meal. The terms for Homeric meals and whether the heroes had two meals a day or three was the subject of lively discussion in Hellenistic scholarship (cf. Plut. *Mor.*726c–d, Ath. 1.11b–f, Schmidt 1976: 191–7, Schironi 2018: 278), and it may be that Euripides' striking use of ἄριστον here points to a classical anticipation of that debate; Homer calls the Cyclops' 'breakfast' δεῖπνον (*Od.* 9.311), so here Euripides pointedly reverses that and uses ἄριστον for the meal which the audience would have called δεῖπνον.

εὖ 'properly'.

215 φάρυγξ appears four times in *Cycl.*, but never in tragedy (or other satyr-play); we will remember *Od.* 9.373–4 φάρυγος δ' ἐξέσσυτο οἶνος/ψωμοί τ' ἀνδρόμεοι.

216 κρατῆρες: words more usually connected with wine appear regularly in *Cycl.* in connection with milk, cf. 217, 218n., 327, 388; in Homer, the Cyclops' milk is stored in ἄγγεα (*Od.* 9.222, 248). Such language might come more naturally to satyrs than to the Cyclops, but it is one of the ways in which the absence of wine and the Cyclops' rejection of Dionysos are marked, cf. 123–4, 204–5, Voelke 2001: 185–9, above pp. 17–18. The conceit perhaps took its cue from *Od.* 9.297, where the Cyclops is said to drink 'unmixed' (ἄκρητον) milk; in Homer it was the substitution of unmixed wine for milk which was to prove his undoing. For an extended comic use of the substitution of milk for wine cf. Lucian, *VH* 2.3.

217 There is enough milk to fill a storage-jar; at 327 the Cyclops claims to wash down his dinner with an 'amphora' of milk. Art represents satyrs as drinking wine straight from the jar (e.g. Lissarrague 2013: Figure 120), and at Sositheus, *TrGF* 99 F 2.7–8, Lityerses, another monstrous figure of satyr-play, is said to drink τὸν δεκάμφορον πίθον, cf. 388.

218–19 The Cyclops is not just a gourmet, but also a 'connoisseur' of milk; 'mixed' would normally be κεκραμένον, used of the mixing of wine with water before drinking, but here μεμειγμένον is used of a 'blend' of two types of milk. If the Homeric Cyclops had wanted 'mixed' milk, this would have to have been sheep's and goats' milk; the possibility of milk from cows draws attention to how far Euripides' Cyclops is from his Homeric predecessor. The three adjectives more naturally refer back to γάλα in 216, but the antecedent of ὅν at the head of 219 must be πίθον; the problem is removed by ὧν (Kaibel) or ὅ γ' (Porson). For verses of the shape of 218 cf. [Aesch.] *PV* 116 (ὀδμά) θεόσυτος ἢ βρότειος ἢ κεκραμένη, which 218 is sometimes thought to parody, Eubulus fr. 6.1 θερμότερον ἢ κραυρότερον ἢ μέσως ἔχον, Alexis fr. 177.1–2 (with Arnott 1996: 518–19).

ὃν ἂν θέλῃς: the near-repetition from 217 marks the satyrs' obsequious eagerness to please the Cyclops.

μόνον: for this colloquial usage cf. 161, 568.

220–1 Repetition of ἄν, particularly when it is placed near the beginning of the sentence and then repeated with an optative verb, is very common, cf. K–G I 246–7, Smyth §1765. Seaford suggested ἐπεί τἄν μ'; for τἄν = τοι ἄν in such sentences cf. 198.

τῶν σχημάτων 'dance-steps', 'positions', cf. Ar. *Wasps* 1485, *Peace* 321–36 (often thought to evoke satyric choruses), Hdt. 6.129.3 (σχημάτια of Hippocleides), Plut. *Mor.* 747c; for satyric dancing and the perpetual movement of the satyrs cf. 37n., 94–5, above p. 96. The image is perhaps of babies 'kicking' in the womb.

222 Cf. 96–100n., 99n. Ar. *Thesm.* 1105 ἔα· τίν᾽ ὄχθον τόνδ᾽ ὁρῶ καὶ παρθένον; κτλ. parodies a verse of Perseus' entrance-monologue from Eur. *Andromeda* (412 BC), ἔα· τίν᾽ ὄχθον τόνδ᾽ ὁρῶ περίρρυτον (fr. 125.1); Euripides may here be responding to the parody by using a very similar line again, cf. Parry 1971: 319–20, Laemmle 2013: 328–9, and (against) Battezzato 1995: 134–5, Wright 2005: 54–5, 2006: 24–5. On the implications of this for the date of *Cycl.* cf. above pp. 39–41.

πρὸς αὐλίοις 'by the sheep-folds'.

223 λῃσταί: cf. *Od.* 9.254 (in the Cyclops' opening questions).

κατέσχον … χθόνα 'put in to land', cf. *Hel.* 1206, LSJ s.v. κατέχω B2. At 348–9 this sense of the verb is used with ἐς and an accusative.

κλῶπες 'thieves', who might come from the local area, whereas λῃσταί suggests, as in Homer, 'raiders' who travel by ship; the difference need not, however, be very great, cf. *Alc.* 766. In *Od.* Odysseus and his men did indeed 'steal' from the Cyclops, but here a proper exchange has been done, though not with the rightful owner.

224 γέ τοι introduces the explanation for the supposition of 223, cf. *Phoen.* 730, *GP*² 550.

225 '… their bodies bound together with twisted withies', a variation on *Od.* 9.427 where Odysseus ties the rams together (συνέεργον) in threes ἐυστρεφέεσσι λύγοισι; in Homer, the purpose was so that they could carry a man suspended beneath them, whereas here they are packed up for simple ease of transport, cf. Laemmle 2013: 337, above pp. 14–15. σῶμα is acc. of respect; the plural would be more regular (K–G I 316), but cf. *Her.* 703. Blaydes suggested σώματ᾽ ἐμπεπλεγμένους, and Seaford 1982: 170–1 wonders whether the bound sheep continue an allusion to the Euripidean Andromeda tethered to a rock, cf. Ar. *Thesm.* 1031–2 (= Eur. fr. 122.4).

226 συμμιγῆ 'jumbled up'.

227 '… his bald head swollen with blows'. μέτωπον φαλακρόν (acc. of respect) is a perfect description of the receding hair line and bald patch on top of the head which is standard in depictions of Silenos and *silenoi*, cf. Soph. fr. 171.3 (almost certainly Silenos), *LIMC* VIII s.v. Silenoi nos. 43a, 54, 88, etc. πρόσωπον and μέτωπον are elsewhere exchanged in transmission, and it is his forehead, not his face, which is bald. Nevertheless, problems remain. If Silenos has been beaten up, rather than, say, hit with a club (cf. 229), then it is his πρόσωπον, 'face', which one would expect to be swollen, not his forehead, cf. Theocr. 22.101 οἰδήσαντος … προσώπου, 110–11 πληγαῖς/πᾶν συνέφυρε πρόσωπον (Amycus); word-order would, however, seem to rule out taking φαλακρόν with γέροντα, a solution which would cut the knot. It may be that Euripides has rather loosely called Silenos' face, rather than his head, 'bald', and that the transmitted reading is correct. Some commentators, however, understand πρόσωπον as 'mask' (cf. perhaps Aesch. *Eum.* 990) and explain that Silenos has changed his mask (to one showing marks of a fight) after entering the *skēnē* at the arrival of the Cyclops (cf. 197n.); Silenos' 'mask' would also indicate his baldness. What the Cyclops actually interprets as the effect of a beating is in fact very difficult to decide. Traditionally, it has been thought that Silenos is flushed (cf. 228) after his first taste of wine for a long time, or perhaps after drinking more from the wineskin while inside the cave (cf. Virg. *Ecl.* 6.15, Martial 5.4.4), and the Cyclops interprets this redness as the result of blows; it seems, however, very hard to see how the audience could understand that. Perhaps Silenos is somehow sporting injuries which the audience have seen him inflict upon himself; at any event, our difficulties here are a good illustration of the fact that we must not assume that all important stage-action in satyr-drama is made explicit in the text. At Aesch. *Dikt.* fr. 47a.788 λιπαρὸν / μιλτόπρεπτον φαλακρόν may refer to Silenos' phallus (cf. also Soph. *Ichn.* 368, Dettori 2016: 139–43), and Seaford 1987 interprets the current passage similarly (cf. also Slenders 2005: 43–6).

228 It is unclear whether Silenos now takes his cue from the Cyclops' misapprehension, or whether his scheming has fooled the Cyclops, see previous n. Arnott 1972: 29–30 suggests a play with συγκοπή as a medical term, cf. LSJ s.v. III. On Silenos' silence about the allegedly wicked stranger's name cf. 103n.

230 οὐκ εἴων: 'I was not allowing' amounts to 'I tried to prevent', cf. 233.

231 θεόν is scanned as a single syllable by synizesis (cf. 286, 605, 624, 679), whereas θεῶν is here disyllabic; for such effects cf. *Andr.* 1258, *Tr.* 1280, Gygli-Wyss 1966: 127, Diggle 1994: 129–36, Battezzato 2000. For the shape of this verse cf. *Alc.* 677 οὐκ οἶσθα Θεσσαλόν με κἀπὸ Θεσσαλοῦ κτλ.

θεῶν ἄπο: in Homer, the Cyclops is the son of Poseidon and the seanymph Thoösa, a daughter of Phorkys (*Od.* 1.69–73).

232 ἐφόρουν, 'they tried to carry off', hardly differs in meaning from ἐξεφοροῦντο in 234. Blaydes proposed ἔφερον, cf. 230. For the scansion here cf. above pp. 36–7.

τὰ χρήματα is suitably vague; we should not ask too closely what 'property' this is, cf. 268, 270.

233 Silenos' lies are here helped by a memory of *Od.* 9.232, where the Greeks do eat some of the Cyclops' cheeses; in one sense these Greeks have indeed eaten his cheese, but in the Homeric version of the story which is here rewritten.

τόν γε τυρόν: Markland's τῶν γε τυρῶν would be a partitive genitive, 'some of the cheeses', cf. *Od.* 9.232.

οὐκ ἐῶντος: sc. ἐμοῦ, cf. Smyth § 2072 for the ellipse.

ἤσθιον: in Eur. ἐσθίειν and its compounds occur only in *Cycl.* (cf. 341) and fr. 907 (a probably satyric description of Heracles eating), whereas θοινᾶσθαι (cf. 248, 550) is common, cf. Arist. *Poet.* 1458b19–24 citing fr. 792 and Aesch. fr. 253.

234 ἐξεφοροῦντο: cf. 232 n. Musgrave proposed ἐξεφροῦντο (< ἐκφρέω, cf. Barrett on *Hipp.* 866–7), 'they were letting out (for their own purposes)', which would also remove a third-foot anapaest, cf. above p. 37.

234–6 'They said that they would bind you in a three-cubit collar and forcibly draw your guts out through your central eye'. The threats which the Greeks are alleged to have made against the Cyclops are a kind of satyric equivalent of Antinoos' horrific threats to the beggar Iros at *Od.* 18.84–7. We might also recall the Philistines' treatment of Samson: 'they cut out his eyes … and bound him in bronze fetters and he was set to grind in the prison' (*Judges* 16.21).

κλωιῶι τριπήχει: 'collars' were worn both by criminals (Xen. *Hell.* 3.3.11, Eupolis fr. 172.16), especially when they were to be flogged, and dogs (Ar. *Wasps* 897, with Biles and Olson's n., Xen, *Hell.* 2.4.41); Plut. *Solon* 24.1 reports that Solon enacted that vicious dogs were to be restrained κλοιῶι τριπήχει, i.e. by a 'three-cubit collar' which allowed them to be held at a safe distance. The Cyclops' teeth, like those of an angry dog, are certainly something to be avoided.

κατὰ τὸν ὀφθαλμὸν μέσον 'out through your central eye'; for this meaning of κατά cf., e.g., Ar. *Wasps* 140–1, *Clouds* 158–9. This vivid interpretation (Gargiulo 1994, following Barnes) is much more horrible, and thus much more likely, than 'right in front of your central eye' (cf. *El.* 910, *Rh.* 421), as most recent commentators understand the preposition. The transmitted κᾶτα produces a split anapaest in the fourth foot (cf. above p. 37), and no other proposal (cf. Biehl 1977: 170–1, Gargiulo 1994) is remotely satisfactory.

ἐξαμήσεσθαι 'will draw out', cf. LSJ s.v. ἀμάω B, and the threat of the female chorus to their male counterparts at Ar. *Lys.* 367 τἄντερ' ἐξαμήσω; it is not necessary to give the verb the special nuance 'harvest', as, e.g., Voelke 2001: 188.

237 ἀπολέψειν 'will strip (the skin) off'; the simple λέπειν is used in comedy as a word for 'thrash', 'whip', cf. Pl. Com. fr. 12, Timocles fr. 31.3, LSJ s.v. II. Silenos' grim fiction may be suitably satyric, if it evokes the fate of the satyr Marsyas, who was flayed alive by Apollo after losing to the god in a musical contest, cf. Hdt. 7.26, Xen. *Anab.* 1.2.8, etc.; it has often been suggested that this story was treated in satyr-drama (cf. *Trag. Adesp.* 381). The transmitted ἀποθλίψειν would be an image from the squeezing of grapes and seems less vivid.

238 συνδήσαντες 'tying you up'.

θἁδώλια: i.e. τὰ ἑδώλια, the quarter-deck at the stern of the ship, cf. *Hel.* 1571, Soph. *Aj.* 1277 (with Finglass' n.). It is likely enough that it is there where the pirates are imagined to have tried to keep Dionysos chained (*HHDion.* 11–15). Others understand 'rowing-benches', but that seems much less probable.

239 ναός: cf. 85n.

239–40 '... (they said that) they would sell you to someone to heave up rocks or would throw you into the mill'. καταβαλεῖν is the last future infinitive in the series.

ἀποδώσειν: the middle is regular in the meaning 'sell', but cf. Thucyd. 6.62.4 (with Dover's n.).

πέτρους μοχλεύειν: it is a suitably absurd fancy that the now 'gutless' Cyclops will be set to the back-breaking task of heaving up boulders, perhaps to build Cyclopean walls. The Homeric Cyclops, we will recall, was very good at heaving up rocks, cf. *Od.* 9.313, 481–2. It is unclear whether we should here sense a reference to the notorious stone-quarries of Syracuse in which Athenian soldiers and later, by repute, the poet Philoxenus were imprisoned, cf. Phaenias fr. 13 Wehrli = *PMG* 816, Hunter 1999: 216–17, Duncan 2012: 138–9, above p. 44.

μυλῶνα: work grinding in a mill was one of the hardest punishments which could be inflicted on a slave, cf. Lys. 1.18 (with Todd's n.), Men. *Aspis* 245, *Heros* 2–3, Apul. *Met.* 9.12, V. Hunter 1994: 171–2. The transmitted πυλῶνα καταβαλεῖν could only be in parallel with πέτρους μοχλεύειν, with καταβαλεῖν as an aorist infinitive, but it is very hard to see what this threat would amount to, even if it brings to mind the scene of the Homeric Cyclops' cave (Laemmle 2013: 341 n.45).

241–3 The Cyclops' instructions are more probably addressed to mute attendants (cf. 83n.) than to Silenos; when the Cyclops enters the cave he does some of these tasks himself (382–7), but such inconsistency and repetition are hardly worrying in a play of this kind, and we might assume that the attendants do depart to do the Cyclops' bidding, but then the whole thing is forgotten, cf. 383–4n., Bain 1981: 2.

ἄληθες; is often ironic in comedy (Collard 2018: 61 (~ Stevens 1976: 23)), but here there is no reason to doubt that the Cyclops believes Silenos: 'Did they really?' In this usage the accent is thrown back to the first syllable; the standard neuter sing. is ἀληθές.

κοπίδας is normally a noun, 'cleavers', but here, unless there is textual disturbance, it functions as an adjective with μαχαίρας, 'knives for chopping'; κοπίδας is, however, placed emphatically at the head of the sentence, because 'chopping' is what matters here. There is something of the comic cook about the Cyclops, as might already have been the case in Epicharmus and Cratinus (cf. above pp. 4–6), cf. 397n., Cratinus fr. 150,

Ar. *Peace* 1017–18, fr. 143 κοπίδι τῶν μαγειρικῶν, Plaut. *MG* 1397 (a threatened castration) *uide ut istic tibi sit acutus, Cario, culter probe*, Wilkins 2000: chapter 8, Worman 2008: chapter 3. κοπίδες are often depicted in art, cf., e.g., Sparkes 1975: Plate XVI a–b.

μέγαν φάκελον ξύλων: cf. *Od.* 9.233–4 φέρε δ᾽ ὄβριμον ἄχθος / ὕλης ἀζαλέης, ἵνα οἱ ποτιδόρπιον εἴη.

ἀνάψεις, like ἀνέκαυσε in 83 and 383, probably means 'get the fire going', by putting fresh wood on it, rather than 'light the fire' in our sense; any home, even a cave-home, will have had a hearth with some heat day and night, cf. *Od.* 9.308, 328, 375–6, 378–9.

243–6 The Cyclops will 'sacrifice' the Greeks by himself and to himself (cf. 334–5), and will then alone enjoy the standard meal which follows sacrifice; δαίς (245, 247), lit. 'a divided/shared meal' (< δαίομαι), sharply marks the paradox, cf. 361, Worman 2008: 137–8. The 'hospitality' which he will offer is like a bizarre parody of the opening of *Od.* 3 in which Telemachos and his colleagues are invited to share the sacrifice and feasting of Nestor and his family. When Telemachos arrives, the σπλάγχνα are already being eaten while the rest of the meat is spitted and roasted (cf. e.g. *Il.* 2.421–9); Telemachos and his colleagues are then invited to join as ξεῖνοι (40). It was standard practice at a sacrifice that the σπλάγχνα were grilled and eaten immediately (cf. perhaps αὐτίκα in 243), with a part set aside for the gods; some meat will then have been grilled on spits over coals and eaten (cf. ἀπ᾽ ἄνθρακος 244, 402–3, *Od.* 14.75–7), with the rest set to boil (cf. 246, 404) or taken away for boiling. The Cyclops' planned meal evokes aspects of sacrificial practice, but it does not follow that practice step by step; whether or not Euripides is here indebted to speculation about the contribution of animal sacrifice and hence of the grilling of meat to the human abandonment of cannibalism (as illustrated much later in Athenion fr. 1) is difficult to establish, but it is amusingly paradoxical that the Cyclops is now keen on cooking and *haute cuisine*, whereas in Homer Odysseus' companions were eaten raw, cf. above p. 7. For sacrificial practices in general cf. Denniston on *El.* 791ff., Meuli 1946: 261–73, Burkert 1983: 5–7, Dunbar on Ar. *Birds* 518–19, von Straten 1995, Hitch and Rutherford 2017.

ὡς introduces the reason for the Cyclops' instructions.

πλήσουσι νηδὺν τὴν ἐμήν: cf. *Od.* 9.296 αὐτὰρ ἐπεὶ Κύκλωψ μεγάλην ἐμπλήσατο νηδύν κτλ., the only instance of νηδύς in *Od.* The Cyclops' foretelling has already been fulfilled in Homer.

διδόντες is a very attractive emendation, though an element of uncertainty about the text must remain; ἔδοντος, sc. ἐμοῦ, seems very weak after 244 and makes τῶι κρεανόμωι difficult to construe.

τῶι κρεανόμωι 'to the distributor of meat', i.e. to the Cyclops himself. A sacrifice would be followed by a distribution of meat (κρεανομία) to the participants, cf., e.g., *Il.* 9.217, Sokolowski 1969: nos. 10A.4, 13.26, 33B.24–5, Theocr. 26.24 (the Dionysiac dismembering of Pentheus), but here the only recipient will be the sacrificer himself, cf., e.g., 356–67; paradoxically, those participating will, like sacrificial animals, supply the meat themselves.

τὰ δ' ἐκ λέβητος κτλ. is either a second object after διδόντες or we must supply ἔσται or something similar, 'the rest will be boiled …'

ἐφθὰ καὶ τετηκότα 'boiled and made tender (lit. "melted")', cf. Antiphanes fr. 1.4 πνικτὰ τακερὰ μηκάδων μέλη, Athenion fr. 1.30 ἐρίφιον ἐτακέρωσε; for the tenderising effects of boiling, as opposed to roasting, cf. Philochorus, *FGrHist* 328 F 173, Arist. *Meteor.* 4.381a23–b13, Ekroth 2017: 46. Regulations for a sacred association in Hellenistic Miletus prescribe ὄπτησις σπλάγχνων κρεῶν ἔψησις among the required duties (Sokolowski 1955: no. 50, line 34).

247 ἔκπλεως 'full and over-full'; at 416 the sense is simply 'stuffed full'. ὡς … γε explains the preceding statement, cf. 439.

248 'Enough of lions in my feasts (lit. 'for me feasting') …' Lions belong to the classical memory of the Bronze Age, and regularly appear in myth; whether or not there ever were lions in Sicily (cf. Hunter on Theocr. 1.72) is not really relevant. In Homer the Cyclops ate 'like a mountain-reared lion' (*Od.* 9.292); here he absurdly claims that lions formed part of the food he hunted 'on the mountains'.

θοινωμένωι suggests a certain pompous self-consciousness about his dining habits: he does not just have a meal, he 'feasts', cf. 233n.

249 Cf. *Or.* 485 βεβαρβάρωσαι, χρόνιος ὢν ἐν βαρβάροις. The verse wrily evokes the gap in time between Homer and Euripides, cf. 251–2n.

βορᾶς: cf. 88n. ἀπ' ἀνθρώπων βορᾶς might be expected to mean 'without the food which men eat'; here the meaning is, more gruesomely, 'without the food consisting of men'.

250 Cf. *Or.* 234 μεταβολὴ πάντων γλυκύ, 'variety is the spice of life'; for the opposition between καινός and ἠθάς cf. *Andr.* 818–19, Ar. *Eccl.* 584–5. γ' 'yes indeed', 'certainly' (*GP*² 130).

ἐκ 'coming after', 'in place of', cf. *Or.* 279 ἐκ κυμάτων γὰρ αὖθις αὖ γαλήν' ὁρῶ, LSJ s.v. II 2.

251–2 again evoke the familiarity of the Homeric story: we should understand that the last such ξένοι were in fact Odysseus and his men in the Homeric version. Such play with the relationship between literary model and copy ('not recently') was to become very common in Hellenistic and Roman poetry.

γὰρ οὖν 'For it is certainly a fact that …', cf. *GP²* 445–6. αὖ makes no comparable sense.

σούσαφίκοντο, i.e. σοι ἐσαφίκοντο with 'synaloephe' (cf. 288, 561, *Ba.* 1256–7 νουθετητέος, πάτερ, / σούστίν [Kirchhoff: σοί τ' ἐστίν], Soph. *Phil.* 812), mends the faulty metre of L, but some uncertainty remains. Wieseler proposed ἄντρα τὰ σ' ἐσαφίκοντο, and Kovacs accepts Heimsoeth's radical πρὸς οἴκους σοὺς ἀφίκοντο.

253 ἄκουσον 'in Euripides usually expresses a (polite) request, a plea or a prayer, rather than an order' and is regularly used 'where the speaker is in no position to simply give orders to his addressee' (Rijksbaron 1991: 34, contrasting the use of the present imperative).

ἐν μέρει evokes the flavour of a rhetorical ἀγών, cf., e.g., *Hec.* 1130, *Hcld.* 182.

254–60 Odysseus' account is basically true to what we have seen; in Homer Odysseus' first speech to the Cyclops (9.259–71) is also broadly in keeping with what the poet and the hero himself have led us to accept, though much more rhetorically elaborated than Odysseus' brief narrative here. Cf. above pp. 9–10 on Euripides' exploitation of the 'truth' of Odysseus' Homeric narrative.

254 βορᾶς χρήιζοντες ἐμπολὴν λαβεῖν: lit. 'wishing to get a trade of food', i.e. 'wishing to receive food in exchange (for other goods)'; ἐμπολή is 'traffic, trade', cf. *IT* 1111, LSJ s.v. II.

256 σκύφου: the implication of (the textually uncertain) 145–7 was that Odysseus was going to give Silenos the whole wineskin in exchange; 'a cup of wine' is thus pointed: Silenos would have sold the lambs for just a cup of wine, cf. 164–5. As transmitted, σκύφος is here masculine (cf. 556, *Alc.* 798, *El.* 499), but in other passages neuter (390, 411, fr. 146); several of those passages, as this one, could be emended to give the other possible gender. The variation in gender was discussed in antiquity, cf. Ath. 11.498a–9b.

257 ἀπημπόλα τε κἀδίδου 'he agreed to sell and was handing over'; ἀπημπόλα is the third pers. sing. imperfect of ἀπεμπολάω. The echo of ἐμπολήν in 254 is intended to lend plausibility to Odysseus' narrative; for the Odysseus of *Cycl.* as a mercantile trader cf. 98n.

πιεῖν λαβών 'receiving (in return) a drink'; for the epexegetic infinitive cf. 404, 520, 561, Xen. *Hell.* 7.2.9, K–G II 16, Smyth §2008.

258 ἑκὼν ἑκοῦσι: a common type of emphatic polyptoton, cf. *Hipp.* 319, fr. 304a.2, *Od.* 3.372; it may here have a legal flavour, thus enforcing Odysseus' claims to tell the truth, cf. Dem. 21.44, 'if someone takes one or two or talents by agreement (ἑκὼν παρ' ἑκόντος) and misappropriates them …'

τούτων 'of these things', i.e. 'of the events I have recounted'. The transmitted τούτω(ι) could only refer to Silenos, 'nothing which happened to him was by violence', but τούτωι βίαι would be stylistically very awkward.

259 'There is not a single sound word in what he says ...', a very emphatic form of expression.

ὑγιὲς οὐδέν: cf. Ar. *Thesm.* 636, *Pl.* 274, Collard 2018: 65 (~ Stevens 1976: 25–6), LSJ s.v. II 3.

φησιν λέγει: for such variation cf. Soph. *Tr.* 346–7 ἀνὴρ ὅδ᾽ οὐδὲν ὧν ἔλεξεν ἀρτίως/φωνεῖ δίκης ἐς ὀρθόν.

260 ἐλήφθη 'he has been caught', cf. *Hipp.* 955, *IT* 100–1, *Med.* 381–2. The transmitted κατελήφθη (cf. Pl. *Apol.* 22b1–2) would give the only instance of Odysseus using a 'comic anapaest' (above pp. 36–7); Odysseus' speech in 253–60 is otherwise entirely 'tragic' and contains only a single resolution (in 259).

261 This is the only case in *Cycl.* of verse-division between speakers ('*antilabē*') that is neither embedded in a *stichomythia* nor occurs in close proximity to one (cf. 546, 669–90nn.). Silenos bursts in at 261 because he realises the danger to him which Odysseus' accusation poses, and Odysseus immediately 'barks back'.

γ᾽ ἄρ᾽ marks 'an exclamatory comment on something said by the previous speaker' (Lowe 1973: 45); it may be that γ᾽ ἄρ᾽ should be read in such cases, cf. Ar. *Birds* 1358.

εἰ ψεύδομαι plays on the fact that, in swearing an oath, it was standard to wish for self-destruction if the oath were ever broken or the declaration proved false, cf. 268–9n.; for such 'self-cursing' cf., e.g., *Hipp.* 1025–31, *Med.* 755, Ar. *Frogs* 586–8, Dem. 54.41, Konstantinidou 2014: 30–7. εἰ <γε> ψεύδομαι would make the point somewhat clearer, but would be unmetrical, and the unclarity led Denniston 1930: 215 to retain γάρ and give the whole verse to Odysseus (but for ἐγώ;). Such buffoonish jesting seems however quite out of character with Odysseus here; this Odysseus really is honest: whatever happened to the ἀνὴρ πολύτροπος?

262–5 Oaths by multiple deities are common in perfectly serious contexts, but are also a frequent source of humour, cf. Ar. *Clouds* 627, *Birds* 194 (with Dunbar's n.), Antiphanes fr. 288, Men. *Dysk.* 666–7. Fletcher 2012: 149–54 suggests that the audience would later understand that Silenos is punished for his 'perjury' by being raped by the Cyclops; nothing in the text supports this. Dover on Ar. *Clouds* 1234 notes that trios of divinities regularly appear in oaths, and here too Silenos' control over his oath seems to run out after the first three invocations.

τὸν μέγαν Τρίτωνα: a son of Poseidon, and hence half-brother to the Cyclops; Hes. *Theog.* 930–3 calls him Τρίτων εὐρυβίης ... μέγας and a δεινὸς θεός.

Νηρέα: 'the old man of the sea', a son of Pontos, cf. West on Hes. *Theog.* 233; Hesiod characterises Nereus as ἀψευδὴς καὶ ἀληθής and as an upholder of justice (*Theog.* 233–6), but here he is used in the service of deceit.

Καλυψώ: Silenos is now scratching around for any marine divinity he can think of; the encounter with Calypso lies in the future for the listening Odysseus, but also in his past (*qua* Homeric character). In Homer Calypso is a daughter of Atlas, but in the *Theogony* she is an Oceanid (359) and has two sons by Odysseus with the suitably nautical names Nausithoos and Nausinoos (1017–18); Apollodorus 1.2.7 lists a Calypso among the Nereids, which is also the company she keeps here.

τάς τε Νηρέως κόρας: Silenos needs as many marine names as he can find, and archaic epic presents two catalogues of the Nereids, *Il.* 18.39–49, Hes. *Theog.* 243–62; Silenos will not go through them all, but he knows that there are a lot of them.

μὰ θαἰερὰ κύματ' 'by the holy waves'; θαἰερά = τὰ ἱερά. There is a second-foot split anapaest in which the short syllables are the final syllables of a polysyllabic word, cf. (probably) 334, Ar. *Birds* 1022, 1363, White 1912: 46, above p. 37. As Silenos searches for anything watery to throw into his oath, so his metre wobbles. L's text is anomalous as repeated μά seems always to be used in asyndeton, and Hermann's τά θ' ἱερά deserves consideration: it avoids the anapaest and has Silenos simply piling as many things as possible in at the end. 'Holy' is a very common epithet of springs and other sources of water, but 'waves' seems a ludicrous distortion, brought on by the mention of sea gods, of the habit of swearing by springs and rivers, cf. *Il.* 3.278, Dittenberger 1915: no. 527 (an ephebic oath from Hellenistic Crete), Dunbar on Ar. *Birds* 194.

ἰχθύων τε πᾶν γένος: an absurd version of the attempt of oaths at inclusivity, cf. *Med.* 746–7 θεῶν τε ... ἅπαν γένος, Ar. *Thesm.* 274 ὄμνυμι τοίνυν πάντας ἄρδην τοὺς θεούς.

266 Silenos' pleading reaches truly comic levels, cf. Ar. *Ach.* 475, *Knights* 726, *Clouds* 746, etc. At Achaios, *TrGF* 20 F 26 (satyric) Heracles is addressed as ὦ κάλλιστον Ἡρακλείδιον, and in another unknown satyr-play he was called by the diminutive Ἥρυλλος (*Trag. Adesp.* 590).

ἀπώμοσ': a performative or instantaneous aorist (cf. 101n.), not uncommon with verbs of swearing, cf. *Hel.* 330 (with Kannicht's n.), Soph. *Phil.* 1289 (with Schein's n.).

267 ἐξοδᾶν 'sell off', cf. 12n.; the present infinitive implies 'trying to sell off, in the process of selling off'.

268–9 Silenos pointedly does not involve himself in his curse, as Odysseus has just done (261). Those swearing oaths regularly invoked destruction upon themselves *and* their children, cf. Lys. 12.10 'When he had sworn, invoking complete destruction upon himself and his children, that he would save me in return for a talent …', Hdt. 6.86, Dem. 23.67–8, 47.70. There is perhaps a similarly wry imprecation from Silenos at Aesch. *Dikt.* fr. 46a.800, ὄλοιτο Δίκτυς.

κακῶς … κακοί: a very common locution in Eur. and comedy, cf. *Med.* 805, 1386, etc.; it need imply no more than 'May they perish miserably …!', but here the adjective κακοί is felt with ironically full force: 'May these wretched sons of mine perish wretchedly …!' In the Cretan ephebic oath (262–5n.), the ephebes invoke destruction κακίστωι ὀλέθρωι upon themselves, and cf. *Suppl.* 1195.

οὓς μάλιστ' ἐγὼ φιλῶ: Silenos can be less complimentary about the satyrs, cf. Soph. *Ichn.* 145–64.

270 αὐτὸς ἔχ' 'Keep that yourself!', i.e. 'Save that curse for yourself', cf. ἐς κεφαλὴν σοί, Ar. *Peace* 1063, *Pl.* 526.

ἔγωγε is both emphatic ('I personally …') and explanatory (*GP²* 144), cf. 273. It is tempting to think that these verses were spoken in unison by the whole chorus (cf. εἰ μὴ 'μοὶ μόνωι in 187, where see n.), though it is normally assumed that trimeters were delivered by the *koryphaios* alone.

271 περνάντα 'selling', masc. sing. acc. participle of πέρνημι.

272 The satyrs return Silenos' curse like-for-like; the comic surprise is perhaps reinforced by the second-foot anapaest. μὴ ἀδίκει is scanned as three syllables with 'synaloephe', cf. 172, 334, *Hec.* 1249, *Hel.* 832.

τοὺς ξένους δὲ μὴ ἀδίκει seems addressed to the Cyclops, who now re-enters the conversation, rather than to Silenos. The theme of 'wronging ξένοι' is central to the Cyclops-story (cf. *Od.* 9.269–71), and to tell the Cyclops not to do this is comically absurd, in light of what the satyrs know about his dietary habits.

273–4 'You're lying! I trust this man [Silenos] more than Rhadamanthys and consider [him] juster [than Rhadamanthys]'.

ψεύδεσθ' · ἔγωγε: the Cyclops decides against Odysseus and all the satyrs, and sides with Silenos; the verb casts Odysseus' words in 261 back at him, and ἔγωγε mockingly echoes the chorus at 270 (where see n.).

τοῦ Ῥαδαμάνθυος/μᾶλλον stands for μᾶλλον ἢ τῶι Ῥαδαμάνθυι by a common type of compression, and then the genitive of comparison is normal with δικαιότερον. The transmitted τοῦδε τοῦ Ῥαδαμάνθυος, 'this Rhadamanthys here' (i.e. Silenos), could stand as a comic designation, if the unmetrical πολλά in 274 concealed a lacuna or deeper corruption, but δικαιότερον makes the text printed here very probable. The Cretan Rhadamanthys was a son of Zeus and early established as δικαιότατος and as a judge in the Underworld, cf. *Od.* 4.564, Pind. *Ol.* 2.75, *Pyth.* 2.73–4, Pl. *Gorgias* 523e8–4a5, *Laws* 1.624b. At *Od.* 7.322–6 Alcinous recalls the Phaeacians conveying Rhadamanthys to Euboea as a precedent for the voyage home they will offer to Odysseus; in the Cyclops' judgement, however, the two could not be more different.

275–6 Cf. *Od.* 9.252 ὦ ξεῖνοι, τίνες ἐστέ; πόθεν πλεῖθ' ὑγρὰ κέλευθα;

τίς ὑμᾶς ἐξεπαίδευσεν πόλις;; a very unexpected question: the ἀπαίδευτος Cyclops (493) is right up-to-date with ideas about the relationship between individual and community and the role of education, cf. Pind. fr.198a M, Thucyd. 2.41.1 (Athens as a παίδευσις to Greece). Later, however, he will reject all communal values as they apply to himself and preach a radical 'self-sufficiency' (316–41).

277–9 A rewriting of Odysseus' response to the Cyclops at *Od.* 9.259–71. The most striking omissions here from the Homeric response are the boastful reference to Agamemnon's μέγιστον ὑπουράνιον κλέος, the size of the city which they had sacked and Zeus's role in their arrival on the Cyclops' island (he is replaced by 'sea winds'); Odysseus here also makes no immediate appeal to his 'rights' under the protection of Zeus ξένιος. This Odysseus is not just a diminished character by comparison with his Homeric model, but he has also learned from *Od.* 9 not to provoke the Cyclops unnecessarily, cf. Hunter 2009: 62–3.

Ἰθακήσιοι: cf. 103n. In Homer, Odysseus concealed his homeland and referred to himself and his men as Ἀχαιοί (*Od.* 9.259).

πέρσαντες ἄστυ: cf. 178n., *Od.* 1.2, 9.265–6.

ἐξωσθέντες 'driven off course', cf. ἐξέβαλεν in 20, LSJ s.v. ἐξωθέω II.

280–4 The Cyclops' paradoxical familiarity with the Trojan War in a notably Euripidean version (cf. 181–6n., 283–4n., *Andr.* 602–6, *Tr.* 368–73) is part of the humorous mixing of temporal levels, cf. above pp. 19–20, as well as part of the self-conscious play with tragic (and particularly Euripidean) traditions.

280 ἦ ... οἳ μετήλθεθ' ... 'Are you the ones who went to punish ...?' μετήλθεθ' is here constructed with two accusatives, ἁρπαγάς and Ἰλίου πόλιν, cf. *Or.* 423, Aesch. *Ch.* 988–9, LSJ s.v. IV 2. Line 280 momentarily suggests that the sense is simply 'went in pursuit of', but 281 makes the meaning more specific.

κακίστης: cf. *Andr.* 595 πασῶν κακίστην (Helen).

281 suggests that the Cyclops also has a knowledge of the geography of the Troad, presumably derived from the *Iliad*; his knowledge of the Trojan river is perhaps appropriate to a son of Poseidon (cf. esp. *Il.* 12.17–29).

282 οὗτοι 'The very ones', cf. K–G I 645.

πόνον τὸν δεινὸν ἐξηντληκότες: cf. 10n., 107n. By δεινόν Odysseus presumably means 'involving terrible effort', but the adjective gives the Cyclops his opening to reinterpret δεινόν, cf. next n.

283–4 A familiar idea, cf. *Tr.* 780–1 τάλαινα Τροία, μυρίους ἀπώλεσας/μιᾶς γυναικὸς καὶ λέχους στυγνοῦ χάριν, *Hel.* 52–3, 109, Paganelli 1979: 92–5, Wright 2006: 35.

αἰσχρὸν στράτευμά γ', οἵτινες ... 'A shameful expedition indeed, given that you ...'; the apparent anacoluthon is very easy, as στράτευμα implies the same people as are the subject of the οἵτινες clause, cf. K–G I 55. γε here is in third position, despite the fact that it primarily refers to αἰσχρόν, cf. GP² 150. There is perhaps a comic echo of these verses at Eubulus fr. 118.6–8 πικρὰν στρατείαν δ' [γ' Hunter] εἶδον, οἵτινες πόλιν / μίαν λαβόντες κτλ.

Φρυγῶν: cf. 296, 199–200n. This designation for the Trojans is standard in Euripides (Hel. 39, 42, etc.), but still paradoxical in the mouth of the Cyclops.

285–346 Odysseus and the Cyclops now exchange speeches in the manner of a Euripidean *agōn* (cf. 285n.). Odysseus' speech is an amusingly inept attempt to appeal to the Cyclops' 'better nature' and his sense of Greek piety and cultural values; for assessments of the speech as a whole cf. above pp. 20–1, Peigney 2015.

285 is in part a way of saying 'we are not going to have a rhetorical *agōn* (in the manner of *Tr.*) about the blame to be attached to Helen and/or Paris'; Gorgias' *Encomium of Helen* was designed to release Helen from αἰτία (2). That the Trojan War was caused by the gods evokes the premise of the *Cypria* that Zeus brought it about to relieve the over-population of the earth (fr. 1), and cf. *Il.* 3.164–5 (Priam to Helen), *Hel.* 36–41, *Or.* 1639–42, etc. The close of Lachesis' speech in Plato's 'Myth of Er', αἰτία ἑλομένου· θεὸς ἀναίτιος (*Rep.* 10.617e4–5), later became quasi-proverbial, and may already have been so for Plato; it is possible that Odysseus here dismisses the subject of the cause of the Trojan War with a twist on proverbial wisdom.

286 Odysseus' wheedling flattery perhaps picks up the Cyclops' pride in his ancestry which Odysseus heard him express at 231. That Poseidon is the Cyclops' father he will have heard at 262, and (of course) this Odysseus knows his *Odyssey*.

θεοῦ is scanned as a single syllable with synizesis, cf. 231n.

287 'We beseech you and we speak freely [about your plans for us]'; Odysseus introduces his speech by singling out its two principal modes and thus suggesting that he recognises that neither supplication nor argument will suffice. The sentence seems somewhat clumsy (contrast the Homeric model in *Od.* 9.266–7), and Kovacs substituted ψέγομεν for λέγομεν (Kovacs 1994: 149–50), arguing that τε καί implies that the second verb should govern σε as well; ψέγομεν seems, however, far too harsh a verb, and σοι is very easy to read out of σε.

288 μὴ τλῆις, 'Do not bring yourself to ...', implies a very negative view of the action about to be recounted.

σοὺςαφιγμένους: cf. 251–2n. The transmitted σοὺς ἀφιγμένους φίλους seems to throw unnecessary specificity upon the claim and draw attention to the implausibility of φίλους (see next n.). Several editors adopt Heimsoeth's conjecture οἴκους for ἄντρα, which attaches σούς to a noun other than φίλους.

φίλους introduces the argument which is to follow and which will explain the Greeks' (absurd) claims to φιλία; a change to ξένους (Kirchhoff) is unnecessary.

289 βορὰν τε δυσσεβῆ θέσθαι γνάθοις 'and to make [the φίλοι] an unholy meal for your jaws', cf. 30–1.

290–1 'Master, we preserved your father in his possession of the seats of temples at the furthest points of the Greek land'. ἐρρυσάμεσθα, a verb which can elsewhere be followed by an infinitive (*Her.* 197, *Or.* 599), here functions almost as a variation on 'we allowed'. This argument, which finds its alleged justification in the verses which follow, implies that the Trojan War prevented a Trojan invasion of Greece (and Sicily), cf. 295–6; this is an absurd transposition to the Bronze Age of the rhetoric of the memory of the Persian Wars, cf. esp. Aesch. *Pers.* 403–5, ἐλευθεροῦτε ... θεῶν τε πατρώιων ἕδη. The Athenian claim to have defended the whole of Greece against the barbarians by the victory at Marathon is particularly evoked, cf. Thucyd. 6.83 (to a Sicilian audience), Lys. 2.20–6, Pl. *Menex.* 240c–e, Thomas 1989: 221–2.

ὦναξ may simply address the Cyclops as 'master' of the dwelling where they are now, but it is a regular address to a god (cf. 189n.), and so here too Odysseus tries to play to the Cyclops' grandiose self-image.

ναῶν ἕδρας 'seats of temples', i.e. temples in which your father can dwell, cf. *Andr.* 303 τυράννων ... δόμων ἕδρας. The simple ἕδρα is often used of shrines (*Andr.* 135, *Ion* 130, LSJ s.v. I 2), and the present circumlocution is perhaps a sign of Odysseus' embarrassment.

μυχοῖς: the four places which Odysseus proceeds to mention are at the tips of promontories, which are naturally associated with Poseidon, in the southern Peloponnese, Attica and Euboea; it seems best, therefore, to understand μυχοί as 'furthest points', as the μυχός of a house is the 'furthest', deepest part (cf. 407, 480), but we should not push Odysseus' vague language too hard. A further implication is that these promontories would most vulnerable to Trojan invasion because they are the first places at which an army coming from the east would make landfall. Plut. *Mor.* 601a suggests that Sounion and Tainaron could be thought of as bounding Greece to the east and the south, and Paus. 1.1.1 presents Sounion as the first piece of the Greek mainland jutting out into the Aegean. In Nestor's narrative at *Od.* 3.276–92, he and Menelaos first reached 'holy Sounion, the furthest cape (ἄκρον) of Athens', the next landmark named is Malea, and Geraistos had already been mentioned at 3.177; Strabo 10.1.7 notes that in that passage 'Homer makes clear that Geraistos, which is close to Sounion, is conveniently located for those crossing from Asia to Attica'.

292 For Poseidon's important cult at Tainaron (Cape Matapan), the southernmost tip of the central Peloponnese, cf. *PMG* 939, Strabo 8.5.1, Paus. 3.25.4–8, Wide 1893: 33–5, 40–5. It was believed that there was an entrance to the Underworld there, and the worship of Poseidon was associated with a sacred cave. Mythical genealogy created a link between the founders of the cults at Tainaron and Geraistos (295), cf. Steph. Byz. s.v. Tainaros, Schumacher 1993.

ἱερᾶς: cf. Pind. *Pyth.* 4.44 Ταίναρον εἰς ἱεράν (in the context of Euphamos, a son of Poseidon).

ἄθραυστος ... λιμήν: Odysseus must mean 'the shrine with adjacent harbour remains undestroyed', but here again the weakness of his argument is revealed in strained language. The harbour for Tainaron was at Psamathos, just around the promontory to the east.

293 Μαλέας τ' ἄκρας κευθμῶνες 'the hiding-places at Cape Malea'; the notorious reputation of Malea among sailors (18n.) made it natural to associate the promontory with Poseidon, cf. Paus. 3.23.2, 'near the cape of Malea (τὴν ἄκραν τῆς Μαλέας) there is a harbour called Nymphaion and an upright image of Poseidon and a cave very close to the sea'. κευθμῶνες might refer to that cave, but more likely to 'hiding-places', perhaps at Nymphaion, where one could wait for the adverse winds to abate. For Μαλέας ἄκρας, 'the headland of Malea', cf. also Pind. *Pyth.* 4.174 ἀπ' ἄκρας Ταινάρου, Soph. *Tr.* 788 Εὐβοίας τ' ἄκραι, LSJ s.v. ἄκρα 1.

293–4 '... and the rock of Sounion with silver beneath it, which belongs to divine Athena, is safe'. The cult of Poseidon at Attic Sounion, famous today because of the remains of the temple, stretched back for centuries before Euripides, cf. Travlos 1988: 404–29; Athena too was worshipped nearby as Athena Sounias, in a temple built in the second half of the fifth century. Poseidon's temple had in fact been rebuilt after being destroyed by the Persians (as many of Euripides' audience will presumably have known); in 413/12 Sounion had been fortified against the Spartans occupying Decelea.

δίας Ἀθάνας: cf. *Hcld.* 850, *Ph.* 666. Poseidon and Athena had competed over possession of Athens, and Odysseus' reference here is singularly inept if the aim is to persuade a son of Poseidon. Pausanias 1.1.1 mistakenly took the famous temple on Cape Sounion to be Athena's; it seems unlikely that *Cycl.* 293–4 was his source, and there is no reason to think that Odysseus here identifies the temple as hers.

ὑπάργυρος: cf. *Rhes.* 970, Xen. *Poroi* 1.5, 4.2 of Attica. Even if Poseidon's temple was 'safe' at the time of the play, the silver mines at Laurion were certainly not, since the Spartan occupation of Decelea, cf. Thucyd. 6.91.7,

7.27.5, 8.4, Conophagos 1980: 104–8. Odysseus' geography is in fact nostalgic, as well as unconvincing, cf. above p. 158.

295 Γεραίστιοί τε καταφυγαί 'the refuges at Geraistos', the promontory at the southern tip of Euboea, which was a regular stopping-point for ships sailing in either direction across the Aegean (cf. 290–1n. on μυχοῖς). καταφυγαί may be essentially synonymous here with κευθμῶνες, i.e. 'places to escape' from the weather (the harbour is at modern Kastri), but Schumacher 1993: 77–80 argues that the sanctuary to Poseidon of Geraistos was specifically a 'refuge' (ἄσυλον) which offered sanctuary to those fleeing persecution or prosecution, cf. *Suppl.* 267–8, ἔχει γὰρ καταφυγὴν θὴρ μὲν πέτραν,/δοῦλος δὲ βωμοὺς θεῶν. Strabo calls the shrine of Poseidon at Geraistos ἐπισημότατον (10.1.7), cf. *Od.* 3.177–9, Ar. *Knights* 560–1 (Poseidon as lord of Sounion and Geraistos), Wide 1893: 43–4.

295–6 The text is completely uncertain: Hermann's proposal of a lacuna after 295 is attractive, though it is not necessary to assume that the lost text concerned Zeus, cf. 320–1n. With or without a lacuna, the unmetrical and barely comprehensible δύσφρον' ὀνείδη cannot stand. Many assume a parenthetic accusative 'we did not hand over to the Trojans the things of Greece – [which would have been] a terrible disgrace'; hence δύσφορά γ' ὀνείδη of apogr. Par. and Diggle's δύσφορον ὄνειδος. Seaford proposed τά θ' Ἑλλάδος,/δύσφορον ὄνειδος Φρυξίν, ἐξεσώσαμεν (1975: 203–7). δύσφορον is certainly an appropriate adjective, cf. Soph. *OT* 783–4 οἱ δὲ δυσφόρως/τοὔνειδος ἦγον κτλ.

297 ὧν καὶ σὺ κοινοῖ 'You too share in these things' makes more rhetorical sense, inept though it is, than the transmitted κοινοῦ 'Share in these things!' What precisely 'these things' are is partly concealed by corruption in the preceding verses. At Hdt. 7.157.2 the Greeks appeal to Gelon of Syracuse for help against the Persians and claim that 'in ruling Sicily [he] has not the least share of Greece (μοῖρα ... τῆς Ἑλλάδος οὐκ ἐλαχίστη)'.

γῆς γὰρ Ἑλλάδος μυχούς picks up 291 to reinforce Odysseus' point that the Cyclops is 'involved' in what he has been talking about, but what Odysseus actually means by μυχοί here is anything but clear. He may wish to suggest that eastern Sicily is 'the very heartland of Greece' (cf. perhaps the formulaic μυχῶι Ἄργεος ἱπποβότοιο, *Il.* 6.152, *Od.* 3.263), but that is unlikely to convince either the Cyclops or an Athenian audience with painful memories of Sicily; on the other hand, to tell the Cyclops that he lives 'in the far reaches of Greece' (Kovacs) would be less than sensible. No wonder Odysseus changes tack in 299: he has more than exhausted geography.

298 Thucyd. 3.116 reports an eruption in 425, but Euripides may have in mind the famous description of Etna at Pind. *Pyth.* 1.21–4 (cf. Peigney 2015: 108): Typhos is also ὑπ' Αἴτνηι, though even more literally than the Cyclops (cf. 7n.), and in v. 22 Pindar uses μυχοί of the depths of Etna.

ὑπ' Αἴτνηι: Hermann's Αἴτνης may be correct, but the transmitted dative, with resulting apposition, seems unproblematic.

πυριστάκτωι πέτραι is perhaps intended to pick up ὑπάργυρος πέτρα (294), again to reinforce the Cyclops' links with mainland Greece. πυρίστακτος occurs only here in Greek literature.

299–303 Odysseus moves to universally recognised cultural norms, from specific arguments appealing to shared Greekness to appeals to shared humanity; it is not, however, obvious why the Cyclops should be moved by an appeal to the customs of θνητοί. The Homeric model is *Od.* 9.266–71, in which Odysseus appeals to the protecting power of Zeus ξείνιος.

299 εἰ λόγους ἀποστρέφηι 'if you turn away from arguments', cf. *Suppl.* 159 τὸ θεῖον ... ἀπεστράφης;, LSJ s.v. ἀποστρέφω B II 1. There is no reason to assume that the Cyclops has literally turned away while Odysseus has been speaking, though the verb commonly indicates that (*Hel.* 78, Ar. *Peace* 683, etc.). The distinction between νόμος and λόγοι is a mild form of the contemporary νόμος/φύσις distinction, so central to, e.g., the humour of Ar. *Clouds*; the distinction between 'persuasion' and what is allegedly universal and self-evident can of course itself be a trope for persuasion.

300 ἱκέτας δέχεσθαι 'receive as suppliants'.

ποντίους ἐφθαρμένους most naturally suggests 'shipwrecked', cf. *IT* 276, Aesch. *Pers.* 451, though the verb can also more broadly suggest suffering and/or wandering (Denniston on *El.* 234); 301 also suits 'shipwrecked' better than any other sense, and a universal νόμος is more likely to be devised for the shipwrecked than for those 'driven off course' (so LSJ s.v. φθείρω II 4) or those 'physically wasted by their time at sea' (Seaford). Odysseus and his men have not been 'shipwrecked', but his rhetoric takes its own course. The misrepresentation in fact repeats the lie he had told the Cyclops in the Homeric narrative (*Od.* 9.281–6); there Odysseus presented his deceit as a mark of his superior intelligence, but here the rhetorical weakness is evident. Epicharmus wrote a comedy entitled Ὀδυσσεὺς ναυαγός.

301 ξένια at *Od.* 9.267 were a mark of hospitality, but here Odysseus pleads that they are required for survival.

πέπλους: elsewhere ἐπαρκεῖν, 'supply with', always takes the accusative of the thing supplied, cf. LSJ s.v. II.

302–3 '... and not that they [i.e. the shipwrecked], their limbs skewered on ox-piercing spits, should fill your belly and your jaw'. The construction changes after 301 ('anacoluthon'), but it is very easy to follow, and it is hardly surprising that this emotional appeal leads to some syntactic incoherence. Kassel 1991: 204 posited a lacuna to mitigate the anacoluthon. Odysseus here picks up the Cyclops' words at 243–9; although the Cyclops did not mention spits, Odysseus is very familiar with Greek sacrificial and culinary practice, cf. 243–6n., 393.

βουπόροισι ... ὀβελοῖσι: the spits are 'ox-piercing', because it is often beef which is cooked, as modern *souvlaki*, cf. Hdt. 2.135.4, Xen. *Anab.* 7.8.14, Sparkes 1962: 129. The Cyclops would be treating the Greeks like animals (which is precisely his plan).

πηχθέντας: aor. pass. participle of πήγνυμι.

μέλη: acc. of respect.

304 ἅλις picks up 248, as the previous verses picked up 244–5.

ἐχήρωσ' Ἑλλάδα 'emptied Greece of men', 'created widows in Greece', cf. *Il.* 5.642 χήρωσε δ' ἀγυιάς (Heracles laying waste to Troy). The theme is common in Eur., cf. *Andr.* 307–8, 611–13, *Hec.* 322–5, etc., but 304–7 may contain a memory of the herald's prayer to Apollo and Hermes at Aesch. *Ag.* 511–17 (511 ἅλις ... 517 τὸν λελειμμένον δορός). ἐχήρωσ' Ἑλλάδα involves a breach of Porson's Law, cf. Seaford 1982: 162, above pp. 37–8, but one which does not seem to disturb the flow of Odysseus' (slightly absurd) rhetoric.

305 πιοῦσα δοριπετῆ φόνον: lit. 'drinking the spear-fallen slaughter ...', i.e. 'drinking the blood shed by the spear ...' δοριπετής occurs three times in Euripides (cf. *Andr.* 653, *Tr.* 1003) and otherwise only in a Hellenistic list of poetic adjectives (*SH* 991.95); it is intended to sound epic and 'grand'. For φόνος as 'blood, gore' cf. LSJ s.v. I 4. The image here is of Death, or the dead, drinking libations of blood (as in *Od.* 11), cf. *Alc.* 843–5, *Hec.* 535–8, Aesch. *Pers.* 735–6.

306–7 Lit. '... and [Troy] has destroyed wives without husbands and old women and grey-haired old fathers without children'. Odysseus clearly means 'and [Troy] has made wives husbandless and old women and grey-haired old fathers childless', cf. the very similar *Andr.* 612–13, but the use of the emotionally powerful verb ὤλεσεν, properly applicable to the soldiers rather than to their wives and parents, instead of, e.g., ἔκτισε (Kayser), destroys the coherence of the rhetoric. Others understand ἀνάνδρους and ἄπαιδας as indeed proleptic, 'has destroyed them <so that they are> husbandless and childless', cf. *Med.* 436–7 (with the nn. of Page and Mastronarde), but in this context ὤλεσεν can hardly be other than 'killed'. Odysseus here mixes up more than one trope about the pity of war, and although ἄπαιδας applies to both γραῦς and πολιούς ... πατέρας, the rhetorical effect of giving each noun an adjective has added to the confusion of his appeal.

τοὺς λελειμμένους, if taken literally, suggests that Odysseus and his men are the last survivors of the expedition to Troy; the Cyclops knows his Homer well enough to know that that is not true.

308 συμπυρώσας 'burning all together'; the compound reinforces the implication that the Cyclops may make the only Greek men left all disappear.

δαῖτ᾽ ἀναλώσεις πικράν 'you will consume a bitter feast'; the verb also suggests 'waste', 'make no proper use of', given that it is the 'survivors' whom the Cyclops will destroy. A δαὶς πικρά should normally be 'bitter, hateful' for the eater, not – as here – for the eaten.

309 ποῖ τρέψεταί τις; is a colloquial expression of horror at the thought of an act, cf. *Hcld.* 595. Here it is mildly absurd, since if all the remaining survivors are eaten, there will be no τις to turn anywhere.

ἀλλ᾽ ἐμοὶ πιθοῦ: ἀλλά marks 'a transition from arguments for action to a statement of the action required' (*GP*² 14), cf. *Ba.* 309 (Teiresias pleading for the acceptance of Dionysiac cult) ἀλλ᾽ ἐμοί, Πενθεῦ, πιθοῦ, fr. 188.1 (Zethos to Amphion). Rijksbaron 1991: 52–3 notes that in such contexts the aorist imperative is regularly used by a subordinate to a superior.

310 μάργον is already used of the belly in Homer (*Od.* 18.2 of Iros), and cf. the compound γαστριμαργία (Pind. *Ol.* 1.52, Pl. *Phd.* 81e5). Aesch. has μαργῶσης γνάθου of the starving Phineus (fr. 258), and Phrynichus μάργοις … γνάθοις of fire (*TrGF* 3 F 5.4).

311–12 offers a closing *gnōmē*, as is very common at the end of monologues, cf. Ercolani 2000: 143–77. The thought is a commonplace, cf. Hes. *WD* 352, Soph. *Ant.* 326, fr. 807, Alexis fr. 68, Men. *Monostich.* 422 Jaekel κέρδος πονηρὸν ζημίαν ἀεὶ φέρει, and here seems to carry a veiled warning to the Cyclops: retribution will follow.

κέρδη is here not so much 'profit' as the short-term pursuit of one's own desires in opposition to the shared values of a community, cf. Cozzo 1988: 58–71. For ζημία and κέρδος as 'opposites', cf. Arist. *EN* 5.1132a10–19.

ἠμείψατο, 'produce in return', gnomic aorist (Smyth §1931).

313–15 A buffoonish intervention by Silenos takes the place of the brief observations of the chorus-leader which regularly divide pairs of speeches in tragedy. What he has heard has merely confirmed his view of Odysseus, cf. 104.

γάρ, after 'an expression denoting the giving or receiving of information' (*GP*² 59), introduces the details of that information, cf., e.g., Soph. *Phil.* 1325–6.

δέ marks the continuation of Silenos' thought and would be much more regular than the transmitted τε, cf., e.g., *Hel.* 479.

τὴν γλῶσσαν plays with the very widespread belief in many cultures that one can acquire the properties of what one eats. The joke also continues the sacrificial imagery that runs throughout this passage: the tongue of the sacrificed animal had a special place in ritual and was regularly set aside for the god or the priest (the Cyclops is both), and might therefore often be 'left over', cf. Ar. *Peace* 1060 (with Olson's n.), *Birds* 1074–5 (with Dunbar's n.). Ar. *Pl.* 1110 suggests a special link between the tongue and Hermes, the god presiding over communication of all kinds, and this would be appropriate in the present context.

κομψός is commonly used in a derogatory way of a 'clever' speaker, cf. *Suppl.* 426, fr. 188.5 (Zethos urges Amphion to abandon τὰ κομψὰ ... σοφίσματα), Chantraine 1945, LSJ s.v. I 2.

λαλίστατος also occurs at Men. fr. 129.1, Lucian, *Dion.* 7 (a Dionysiac context) and very probably at Soph. *Ichn.* 135 (Silenos about the satyrs); the comparative is found at Ar. *Frogs* 91 and Alexis fr. 96.1. Cf. Mastronarde 2010: 207 n.1, and for the related λαλεῖν cf. 175n.

316–46 For general assessments of the Cyclops' speech cf. Paganelli 1979: 21–60, O'Sullivan 2005, Hunter 2009: 67–77, above pp. 20–1.

316–17 The Cyclops shares a fifth-century habit, fostered by the cultural speculations of Prodicus and the sophists, for the divinising of abstract notions, cf. *Ph.* 506, 531–2, 782–3, *Or.* 213–14, Kannicht on *Hel.* 559–60. The divinisation of wealth here, as that of the belly at 335–8, takes that trope to a comic extreme. Perhaps some twenty years after *Cycl.* (above pp. 38–47), personified Ploutos was the eponymous central figure of Ar. *Wealth*, a δαίμων (vv. 123, 230) whose power was shown to be far greater than Zeus's (vv. 127–201), just as the Cyclops too claims in this speech. Euripides' audience, however, are here given no reason to hear Πλοῦτος rather than πλοῦτος, and the Cyclops offers extravagant praise of wealth/property, rather than recognising a rival 'god' to himself, let alone wasting any time on the temples which Odysseus had made central to his claim. For him πλοῦτος is what promotes the radical self-sufficiency which he claims, cf. Hunter 2009: 74; like κέρδος, with which Odysseus finished his speech (311–12n.), personal πλοῦτος is in such contexts opposed to any sense of shared communal values. Wealth is in fact what allows the unchecked indulgence of the physical appetites on which the Cyclops prides himself (334–8), cf. Pl. *Laws* 8.831d–e, von Reden 1995: 140–1, O'Sullivan 2005: 135–6. For related praise and censure of money and wealth cf. *Ph.* 439–40, fr. 20 μὴ πλοῦτον εἴπηις· οὐχὶ θαυμάζω θεόν,/ὃν χὠ κάκιστος ῥαιδίως ἐκτήσατο, Pind. *Isth.* 2.11, Soph. fr. 88, etc.

ἀνθρωπίσκε: for the dismissive diminutive cf. Ar. *Peace* 751, Pl. *Phdr.* 243a1, and the Cyclops' description of Odysseus as δριμύτατον ἀνθρώπιον in *PMG* 818 (cf. 104n.). For the use of diminutives in satyr-play cf. above p. 35, 185–6n., 266n.

κόμποι 'fine words', 'self-serving rhetoric'. In Alexis fr. 25 a slave declares the stomach to be 'father and mother', whereas holding high office as an ambassador or general is merely κόμποι κενοί; at Ar. *Clouds* 365 Socrates declares that the Clouds are the only gods, τἄλλα δὲ πάντ' ἐστὶ φλύαρος.

λόγων εὐμορφία is essentially synonymous with κόμποι, cf. Thucyd. 2.41.2, the opposition between λόγων ... κόμπος and ἔργων ἀλήθεια. 'Beautiful' words are almost inevitably untrue, cf. fr. 206, Pl. *Apol.* 17b9–10, Dem. 18.149 λόγοι εὐπρόσωποι. The transmitted εὐμορφίαι is not impossible, but the singular seems much more natural; the error was an easy one in a verse full of plurals.

318–19 ἄκρας ... κελεύω 'I care nothing for the sea-girt headlands on which my father is established'; the transmitted ἅς would necessitate 'established' for καθίδρυται (cf. LSJ s.v. 2), but the passive form would be unwelcome and 'establish' is not something one does to headlands.

χαίρειν κελεύω: for such brusque phrases of dismissal cf. 340, 172–4n., *Hipp.* 113, *El.* 400, Collard 2018: 65–6 (~ Stevens 1976: 26).

τάδε, 'these matters', suggests that the Cyclops is thinking of Odysseus' arguments more generally, not just the headlands, though a masculine or feminine noun denoting non-living objects is often picked up by a neuter demonstrative (K–G I 60–1). Cf. the not dissimilar rhetoric of Lykos at *Her.* 151–6.

προυστήσω λόγου 'did you put at the head of your speech', a reference to Odysseus' plea at 290–6, cf. Dem. 18.15, Barrett 2007: 484. The transmitted dative would mean 'did you bring forward in your speech' i.e. 'gave prominence to in your speech', and seems more awkward than the genitive. There is perhaps an amusing suggestion that the Cyclops criticises the ordering of Odysseus' speech with the judgement of a skilled rhetorician.

320–1 have been taken to show that a passage has dropped out from Odysseus' speech in which he referred to Zeus and warned the Cyclops of the consequences of his actions. The Cyclops' retort may, however, be seen as a response to Odysseus' closing verses, and in any case he reacts not just to the speech he has heard, but also to Odysseus' appeal to Zeus in the Homeric model (*Od.* 9.270–1); lines 320–1 rewrite *Od.* 9.275–6, the Cyclops' dismissal of Zeus and the gods in response to Odysseus, cf. Hunter 2009: 62–3. The verses fashion the Cyclops as a boastful θεόμα-χος in the mould of Capaneus (cf. *Ph.* 1180–6, hit by a lightning-bolt, Aesch. *Sept.* 425 his κόμπος), Typhoeus (cf. [Aesch.] *PV* 358–61, 372) or Salmoneus (cf. 328n.). There may be an echo of these verses at Ovid, *Met.* 13.857–8 (Cyclops to Galateia) *quique Iouem et caelum sperno et penetrabile fulmen,/Nerei, te ueneror ...*, cf. above p. 51 n.173. For a comic version of such claims cf. Ar. *Wasps* 619–30.

κεραυνόν: despite 332–8, the Cyclops is here not eliminating Zeus altogether by claiming that the lightning-bolt is no more than a natural phenomenon (cf. Critias, *TrGF* 43 F 19.12–15, Ar. *Clouds* 366–407, with Dover's n. on 404–7 for such fifth-century speculation); rather, he puts himself forward as rivalling, or surpassing, Zeus in power. The inconsistencies of the speech allow him both boastful self-aggrandisement and persuasive arguments.

φρίσσω may convey a sense of religious awe or fear (cf. φρικτός), and that is appropriate here.

οὐδ' οἶδ' ὅτι Ζεύς κτλ.: οὐδ' οἶδ' has an understated, almost ironic tone 'I am not aware …' Several editors prefer ὅ τι 'in what respect', but cf. *Suppl.* 518–19 οὐκ οἶδ' ἐγὼ Κρέοντα δεσπόζοντ' ἐμοῦ/οὐδὲ σθένοντα μεῖζον.

322 οὔ μοι μέλει τὸ λοιπόν: the Cyclops is presumably saying something similar to Prometheus' challenge at [Aesch.] *PV* 938 ἐμοὶ δ' ἔλασσον Ζηνὸς ἢ μηδὲν μέλει, but the exact text and sense are uncertain. 'The future does not concern me' makes excellent sense (cf. also 331n., *Anacreontea* 8.9–10 West τὸ σήμερον μέλει μοι,/τὸ δ' αὔριον τίς οἶδεν;), and may be thought to respond to Odysseus' closing warning, but τὸ λοιπόν is almost always adverbial in Euripides (e.g. 709), and so the words more likely mean 'I have no concern for Zeus in the future' or (cf. LSJ s.v. λοιπός 4) 'I have no concern for Zeus in other respects', with either μέλει impersonal (cf. 331) and τοῦ Διός understood by an easy process after 320–1, or with Ζεύς as the subject of μέλει (cf. *Hipp.* 104); this also suits the fact that Zeus is the unexpressed subject of the ὅταν clause in 323. Cf. further Diggle forthcoming.

323–31 The Cyclops' account of how the weather does not affect him has something in common with Bdelycleon's offer to his father of the chance for jury-service at home, regardless of the weather and with food laid on (Ar. *Wasps* 771–8). Accounts of human progress regularly made protection against the elements and the cold an important step in human progress, cf. *Suppl.* 207–8, Pl. *Prt.* 321a3–6 (animal skins against the cold), Xen. *Mem.* 4.3.7, but the Cyclops sees himself as quite immune from such discomforts.

323 ἐκχέῃ: sc. ὁ Ζεύς.

324–5 Many editors prefer ἔχω … καὶ μόσχον κτλ., but the accumulation of participles suggests the very number of the Cyclops' 'pleasures', and ἤ … ἤ comically evokes the discernment of a connoisseur.

στέγν' … σκηνώματα 'water-tight cover'. Tragedy uses the form στεγανός.

μόσχον ὀπτόν: 'roasted calf' (cf. 389, 121–2n.) would be a rare treat for most of the audience, but the Cyclops has such pleasures ready to hand.

θήρειον δάκος 'a wild beast', the result of the Cyclops' hunting; cf. *Hipp.* 646–7 δάκη/θηρῶν.

326–8 have produced an extraordinary array of emendations and interpretations, usually involving flatulence and/or masturbation; cf. the surveys in Di Marco 2013: 253–63 and Diggle forthcoming. For the corrupt ἐν στέγοντι, a corruption stemming from στέγ' ἔχων in 324, Reiske's εὖ τέγγων τε is very attractive, cf. 574, Alcaeus fr. 347.1 τέγγε πλεύμονας οἴνωι, Petr. *Sat.* 34.7, 73.6 *tangomenas faciamus*; for further possible echoes of

Alcaeus cf. 331n. No other plausible suggestion has been made: ἐκτείνων τε (Faehse) is perhaps the next best, cf. *Od.* 9.298. γαστέρ᾽ ὑπτίαν suggests that he is now lying on his back, cf. *Od.* 9.371 (the Cyclops *after* drinking), Hor. *Sat.* 1.5.85 *uentremque supinum*; this is not the obvious posture in which to drink, even for the Cyclops, but the slight awkwardness is outweighed by the attractions of Reiske's conjecture. Others have tried to introduce a finite verb (ἐμπίπλημι Kovacs 1994: 151, cf. *Od.* 9.296). The evocation of *Od.* 9.371 shows that this Cyclops claims to surpass his Homeric model; Virgil's Cyclops similarly kills and eats Odysseus' men *medio resupinus in antro* (*Aen.* 3.624).

ἐπεκπιὼν γάλακτος ἀμφορέα 'drinking completely (ἐκ) an amphora of milk after/on top of (ἐπί) [my meal]', cf. *Od.* 9.297 ἐπ᾽ ἄκρητον γάλα πίνων.

ἐπεκπίνειν occurs only here (Musgrave conjectured εἶτ᾽ ἐκπιών, cf. 563); ἐκπίνειν occurs five times in *Cycl.* and nowhere else in Euripides. For the language of wine transferred to milk cf. 216n.; the size of amphorae varied considerably, but the Cyclops is probably claiming to drink at least 25 litres of milk, cf. further 388.

πέδον/κρούω is most plausibly explained by Diggle forthcoming: while lying on his back the Cyclops beats the ground, presumably with both hands and feet, to make an earthly thunder to rival that of Zeus. The Cyclops' father Poseidon was standardly associated with the 'thunder' of earthquakes, though in satyr-play it was probably the chorus which regularly thumped upon the earth (cf. Soph. *Ichn.* 217–20). The transmitted πέπλον/κρούω offers no plausible interpretation (despite Catullus 32.10–11 *nam pransus iaceo et satur supinus/pertundo tunicamque palliumque*, cf. above p. 51 n.173); it would also be surprising (despite 301) to find the Cyclops claiming to wear a πέπλος, which, in tragedy at least, normally refers to a woven high-status robe. For the Cyclops' costume cf. above p. 30.

Διὸς βρονταῖσιν εἰς ἔριν κτυπῶν 'crashing in rivalry with the thunderings of Zeus'. The Cyclops here presents himself as a θεόμαχος who seeks to rival Zeus, but his claims specifically evoke the Aeolid Salmoneus, who used a machine to imitate thunder and lightning and was put down by Zeus, cf. Diod. Sic. 6.6.4–7.4 (Salmoneus was ἀσεβής and claimed to surpass Zeus, and he mocked the gods and would not sacrifice to them), Virg. *Aen.* 6.586–94; Hes. fr. 30.23 perhaps (text uncertain) says that Salmoneus was sent to Tartarus so that no other mortal 'might rival Zeus (ἐρίζοι Ζηνὶ ἄνακτι)'. Sophocles wrote a satyr-play about Salmoneus (frr. 537–41a), and Poseidon was said to have slept with Salmoneus' daughter, Tyro, so that this θεόμαχος is already within the orbit of the Cyclops.

329 The north wind is associated with snowy Thrace from the earliest period, cf. *Il.* 9.5, Hes. *WD* 553, Ibycus, *PMG* 286.9; it is perhaps tempting to understand Βορέας, rather than βορέας, as this would be one more divinity who can do no harm to the Cyclops.

330 Cf. the preventative measures at Hes. *WD* 543–53.

331 The anacoluthon (nominative participles and then an impersonal construction with μοι) is of a familiar type, cf. *Hipp.* 22–3 (with Barrett's n.), *IT* 947–8, K–G II 105–6. Burzacchini 1979 suggests a memory here of Alcaeus 338 in which a fire, good wine and a soft pillow are the poet's remedy for Zeus's bitter winter storm; χιόνος οὐδέν μοι μέλει would be a variation for the Alcaean κάββαλλε τὸν χείμων'; Horace *c.* 1.9 reworks the Alcaean poem as a lesson about avoiding unnecessary care about the future (*quid sit futurum cras fuge quaerere*) and enjoying the present; this too is an attitude the Cyclops would share (cf. 322 and *Anacreontea* 8 West).

332–3 represent a 'contemporary' version of the 'Golden Age' description of the Cyclopes at *Od.* 9.107–11. ἀνάγκη, the necessity of nature, of just 'what happens', had an important place in Presocratic science, cf. *Tr.* 886, where ἀνάγκη φύσεος is one 'modern' name for Zeus, Ar. *Clouds* 377 (with Dover's n.), 405, Paganelli 1979: 36. Understood in this way, ἀνάγκη also had an important role in the debates around νόμος and φύσις, cf. Antiphon B 44 A I D–K = fr. 44 (a) Pendrick. Earth itself could be considered a goddess, but here all is simply a matter of natural process, and the divine has nothing to do with the benefits which the earth bestows (contrast, e.g., Xen. *Mem.* 4.3.5); Plutarch in fact cites these verses as an example of how over-reliance on physical explanation can lessen respect for the divine (*Mor.* 435b, cf. above p. 51).

κἂν θέληι κἂν μὴ θέληι: cf. *Suppl.* 499, Aesch. *Sept.* 427–8, both with reference to Capaneus.

τίκτουσα: τίκτειν is not uncommon of such natural processes, cf. fr. 839.5, Aesch. fr. 44.4 (in both of these passages the 'birth' metaphor is still active), Aesch. *Ch.* 127.

334 For the Cyclops eating is making 'sacrifice' to himself and his stomach.

ἀγώ: i.e. ἃ ἐγώ; the antecedent is βοτά.

ἀγὼ οὗτινι θύ- forms the first metron, with 'synaloephe' of -ω ου- (cf. 172, 272, Soph. *OT* 332, *OC* 939, *Ichn.* 9) and a split anapaest in the second foot, cf. 262–5n., above p. 37. Hermann proposed οὔτι, 'in no way at all', which would remove the metrical anomaly.

335 Cf. 316–17n. Odysseus, if anyone, should know about γαστήρ, cf. *Od.* 7.216–18, 17.228, 286–9, 473–4, etc.; a character in Eupolis used the term κοιλιοδαίμων ('with stomach as god') of κόλακες (fr. 187). The Cyclops is, in part, a brutal representative of the views put in Callicles' mouth in Pl. *Gorgias*: 'the person who would live properly should allow his appetites to grow as powerful as possible (ὡς μεγίστας) and should not check them, should serve them when they are at their height through manliness and intelligence, and should satisfy them as they arise' (491e8–2a3), cf. Hunter 2009: 68–9. A slave in Alexis' *Galateia* relates how his master, very probably Polyphemos, was in his youth a student of Aristippos of Cyrene, renowned as a carefree hedonist (fr. 37).

336 τοὐμπιεῖν: i.e. τὸ ἐμπιεῖν, 'enjoying a drink', 'being able to drink', cf. Ar. *Peace* 1143, 1156, Renehan 1976: 20, Arnott 1996: 763–4; this compound is more urbane and suitable here than τοὐκπιεῖν (Heath, Paganelli 1978/9: 201–2). The definite article colours also φαγεῖν and λυπεῖν; the transmitted genitive would have no syntactical construction.

τοὐφ' ἡμέραν, i.e. τὸ ἐφ' ἡμέραν, adverbial, 'each day, on a daily basis', cf. fr. 835.1. The need of and pleasure in having enough to get through each day without trouble is a richly attested piece of popular wisdom, cf. *Alc.* 788–9 (Heracles) πῖνε, τὸν καθ' ἡμέραν/βίον λογίζου σόν, τὰ δ' ἄλλα τῆς τύχης, Aesch. *Pers.* 840–2, Bond on *Her.* 503–5. There is an important overlap with elements of Dionysiac lore presented in *Ba.*, cf. *Ba.* 417–25 (τέρψιν ἄλυπον), 911 τὸ δὲ κατ' ἦμαρ ὅτωι βίοτος/εὐδαίμων, μακαρίζω.

337 τοῖσι σώφροσιν makes the claim particularly paradoxical; a character in Alexis fr. 273 regards drinking, eating and sex as the three pleasures which make life complete, and it is these which ὁ σώφρων should pursue. More commonly, of course, σωφροσύνη could be associated with denial of such pleasure, cf. Ar. *Clouds* 1060–2, 1071–4.

338 λυπεῖν δὲ μηδὲν αὐτόν continues the traditional theme of 336. Antiphon is said to have devised a τέχνη ἀλυπίας, but if there is anything to this report (87 A6 D–K = T 6(a) Pendrick), the τέχνη is likely to have concerned relief from grieving and had little to do with what the Cyclops has in mind here, cf. Pendrick 2002: 241.

338–9 οἱ δέ 'As for those who …' 'Speaking against *nomoi*' is one of the pleasures of the Lesser Argument in Ar. *Clouds*, cf. v. 1040, and in Pl. *Gorgias* Callicles attacks the self-serving motives of those who make *nomoi* to restrict the freedom of the strong (483b–d). In such passages the distinction between νόμος as 'law' and νόμος as 'convention' breaks down; both are covered. Sisyphos offers a different view of the pointlessness of νόμοι at Critias, *TrGF* 43 F 19.5–8, cf. above pp. 20–1.

ποικίλλοντες 'complicating', 'adding fancy bits to …', cf. Pl. *Gorgias* 492c6–8, 'All these other embellishments (καλλωπίσματα, i.e. justice and σωφροσύνη), namely the agreements which men make contrary to nature, are worthless nonsense'. Life should be simple, not ποικίλον; the Homeric Cyclopes had no ἀγοραὶ βουληφόροι and no θέμιστες (*Od.* 9.112), and the Euripidean monster would like to get back to that 'Golden Age'. ποικίλον and related words often carry a negative charge, cf. Collard on *Suppl.* 187.

340 κλαίειν ἄνωγα: cf. 172–4n., 318–19n. Here the high-style ἄνωγα (cf. 701) adds an amusing pomposity to the Cyclops' brusque, colloquial dismissal; ἄνωγα never occurs in comedy.

τὴν ⟨δ'⟩ ἐμὴν ψυχήν: emphatic asyndeton here is possible (K–G II 342), but δέ offers a contrast between 'those who introduce νόμοι' and 'my ψυχή', which here stands on the side of φύσις. 'Bringing pleasure to the ψυχή' is another element of popular wisdom which the Cyclops takes to extremes, cf. Aesch. *Pers.* 841 (with Garvie's n.), Simonides fr. 8.13–14 West, Theocr. 16.24 (with Gow's n.), *GVI* 1368. Arist. *Pol.* 5.1311a4–5 notes that 'pleasure' (τὸ ἡδύ), supported by the accumulation of wealth, is the aim of tyrants, whereas kings aim at τὸ καλόν; for Polyphemos as in part a depiction of the tyrant cf. O'Sullivan 2005, above p. 20. νόμοι (cf. 338) have no place in a tyranny, cf. *Suppl.* 430–1.

341 κατεσθίων γε σέ: cf. 233n.; with shocking surprise, the Cyclops reverts from generalities to Odysseus, who has not been explicitly mentioned since 320.

342 Cf. 550–1, *Od.* 9.369–70.

τοιάδ' looks forward, 'the following …', cf. 196 τόδ'.

ὡς ἄμεμπτος ὦ: never let it be said that the Cyclops failed in his responsibilities as host; he will in fact pay heed to the νόμος to which Odysseus appealed (299–301).

343 The transmitted πατρῷον τόνδε λέβητά γ' offers an anapaest in the fourth foot split after the first short syllable (cf. above p. 37) and a superfluous γε; Jackson 1955: 91–2 cut the knot by assuming that λέβητα was originally a gloss for χαλκόν, which is used by itself in Homer to refer to a cauldron (*Od.* 8.426, 13.19), and that γε, as often, was added to mend the metre. This attractive solution, which we adopt with some hesitation, assumes that the cauldron is currently visible on stage (τόνδε) and is carried into the cave at the end of the scene, probably by the Cyclops himself; there would be a certain comic grimness in Odysseus being shown the 'guest-gift' in which he will be cooked. There would also be the added irony that cauldrons and tripods are indeed offered as guest-gifts in the Homeric poems (cf., e.g., *Od.* 13.13). πατρῷον inevitably suggests Poseidon; the Cyclops is apparently boasting of the value of the gift which he is offering. Others have wanted to introduce a reference to water into the verse (e.g. πατρῷον τόδε λέβητά θ' Hermann), as this too will be part of Odysseus' guest-gifts when he is boiled, and water may be more appropriate to πατρῷον than a cauldron, cf. Kovacs 1994: 154–5.

344 No convincing substitute for the meaningless δυσφόρητον has been suggested. Scaliger's διαφόρητον, 'torn in pieces' (cf. διαφορεῖν at *Ba.* 739, 746, 1210), is not otherwise attested; Seaford suggests δυσφόρητος, 'hard to wear', with a grim joke on Odysseus' apparent request for clothes at 301, reinforced by ἀμφέξει 'will clothe'. Corruption may, however, conceal an adjectival expression, perhaps used predicatively, meaning 'softened/ made tender', cf. 246; ἀμφέξει need not be as specific as 'clothe', but merely 'contain', 'offer space for'.

καλῶς, 'nicely', has a colloquial ring, cf. 631, Collard 2018: 119 (~ Stevens 1976: 55).

345–6 τοῦ κατ' αὔλιον θεοῦ '[the altar] of the god of the stall'; the transmitted dative 'in honour of (?) the god of the stall', is very awkward. The Cyclops makes another joke about his divine standing and about the meal he is to enjoy as a 'sacrifice': the altar he has in mind is simply a blazing cauldron, here taking the place of a real altar, such as that to Zeus ἑρκεῖος inside houses (*Her.* 922, *Od.* 22.334–5, etc.). The verses perhaps evoke tragic scenes in which those who are to be killed are urged to enter the house to share in sacrifice, cf. Aesch. *Ag.* 1035–9 (Clytemestra to Cassandra). Others understand αὔλιον as 'cave', cf. 593, Soph. *Phil.* 19, 954, but the fact that the 'altar' will be inside the cave does not require that meaning for the Cyclops' humour here. There is evidence from eastern Thrace and Phrygia for cults of Zeus ἐναύλιος and ἐξ αὐλῆς, where the epithet seems to refer to 'the stall' (rather than 'the cave') and to be connected to the fertility of flocks (Robert 1955: 33–7); this too does not prove the meaning here, but it would be typical of the Cyclops to play with his position as an alternative 'Zeus'.

ἀμφὶ βωμὸν στάντες may echo the formal language of cult to describe those sharing in sacrifice, cf. *El.* 792.

εὐωχῆτέ με: another grim joke. 'Entertain me splendidly' would normally mean 'offer me (your guest) a splendid meal'; here it is the 'guests' (ξένοι) who will offer the host a meal. A feast (εὐωχία) regularly followed a sacrifice.

347 πόνους ... Τρωϊκούς: cf. 107n.

ὑπεξέδυν 'I escaped from, slipped out from'; construction of such a verb with the accusative is attested (K–G I 300), though the genitive is more common. The verb perhaps varies ὑπέκφυγον at *Od.* 9.286 (Odysseus lying to the Cyclops about his 'escape' from shipwreck), but it does not offer a heroic picture of Odysseus' survival, cf. Hdt. 1.10.2 (Gyges in the bedroom), Men. *Epitr.* 904. Plutarch, *Mor.* 642b uses ὑπεκδιδράσκειν of Odysseus' escape from the Cyclops.

348 θαλασσίους τε evokes *Od.* 1.4; Odysseus' 'troubles at sea' in Homer in fact came about because of what he did to the Cyclops. This is thus another instance where Euripides positions his play both before and after Homer.

349 ὠμήν: the Cyclops has a 'savage' heart, lacking all civilised feeling, cf. Pl. *Laws* 4.718d3, ὠμόν opposed to ἡμερώτερόν τε … καὶ εὐμενέστερον, LSJ s.v. II. Although the Cyclops will cook the Greeks, it is hard not to feel also the sense 'raw': the Homeric Cyclops eats his victims raw, and cf. the Dionysiac ὠμοφαγία. The transmitted γνώμην is very weak in comparison.

κατέσχον 'I have put in at', cf. 223n.

ἀλίμενον 'without a harbour', i.e. 'inhospitable', continues the metaphor of κατέσχον; there is a milder metaphorical use at *Hec.* 1025.

350–5 Such end-of-scene prayers, which also offer a challenge to divinity, are common in Euripides' later plays, cf. 599–607, *Hel.* 1093–1106, *Ph.* 84–7, Dale 1969: 183–4. They have some of the force of a 'cliff-hanger', by focusing attention and expectation on what will happen at the next stage.

350–1 A formal, high-style address. At *Od.* 9.317 Odysseus involves Athena in his plotting, εἴ πως τισαίμην, δοίη δέ μοι εὖχος Ἀθήνη, but she does not otherwise appear in that book, and at 13.318–21 he tells her that she was nowhere to be seen during his ἄλγεα; 'now' is her chance to make up for her Homeric absence.

νῦν νῦν: an emphatic, urgent repetition, cf. *Ph.* 190 μήποτε μήποτε in a prayer to Artemis.

351–2 Odysseus is now facing his toughest hour, just like Silenos (10).

κινδύνου βάθρα, 'the base/foundations of danger', is both striking and hard to understand (Musgrave proposed βάθη). Many assume a reference to the base of an altar, next to which the sacrificial victims would be placed, but the image is perhaps rather of the foundations of a wall or a city (cf. *Her.* 944 Κυκλώπων βάθρα, *Suppl.* 1198), which are the most solid part and the hardest to destroy: this is 'as dangerous as it gets'.

353–5 The appeal to Zeus who dwells in the stars to 'see' what is happening suggests the familiar notion of the stars as Zeus's eyes and as preservers of justice, cf. Plautus, *Rudens* 1–82, Plut. *Mor.* 161e–f, Hunter 2008: 175–81. What Odysseus and his men are about to suffer is so outrageous that a Zeus who does not 'see' it is no Zeus at all. The current verses may, but need not, imply that the stars are now visible, cf. 213, 214n.

φαεννάς offers a higher, more solemn style than the transmitted genitive, cf. *El.* 726, *Ph.* 84.

ἄλλως … θεός 'You are considered a god in vain, Zeus, when you are nothing'; θεός is best taken with νομίζηι, rather than with τὸ μηδὲν ὤν, 'being nothing/worthless', cf. *El.* 370, Barrett on *Hipp.* 638–9. The transmitted Ζεύς could be taken either with νομίζηι, e.g. 'in vain are you considered Zeus, when you are a worthless god', or with what follows, so (Kovacs) 'men mistakenly worship you as a god, when you are in fact Zeus the worthless'. For the thought cf. *Hec.* 488–91, *Her.* 339–47.

356–74 FIRST STASIMON

The Cyclops' deadly meal is covered by a lively song, and presumably much dancing and miming, by the chorus. The song falls broadly into two parts. A strophic pair imagines and foreshadows the dreadful events off-stage which Odysseus is soon to relate; there is particular emphasis upon the Cyclops' brutal munching on human flesh. The dramatic pattern resembles that of *Ba.* 977–1023 where the chorus in lyric song evoke (and wish for) the terrible fate of Pentheus, which will be narrated immediately afterwards by a messenger. In both these plays Euripides seems to be experimenting with the interplay between narrative or epic modes and dramatic song, cf. Laemmle and Scheidegger Laemmle 2012: 150–2.

The strophic pair is separated by a mesode, or non-corresponding stanza (cf., e.g., 49–54, *El.* 125–6, 150–6), in which the chorus expresses its horror at the Cyclops' sacrifice and its wish to have nothing to do with it. Some critics believe that the mesode was repeated after the antistrophe (one verse is certainly missing at the end of the antistrophe), but has been completely lost. This is not impossible, but only the lacuna at the end of the antistrophe suggests it; there is no reason to think that, in the mode of satyr-drama and in the marked speed of this play, the brevity of the song is insufficient for the action which Odysseus will describe in the following scene.

The song is textually and metrically very uncertain; any reconstruction will need to depart significantly from the transmitted text. Despite these difficulties, there are enough clear signs of responsion between 356–60 and 370–4 to make all but certain that those stanzas correspond metrically, as they do significantly in language and ideas. The principal metrical and textual problem of the song concerns the opening (356–7 ~ 370–1) of the strophic pair, and this needs to be considered first. Our discussion is based on Diggle's colometry. Cf. further Cerbo 2015: 78–9, 96–7.

In 356 the transmitted text is

$$- - - \cup - \cup - \cup -$$

εὐρείας φάρυγγος, ὦ Κύκλωψ

which may be read as an iambic trimeter with syncopation in the first two metra, or as *sp lek*; as 357 and 371 seem certainly to be iambic trimeters, this is attractive. Elsewhere, however, φάρυγος is the metrically guaranteed genitive (410, 592), and the same is true in other texts; φάρυγγος standardly replaces φάρυγος in MSS. With Hermann's correction, therefore, we have

‒ ‒‒ ◡◡◡ ‒ ◡ ‒
εὐρείας φάρυγος, ὦ Κύκλωψ

which may be read as *sp cr* (with resolution) *cr* or perhaps as an iambic trimeter with double syncopation in the first two metra. The difficulty of this analysis led Seaford (followed by Kovacs) to suggest λάρυγγος in place of φάρυγγος, but elsewhere the Cyclops' greedy throat is always φάρυγξ (contrast 158 of Silenos). It may be worth noting that deletion of ὦ would produce a glyconic.

As transmitted 370 reads

‒ ‒ ‒ ‒ ◡ ‒ ‒ ‒ ◡ ‒
νηλὴς ὦ τλᾶμον ὅστις δωμάτων

This may be read as *mol lek* or as a spondee followed by an iambic dimeter (an iambic trimeter with double syncopation in the first metron). Deletion of ὦ (Wecklein) would allow analysis as *sp* followed by a catalectic trochaic dimeter. This is close to 356, but not close enough, and we have therefore retained Diggle's obeli. Among attempts to heal the verse are:

(a) Kovacs adopts deletion of ὦ and replaces ὅστις by ὅστε:

‒ ‒ ‒ ◡ ‒ ◡ ‒ ‒
νηλὴς τλᾶμον ὅστε δωμάτων

This gives perfect responsion with the text of 356, but does not solve the problems there.
(b) Seaford offers an analysis of 356–7 ~ 370–1 as syncopated trochaic dimeters.
This has some attractions, but it depends upon retention of φάρυγγος (or λάρυγγος or the replacement of ὅστις by ὅς) and the deletion of ὦ:

εὐρείας λάρυγγος,
ὦ Κύκλωψ, ἀναστόμου τὸ
χεῖλος· ὡς ἕτοιμά σοι

νηλὴς τλᾶμον ὅστις
δωμάτων ἐφεστίους ἱκτ-
ῆρας ἐκθύει ξένους.

(c) Willink 2001: 523–5 seeks to bring the strophic pair closer to the rhythm of the mesode by deleting Κύκλωψ and (with Murray) δωμάτων, and accepting Diggle's ὅς γ᾽ in 370:

εὐρείας φάρυγος, ὦ
νηλὴς ὦ τλᾶμον ὅς γ᾽

The result is *mol cr* in both places, but the first deletion in particular fails to convince. The address to the Cyclops perfectly prepares for σοι which immediately follows.

The other principal difficulty lies in 365, but we assume that the correct text (whatever that was) was an anapaestic dimeter. The pattern of the whole song is therefore as follows:

— —— ∪ ∪ ∪ — ∪ —
εὐρείας φάρυγος, ὦ Κύκλωψ,   ? *sp 2 cretics*   356

∪ — ∪ — ∪ — ∪ — ∪ — ∪ —
ἀναστόμου τὸ χεῖλος· ὡς ἕτοιμά σοι   *ia trim*

— ∪ ∪— ∪ ∪ —∪ ∪ — ∪
ἐφθὰ καὶ ὀπτὰ καὶ ἀνθρακιᾶς ἄπο ⟨θερμὰ⟩   *5 da*

— — — —
χναύειν βρύκειν   *sp sp*

∪∪ ∪ — ∪ — ∪ —
κρεοκοπεῖν μέλη ξένων   *tr dim cat (lekythion)*

∪ ∪ ∪ — ∪∪ — ∪ ∪ —
δασυμάλλωι ἐν αἰγίδι κλινομένωι.   *anap dim*   360

— — — — — —
μή 'μοὶ μὴ προσδίδου·   *ia dim (molossus cretic)*

∪ — ∪ — ∪ —∪ ∪— ∪ —
μόνος μόνωι γέμιζε πορθμίδος σκάφος.   *ia trim*

— ∪ — ∪ — ∪ —∪
χαιρέτω μὲν αὖλις ἅδε,   *tr dim*

— ∪ — ∪—∪ —
χαιρέτω δὲ θυμάτων   *tr dim cat (lekythion)*

∪ ∪ —∪ ∪ <   >
ἀποβώμιος †ἃν ἔχει θυσίαν†   ? *anap dim*   365

— — — —— ∪∪ —
Κύκλωψ Αἰτναῖος ξενικῶν   *wil*

∪ — ∪ —∪ — ∪ —
κρεῶν κεχαρμένος βορᾶι.   *ia dim*

†νηλὴς ὦ τλᾶμον ὅστις δωμάτων† ?   370

∪ — ∪— — ∪ — — ∪— ∪ —
ἐφεστίους ἱκτῆρας ἐκθύει ξένους   *ia trim*   371

— ∪ ∪ —∪ ∪ — ∪ ∪ —∪ ∪ —
ἐφθά τε δαινύμενος μυσαροῖσί τ' ὀδοῦσιν   *5 da*   373

— — — —
κόπτων βρύκων   *sp sp*   372

```
 _   ⌣   _   ⌣   _   ⌣   _
```
θέρμ' ἀπ' ἀνθράκων κρέα   *tr dim cat* (*lekythion*)   374
<   >

356–7 'Throat', 'mouth' and 'lips' are combined in a vision of what is to come: the Cyclops has become 'all mouth'.

εὐρείας φάρυγος: φάρυγξ is here feminine, as more regularly; contrast 215.

ἀναστόμου: the verb is first found here and (presumably earlier) at Callias fr. 24 (Callias happens to have written a comic Κύκλωπες, cf. above p. 5). Wilamowitz proposed the middle ἀναστομοῦ, but the active seems perfectly in order.

358 For the Cyclops' varied methods of cooking cf. 243–6n., 403–4, Cratinus fr. 150 φρύξας χάψήσας κἀπανθρακίσας κὠπτήσας κτλ. (cf. above pp. 5–7 on Cratinus' play).

ὀπτά may refer to the use of spits (cf. 303, 393) rather than placing the meat directly over the coals on a griddle; Posidonius reported that the Celts ate κρέα ... πολλὰ ἐν ὕδατι καὶ ὀπτὰ καὶ ἐπ' ἀνθράκων ἢ ὀβελίσκων (fr. 67 Edelstein and Kidd).

⟨θερμά⟩ is not strictly necessary for sense, but is so for responsion with 373, and is strongly suggested by 245 and, above all, 374.

358–9 The infinitives depend upon ἕτοιμα, 'ready for the munching etc.', but by the time we reach μέλη ξένων we may well think of that phrase as the object, rather than the subject.

χναύειν, 'to munch on', is otherwise restricted to comedy.

βρύκειν 'to bite on, tear with the teeth', cf. 372.

κρεοκοπεῖν looks back to the chopping-knives and meat-distribution of 241–5 (cf. 241–3n.) and forward to the image of the Cyclops as μάγειρος at 397. The verb is found only here and at Aesch. *Pers.* 463 (slaughter of the Persians) παίουσι κρεοκοποῦσι δυστήνων μέλη; despite μέλη, a deliberate echo of Aesch. here (so, e.g., Citti 1994: 131–2) is far from certain.

360 '... as you recline <dressed> in a thick-fleeced goatskin' picks up the Cyclops' own claim at 330 to keep himself warm with animal skins; the grotesque mixture of primitive savagery and refinement ('reclining', cf. 543) suits the atmosphere of absurdity which Euripides creates. Haupt proposed ἐπ' αἰγίδι, so that the Cyclops is reclining 'on' a goatskin, and this sense – despite 386–7 – is still worth considering, with or without Haupt's emendation; it is not the most natural meaning of the transmitted ἐν αἰγίδι (cf. Diggle 1994: 39), but hardly seems impossible for that preposition. On the Lucanian *kratēr* (above pp. 46–7) the drunk Cyclops seems to have a skin under him as he sprawls on the ground. Archilochus fr. 2.2 West πίνω δ' ἐν δορὶ κεκλιμένος is only superficially similar.

δασυμάλλωι is found elsewhere only at *Od.* 9.425 of the Cyclops' sheep, cf. above p. 18 n.55; Euripides has transferred this rare epithet to his goat-skin. Hes. *WD* 516–18 observes that goats are in fact less protected against cold wind than sheep, which have thicker fleeces; goatskin too probably keeps wearers less warm than sheepskin.

κλινομένωι is an all but certain emendation. Diggle 1994: 39–40 tenta-tively suggested κλινόμενος, which would give a syntactical anacoluthon of a familiar kind (cf. 331n.) and would mean that if, as Haupt suggested, 360 was repeated after 374, it would require no textual change at all.

361 προσδίδου 'give me a share', cf. 531n. 'Sharing' is exactly what one would expect at the meal following a sacrifice, cf. 243–6n. At *Ba.* 1184 the horrified chorus refuse to share in Agaue's θοίνα.

362 'By yourself cram the hull of your own boat!'

μόνος μόνωι: juxtaposed forms of μόνος are a common mode of empha-sis, but the two forms usually refer to different persons, cf. Finglass on Soph. *Aj.* 466–8. The satyrs' rejection of the Cyclops is thus very emphatic.

γέμιζε πορθμίδος σκάφος 'load up the hull of your vessel', i.e. fill your stomach, cf. Worman 2008: 144. The Cyclops himself picks up the cho-rus' imagery at 505–6, which also makes γέμιζε, the *uox propria* for loading a ship (cf. LSJ s.v.), a certain emendation here. For nautical imagery in Euripides more generally cf. Breitenbach 1934: 145–50. As 505 makes clear, πορθμίς must refer to a merchant-vessel or 'freighter', rather than to a passenger-boat or ferry, the expected sense of the term (cf. *Hipp.* 753, *IT* 355, *Hel.* 1061); emendation to φορτίδος or ὁλκάδος carries no con-viction. The image depends both upon the use to which merchant-ships were put, as large containers, and the much more rounded hull that was typical of them in comparison to a warship (cf. Casson 1971: 65–8), thus allowing the likeness to 'bellies'; cf. the term γαῦλοι, 'pots', for certain types of eastern merchant-ships. Large drinking-cups could also be com-pared to both merchant-ships and bellies, cf. Pherecrates fr. 152.4–5 and perhaps Cratinus fr. 202 (*Pytine*). Later at least, γαστήρ or γάστρα was a standard term for the hold of a ship below the waterline (and is used in this way in modern Greek), cf. *Rhet.* 3.208.26, 247.5 Spengel, Schol. *Od.* 5.249, Schol. Thucyd. 1.50, Eustath. *Hom.* 1532.61; lines 362 and 505–6 suggest that the term may have been current in classical times. Homer already uses γάστρη for the 'belly' of a tripod (*Il.* 18.348), just as 'cooking pot' is another standard meaning of γάστρα in modern Greek. A specula-tive reconstruction might be that the description of the Cyclops' staff at *Od.* 9.322–3 as like the mast 'of a broad merchant-ship' (φορτίδος εὐρείης) either itself led Euripides to this image or reminded him of *Od.* 5.249–50, where Odysseus constructing the raft is compared to a man crafting 'the

bottom of a broad merchant-ship'; ἔδαφος … φορτίδος εὐρείης was, as the
scholia explain, the γάστρα/γαστήρ of the ship, at least in later times.

363 For μέν … δέ linking balanced verbs in anaphora cf. *Rhes.* 906–7,
Aesch. *Pers.* 694–5, Diggle 1981: 55–6.

αὖλις 'lodging, stall', a suitably dismissive way to refer to where the satyrs
are now forced to live. The term picks up the Cyclops' reference at 345
(τοῦ κατ' αὔλιον θεοῦ), just as the following verse picks up 346.

364–5 No textual restoration can be more than plausible. θυμάτων …
θυσίαν might raise the suspicion that θυσίαν is a gloss, but the grammatical
tradition explains ἀποβώμιος (found only here) as a reference to sacrifices
not conducted at an altar and thus, by extension, unholy (cf. Ar. Byz. fr.
48C Slater, Hesych. α 6269), and this suggests that θυσίαν is not lightly
to be removed. Rhythmically, the transmission is only one syllable short
of an anapaestic dimeter, which can easily be restored by emending ἔχει
to, e.g., ἀνέχει (Spengel), though 'uphold, preserve' (cf. Ar. *Thesm.* 948)
is not quite right here, or ἀνάγει (Jackson), which is the standard verb in
Hdt. for 'conducting' a sacrifice, cf. LSJ s.v. I 5. If this is on the right lines,
then ἀποβώμιος … θυσίαν may be the subject of χαιρέτω δέ, with the noun
attracted into the accusative from its place in a dependent relative clause
(cf. perhaps Soph. *El.* 160–3), but Hartung proposed θυσία. The sense of
the whole would then be 'and farewell to the unholy sacrificing of victims
which the Cyclops … conducts'.

366 ξενικῶν refers primarily to '[the meat] of strangers', but it is tempting to hear also 'strange, exotic [meat]', which would suit this connoisseur of a Cyclops. ξενικόν is used of 'foreign' wine at Alexis frr. 232.5,
292.1, Diphilus fr. 31.27.

367 βορᾶι: cf. 88n.

370 On the metrical problems of this verse cf. above p. 174.

νηλής, 'pitiless', is a repeated epithet for the Cyclops in *Od.*, cf. 9.272,
287, 368.

ὦ τλᾶμον: as transmitted, this must be addressed to the Cyclops, with
τλήμων in its rarer negative sense 'outrageous', cf. 288 μὴ τλῆις κτλ., *Hec.*
775 (Agamemnon's reaction to learning what Polymestor has done) ὦ
τλῆμον, LSJ s.v. τλήμων I 2.

371 ἐφεστίους ἱκτῆρας … ξένους 'suppliant strangers at the hearth',
which was a special place of protection for suppliants, cf. Gould 1973:
97–8, Hunter on Ap. Rhod. *Arg.* 4.693–4. ξένους cannot be counted a
certain emendation, but either δωμάτων or δόμων has to go and δόμων
may easily have arisen from a gloss or paraphrase, particularly after ξενι-
κούς had entered the text; ξένους increases the outrageousness of what the
Cyclops does, and the theme is insistent throughout the play, cf. 89, 91,
126, 301, 342, 610, 658.

373 μυσαροῖσι: Eur. is fond of this adjective, 'abominable', which suggests religious defilement (cf. μύσος); it is often used of abhorrent bloodshed, cf., e.g., *Med.* 1393, *IT* 1224, *Or.* 1624.

372 κόπτων picks up κρεοκοπεῖν (359) and suits ὀδοῦσιν better than would χναύων. Haupt's suggestion (cf. 360n.) that 360, with κλινόμενος, was repeated after 372 has been adopted by many recent critics.

375–482 SECOND EPISODE

Odysseus re-emerges from the cave (there is no boulder blocking the entrance, cf. above pp. 13–14). He reports to the chorus on the death of two of his comrades, and explains his plan for revenge and escape by making the Cyclops drunk. Odysseus' role in this scene contains elements both of a tragic messenger (cf. 375–6, 377–8, 379–80, 382, 407–8 nn.) and of the cunning plotter most familiar from the slaves of New Comedy, particularly Plautus. It is striking that Odysseus' narration of what has happened off-stage out of our sight is as close to the Homeric model as anything in the play; when the play, however, allows us to see events, we realise that the Homeric version was indeed very much Odysseus' version, cf. above pp. 9–10.

375–6 play with the familiarity and status of the Cyclops story, cf. Laemmle 2013: 336–7, above pp. 9–10. The Homeric story has indeed become a μῦθος βροτῶν, 'a story which men tell'; the opposition between μῦθος and ἔργον involves a developing sense of what we call 'fictionality'. For 'metamythology' more generally in Euripides cf. Wright 2005: 133–57. Just as the messenger of *Ba.* comes to report of the women of Thebes ὡς δεινὰ δρῶσι θαυμάτων τε κρείσσονα (*Ba.* 667), using language evocative of Dionysiac cult, so here 376 evokes what was to become a standard rhetorical and critical classification of poetic 'myth' as opposed to 'truth'. By οὐ πιστά Odysseus means '<real, but so terrible that they are> beyond belief', but the audience will understand that the events are 'beyond belief' in another sense. For a very similar allusive technique in a different genre cf. Clitophon's declaration at Ach. Tat. 1.2.2 σμῆνος ἀνεγείρεις ... λόγων· τὰ γὰρ ἐμὰ μύθοις ἔοικε. Messengers often have 'incredible' events to relate, and Odysseus is here already 'playing the messenger', cf. the chorus' reaction to the reunion of Orestes and Iphigeneia at *IT* 900–1, 'I myself have seen these things which are wondrous and surpass myth (ἐν τοῖσι θαυμαστοῖσι καὶ μύθων πέρα) and I did not hear them from messengers'. There is little sign that satyr-play used 'messenger-speeches' by minor characters in the manner familiar from tragedy, cf. Griffith 2015: 25, 48.

ὦ Ζεῦ: Odysseus' last words before he entered the cave (354–5) were a challenge to Zeus's wisdom and divinity; the exclamation now suggests that Zeus has not met that challenge.

κοὐ πιστά … βροτῶν 'and not to be believed, like myths, not <like> deeds of mortals'; the asyndeton is expressive of Odysseus' shock (Dawe proposed μύθοις <δ' >). οὐδέ here 'holds apart incompatibles' (*GP*² 191).

377–8 μῶν … Κύκλωψ 'The most unholy Cyclops hasn't feasted on your "dear comrades", has he?'

μῶν indicates feigned surprise, cf. 36–8n., 158, K–G II 525; the satyrs know exactly what will have happened in the cave (cf. the previous ode), but – more importantly – they too, like the audience, know the Homeric script. The effect is something like 'You're not going to tell us that …?' Odysseus 'plays the messenger', but the gist of what he will say is already very well known.

τεθοίναται: the Cyclops' wish of 248 has come true.

φίλους ἑταίρους picks up a Homeric phrase which occurs repeatedly in the *apologoi* of *Od.* 9–12 (and only there) and always in the context of the loss of Odysseus' companions, cf. *Od.* 9.63, 566, 10.134, 12.309. The satyrs continue to exploit their knowledge of Homer.

379–80 Like a good messenger, Odysseus briefly summarises the news he brings before yielding to a request (381) to tell the story in detail. In Homer, the Cyclops' first meal was also of two men (*Od.* 9.289, rewritten in *Cycl.* 397–8), but they were apparently chosen at random; the Euripidean Cyclops is too much of a gourmet to leave such things to chance.

γ' 'Yes, he did …'

ἀθρήσας 'inspecting'. The verb is found elsewhere of 'inspecting' the entrails of sacrificial animals (*El.* 826–7, 839), and it is tempting to sense that resonance here; in *IG* XII 1,694 (fourth-century Rhodes) ἀθρεῖν τὰ ἱερά is used in a description of sacred activity. For γ' ἀθρήσας Pierson suggested σταθμήσας, 'measuring, checking the weight of'.

κἀπιβαστάσας χεροῖν 'and by hands-on examination', cf. *Od.* 21.405 (Odysseus checks the bow), Soph. *Phil.* 657, Fraenkel on Aesch. *Ag.* 35; the compound with ἐπι- occurs only here. At Ar. *Ach.* 766 the Megarian invites Dikaiopolis to test his 'pigs', ὡς παχεῖα καὶ καλά.

εὐτραφέστατον: εὐτραφ- and εὐτρεφ- are standardly confused in MSS; both are possible here, but the MSS of Euripides regularly present the -τραφ- form (cf. *IT* 304), and εὐτραφέστατον perhaps carries a more expert resonance (cf. LSJ s.v.), thus reinforcing the idea of the Cyclops as a connoisseur. At *Od.* 9.425 Odysseus calls the Cyclops' rams εὐτρεφέες.

πάχος occurs only here in Euripides and never in Aeschylus (who has παχύνειν, *Suppl.* 618, *Sept.* 770) or Sophocles; παχύς is also entirely absent from tragedy. The only Homeric occurrence of πάχος is *Od.* 9.324 (the Cyclops' staff), cf. above p.18 n.55.

381 'How, wretched man, did you (plural) come to suffer these things?' ἦτε πάσχοντες is a periphrastic form for ἐπάσχετε, cf. 23, 636, *Hec.* 1179, Aesch. *Ag.* 1179, Smyth §1961, K–G I 38–9.

382 ἐπεί is the first word of very many Euripidean messenger-speeches, cf., e.g., *El.* 774, *IT* 260, 1327, *Ba.* 1043.

†χθόνα†: Musgrave's στέγην is often printed (cf. 29n.), but there are other possibilities. The corruption perhaps arose from the familiarity of forms of χθών at verse-end, as in *Ba.* 1043 (the opening verse of the messenger-speech).

383–4 Cf. *Od.* 9.233–5, 308. Dramatic staging allows the audience to feel a mismatch between Odysseus' reports of the deeds of what must be a giant of superhuman strength and the Cyclops they have actually seen on stage; the effect is humorously to cast doubt at least upon the rhetorical elaboration of Odysseus' narratives both here and in *Od.* 9, cf. Laemmle 2013: 336, above pp. 9–10. On the other hand, the familiarity of the Homeric version smooths over any inconsistency between the Cyclops' preparations in 383–9 and the fact that milk and fire should both be ready for him (216–19, 241–3), cf. 241–3n.

ἀνέκαυσε: cf. 241–3n.

μέν will be answered by ἔπειτα (386), cf. 3–5, *GP*² 376–7.

ὑψηλῆς ... βαλὼν ἔπι 'throwing logs from a tall oak on to the broad hearth'; the adjectives create a grand 'epic' style, appropriate to the Cyclops. For the availability of oaks to the Cyclops cf. *Od.* 9.186. δρῦς may be used more generally for any tree (cf. 615, LSJ s.v. II, Bond on *Her.* 241), but Odysseus' speech is full of lively and specific detail.

385 '... roughly a portable weight for three wagons', in apposition to κορμούς. At *Od.* 9.241–2 Odysseus says that 'twenty-two strong, four-wheeled wagons' could not have lifted the Cyclops' door-stone, whereas the amount of firewood which the monster brings is simply ὄβριμον ἄχθος (9.233), of which ἀγώγιμον βάρος may be a kind of verbal echo. The Homeric Odysseus also uses ὄβριμον of the door-stone (9.241), and here Euripides picks up that link between firewood and door-stone by transferring the wagon-comparison to the Cyclops' firewood (there is no longer a door-stone). Such allusive rewriting of a model was to become very common in Hellenistic and Roman poetry.

ἁμαξῶν: cf. 473; the noun does not appear in tragedy (except for the very doubtful Aesch. fr. 214), though Euripides has ἁμαξήρης (*Or.* 1251), ἁμαξιτός (*El.* 775), and ἁμαξοπληθής (*Ph.* 1158).

ὡς, 'about, approximately', is common in prose with numerals (LSJ s.v. E), but the usage seems confined in poetry to *Cycl.* (cf. 388), except perhaps for Stesichorus fr. 22.1 Finglass.

ἀγώγιμον is never found in tragedy.

392 Where this verse is transmitted, ἐπέζεσεν would also govern ὀβελούς (393), which is impossible, unless another verb or a lacuna is concealed in the corrupt 395. The verse is plausibly placed either here or after 394 or 395; the homoioteleuton with 393 (πυρί) may have originally caused the displacement. It makes sense for the Cyclops to 'put the cauldron on' early in his preparations, as the water will take some time to boil, cf. *El.* 801–2.

ἐπέζεσεν 'set to boil', a very rare transitive use (cf. Parker on *IT* 987); ἀναζεῖν is transitive at Hippocr. *Acut.* 21, but transitive ζεῖν does not occur before Hellenistic poetry (Campbell on Ap. Rhod. *Arg.* 3.273). Lobeck proposed ἐπέστησεν.

386–7 The Cyclops' couch of leaves suggests a peaceful idyll, quite in contrast to the violence we are about to witness, cf. Pl. *Rep.* 2.372b4–5, Theocr. 13.32–5, Ap. Rhod. *Arg.* 1.453–5; he will drink (milk) by the fire, as others took pleasure in drinking wine, cf. Alcaeus fr. 338, Xenophanes fr. 22 D–K (= D54 Laks–Most), Ar. *Ach.* 751–2.

ἐλατίνων: the silver-fir (cf. Theophr. *HP* 3.9.6–8) perhaps takes the place of the pines of *Od.* 9.186.

χαμαιπετῆ 'on the ground', cf. *Tr.* 507 στιβάδα ... χαμαιπετῆ (for a slave).

388 κρατῆρα: cf. 216n.

ὡς 'about', cf. 385n.

δεκάμφορον: cf. 326–8n. Another 'satyric' monster, Lityerses, is described as drinking a δεκάμφορος πίθος of wine (Sositheos, *TrGF* 99 F 2.8).

389 μόσχους cf. 325, *Ba.* 736.

λευκὸν ... γάλα: cf. Arist. *Rhet.* 3.1406a12–13 'In poetry it is appropriate to call milk white, in prose it is less so'; for an example cf. Empedocles fr. 33 D–K (= D72 Laks–Most). Odysseus tells his story in a relatively ornate style, in which nouns are given adjectives, even when they are hardly 'necessary'.

ἐσχέας: this compound is very rare, and ἐγχέας (cf. 556, 568) may be correct.

390–1 σκύφος ... κισσοῦ: cf. 256n. At *Alc.* 756 Heracles drinks ποτῆρα ... κίσσινον λαβών (cf. Parker ad loc.). Whatever the real etymology of the κισσύβιον in which Odysseus served wine to the Cyclops (*Od.* 9.346, cf. Timotheus, *PMG* 780.1), by Euripides' time the explanation 'a bowl made of ivy-wood' was certainly current, cf. fr. 146 (rustics bring along γάλακτος κίσσινον ... σκύφος), Dale 1969: 98–102, Halperin 1983: 167–74, Hunter on Theocr. 1.27. Cf. further 620n.

εἰς εὖρος ... ἐφαίνετο 'measuring three cubits with regard to breadth, and it seemed <to be> four cubits in depth'. There is no real difference between understanding βάθος as an accusative of respect or as <εἰς> βάθος; for the genitives of measure cf. Smyth §1325. Odysseus' amusing concern for estimating sizes (cf. 385) suggests the implausibility of the whole narrative (cf. 375–6n.), but also varies his Homeric counterpart's description of the Cyclops' staff, which was like 'the mast of a twenty-oared ship, a broad (εὐρείης) merchantman' (*Od.* 9.322); the Homeric Odysseus deals in μῆχος and πάχος (9.324), rather than εὖρος and βάθος, but there too we have an estimate of size to the naked eye. πήχεων varies the Homeric ὄργυιαν, as παρέθετ' picks up παρέθηχ' (*Od.* 9.326); in *Od.* 9.346 there is no indication of the size of the cup, but the Euripidean Odysseus exaggerates the 'gigantic' narrative. There is no reason to think that Euripides is here parodying the Homeric 'cup of Nestor' (*Il.* 11.632–7), as OSC suggest, but Epicharmus fr. 70 from the *Cyclops*, ναὶ τὸν Ποτειδᾶν, κοιλότερος ὅλμοῦ πολύ, may also describe the Cyclops' oversize drinking-cup.

393–4 '... and <he set out> spits, made of branches of thorn-tree, burned at their tips in the fire, and the rest smoothed off with a scythe'. For the transposition of 392 cf. 392n. (after 385n.). Just as Odysseus' description of the Cyclops' bowl reworked the Homeric description of his staff (390–1n.), so these spits (presciently foreshadowed by Odysseus at 302–3) recall the immediately following Homeric verses, in which Odysseus orders his men to smooth the staff while he sharpens the tip and hardens it in the fire (*Od.* 9.326–8). Those Homeric verses are more directly recalled at 456–7.

ἄκρους μὲν ... τἄλλα: a mannered chiasmus in keeping with the pretensions of the narrative, cf. 389n.

ἐγκεκαυμένους: this compound appears nowhere else in classical poetry; it is largely confined to Hellenistic prose.

δρεπάνωι is more probably a 'scythe' (cf. *Od.* 18.368) than a 'pruning-hook', as befitting the monstrous size of everything connected with the Cyclops.

παλιούρου 'of Christ's thorn', 'an extremely spiny shrub with zig-zag branches' (Polunin and Huxley 1965: 122), and therefore certainly in need of planing; Theophrastus calls it πολύκλαδος and ἀκανθώδης (*HP* 1.3.1, 1.5.3), and cf. Virg. *Ecl.* 5.39 *spinis surgit paliurus acutis*.

κλάδων 'made of branches ...', although κλάδους, in apposition to ὀβελούς, is attractive, if palaeographically more difficult.

395 is corrupt beyond convincing restoration and may also conceal a lacuna; Diggle prefers to delete the verse entirely. As transmitted, 'Aitnaian sacrificial bowls' would be another object with παρέθετ' (390), but 'for the jaws of axes' makes no obvious sense. Seaford suggests that Αἰτναῖα σφαγεῖα is a 'grim periphrasis' for the cauldron, but a further reference to the cauldron (cf. 392) is unnecessary.

Αἰτναῖα: if sound, this presumably means both 'of Etna' (near where the play is set) and 'monstrously large', cf. Ar. *Peace* 73 Αἰτναῖον μέγιστον κάνθαρον, a reference to the belief that Mount Etna was home to huge beetles, cf. Olson's note ad loc., Epicharmus fr. 65, Laemmle 2013: 418–22.

σφαγεῖα are bowls for catching the blood of sacrificial victims, cf. *El.* 800, *IT* 335.

396 θεοστυγεῖ 'hated by the gods', cf. 602, *Tr.* 1213 (Hecuba about Helen), *Or.* 19–20 τὴν θεοῖς στυγουμένην ... Ἑλένην; θεοῖς ἐχθρός is the more common expression, cf. Soph. *OT* 1345–6, Ar. *Clouds* 581, Biles and Olson on Ar. *Wasps* 418, Orth 2009: 262–3.

397 Ἅιδου μαγείρωι 'cook from hell', cf. 241–3n., *TrGF* 9 F 3, Ἅιδου τρα-πεζεύς. Ἅιδου is commonly added to nouns in this derogatory manner, cf. *Hec.* 1076, *Her.* 562, 1119, Fraenkel on Aesch. *Ag.* 1235. μάγειρος occurs nowhere in tragedy (except for the very doubtful Soph. fr. 1122).

397–402 rewrite *Od.* 9.288–90, ἀλλ' ὅ γ' ἀναΐξας ἑτάροισ' ἐπὶ χεῖρας ἴαλλε,/ σὺν δὲ δύω μάρψας ὥς τε σκύλακας ποτὶ γαίηι/κόπτ'· ἐκ δ' ἐγκέφαλος χαμάδις ῥέε, δεῦε δὲ γαῖαν, cf. Virg. *Aen.* 3.623–6 *uidi egomet duo de numero cum corpora nostro/prensa manu magna medio resupinus in antro/ frangeret ad saxum, sanieque aspersa natarent/limina.* συμμάρπτειν appears in *Od.* only in this passage and the repetition at 9.311 and 344, and in drama only here.

The text of this passage remains very uncertain; it seems to describe one of Odysseus' comrades sacrificed either by being thrown into the boiling cauldron or by having his throat cut so that the blood runs into the cauldron, whereas the brains of a second comrade are smashed out against a rock. We have tentatively adopted Diggle's lacuna after 399, in which the action of throwing the first comrade into the cauldron will have been made clear; the imperfect ἔσφαζ' will mean 'set about the sacrifice/began to slaughter'. Seaford proposed transposing 398 and 399, but this would seem to require the aorist ἔσφαξ' and leaves ἑταίρων τῶν ἐμῶν awkwardly misplaced. There can be no confidence that the correct solution has been identified.

398 †ῥυθμῶι τινι†: both text and meaning are uncertain. 'With a certain rhythm' might perhaps refer to the practised skill (admired even by Odysseus) with which the Cyclops sacrifices one of the Greeks; there would then be a pointed contrast between this act of a skilful μάγειρος and the 'primitive' brutality with which the second Greek is killed, and that contrast would reflect one of the central paradoxes of Euripides' portrayal of the monster. Cf. Theocr. 26.23 Αὐτονόας ῥυθμὸς ωὗτός in the dismemberment of Pentheus. On this reading, ῥυθμός comes near in sense to εὐρυθμία (cf. 563, Ar. *Wasps* 1210 εὐσχημόνως); Plut. *Mor.* 67e–f notes that when a doctor is cutting into flesh his work should be marked by εὐρυθμία τις and καθαρειότης (cf. also Hippocr. *Decorum* 8). Nevertheless, ῥυθμῶι τινι is difficult to construe (cf. Diggle 1994: 40–2) and Wilamowitz's ῥυθμῶι θ' ἑνί, 'with a single movement', is very attractive, cf. Aesch. *Pers.* 462, 975. For a survey of interpretations of the phrase cf. Laemmle 2013: 289.

399 λέβητος ἐς κύτος χαλκήλατον 'into the bronze-hammered hollow of the cauldron', a grandiose circumlocution for a cooking utensil, cf. *Ba.* 799, Soph. fr. 378, Ar. *Frogs* 929 (parody of Aeschylus).

400 τένοντος ἁρπάσας ἄκρου ποδός 'snatching [him] by the tendon at the end of the foot', i.e. the heel. The genitive is regular for the part of the body by which someone is seized, cf. *Il.* 1.591, Soph. *Tr.* 779 (μάρψας ποδός νιν, Heracles killing Lichas), Smyth §1346.

401 στόνυχα, 'sharp point', cf. Hesych. σ1927. The noun appears only here before Hellenistic poetry; Ap. Rhod. *Arg.* 4.1679 uses it of a jagged rock, and Lyc. *Alex.* of a boar's tusk (486), a spear-point (795) and a tapering promontory (1181).

πετραίου λίθου: cf. fr. 176.3 πετραῖον σκόπελον. The 'redundant' adjective perhaps intensifies the Cyclops' brutality, as does the emotional elaboration on the simple ποτὶ γαίηι of *Od.* 9.289.

402 ἐγκέφαλον ἐξέρρανε: ἐκραίνειν is certainly found elsewhere only at Soph. *Tr.* 781 κόμης δὲ λευκὸν μυελὸν ἐκραίνει (Heracles' very similar killing of Lichas, which some commentators think is echoed by Euripides here, cf. Garner 1990: 155).

†καθαρπάσας† presumably conceals a verb meaning 'cutting, slicing, chopping', cf. *Od.* 9.291 τοὺς δὲ διὰ μελεϊστὶ ταμὼν ὁπλίσσατο δόρπον, Hdt. 1.119.3 (Astyages) σφάξας αὐτὸν καὶ κατὰ μέλεα διελὼν τὰ μὲν ὤπτησε, τὰ δὲ ἥψησε τῶν κρεῶν; Paley suggested διαρπάσας or διαρταμῶν. Other attempted remedies keep καθαρπάσας, perhaps 'grabbing hold of', and change μαχαίραι to the accusative, with λάβρωι referring to the fire (Meurig Davies 1949) or changed also to λάβρον (Ussher); word-order seems decisively against the first.

403–4 The Cyclops now carries out his earlier threat, cf. 243–6n.

λάβρωι 'cruel, pitiless'.

ἕψεσθαι 'to be boiled'; for such epexegetic infinitives cf. 257n.

405 For Odysseus' tears cf. *Od.* 9.294.

ἐγὼ δ' ὁ τλήμων might sound almost comically self-regarding, when we consider the fate of his two comrades, but having to help the Cyclops (as Silenos had done, 30–1) meant that Odysseus really was 'wretched', 'miserable', not that his fate was worse than those who were eaten. At *Od.* 9.345–6 Odysseus tells the Phaeacians that he 'stood near to' the Cyclops to offer him the marvellous wine, and the scholia comment on Odysseus' bravery in getting close to the monster who had eaten his comrades. Odysseus' telling here allows the Homeric ἄγχι παραστάς to suggest the behaviour of a servile wine-pourer; Silenos is soon to be the Cyclops' Ganymede (582–9).

407–8 A brief simile imitates a feature of messenger-speeches, in which such comparisons, often drawn from the animal world, are common, cf. *Andr.* 1140–1, *IT* 297, *Ba.* 748–9, de Jong 1991: 87–94; for the present simile cf. *Her.* 974 (the killing of the children) ἄλλος δὲ βωμὸν ὄρνις ὣς ἔπτηξ᾽ ὕπο, Finglass on Soph. *Aj.* 171. Odysseus' comparison certainly does not cast his comrades in a good light. Cratinus fr. 148 οἱ δ᾽ ἀλυσκάζου-σιν ὑπὸ ταῖς κλινίσιν perhaps derives from a similar account in the *Odysseis*, cf. above p. 6.

ἐν μυχοῖς πέτρας varies *Od.* 9.236 ἐς μυχὸν ἄντρου, cf. 195–7n.

πτήξαντες εἶχον 'stayed cowering'; the periphrasis 'emphasises the permanence of the result' (Smyth §1963), cf. *Med.* 33, *Hipp.* 932, Bentein 2016: 118–25.

αἷμα δ᾽ οὐκ ἐνῆν χροΐ: paleness, here understood to reflect a lack of blood, is a marker of fear from Homer onwards, cf. *Suppl.* 599, Aesch. *Suppl.* 566, LSJ s.v. χλωρός II 2. The almost identical half-verse at *Med.* 1175 refers not to fear but to the effect of Medea's poison.

409 Cf. *Od.* 9.296–7.
βορᾶς: cf. 88n.

410 begins with two tribrachs, cf. 436; the transmitted later form φάρυγ-γος would produce a 'split anapaest' in the second foot, which is very unlikely in the style of Odysseus' speech, cf. 262–5, 334nn.

φάρυγος αἰθέρ᾽ ἐξανεὶς βαρύν 'sending up from his throat a blast of air from the deep', i.e. he belched vigorously. αἰθήρ is virtually unparalleled in this sense. The principal Homeric model is *Od.* 9.371–4 (the Cyclops drunk) ἦ, καὶ ἀνακλινθεὶς πέσεν ὕπτιος, αὐτὰρ ἔπειτα/κεῖτ᾽ ἀποδοχμώσας παχὺν αὐχένα, κὰδ δέ μιν ὕπνος/ᾕρει πανδαμάτωρ· φάρυγος δ᾽ ἐξέσσυτο οἶνος/ψωμοί τ᾽ ἀνδρόμεοι· ὁ δ᾽ ἐρεύγετο οἰνοβαρείων.

ἐξανεὶς: a 'coincident' aorist participle, cf. 152n. ἐξανίημι, the compound found (though in the present participle) in Athenaeus' citation of this verse, is appropriate for this action; contrast *Ba.* 1122 (the crazed Agaue) ἀφρὸν ἐξιεῖσα. Athenaeus' ἐξανιείς (present participle) would create a fifth-foot anapaest in Odysseus' verse (cf. above p. 36).

411 In Homer the idea of making the Cyclops drunk is the result of Odysseus' plotting and μῆτις (*Od.* 9.316–18), as the bringing of the wine to the cave was the result of his forethought (9.213–14). These themes are played down in *Cycl.* (cf. 88n., above p. 14), but the idea of 'divine inspiration' is found in the Homeric Cyclops' decision to bring all the sheep into the cave at night, ἤ τι ὀϊσάμενος ἢ καὶ θεὸς ὣς ἐκέλευεν (9.339); that is immediately before Odysseus offers him wine, and this motivation has here been transferred from the Cyclops to Odysseus. Anything to do with wine is θεῖον because of Dionysos' identification with the liquid (cf. the echo of this verse in 415), but any suggestion that we are to understand Dionysos as behind Odysseus' 'bright idea' here (cf., e.g., Konstan 1990: 224) is very faint. For the verbal expression cf. *El.* 619 ἄρτι γάρ μ᾽ ἐσῆλθέ τι.

σκύφος: cf. 256n.

412 Μάρωνος ... τοῦδε 'of this Maron here', cf. 141–3n.; apparently Odysseus is still carrying the wineskin, cf. 446.

πιεῖν: cf. 257n.

413–15 Quotations of direct speech are very common in messenger-speeches (cf. de Jong 1991: 131–9, who notes that the average length of such quotations in Euripides is two verses), but it is very rare for messengers, who normally have no other role in the action, to quote their own words: *Hec.* 532–3 (del. Battezzato) and *Or.* 875–6 are the nearest parallels. Odysseus in *Cycl.* is a very experimental messenger.

413 ʾΏ ... Κύκλωψ: for the omission of παῖ in such addresses cf., e.g., *IT* 1230, *Ion* 1619. Odysseus here reprises the wheedling tone of 286.

414 Cf. *Od.* 9.348–9 (Odysseus to Cyclops) ὄφρ' εἰδῇις οἷόν τι ποτὸν τόδε νηῦς ἐκεκεύθει / ἡμετέρη.

415 θεῖον ... πῶμα: the 'divinity' of the wine is over-determined. It comes from the priest Maron, is associated with (or in fact *is* (cf. 521–7)) Dionysos, and is 'marvellous' enough to be drunk by the son of a god such as the Cyclops. In *Od.* Odysseus says that he has brought the wine as a 'libation' for the Cyclops (9.349), and after tasting it the monster describes it as ἀμβροσίης καὶ νέκταρος ... ἀπορρώξ (9.359).

κομίζει 'provides, produces'.

Διονύσου γάνος 'the delight of/from Dionysos'. γάνος probably originally referred to the bright glitter of wine (cf. Beekes s.v. γάνυμαι), and the noun is commonly found in connection with wine, cf., e.g., *Ba.* 261, 382–3, Ar. *Frogs* 1320.

416 essentially repeats 409, but behind this lies *Od.* 9.347, where Odysseus suggests to the Cyclops that, having eaten human flesh, he should now taste the wine brought by the ship which (though Odysseus does not spell this out) had also brought the men who provided the Cyclops' meal. In classical Greece wine-drinking habitually followed rather than accompanied the consumption of food.

417 ἔσπασέν ⟨τ'⟩ ἄμυστιν ἑλκύσας 'he gulped it down, draining it in one go', an elaboration of the simple Homeric ἔκπιεν (*Od.* 9.353, 361). Both σπᾶν and ἕλκειν are common expressions for rapid and deep drinking, cf. 571, Ar. *Knights* 107, Alexis frr. 5, 88.3, Eubulus fr. 56.7, Clem. Alex. *Paed.* 2.2.31 (the denunciation of drunkenness) ἅδην σπάσαντας ... ἀμυστὶ ἕλκοντας ὑπὸ ἀκρασίας. ἑλκύσας is a 'coincident' aorist, cf. 410n.

ἄμυστιν is an adverbial accusative 'in one long draught', cf. 565, Ar. *Ach.* 1229, Anacreon, *PMG* 356a.2, Antiphanes fr. 75.14 ἕλκειν ἀπνευστί, Harder 2012: 2.969–70, Hunter 2017: 194. ἄμυστις is also used as a term for a large drinking-cup, cf., e.g., Ameipsias fr. 21.3.

418 ἄρας χεῖρα: there is Roman evidence for raising the hand as a gesture of admiration (Cic. *Acad.* 2.63, *Ad fam.* 7.5.2, Cat. 53.4), but no clear Greek literary evidence, although similar gestures in vase painting are sometimes interpreted in this way, cf. Wilson 2010: 210–12; Sittl 1890: 13 takes the current passage as marking admiration and surprise. Others understand that the Cyclops holds up the cup for another drink.

Φίλτατε ξένων: an amusing extension of the Cyclops' sarcastic humour at *Od.* 9.355–6.

419 '… excellent <is> the drink <which> you offer on top of an excellent meal'.

420 ἡσθέντα: cf. 446, *Od.* 9.353–4 ἥσατο δ᾽ αἰνῶς/ἡδὺ ποτὸν πίνων.

421–2 Odysseus now asserts the controlling power of his intelligence, cf. 411n.

τρώσει: cf. *Od.* 21.293 (Antinoos to Odysseus) οἶνός σε τρώει μελιηδής. χανδόν in the following Homeric verse has here been replaced by ἄμυστιν in 417. *Od.* 21.293–4 are also evoked in 524, where see n.

οἶνος = ὁ οἶνος.

δίκην δώσει: cf. 441–2n.

423 καὶ δή adds a vivid immediacy (cf. 488), almost proving correct Odysseus' prediction of the previous verse, cf. *GP*² 248.

πρὸς ὠιδὰς εἶρπ᾽: cf. *Hel.* 316 ἐς ποῖον ἔρπεις μῦθον ἢ παραίνεσιν;, *Ion* 1177 ἐς αὐλοὺς ἧκον.

ἐπεγχέων 'pouring in after/on top of another'.

424 σπλάγχν᾽ ἐθέρμαινον ποτῶι: cf. *Alc.* 758–9 (Heracles) ἕως ἐθέρμην᾽ αὐτὸν ἀμφιβᾶσα φλὸξ/οἴνου, Hor. *Sat.* 2.1.24–5 *saltat Milonius, ut semel icto/ accessit feruor capiti*, *Anacreontea* 50.1–4, the poet's heart, 'warmed' by wine, turns to song. Doctors indeed believed that too much wine increased body-temperature, cf., e.g., [Hippocr.] *Epidemics* 3.4, 5, 16, Pl. *Tim.* 60a5. At Ar. *Frogs* 844 Dionysos tells Aeschylus μὴ πρὸς ὀργὴν σπλάγχνα θερμήνηις κότωι, and the current verse increases the likelihood that Ar. there echoes a verse of Aesch. (= fr. **468 Radt). Ancient literary gossip also reported that Aesch. composed his plays when 'warmed' with wine (T117e–f Radt). Euripides' parody here (if that is what it is) suits the sympotic jollity of what is being described; citations and distortions of well-known verses were a regular feature of symposia.

425–6 Cf. 488–90. At *Alc.* 755–64 there is a very similar description of Heracles drinking and ἄμουσ᾽ ὑλακτῶν (cf. also fr. 907), while Admetus' servants silently weep for Alcestis; cf. also Theognis 1041–2, 1217–18, Xen. *Cyr.* 1.3.10 (the young Cyrus reproves the Median court for singing μάλα γελοίως when drunk). Singing (then as now) can be a 'natural' result of too much alcohol (cf. *Od.* 14.464–5), and drunken singing may have been something of a satyric topos; in Tzetzes' summary of Eur. *Syleus* (Eur. T 221b), Heracles is described as 'singing while he ate and drank'. The switch to present-tense verbs emphasises the contrast and cunning of Odysseus' silent exit.

κλαίουσι: cf. *Od.* 9.294 (after the first deaths of Odysseus' crew) ἡμεῖς δὲ κλαίοντες κτλ.

ἄμουσ᾽ is of a piece with the Cyclops' ἀμαθία, cf. 172–4n., 490n.; the great majority of fifth-century examples of ἄμουσος occur in Euripides, cf. Halliwell 2012.

427–36 Odysseus addresses the *koryphaios* (σέ, cf. 434–5, 442), but he clearly means to save all the satyrs (cf. the plural verbs in 428); they could all just run away now, but that would leave Silenos and some of Odysseus' comrades behind and also spoil the fun. Throughout these verses, Odysseus envisages a future for the satyrs (countryside, nymphs, their 'old friend' Dionysos rather than the Cyclops, etc.) as though he has heard their longing in the epode of the parodos (or been to a satyr-play).

429–30 ἄμεικτον 'savage', cf. *Her.* 393 (the monstrous Kyknos), Soph. *Tr.* 1095 (Centaurs), Anaxilas fr. 22.3 (a δράκαινα); the satyrs may well also hear the resonance 'unsociable', which is reinforced by what Odysseus proceeds to add and by 436.

τὰ Βακχίου ... μέλαθρα 'the halls of the Bacchic one', i.e. the open countryside, where satyrs might hope to find 'Naiad nymphs'. Naiads are, strictly speaking, nymphs of streams and rivers, but neat distinctions between types of nymph constantly break down, cf. 69–72, Pratinas, *PMG* 708.3–4 ἐμὲ δεῖ παταγεῖν ἀν᾽ ὄρεα σύμενον μετὰ Ναϊάδων, Aesch. fr.204b.4–8, Larson 2001. For μέλαθρα cf. 491n.

432 ἀλλ᾽ ἀσθενὴς γάρ 'but he <is> weak and therefore ...'; γάρ shows that this explains what follows, cf. 434, *GP²* 98–9.

κἀποκερδαίνων ποτοῦ 'and getting enjoyment from the drinking'; the compound verb allows the simple genitive, whereas κερδαίνειν is normally followed by ἐκ or ἀπό.

433–4 '... having been caught (perf. pass. participle of λαμβάνειν) by the cup as if by bird-lime, he struggles with his wings', a marvellous picture of Silenos 'flapping' with the exciting nearness of alcohol. Sticky bird-lime was usually made from mistletoe or oaK–Gum which was smeared on rods which were then brought into contact with birds; the birds which had been thus rendered immobile would then be seized by hand or with nets, cf. Dionysius, *Ixeutika* 1.1, 3.1 Garzya, Longus, *D&C* 3.5–6, Butler 1930: 184–91. Metaphors and similes are often drawn from this activity, particularly in erotic contexts, cf. Meleager, *AP* 5.96.1 (= *HE* 4296), 12.132a.2 (= *HE* 4105), LSJ s.v. ἰξός II 2.

πτέρυγας: accusative of respect, cf. fr. 908.7–8 οὐκ ἀρκεῖ μίαν/ψυχὴν ἀλύ-
ειν. Others understand the accusative with λελημμένος, 'caught by the wings
is beside himself'.

νεανίας γὰρ εἶ: all satyrs are young in comparison with Silenos, cf. above
pp. 27–30.

435 τὸν ἀρχαῖον φίλον 'your *philos* of former days', cf. 73, 81, Xen. *Mem.*
2.8.1 ἄλλον δέ ποτε ἀρχαῖον ἑταῖρον διὰ χρόνου ἰδών κτλ.

436 οὐ Κύκλωπι προσφερῆ: a kind of litotes: the Cyclops could not be
less like Dionysos. Negatived adjectives are often used in this way, cf. *Hipp.*
1, *Hel.* 16, *Ph.* 425, Smyth §2694.

437–8 For such wishes cf., e.g., *Or.* 1100, *Rhes.* 464–5, Ar. *Peace* 346. γὰρ
marks assent to the previous speaker, cf. *GP²* 92–3.

τήνδ' ... ἡμέραν 'the day you mention'.

Κύκλωπος ... ἀνόσιον κάρα: a very common type of periphrasis, cf. *Tr.*
661, LSJ s.v. κάρα 3. At *Or.* 481 Tyndareos refers to Orestes as ἀνόσιον κάρα.

439–40 The text is corrupt beyond probable restoration. The first syllable of σίφων, 'siphon/hose', for drawing off wine, etc., seems to have been
long (cf. Ar. *Thesm.* 557, Meleager, *AP* 5.151.2 (= *HE* 4167)), but as transmitted here it is short. It is standardly understood here as a euphemism
for the penis, either as the object of χηρεύομεν, a construction nowhere
attested, or as an accusative of respect (cf. *Alc.* 1089). Biehl and Kovacs
1994: 156 take σίφων as either an affectionate term for Dionysos or as
actually a name for him, and Scaliger suggested θηρεύομεν for χηρεύομεν;
that the only Homeric instance of χηρεύειν is used of the lush island near
the Cyclopes (*Od.* 9.124) is, however, one further reason for retaining it.
Cf. further Di Marco 2013: 265–75.

ὡς διὰ μακροῦ γε 'It has – you see – been a long time that ...'; ὡς ... γε
explains the preceding statement, cf. 247. For διὰ μακροῦ [sc. χρόνου],
'after a long interval' or 'after a long time', cf. *Hec.* 320, *IT* 480, *Ph.* 1069
(with Mastronarde's n.). At Ar. *Lys.* 904 Kinesias begs Myrrhine to sleep
with him διὰ χρόνου.

441–2 In *Od.* the blinding of the Cyclops is not explicitly 'punishment',
though it certainly is within the moral frame of the narrative, but here the
theme is given prominence (cf. 422, 693n.) because Odysseus and the
satyrs could just escape at this very moment; that, however, would leave
the Cyclops 'unpunished', as the Dionysiac pattern of the play demands
he must be. The theme of 'the monster punished' was a recurrent trope
of satyr-play, cf. fr. 678 (*Skiron*) 'it is a fine thing to punish the wicked',
Laemmle 2013: 266–72.

τιμωρίαν ... φυγήν: chiasmus marks Odysseus' pride in his plan. The
two nouns function as shorthand for '<plan for> punishment' and '<plan
for> your escape'.

θηρός: cf. 602, 658.

πανούργου, 'rascally, wicked', has a colloquial ring, cf. *Alc.* 766 πανοῦργον κλῶπα of Heracles, *Hec.* 1257, *Ion* 1279; the use is very common in comedy. There is also an ironic resonance: Odysseus himself was often portrayed in drama and elsewhere as πανοῦργος, lit. 'willing to do anything'.

δουλείας φυγήν: in another sense, the satyrs will never escape from slavery, cf. 709, 23–4n.

443–4 'Tell me, as I would not listen to the sound of the Asian cithara with greater pleasure than to (news of) the Cyclops' death'.

Ἀσιάδος … κιθάρας: the kithara is frequently designated 'Asian', and such eastern associations are appropriate for Dionysiac cult, cf. *Hyps.* fr. 752g.9–10, 759a.1622, Austin and Olson on Ar. *Thesm.* 120, Cassio 2000: 105–10; Plut. *Mor.* 1133c explains that the kithara was called 'Asian' because it was used by 'the kitharodes of Lesbos, who live beside Asia'. The kithara normally had seven strings, but the word is used for a variety of types, cf. Maas and Snyder 1989: 53–78, West 1992: 50–6, Power 2010. For paintings of satyrs playing the kithara cf. Maas and Snyder 1989: 72 Figure 3, 75 Figure 12, Taplin and Wyles 2010: Figure 12.6. Power 2018: 358–9 suggests an allusion here back to the invention of the lyre in Soph. *Ichn.*

Κύκλωπ' ὀλωλότα '(the news of) the Cyclops' death'.

445–6 raise the possibility that Odysseus is going to encounter a large group of Cyclopes. That the Cyclops' first thought is to share the wine with his brothers (contrast 243–6, 316–17nn.) both illustrates the communal force of Dionysiac wine and reminds us that already in Homer the Cyclopes were not quite as anti-social as Odysseus had made them out to be (9.112–15). The Homeric motif of the group coming to help their neighbour (a βοή, 9.399–413) is here rewritten as the possibility that the single Cyclops will go to the group (a κῶμος); that the Homeric Cyclopes spoke to Polyphemos through a closed door-(stone) perhaps activates the reworking as a κῶμος.

ἐπὶ κῶμον ἔρπειν is a standard phrase for 'go on a *kōmos*' (cf. 508) and ἐπί … πρός is not awkward; Wecklein proposed ἐπίκωμος (cf. Aristias, *TrGF* 9 F 3). On the Cyclops' apparently paradoxical knowledge of sympotic practice (cf. 537) cf. above p. 18.

ἡσθεὶς τῶιδε Βακχίου ποτῶι: cf. 420n.

447–8 The satyrs' assumption that Odysseus wants to ambush the Cyclops probably draws, not just on Odysseus' own reputation (cf., e.g., *Il.* 10, *Od.* 13.268), but also on familiar themes of satyr-play, cf. Laemmle 2013: 288–90. Euripides' satyric *Skiron* concerned a monster who threw passers-by over a cliff to be eaten by a giant turtle, only himself then to be killed by Theseus in identical fashion; the same play (cf. fr. 679) may have mentioned Sinis/Pityokamptes, 'The Pinebender', who killed his victims in wooded areas, cf. Barrett on *Hipp.* 976–80.

δρυμοῖσι: the transmitted ῥυθμοῖσι or ῥυθμῶι τινι (Dobree)/σφάξαι would pick up the textually problematic 398 (where see n.) and suggest that there was to be 'poetic justice' in the Cyclops' fate; the idea of a recurring ῥυθμός in such violent acts is attractive (cf. Laemmle loc. cit.), but δρυμοῖσι forms a neat pair with πετρῶν, and we print it with some hesitation. Kassel suggested ἐρημοῖς ... δρυμοῖσι, cf. Soph. fr. 581.10 and the setting of Eur. *Skiron* described as ἐρημία (T iia.12).

σφάξαι: presumably with a sword or axe (we should not enquire too closely as to how the satyrs imagine that Odysseus will be able to over-power the Cyclops). Their fantasised scenario is not unlike the treacher-ous killing of Apsyrtus on a lonely island at Ap. Rhod. *Arg.* 4.456–70.

πετρῶν ... κάτα 'down from rocks', cf. *IT* 1429–30, Pl. *Phdr.* 229c7–8; the recessive accent on κάτα is regular when disyllabic prepositions follow their noun ('anastrophe'). The transmitted κάτω as a preposition means 'under, below', cf. *Alc.* 45, *El.* 677.

449 δόλιος ἡ προθυμία 'my intention is cunning', cf. *Her.* 310 πρόθυμός ἐστιν, ἡ προθυμία δ' ἄφρων. For προθυμία, a very common Euripidean word, in this sense cf. *Alc.* 51, 1107. The transmitted ἐπιθυμία is perhaps not impossible, but the noun is not certainly found in drama (*Andr.* 1281 being the only other possible case).

450 is a rather politer version of Silenos' retort at 104 (where see n.). Odysseus is of course known as both δόλιος and σοφός principally from *Od.* (cf. esp. 9.19–20), and there is here again the suggestion that this is the source of the satyrs' knowledge, cf. Wright 2006: 36.

πῶς δαί;: the particle expresses surprise and/or curiosity after a rejected suggestion, cf. *Hel.* 1246, Ar. *Wasps* 1212, *GP²* 263, Collard 2018: 101–3 (~ Stevens 1976: 45–6).

τοι 'you know', 'let me tell you', cf. *GP²* 540–1.

451 '<My intention is> to remove him from this <idea of> a revel', i.e. I will make him give up the idea. In the passive ἀπαλλάσσειν can mean 'give up/be released from', cf. Ar. *Pl.* 316 τῶν σκωμμάτων ἀπαλλαγέντες. At Theognis 1351–2 the poet seeks to dissuade a young man from going on a revel (οὔτοι κωμάζειν σύμφορον ἀνδρὶ νέωι), but presumably for very different reasons.

452-3 Odysseus' plan will play on the Cyclops' previous sense of superi-ority and self-sufficiency, cf. 532–3n.

454 ὑπνώσσηι 'gets drowsy', 'wants to sleep', pres. subj. of ὑπνώσσειν, cf. *Or.* 173 (with Willink's n.), Aesch. *Eum.* 121. ὑπνώσηι would be the aor. subj. of ὑπνοῦν, a verb not otherwise found in Euripides. The Homeric model is *Od.* 9.372–3.

Βακχίου νικώμενος: the god will triumph over his adversary (cf. above pp. 18, 26), but we should not seek to draw a clear distinction here between the god and his wine, cf. 519–20n. The construction is parallel to that of ἡττᾶσθαι followed by the genitive, cf. *Med.* 315, *Tr.* 23, Smyth §1402, K–G I 392; this is usually explained as a genitive of comparison.

455–82 Vestiges of the ends of 455–71 and of the beginnings of 479–81, together with more substantial parts of 484–96, survive on *POxy* 4545 (= Π¹), the only papyrus of *Cycl.* yet known, cf. above p. 48.

455 The syntax does not follow 454, but such an anacoluthon, imitative of everyday speech, is very easy. The olive-branch derives from *Od.* 9.320, 382.

456 ὃν ... ἐξαποξύνας ἄκρον 'after sharpening its tip', cf. *Od.* 9.382 ὀξὺν ἐπ' ἄκρωι. As transmitted, the verse is a syllable short. ἐξαποξύνειν is unattested elsewhere, but ἐκ- regularly forms compounds to denote the completeness of an act (cf. 327, Bond on *Her.* 18); Zuntz 1965: 54 noted that the rarity and appropriateness of this double compound suggest that Triclinius derived it from the manuscript from which L was copied, rather than by emendation. Murray suggested φασγάνωι ‹γώ›. At *Od.* 9.326–7 Odysseus tells his comrades ἀποξῦναι the great staff, and then 'they made it smooth, while I beside them sharpened (ἐθόωσα) the tip (ἄκρον)'. This suggests that ἀποξύνειν, which should mean (as here) 'sharpen to a point', is in the Homeric model used to mean 'plane' (as it must also at *Od.* 6.269); for this reason some modern editors accept ἀποξῦσαι (from ἀποξύω) at *Od.* 9.326. Euripides' Odysseus has removed any uncertainty: there is no mention of a role for Odysseus' comrades (thus putting all the emphasis upon Odysseus himself), but the verb which was used for what they did in *Od.* is now given its 'natural' meaning in reference to Odysseus' own action. Such attention to the meaning of Homeric words strikingly foreshadows the 'philological' poetry of the Hellenistic age.

φασγάνωι τῶιδ': that Odysseus is carrying a sword has not previously been mentioned, but cf. *Od.* 9.300.

457 Cf. *Od.* 9.328 ἐπυράκτεον ἐν πυρὶ κηλέωι, 9.378–9. The repeated κ-sounds in this verse are perhaps a memory of *Od.* 9.329 καὶ τὸ μὲν εὖ κατέθηκα κατακρύψας ὑπὸ κόπρωι.

κεκαυμένον 'scorched'.

458–9 Although the plural is elsewhere used of the Cyclops' eye (cf. 463, 470, 611), ἄρας ... βαλών would be a very awkward asyndeton (much more so than, e.g., 238–9), and Pierson's reconstruction is very attractive. The plural βλέφαρ' ἀμφὶ καὶ ὀφρύας of the Cyclops at *Od.* 9.389 attracted the attention of keen-eyed grammarians (cf. Schol. *Od.* 9.383).

ὄψιν, 'vision', is more abstract than 'face' or 'eyes', cf. 463, 595, 627–8 ὄμματος/ὄψις, LSJ s.v. II c2. ὄμμα here is the physical 'eye', cf. ὀφθαλμός at *Od.* 9.397.

ἐκτήξω 'I shall melt ‹the eye›'; for the rare use of the active in a literal sense, cf. Ar. *Clouds* 772.

456–64 Five future tense verbs (καθήσω, βαλῶ, ἐκτήξω, κυκλώσω, συναυανῶ) draw on the certainty which the Homeric script gives to the action.

460–4 'Just as a man who puts together the construction of a ship moves the drill like an oar by means of two straps, so I will rotate the torch in the light-bearing eyes of the Cyclops and wither his eyeball', a remarkable reworking of Odysseus' account of the blinding of the Cyclops (*Od.* 9.383–90):

> ἐγὼ δ' ἐφύπερθεν ἐρεισθεὶς
> δίνεον, ὡς ὅτε τις τρυπᾶι δόρυ νήϊον ἀνὴρ
> τρυπάνωι, οἱ δέ τ' ἔνερθεν ὑποσσείουσιν ἱμάντι   385
> ἁψάμενοι ἑκάτερθε, τὸ δὲ τρέχει ἐμμενὲς αἰεί·
> ὡς τοῦ ἐν ὀφθαλμῶι πυριήκεα μοχλὸν ἑλόντες
> δινέομεν, τὸν δ' αἷμα περίρρεε θερμὸν ἐόντα.
> πάντα δέ οἱ βλέφαρ' ἀμφὶ καὶ ὀφρύας εὗσεν ἀϋτμὴ
> γλήνης καιομένης· σφαραγεῦντο δέ οἱ πυρὶ ῥίζαι.

The shared elements (ship-building, τις ... ἀνήρ, drilling, the strap or straps) do not conceal an important difference: the Euripidean Odysseus offers no role for his comrades but envisages acting alone. Both here and in Homer the craft simile stresses Odysseus' pride in his superiority to the Cyclopes, who have no ships or carpenters (*Od.* 9.125–9). At *Od.* 5.250 (the building of the raft) Odysseus is compared to a man 'who is a master carpenter' (εὖ εἰδὼς τεκτοσυνάων); the idea is picked up in 477. A simile describing a prospective act in the future is itself very remarkable (cf. 469–71n., 475), and seems to have only one Homeric precedent (*Od.* 4.335–40, cited verbatim at 17.126–31). In *Cycl.*, however, the action is both future and past, because it is already in the Homeric text, and Euripides' play with the narrative of his drama as both post- and pre-Homeric is here at its most overt. Later at least, similes were to be very marked sites of poetic and intertextual display, as assertions (and disavowals) of 'likeness' suggest relations between texts within a mimetic literary practice (cf., e.g., Hunter 2006: chapter 3), and we sense something of that spirit already here.

460 ναυπηγίαν δ' ὡσεί ... ἀνήρ would in prose be ὡς ἀνήρ τις ναυπηγός; the slightly awkward expression, 'puts together the construction of a ship', stresses the skill (τέχνη) involved in what Odysseus will do. Others understand ναυπηγία here as simply 'ship' (cf. ναυκληρία at *Hel.* 1519, where see Kannicht's n.), but that does not do justice to the resonance of Odysseus' language. The specific reference of the simile is perhaps to the drilling of holes for the cords which held the planks together, cf. Morrison and Williams 1968: 199.

461 διπλοῖν χαλινοῖν: χαλινός may be used of anything which ties or binds (LSJ s.v. I 2), and so 'strap, thong' is not a difficult extension. In Homer, Odysseus' comrades power the drill by pulling on a strap on either side (ἱμάντι/ … ἑκάτερθε, here varied by διπλοῖν), but Odysseus apparently envisages operation by a single craftsman, unless he has simply elided the necessary role of helpers for the shipwright.

κωπηλατεῖ introduces into the simile a further image from the nautical world, cf. 484. The movement of the straps in and out, which gives the drill its rotational power, is compared to the rhythmical backwards and forwards movement of a rower. The ancient variant τροχηλατεῖ, 'drive, cause to wheel around', introduces a common Euripidean word (*El.* 1253, *Or.* 36, *Ph.* 39, etc.) and a much less striking image.

462 κυκλώσω varies the Homeric δίνεον … δινέομεν (*Od.* 9.384, 388). The etymological play with Κύκλωψ (cf. Hes. *Theog.* 144–5) carries a savage relish; there is perhaps a suggestion in 463 that Κύκλωψ is formed from κύκλος + ὄψις.

φαεσφόρωι: cf. 611 φωσφόρους ὀλεῖ κόρας, 486 λαμπρὰν ὄψιν, 663 ὀφθαλμοῦ σέλας; a torch which normally brings light will here bring eternal darkness to the Cyclops. Pl. *Tim.* 45b3 has φωσφόρα … ὄμματα as the first organ constructed by the gods, and Plato explains that our eyes are the organ through which pure inner fire streams out into the light of day, thus enabling vision. Behind Plato lies Empedocles, whose hexameter account of the construction of the eye has several features suggestive of the present passage. Aphrodite 'constructed' (ἔπηξεν, cf. ναυπηγία) the eye using γόμφοι, 'pegs' (fr. 86–7 D–K = D213–14 Laks–Most), a standard term of ship-building (already at *Od.* 5.248, the building of the raft), and Empedocles describes the eye through the simile of a lamp which sends its light out into the darkness (fr. 84 D–K = D215 Laks–Most, cf. Lloyd 1966: 325–7); most strikingly in this last passage, Empedocles has both fire and water within the eye (cf. also A86 D–K = D218 Laks–Most), which he calls κύκλοπα κούρην. It would be typical of Euripides to 'update' Homer's Odysseus by the evocation of much more recent scientific speculation, and no one would better suit *Cycl.* than the Sicilian Empedocles, cf. 663n., D'Alfonso 2006: 22–3. Rashed 2007: 33–5 argues that Empedocles' description of Aphrodite's construction of the eye is in turn indebted to *Od.* 5.247–59 (the building of the raft). Presocratic science, and perhaps Empedocles, lies behind the comic Euripides' ὀφθαλμὸν ἀντίμιμον ἡλίου τροχῶι at Ar. *Thesm.* 17, cf. Clements 2014: 25–6.

463 συναυανῶ 'I shall wither, cause to dry up completely'; the choice of verb perhaps reflects theories about the moisture of the eye (cf. previous n.), although scientific speculation is not needed to link eyes with moisture (cf. *Od.* 19.204–9, etc.).

κόρας: cf. 458–9n.

464 ἰού ἰού: the satyrs presumably dance a jig of celebratory pleasure here. At *Clouds* 543 Aristophanes implies that this exclamation is typical of lowbrow comedy. Later grammarians sought to distinguish joyful ἰοῦ from ἰού of lamentation (Schol. Ar. *Peace* 317, *Suda* ι 427), but it is quite uncertain whether classical authors recognised the distinction.

465 The asyndeton (cf. Mastronarde on *Ph.* 1193) is here a marker of enthusiasm. Mastronarde notes that in such cases 'the two verbs are often synonymous, or the second is more specific and colourful than the first'; this verse fits that pattern. For the change from singular to plural cf., e.g., 212–13, 427–8, 643–4, above p. 24. Both verbs may be constructed with the simple dative, although the dative is more natural after μαινόμεσθα; this meaning (as in colloquial English 'to be crazy about') is not unusual, but μαίνεσθαι is a good Dionysiac word for the chorus to use, cf. 164–7, 168nn.

εὑρήμασιν: the implication is both 'We love your devisings!' and 'We love inventions!', which seems to have been a regular theme of satyr-drama; the chorus again suggests its metatheatrical consciousness, cf. Laemmle 2013: 371–80. This rather surprising word may also reinforce the suggestion of a modern 'scientific' flavour to Odysseus' proposal (cf. 460–4n.). It is wrily ironic that Odysseus has 'invented' nothing here – he is simply following the Homeric script.

466 σέ: by a familiar convention, all the chorus-members are covered by the singular address to the *koryphaios*.

φίλους: i.e. Odysseus' 'dear comrades' (377–8n.), cf. 650–3.

467 νεὼς μελαίνης κοῖλον … σκάφος 'the hollow hull of (my) black ship'; although σκάφος is not a Homeric term, Odysseus is here at his most epic. κοῖλος and μέλαινα are both standard Homeric epithets for ships, sometimes found, as here, together (cf., e.g., *Od.* 4.731).

ἐμβήσας, 'causing to embark upon' (cf. LSJ s.v. ἐμβαίνω II), takes a double accusative, cf. *Hcld.* 844–5, *IT* 742.

468 διπλαῖσι κώπαις, 'with double [banks of] oars', presumably means 'with all possible speed'; in the classical period warships of the heroic age were assumed to have been penteconters with two banks of oars, cf. *IT* 1124, *Hel.* 1412, Thucyd. 1.14.1, Morrison and Williams 1968: 194–5, 309–10.

ἀποστελῶ 'I shall get <all of us> away from …'; as parallels for an intransitive active, 'I shall set off', are lacking, it is better to understand ἀποστελῶ as transitive, with the persons of 466 as the objects of both ἐμβήσας and the verb.

469–71 are difficult and disputed verses. As transmitted, the satyrs ask to 'touch the torch, as after a libation'. In preparation for a sacrifice, a burning torch was dipped into water (χέρνιψ), which was then sprinkled over the participants, hence making them sharers in the ritual act, cf. *Her.* 928–9, Ar. *Peace* 959 with scholia, *Lys.* 1129–30; as this act did not take place *after* libations, Reiske here proposed ὥσπερ ἐν σπονδαῖς. Although there is no evidence that the ritual act involved a shared touching of the torch, we need not demand absolute ritual accuracy from the satyrs; they claim to want a share in the act, just as Electra asserts that she too had her hand on the sword which killed Clytemestra (*El.* 1225, *Or.* 1235). An allusion to the dousing of a torch in water evokes Odysseus' second simile for the blinding of the Cyclops at *Od.* 9.391–4:

ὡς δ’ ὅτ’ ἀνὴρ χαλκεὺς πέλεκυν μέγαν ἠὲ σκέπαρνον
εἰν ὕδατι ψυχρῶι βάπτηι μεγάλα ἰάχοντα
φαρμάσσων· τὸ γὰρ αὖτε σιδήρου γε κράτος ἐστίν·
ὡς τοῦ σίζ’ ὀφθαλμὸς ἐλαϊνέωι περὶ μοχλῶι.

If 469–70 evoke these verses, then the rewriting is utterly different in kind from the preceding simile of ship-building; our memory is activated by the expectation raised by the Homeric passage, not by specific verbal clues in *Cycl.*

If the reference is not to the dipping of a torch into ritual water, then the most likely alternative is that the satyrs ask for a role as helpers comparable to that of those who share in the pouring of libations together, often in connection with the swearing of an oath, cf. *Ph.* 1240–1, Aesch. *Sept.* 42–8, Ar. *Peace* 431–58 (Trygaios and the chorus), *Lys.* 195–7, 209–11, where all members of a group touch the blood of a victim or a large drinking bowl in making an oath, Torrance 2014: 147–8. With this interpretation, Reiske's ὡσπερεί mends the syntax and provides the satyrs with a suitably secondary role, cf. Aeschines 2.84 τοὺς ὥσπερ συνεφαπτομένους τοῖς σπένδουσι τῶν ἱερῶν, Dio Chrys. 34.34 οἱ σπονδῆς θιγγάνοντες. We hesitantly adopt this text and interpretation, but the matter remains uncertain.

ἔστ’ οὖν ὅπως ἄν ... 'Is there some way that I might ...?', cf. *Alc.* 52 (without ἄν), Smyth §2552, K–G II 375.

ὄμματα: cf. 458–9n.

φόνου: the satyrs want the Cyclops dead and so exaggerate wishfully, 'bloodletting'; there is no need to understand φόνου either as 'gore' (*Hec.* 241, LSJ s.v. I 4) or as a reference to sacrificial killing (Seaford 1981: 273–4, citing Porphyry, *De abst.* 2.29.5 on the sharing of responsibility for sacrifice, κοινωνήσουσι τοῦ φόνου). Nauck's πόνου deserves serious consideration, cf. *Ion* 331 εἰ πόνου μοι ξυλλάβοι κτλ., Laemmle 2013: 164 n. 28.

472 δεῖ γοῦν 'Yes, you must!', cf. *GP*² 454.

μέγας γὰρ δαλός: cf. *Od.* 9.319–26 Κύκλωπος γὰρ ἔκειτο μέγα ῥόπαλον κτλ.

οὗ ξυλληπτέον 'which we must take up together', cf. Ar. *Peace* 437, LSJ s.v. συλλαμβάνω II 1a. The transmitted ὃν ξυλληπτέον would be 'which we must stop/grab'.

473 ὡς '<Be assured> that ...', cf. Smyth §3001, Diggle 1981: 88.

ἁμαξῶν ἑκατόν: cf. 385n. Hyperbole is the satyrs' natural mode of speech, as well as Odysseus'.

ἀραίμην: aor. mid. opt. αἴρειν, cf. Ar. *Frogs* 1406 ὅσ᾽ οὐκ ἂν ἄραιντ᾽ οὐδ᾽ ἑκατὸν Αἰγύπτιοι.

474 τοῦ κακῶς ὀλουμένου 'cursed, who will come to a bad end', cf. *Hcld.* 874–5. This colloquial expression (never in Aeschylus or Sophocles) is very common in comedy, which however prefers the compound ἀπολού-μενος; the simple verb 'may make the phrase slightly less colloquial' (Collard 2018: 49 (~ Stevens 1976: 15)).

475 ἐκθύψομεν 'we will smoke out', the future of the rare ἐκτύφω; for the simple verb cf. 655, 659. Smoke was regularly used to clear bee-hives and wasps' nests, cf. Ar. *Wasps* 457 (with the n. of Biles and Olson), *Lys.* 475, Ap. Rhod. *Arg.* 2.130–4. The very lively image suits the rustic, comic imagination of satyrs. The transmitted ἐκθρύψομεν (an unattested compound), 'we will shatter', is much inferior. It is at least curious that at Ar. *Wealth* 301 (the parody of Philoxenus' *Cyclops*, cf. above pp. 8–9) the chorus threaten to catch the Cyclops and μέγαν λαβόντες ἡμμένον σφηκί-σκον ἐκτυφλῶσαι. σφηκίσκος, which occurs only in that passage in this sense, apparently (cf. the scholia) refers to a piece of wood sharpened like a wasp's sting. Philoxenus perhaps echoed and varied *Cycl.* in this detail, or perhaps both were indebted to an earlier version; ἐκτυφλοῦν is in sound very close to ἐκτύφειν.

476 σιγᾶτε: a brief allusion to the familiar tragic motif whereby a character asks the chorus to keep silent about a plot which is being hatched (Barrett on *Hipp.* 710–12, Mastronarde on *Med.* 263). The allusion is humorous as silence never comes easily to a group of satyrs, but satyr-drama is characterised by constant threats to the Dionysiac life, includ-ing choral dancing and noise, cf. Laemmle 2019a. Odysseus is the only character in Homer who uses the imperative σῖγα (*Il.* 14.90, *Od.* 14.493 (Odysseus making up a story about Odysseus), 19.42, 486 (Odysseus to Eurycleia)), and such an instruction may be seen as characteristic of him, cf. 624n.; the closest early parallel is the young Hermes, a god who stands very close to Odysseus, at *HHHermes* 93. For the alternation of singular and plural verbs cf. 427–8, 465, above p. 24.

477 τοῖσιν ἀρχιτέκτοσιν: i.e. Odysseus himself, a rather grandiose plu-ral for singular. For this metaphorical use, which looks forward to the self-aggrandisement of scheming Plautine slaves, cf. Ar. *Peace* 305, Dem. 56.11 τῶι ἀρχιτέκτονι τῆς ὅλης ἐπιβουλῆς, Arnott 1996: 450–1; the simple τέκτων is often used metaphorically, cf. *Med.* 409, Aesch. *Ag.* 153, LSJ s.v. 3–4. Odysseus here continues the language of ship-building from 460–1 (cf. Arist. *Ath. Pol.* 46.1, publicly elected naval ἀρχιτέκτονες), cf. 460–4n. At least somewhat later, however, the Theatre of Dionysos and other theatres had ἀρχιτέκτονες, who leased the theatre and were then in charge of seating, ticket prices, etc., cf. Dem. 18.28 (with Wankel's n.), Pickard-Cambridge 1968: 266 n.3, Csapo and Slater 1995: 288–9, Diggle 2004: 509. How early this system was in operation we do not know, but it is tempting to see a theatrical joke here as well. Torrance 2013: 257 interprets the metaphor as casting Odysseus as a master-poet.

478–9 Cf. Pylades' sentiments at *IT* 676–9. The Homeric Odysseus always presented himself as concerned with the fate of his comrades (*Od.* 9.421, 430, 10.383–7, etc.). οὐ μόνος σωθήσομαι would make a stirring closure to the scene, cf. next n.

480–2 are a very puzzling repetition of 478–9, although they do not appear to be a simple alternative for them, as they are three complete trimeters and καίτοι hooks them to what has preceded as an objection raised by the speaker himself, cf. *GP*² 556–7. The repetition might make Odysseus look absurd in his efforts to appear heroic (cf. Laemmle 2013: 346–7), but it is perhaps better to see a post-Euripidean attempt to draw explicit attention to (and make theatrical capital out of) the un-Homeric ease with which Odysseus can come and go from the cave, cf. Zwierlein 1967: 451–2.

φύγοιμ' ἄν 'I could flee', potential optative.

κἀκβέβηκ' 'and I have come out from …'; we might rather have expected a verb meaning 'I have slipped out from …', cf. 347n.

ἄντρου μυχῶν: in 407 Odysseus' comrades are cowering ἐν μυχοῖς πέτρας while he serves the Cyclops; here again Odysseus distinguishes himself from them.

483–518 SECOND STASIMON AND SONG EXCHANGE

The chorus react to Odysseus' plan by imagining, and probably miming out, the blinding to come (483–6), in verses which rework Odysseus' fore-shadowing at 460–3. The sound of the Cyclops' singing alerts them, however, to the fact that the monster is about to set off on his *kōmos* (cf. 445–6) and so they decide to 'educate' him in such sympotic practice by singing an appropriate song (488–94). The two stanzas of their song (494–502, 511–18) are separated by a metrically identical strophe sung by the inebriated Cyclops who has emerged from the cave, probably wearing a wreath (cf. 517–18n.) and followed by Silenos carrying a mixing-bowl (cf. 545) and Odysseus with the wineskin.

483–94 form an anapaestic system which may be performed either by the *koryphaios* (cf. Garvie on Aesch. *Pers.* 532–97) or, more probably, the entire chorus; σῖγα σῖγα in 488 has been taken as a sign that the two sections of the anapaests are performed by two half-choruses, but the singular imperative is more likely self-admonition by the entire chorus (cf., e.g., *Suppl.* 271, *Her.* 819, *Tr.* 1235). The choral pattern of anapaests introducing lyrics is familiar from Aesch. (cf., e.g., *Pers.* 532–47, 623–32, *Sept.* 822–31), and there, as here, the anapaests serve in part as a self-conscious introduction to what follows: the chorus announce the plan to 'educate' the Cyclops, and the lyrics which follow are part of that education. The initial resonance of the anapaests may be comically martial: the inevitably unwarlike satyrs imagine themselves 'drawn up' to fight, cf. Lissarrague 2013: 183–9 for images of soldier-satyrs. For such anapaestic systems in satyr-drama cf. Aesch. *Dikt.* fr. 47a.821–32, Cerbo 2015: 72–7; in Aeschylus too the suggestion of semi-choruses has been made (cf. Dettori 2016: 186). In Cratinus' *Odysseis* (cf. above pp. 5–7), the chorus of sailors seem to have introduced themselves in stichic paroemiacs (fr. 151): σῖγα νυν πᾶς, ἔχε σῖγα,/καὶ πάντα λόγον τάχα πεύσηι·/ἡμῖν δ᾽ Ἰθάκη πατρίς ἐστι,/πλέομεν δ᾽ ἅμ᾽ Ὀδυσσέι θείωι.

The anapaests here are, as is conventional, divided into dimeters. The first section and the system as a whole are concluded (486, 494) by catalectic dimeters ('paroemiacs') of identical shape: – – – – ‿‿ – –. The utterance immediately before the close (492–3) forms three metra, rather than the expected multiple of two, and this suggests the colometry adopted here, a dimeter followed by a monometer; exactly the same pattern closes an anapaestic sequence at *Med.* 1114–15. Π¹ offers a different colometry (monometer followed by dimeter):

φέρε νιν κώμοις
παιδεύσωμεν [τὸν ἀπαίδευτον·
πάντως μέλλει [τυφλὸς εἶναι.

In performance hardly any difference would be felt, but it makes sense to give special emphasis to τὸν ἀπαίδευτον as in the colometry adopted here.

483–4 On the difference from *Od.*, in which Odysseus orders his men to draw lots for a role in the blinding, cf. above p. 10, 632–4n.

τίς δ᾽ ἐπὶ πρώτωι 'who after/in sequence to the first …'; for this, perhaps martial, sense of the preposition cf. Xen. *Cyr.* 8.3.16–18 (17 ἐπὶ δὲ τούτοις … τεταγμένοι). δέ is not uncommon in the second limb of an anaphoric sequence, without preceding μέν, cf. *GP*² 163, Diggle 1981: 55–6.

δαλοῦ κώπην, 'the oar of the torch', picks up Odysseus' nautical image at 460–1. κώπη primarily means 'handle, grip', as of a sword, etc., but in the present context 'oar' is unavoidable.

ὀχμάσαι 'to grip firmly', dependent upon ταχθείς, cf. λαβόντας in 633. The transmitted participle is not impossible – for such sequences of participles in asyndeton cf. K–G II 104 – but the infinitive provides a clearer sequence.

485–6 recall both 462–3 and *Od.* 9.389–90.

βλεφάρων: for the plural with reference to the one-eyed Cyclops cf. 458–9n., *Od.* 9.389 βλέφαρ' ἀμφὶ καὶ ὀφρύας.

διακναίσει 'will destroy utterly', lit. 'will grind/scrape thoroughly', cf. *El.* 1307, *Med.* 164.

487 ᾠδὴ ἔνδοθεν 'singing within (the *skēnē*)' is a surviving stage-direction (παρεπιγραφή); the indentation in the text matches that in Π¹. For examples in satyr-play cf. (probably) ποππυσμός at Aesch. *Dikt.* fr. 47a.790, 803. Close to the current example are instances such as Ar. *Birds* 222 αὐλεῖ, *Frogs* 311 αὐλεῖ τις ἔνδοθεν. Such stage-directions may have entered written texts at a relatively early date, but it is unlikely that many, if indeed any, are contemporary with the poet, although that question raises the very complex issue of how dramatists actually scripted their plays. Most, but not all, such παρεπιγραφαί are readily inferrable from the text itself; in the present case reference has already been made to the Cyclops' singing (425), and 489–90 pick up the description of 425–6. Cf. further Taplin 1977b.

488 σῖγα σῖγα picks up Odysseus' instruction at 476, where see n.

καὶ δή marks the arrival of a new character, cf. *Med.* 1118, Ar. *Birds* 268, *GP*² 251.

489 ἄχαριν κέλαδον μουσιζόμενος is a mocking paradox: music, particularly in the manner of Anacreon (cf., e.g., Anacreon T 13 Campbell), should be full of χάρις, just as the Graces (Χάριτες) and the Muses together form the 'sweetest company' (*Her.* 675). The effect is something like 'making music which is a graceless din', a variant of 425–6 ᾄδει ... ἄμουσ'. κέλαδος (cf. 7n.) here bears its negative sense, though it can also be used of tuneful melody (cf., e.g., *IT* 1129). The mockery is heightened by the verb μουσίζεσθαι, which is found only here before Theocr. 11.81 (the Cyclops again) and 8.38, both active, rather than middle; perhaps Euripides coined a strange verb to describe a very strange sound (and Theocritus noticed).

490 σκαιός, lit. 'on the left', i.e. 'clumsy', 'gauche', like ἀμαθής (cf. 172–4n.) and ἄμουσος (cf. 426), covers a broad range of intellectual, cultural and social ineptitude (cf. Halliwell 2012: 20–1); the chorus see themselves as sophisticated judges of song (cf. Pratinas' angry chorus, in all likelihood satyrs, at *PMG* 708), and the Cyclops here falls well short. At Ar. *Wasps* 1183 the exasperated son addresses his reprobate father as ὦ σκαιὲ κἀπαίδευτε, Socrates sees Strepsiades as σκαιός (Ar. *Clouds* 629), and at Pl. *Rep.* 3.411d7–e2 the voracious athlete who has no interest in μουσικὴ καὶ φιλοσοφία is ἄμουσος and lives ἐν ἀμαθίαι καὶ σκαιότητι μετὰ ἀρρυθμίας τε καὶ ἀχαριστίας (cf. ἄχαριν in 489).

ἀπωιδός may be understood as an adjective, 'singing unmusically', or a one-off noun 'non-singer' (Halliwell 2012: 21), another lexical rarity to match the unmatched awfulness of the Cyclops' singing. The term does not re-appear before Hellenistic and imperial prose.

καὶ κλαυσόμενος 'and who will come to a sorry end'; for this colloquial use of κλαίειν cf. 172–4, 554nn. The third and least expected member of the crescendo is given emphasis both by καί and by the switch to the future tense; the certainty of the Cyclops' suffering is written in the Homeric script. A certain awkwardness remains, however, which some have sought to remove by emendation: κατακλαυσόμενος (Hermann), although κατα-κλαίειν does not seem to occur in this sense, τάχα κλαυσόμενος (Fix). One might consider interchanging 490 and 491, to give 490 even greater surprise effect.

491 πετρίνων ... μελάθρων: a mockingly high-style variant for πέτρα, although μέλαθρα is used by Electra's husband of his hut (*El.* 78) and by Philoctetes of his cave (Soph. *Phil.* 1453); in *Cycl.* it appears also at 430, 'the halls of the Bacchic one', a grand phrase to tempt the satyrs, and 512 which picks up the current verse in a lyric context. In Ar. it occurs only in paratragedy (*Birds* 1247, *Thesm.* 41, 874).

492–3 For the theme of the Cyclops' education cf. above p. 18. Part of turning the ἄμουσος into a μουσικός is to teach him to perform lyric verse. There is a close analogy in the education into sympotic practice of Philocleon in Ar. *Wasps*. For other links between *Cycl.* and *Wasps* cf. 156, 203, 320–1, 323–31, 475, 490, 492–3, 543 nn.

φέρε νυν: the transmitted νιν would be picked up by τὸν ἀπαίδευτον, 'him ... the boorish one'; such a pattern is common (K–G I 658), though it cannot be exactly paralleled in Euripides. The urgency of φέρε νυν (cf., e.g., *Or.* 1281), however, well suits the situation.

κώμοις 'with revel-songs', to be taken with παιδεύσωμεν, cf. Ar. *Thesm.* 988–9, LSJ s.v. II; this song is in fact to be about the κῶμος.

ἀπαίδευτον: both 'uneducated' and 'boorish, stupid', cf. 490n., LSJ s.v.; at *Ion* 247 οὐκ ἀπαιδεύτως refers to the proper sensitivity of a decent person. The Cyclops is probably the character referred to in Nicochares frr. 4–5 (from the *Galateia*) as 'more uneducated' (ἀπαιδευτότερος) than a notoriously stupid person and also described as 'illiterate' (τὸν ἀναλφά-βητον). Despite the satyrs' scorn, Euripides' Cyclops is in fact surprisingly 'well educated', cf. 275–6n., 316–46, etc.

494 πάντως 'at any rate, at all events'. The implication seems to be that educating the Cyclops in komastic practice will not have any harmful effects, despite Odysseus' plan to dissuade him from the *kōmos* (451–2), because the blinding is a certainty; one of the reasons they (and we) know that is because we all know the Homeric script. This interpretation has important implications for the song which follows, cf. 495–502n.

495–518 The 'revel-song' consists of three metrically identical stanzas (cf. 510n.), two performed by the chorus and one by the Cyclops; such a structure is very rare in drama and is probably resonant not just of the poetry of Anacreon, but also more generally of popular and sympotic song-culture, in which guests took turns to recite small snatches of song. On the song in general cf. esp. Rossi 1971a: 11–23, Bing 2014.

The metrical form of the stanzas falls broadly into two parts:

(i) Each stanza begins with six pure 'anacreontics':

⏑⏑ – ⏑ – ⏑ – –

The 'anacreontic' may be seen as an 'anaclastic' version of the ionic dimeter, ⏑⏑ – – ⏑⏑ – – ; 'anaclasis' refers to the redistribution of syllables. In the present case ⏑ – replaces – ⏑ in positions 4 and 5.

(ii) The six anacreontics are followed by three ionics (⏑⏑ – – ⏑⏑ – – ⏑⏑ – –) and then the closural sequence ⏑⏑ – ⏑ – – –. Different interpretations of this cluster are possible (cf. Willink 2001: 526), but most probably we have:

| ⏑⏑ – – ⏑⏑ – – | *2 ion* |
| ⏑⏑ – – ⏑⏑ – ⏑ – – – | *ion anacr (syncopated)* |

The closural sequence ⏑⏑ – ⏑ – – – occurs also at *Ba.* 72, where it is preceded by an ionic dimeter. In Anacreon, *PMG* 395 eleven anacreontics are followed by an ionic dimeter and then a further anacreontic.

Ionic rhythms are particularly associated with ritual and cultic contexts, most notably *Ba.* 64–134 and Ar. *Frogs* 323–53 (cf. Dodds 1960: 72–3), but the principal resonance here will be with the sympotic songs of Anacreon of Teos, although the name 'anacreontic' for this verse form goes back only to much later metricians. Athenian tradition recorded that Anacreon had been brought to Athens by Peisistratos' son Hipparchos ([Pl.] *Hipparchos* 228c1–2, Arist. *Ath. Pol.* 18.1) and that he had written poetry for elite families (Pl. *Charm.* 157e6, cf. Schol. [Aesch.] *PV* 128); it is not unlikely that he influenced some of Aesch.'s lyrics. Pausanias (1.25.1) records a statue of the poet on the Acropolis in which he was represented like 'a man singing while drunk', but both the date of this statue and the reliability of Pausanias' report are disputed (cf. 503–10n., Rosenmeyer 1992: 27–9). Comedy shows that both the poet's name and some at least of his verses would have been recognised by a late fifth-century audience (cf. Ar. *Ach.* 850, *Birds* 1372–4, *Thesm.* 161); in Ar. fr. 235

(*Daitaleis*) a character asks someone to sing him a *skolion* of Alcaeus or
Anacreon, and 495–502 would well fit such a request. A good notion of
the 'idea of Anacreon' in late fifth-century Athens can be gained from
a hexameter poem about him by the oligarchic politician Critias (fr. 1
D–K = *PMG* 500): Anacreon is depicted precisely as a poet of love and
wine, a φιλοβάρβιτος whose fame will last as long as do sympotic practices.
The satyrs too are creatures given to wine and the pursuit of sex and are
also players of the βάρβιτος (cf. 40n.); it is no wonder that Anacreon, like
them a 'servant of Dionysos' (Leonidas, *APl*. 306.10 (= *HE* 2160)), was
one of their favourite poets. Later rhetorical and stylistic theory identified 'simplicity' (ἀφέλεια) as characteristic of Anacreon, cf. Hermogenes
322–3 Rabe; this stylistic feature suited 'innocent, childish natures', such
as Theocritus' herdsmen (the Cyclops of *Idyll* 11 is a paradigmatic example of such 'simplicity'), and here too we may see an affinity between the
lyric poet and his satyric fans. Anacreon is depicted and named on three
Attic vases of the late sixth century, on one of which he appears to be
taking part in a *kōmos*, which is the context of the current performance.
On Anacreon's reputation at Athens cf. Rosenmeyer 1992: 15–33 (with
Plate II), Yatromanolakis 2007: 110–43 (with Figures 8–10), Bing 2014,
Bernsdorff 2016, and for Athenian knowledge of archaic lyric more gen-
erally cf. Carey 2011: 447–54, D'Alessio 2016.

495–502 The chorus perform a song describing the pleasures and purpose of the *kōmos*; for this theme in early lyric cf. Alcaeus fr. 374 and perhaps
Anacreon, *PMG* 442. Antipater of Sidon later called Anacreon ὁ Διωνύσου
μεμελημένος εὐάσι κώμοις (*AP* 7.26.5 = *HE* 256), and an epigram ascribed
to Simonides calls him φιλόκωμος (*AP* 7.24.5 = *FGE* 960). In *Alc*. Heracles'
drunkenness is likened to a κῶμος, cf. 804, 815, and the messenger in *Ion*
likens the doves who interrupt the celebration in the tent to a κῶμος burst-
ing into a house (1196–7). We should imagine, however, the 'real' analogies of such a song being performed at a symposium, rather than by a
komast already on his way through the streets. Textual corruption in 499
and difficulties of interpretation enjoin caution, but there is no reason to
believe, as commonly argued (e.g. Voelke 2001: 95–6), that the purpose
of the song is to make the Cyclops realise that he has available already all
that he needs and so deter him from the *kōmos*; rather, the satyrs 'educate'
him, in the certain knowledge of his fate (cf. 494n.). Odysseus' plan is
then enacted at 530–44. The principal difficulty arises from uncertainty as
to whether the song describes someone on his way to the beloved's house
or someone, together with appropriate company, still at the symposium, or
whether both situations are somehow evoked and combined.

The language and themes of the first stanza are not obviously parodic
of extant anacreontic or sympotic song more generally; the humorous

incongruity rather arises from the disjunction between the *makarismos* of a happily drunken komast and the actual situation of the Cyclops.

495 The generalising assertion of blessedness or happiness, 'lucky the man who …', the so-called *makarismos*, is frequently found in contexts of cult and the mysteries, cf. *Ba.* 72–4 ὦ μάκαρ, ὅστις εὐδαί-/μων τελετὰς θεῶν εἰ-/δὼς κτλ., 902–4 (with Dodds 1960: 75, Richardson 1974: 313). In describing the 'blessedness' of the happy komast, this form therefore suggests how easily obtainable 'blessedness' is. The satyrs begin with a formulation, μάκαρ ὅστις εὐιάζει, which would be perfectly at home in the mouths of the chorus of *Ba.*, but they soon move away to a different vision; theirs is a Dionysiac κῶμος, but not that in which the chorus of *Ba.* long to take part. This is one of the passages which make the relationship between *Ba.* and *Cycl.* particularly intriguing, cf. above pp. 45–6. *Makarismos* is also a familiar form in wedding-songs (Diggle on *Phaethon* 240, Hunter 1983: 195), and as such the formula here may look forward to the third stanza; a number of motifs are shared with the comic *makarismos* of a bride in Eubulus fr. 102.

εὐιάζει 'shouts the Bacchic cry', cf. 25–6n., *Ba.* 67, 104, Soph. *Ichn.* 227. The more common form is εὐάζειν.

496 βοτρύων φίλαισι παγαῖς most likely depends upon ἐκπετασθείς; φίλαισι is presumably focalised both by the komast and by the performing satyrs. Choice between Attic/Ionic and Doric forms is difficult in this ode, cf. 500, 504, 515. In a poem resonant of Anacreon, it may seem mistaken to seek to eliminate Attic/Ionic forms, but Doric νύμφα (515) seems unlikely to have been introduced by error, and Doric forms have thus been accepted throughout.

497–8 '… spread out (< ἐκπετάννυμι) for the revel, his arms around a dear friend'. Interpretation is disputed. 'Spread out' may refer to the sails of a ship, with the 'dear grape-streams' taking the place of the breeze (cf. *Anacreontea* 50.10–12); if so, the image of the drunken komast as a ship fits with a familiar and recurrent pattern of imagery, which the Cyclops also picks up in the next stanza, cf. 362n. For the emotional elation suggested by ἐκπετασθείς cf. perhaps *Od.* 18.160–1 (Penelope) ὅπως πετάσειε μάλιστα/θυμὸν μνηστήρων (with Steiner's n.). If the κῶμος is already under way, ὑπαγκαλίζων will mean 'embracing for support', rather than the more erotic sense, 'cuddling', which the verb might otherwise suggest; at Pl. *Symp.* 212d6 an aulos-player brings in the drunken Alcibiades ὑπολαβοῦσαν, 'supporting him'. On balance, this interpretation seems the most natural. Wilamowitz (on *Her.* 890) read ἐπίκωμος and took the participle as an image from wrestling (cf. 678n.), 'overcome (*bezwungen*) by the wine', though he did not think that the komast was here depicted as lying on the ground; as a wrestling term, however, ἐκπετασθείς could hardly mean anything other than that the komast was flat on his back (in a κῶμα rather than a κῶμος). Others understand that he is indeed 'spread out', but on a dining-couch rather than the ground; this, however, makes ἐπὶ κῶμον very difficult to construe ('ready for a revel' OSC, cf. Voelke 2001: 94–6).

499–500 499 is unmetrical as τε ξανθόν gives – – – in place of ⏑ – –. Several of the many suggestions (cf. Di Marco 1980b) seek to find some form of ἄνθος behind ξανθόν: ἐπὶ δεμνίοισί τ' ἄνθος (Meineke), '[having] on the bed the flower of a voluptuous companion …', ἐπὶ δεμνίοισί τ' ἀνθέων/χλιδανὰν ἔχων ἑταίραν (Seaford), 'having a voluptuous companion on a bed of flowers'. If this is a description of a κῶμος already under way (cf. 497–8n.), then ἔχων will mean 'having [i.e. waiting for him, in prospect]', which is an awkward extension, unless the corruption in 499 conceals a wording which made that sense easier. If, however, the verses refer to a reclining symposiast, then comprehension is admittedly easier, cf. *Anacreontea* 50.17–20, ὅτ' ἐγὼ πίω τὸν οἶνον,/μύρωι εὐώδει τέγξας/δέμας, ἀγκάλαις δὲ κούρην/κατέχων, Κύπριν ἀείδω, behind which may lie poetry of Anacreon (cf. *PMG* 444).

χλιδανᾶς occurs only here in Euripides, although χλιδή is not uncommon. Sappho seems to have used the adjective (fr. 60.8), and there may be archaic lyric lying behind the use here. For the Doric form cf. 496n.

501 Men used perfume, like garlands, most notably at symposia and weddings, cf. Ar. *Peace* 862 (with Olson's n.), Blech 1982: 63–81, Laemmle 2013: 354–8.

μυρόχριστον λιπαρός is perhaps to be preferred to μυρόχριστος λιπαρόν (Scaliger), as giving a more stylised word-order.

502 The komast calls out to be admitted when he has reached the house of the beloved; as with the Cyclops' imitation in 510, there may be specific lyric models (? Anacreon) behind this verse, cf. Alcaeus fr. 374 δέξαι με κωμάσδοντα, δέξαι, λίσσομαί σε, λίσσομαι. Such songs outside the door of the beloved, familiar above all from Hellenistic epigram and Roman elegy, are usually given the generic name *paraklausithyron* (from Plut. *Amatorius* 753b), cf. Headlam on Herodas 2.34–7, Copley 1956, Hunter 1999: 107–8. There may here be a sexual *double entendre*, with θύρα suggesting the female genitalia, cf. Ar. *Eccl.* 962, 990 where both literal and metaphorical senses occur in a short space, Archilochus fr. 196a.21 West πύλαι 'gates', although nothing else in this song prepares for such coarseness, which seems different in kind from the allusiveness of songs such as Anacreon, *PMG* 417. Those who see these verses describing a sympotic rather than a komastic scene explain that the reclining symposiast uses the komastic phrase to issue a sexual invitation to his companion (or companions). In either case, the conventional question calls amusing attention to the fact that the Cyclops' cave has no door which could be locked against (or opened for) a lover.

503–10 The Cyclops' song takes its cue from the chorus' stanza: such an amoeboean technique is a familiar part of sympotic song-making. The Cyclops' song is typically about himself (cf. 322–38), but he is a comic version of the 'blessed' komast whom the chorus has just invoked; his 'anacreontic' performance foreshadows the standard representation of Anacreon in Hellenistic epigram as swaying under the influence of drink, cf. Gutzwiller 2014, and Most 2014 for the subsequent history of such *mimesis*. The Cyclops' performance may conceivably have recalled for the audience representations of Anacreon in art (cf. 495–518n.). The imagery of the Cyclops' song is more obvious and coarse than is normal in sympotic lyric, but that is just what we would expect; the Cyclops' first anacreontic begins in fact with a very down-to-earth and inarticulate exclamation. In Philoxenus' dithyrambic *Cyclops* (cf. above pp. 8–9), the Cyclops danced and imitated lyre-playing (Ar. *Pl.* 290–5, *PMG* 819, Theocr. 7.153), and here too the Cyclops may have performed some drunken dance-steps while singing. At Hor. *Sat.* 1.5.60–4 an ugly clown is asked 'to dance (the part of) the shepherd Cyclops' and the context is dramatic (cf. Gowers on v. 63). A scholium on Theocr. 7.153 reports that Theocritus 'took over (μετήνεγκε) from Euripides the fact that the Cyclops danced'; as the Cyclops does not dance in *Od.* 9, grammarians needed to find an alternative origin for Theocritus' reference. The scholium can hardly be other than a reference to this passage (hardly to Silenos' dance at 156); it may just be 'a guess' (Seaford), but it would be a remarkable dramaturgical observation, given that there is no explicit reference in the text to dancing. Εὐριπίδου may, however, be a slip for Φιλοξένου or Ἀριστοφάνους.

503 παπαπαῖ: cf. 153, 572, Ar. *Thesm.* 1191 (a cry of pleasure from the Scythian archer).

πλέως μὲν οἴνου: for the common omission of the verb 'to be' cf. *El.* 37 with Denniston's n., K–G I 40–1, Smyth §945.

504 γάνυμαι ⟨δὲ⟩ δαιτὸς ἥβαι 'I rejoice in the merriment of the feast'; for the Doric form cf. 496n. ἥβη is very hard to illustrate in this sense, but cf. Pind. *Pyth.* 4.295 θυμὸν ἐκδόσθαι πρὸς ἥβαν, 'give the spirit over to youthful merriment' (in a sympotic context). Stephanus proposed ἥδη, but one might consider ἥδει or ἅδει from ἥδος, 'I delight in the pleasure of the feast', cf. *Il.* 1.575–6 (= *Od.* 18.403–4) οὐδέ τι δαιτός/ἐσθλῆς ἔσσεται ἥδος; the Cyclops' feast has been anything but 'pleasurable' by ordinary standards. Some have wanted to see in the transmitted text puns on Ganymede and Hebe, cf. Ambrose 2005: 23.

505–6 '… stuffed in my hull (σκάφος) like a merchant-ship up to the deck at the top of my belly'; the Cyclops pictures himself as a ship so crammed with merchandise, presumably amphorae of wine, that it fills the whole hold below deck-level, cf. 362n. The vividly explicit and almost repetitious detail, continued in φόρτος in the next verse, is a hallmark of Cyclopean lyric.

507 ὑπάγει 'leads on', almost 'entices me to …', cf. *Andr.* 428, LSJ s.v. III.

ὁ φόρτος εὔφρων 'the cargo of delight', cf. *Il.* 3.246 οἶνον εὔφρονα, Xenophanes fr. 1.4 West κρητὴρ … μεστὸς εὐφροσύνης, Fraenkel on Aesch. *Ag.* 806. εὐφροσύνη is a key ingredient of the proper symposium, cf. *Od.* 9.6, Hunter 2018: 103, 106.

508 ἦρος ὥραις: springtime may perhaps evoke both the time of the original performance at the Great Dionysia (in the month of Elaphebolion, i.e. late March) and the opening of the sailing season, when very many merchant-vessels were indeed launched after the winter pause; the two events are linked at Theophr. *Char.* 3.3 (where see Diggle's n.). It is possible also that there was a tradition linking symposia and sympotic song to springtime, cf. Alcaeus fr. 36, Hor. *c.* 1.4. Wecklein proposed ἐπίκωμον, 'me … revelling' (cf. 497–8n.), but cf. 445.

509 ἐπὶ Κύκλωπας ἀδελφούς: cf. 445–6n.

510 The Cyclops concludes with a direct address, as had the chorus. It is very likely that there are specific verses of Anacreon in the background here, cf. *PMG* 356a ἄγε δὴ φέρ' ἡμῖν ὢ παῖ/κελέβην κτλ., 396 φέρ' ὕδωρ φέρ' οἶνον ὢ παῖ φέρε δ' ἀνθεμόεντας ἡμῖν/στεφάνους κτλ. The reference to the wineskin lowers the tone appropriately. Triclinius' emendation restores exact responsion with 502 and 518, in place of the anaclastic sequence offered by <L>P. Exact responsion seems to offer a funnier performance by the newly trained Cyclops, but some retain the MS reading as either a licence or a marker of the Cyclops' imperfect metrical control, cf. Zuntz 1965: 53–4, Meriani 1999: 164–8.

ξεῖνε: cf. 102n.

ἔνδος μοι 'pass me', 'put into my hands', cf. *IT* 167.

511–18 The chorus now depict the Cyclops with hymeneal motifs obviously designed to mock him; after the κῶμος comes the longed-for union. Textual corruption and loss make the stanza extremely difficult to interpret, but it seems certain that the chorus allude riddlingly to the coming blinding, in portraying the Cyclops as a bridegroom about to lie with a 'tender bride within dewy caves'. As with the chorus' first stanza, there is no reason to think that these verses are designed to deter the Cyclops from going on his κῶμος, cf. 495–502n. Bing 2014: 43–4 attractively suggests that this stanza is modelled on hymeneal poetry written by Anacreon for female choruses, cf. Critias fr. 1.8 D–K (*PMG* 500) παννυχίδας θ' ἱερὰς θηλεῖς χοροὶ ἀμφιέπωσιν; Dioscorides, *AP* 7.31.2 (= *HE* 1576) addresses

Anacreon as κώμου καὶ πάσης κοίρανε παννυχίδος. There is, however, very little evidence for any such compositions by Anacreon.

511 The material gathered in 553n. suggests that there may be specific forebears for this verse in archaic lyric; Leonidas of Tarentum describes the drunken Anacreon as ὑγρὰ δεδορκώς (*APl.* 306.3 (= *HE* 2153)). Praise of the beauty of both bride and groom was of course conventional in hymeneal contexts, cf., e.g., Fedeli 1983: 122–4.

ὄμμασιν: the conventional reference to 'eyes' (plural, cf. 458–9) reminds us that the one-eyed Cyclops is not like the bridegrooms normally celebrated in song.

512 picks up the announcement of the Cyclops' entry at 491; it does not necessarily suggest that the Cyclops enters at this point – he may well have been on stage since the anacreontic song began. The second half of the stanza will address him in the second person, but there is no need for ἐκπερᾶις (Heath) or ἐκπέρα (Scaliger). The verse may in fact draw on hymeneal poetry describing the appearance of bride and/or groom for the wedding-procession, cf. Sappho frr. 111.5 γάμβρος †ἔρχεται ἶσος Ἄρευι†, 112, Ar. *Birds* 1709 προσέρχεται, Cat. 61.91–100, 176–88.

513 The lacuna at the start of the verse leaves its interpretation entirely uncertain, whether we read τίς or τις. Diggle (1972: 345) suggested a participle such as κελαδῶν, 'crying out', but why the Cyclops (or any komast or bridegroom) should be depicted shouting 'Who/someone loves me' remains unclear, even in the context of the familiar banter and jesting associated with weddings. We might consider something like a simple καλὸς ὤν; Hermann proposed φίλος ὤν.

514–15 are corrupt beyond even plausible restoration; for surveys of attempted solutions cf. Diggle 1972, Stinton 1977: 138–9. 'Torches' suit the hymeneal context and perhaps also evoke the firebrand which awaits the Cyclops (many have sought to connect δαῖα with δαΐς, 'torch'); Seaford proposed λύχνα σ᾽ ἡμμέν᾽ ἀμμένει καὶ/ῥοδόχρως τέρεινα νύμφα, where the epithet would indeed suit a hymeneal context (cf. Theocr. 18.31, Hunter 1983: 126). Several suggestions find χρώς concealed within the transmitted χώς. Comparisons and similes are very common in hymeneal contexts (cf., e.g., Sappho fr. 115, the bridegroom compared to a 'slender branch', Feeney 2013), and corruption here may conceal such a 'likeness'. The 'tender bride' may evoke the tree-branch which has become a red-hot stake.

ἀμμένει: i.e. ἀναμένει with apocope of the disyllabic prefix; the verb can be used of both pleasant and very unpleasant things in store, cf. *Hec.* 1281 φόνια λουτρά σ᾽ ἀμμένει. It is obviously tempting to see an allusion to Alcaeus fr. 346.1 πώνωμεν· τί τὰ λύχν᾽ ὀμμένομεν; δάκτυλος ἀμέρα, but no reconstruction yet suggested offers a plausible text or purpose for such an allusion.

νύμφα: cf. 496n.

516 'Dewy caves' suggests both a *locus amoenus* for love-making (perhaps again evocative of Anacreon, cf. Dioscorides, *AP* 7.31.8 (= *HE* 1582)), and (ironically) the blood-spattered cave of the Cyclops, cf. *IT* 443 δρόσον αἱματηράν, Aesch. *Ag.* 1390. There may again be a sexual *double entendre* (cf. 169–73, 502nn.), but despite all that has been written about the relationship of women and caves in the Greek male imagination (Calypso, Theocr. 3 etc.), such a usage here would be hard to parallel.

517–18 Lit. 'no single colour of garlands around your head will soon keep you company'; ἐξομιλήσει is very remarkable, but 'no remotely plausible substitute has been suggested' (Diggle 1972: 345). Bridegrooms, like symposiasts, wore garlands, and garlands are a constant theme in sympotic poetry, cf., e.g. Anacreon, *PMG* 410, 434, Blech 1982: 63–74; the meaning seems to be that, whatever wreath the Cyclops is currently wearing, it will soon be joined by another 'crown' of blood-red. There is no good evidence, as sometimes asserted, that bridegrooms were particularly indicated by wreaths of several colours or of one.

519–607 THIRD EPISODE

In a long stichomythic exchange, Odysseus and Silenos seek to educate the Cyclops about wine, while dissuading him from going on a κῶμος to his brother-Cyclopes; Silenos uses the occasion to drink as much as he can. The wine goes to the Cyclops' head, and he chooses Silenos as the appropriate sexual partner to complete the party. They disappear into the cave (Silenos never to return), and Odysseus seeks to strengthen the chorus' resolve and prays for divine help.

519–20 ἄκουσον: cf. 253n.
ὡς '[You should listen to me] because …'
τοῦ Βακχίου: the identity of the god and his wine, which forms the basis for the interchange of 519–29, is very familiar, cf. 454, *IT* 953, *Ba.* 284 οὗτος θεοῖσι σπένδεται θεὸς γεγώς (with Dodds's n.); in Timotheus' *Cyclops* (*PMG* 780.4) wine is αἷμα Βακχίου, cf. Obbink 1993, above pp. 17–18 and 521–2n.
τρίβων 'an old hand with', 'very experienced in', cf. *Med.* 686, *Ba.* 717; the term is not found in Aeschylus or Sophocles and probably has a colloquial flavour, cf. Collard 2018: 112–13 (~ Stevens 1976: 50–1), Biles and Olson on Ar. *Wasps* 1429. Odysseus never needs a particular reason to claim expertise in any sphere of activity, but it is the *Odyssey* and, above all, the Cyclops-story of Book 9 which have demonstrated his knowledge of wine; here again (and cf. 567) Odysseus perhaps teases the Cyclops with the well known Homeric story.
πιεῖν: cf. 257n.
521–2 The Cyclops' awkward (and somewhat unexpected) questions call attention to the potential ambiguity of 519–20: is Odysseus referring

to the 'Bacchic one' *qua* wine or *qua* divine figure? It is tempting for us to translate this into a difference between βάκχιος and Βάκχιος, but that distinction is naturally blurred in oral performance (cf., e.g., ἔρως and Ἔρως). Despite 204–5, the Cyclops seems not to have made the link between the 'Bacchic one' and the wine he has been drinking; in his reported conversation with the Cyclops within the cave, Odysseus used only the name 'Dionysos' (415). The awkwardness of taking 521 as a single question is overcome by Nauck's punctuation into two halves (cf. *Med.* 701 for strong punctuation at the centre of the trimeter), but θεὸς νομίζεται; remains an unexpected question for the Cyclops to ask (Hermann suggested θεοῦ for τούτου in 520 to explain the question). Some editors follow Wieseler in giving these words (and 522) to Odysseus; the absence of any assenting particle in 522, 'Yes, he is …', is indeed surprising (cf. K–G II 541).

μέγιστος … βίου: cf. *Ba.* 278–83, 421–3 (οἴνου τέρψιν ἄλυπον), 769–74, *Il.* 14.325, etc.

523 ἐρυγγάνω never occurs in high poetry, which restricts itself to ἐρεύγομαι, the verb used of the Cyclops in *Od.* 9.374; neither verb appears in tragedy.

γοῦν confirms Odysseus' claim, cf. *GP*[2] 451–2; the pleasure (ἡδέως) the Cyclops takes in vomiting is an example of the god's contribution to τέρψις βίου.

524 A flat contradiction, not just of what every audience-member knew (cf. *Ba.* 860–1), but also of *Od.* 21.293–4, spoken by Antinoos to Odysseus, οἶνός σε τρώει μελιηδής, ὅς τε καὶ ἄλλους/βλάπτει, ὃς ἄν μιν χανδὸν ἕλῃ μηδ' αἴσιμα πίνῃι, cf. 421–2n. In instructing the Cyclops about wine, Odysseus is as economical with the truth as ever.

525 δ' expresses the Cyclops' surprise, cf. *GP*[2] 175. The Cyclops is still confused by the notion that the wine is (also) the god. For a rather similar joke cf. Plaut. *Amph.* 341 *quo ambulas tu, qui Volcanum in cornu conclusum geris?*

526 εὐπετής, 'easy-going, unperturbed', lit. 'falling well' (probably a metaphor from dicing), refers both to Dionysos' familiar smiling calm (cf. *Ba.* 439–60, 622, etc.), and to the liquidity of wine, which will 'happily' sit in any space into which it is poured; Odysseus is again teasing the ignorant Cyclops.

527 However familiar the Cyclops may be with animal-skins, he, like many of Euripides' audience, regards them as the dress of poor rustics and thus ill befitting gods, cf. Ar. *Clouds* 72; he is perhaps thinking particularly of goat-skins, cf. 80n. Whether or not gods had 'bodies' and what they looked like had long been debated by intellectuals, cf. Xenophanes fr. 23 D–K = D16 Laks–Most 'one god, the greatest (μέγιστος) among gods and men, alike to mortals neither in form (δέμας) nor thought', Osborne

2011: chapter 7; the Cyclops is, however, somewhat theologically chal-
lenged. σῶμ' ἔχειν in this sense is an unusual phrase, and Pierson suggested δῶμ' ἔχειν, which would have the Cyclops continuing his line of
thought from 525.

528 τί δ' …; 'Why so …?', cf. *Hipp.* 784, *Hec.* 886, Barrett on *Hipp.* 608.

529 The Cyclops probably takes another drink before or after this verse.
The point seems to be that the now childlike Cyclops thinks that it is the
wineskin which is keeping him from the wine and placing a constraint
upon the god; he does not understand that, without the skin, he would
have nothing to drink.

530 κεὐθύμει 'and have a good time'. εὐθυμία, 'good cheer', is appropriate to the symposium, cf. Aesch. *Ag.* 1592 (with Fraenkel's n.), Ion fr.
26.14 West, Dionysos addressed as εὐθύμων συμποσίων πρύτανι, Philemon
fr. 98.4; Pindar personifies Εὐθυμία and connects her with the Muses (fr.
155 M). In such contexts, the meaning is very close to εὐφροσύνη, cf. *Od.*
9.6, Xenophanes fr. 1.4 West, 507n.

531 προσδοῦναι 'give a share of', cf. 361, *Hel.* 700, Ar. *Knights* 1222.

532–3 show Odysseus and the Cyclops involved in a kind of sympotic
capping (τιμιώτερος is capped by χρησιμώτερος), cf. 536–7, 538n., Collins
2004: 44–8. Odysseus appeals to the epic and aristocratic motive of τιμή:
the possession of valued goods, such as wine would be in a country which
has not known it before, will increase the prestige of an individual; in
the only occurrence of τίμιος in Homer, Odysseus' men grumble that
Odysseus is πᾶσι φίλος καὶ τίμιος, to judge by the gifts and property he
collects, whereas they are returning home empty-handed (*Od.* 10.38).
Against this, the Cyclops sets the communal, 'democratic' virtue of being
χρήσιμος (or χρηστός) to one's φίλοι (or indeed one's fellow-Cyclopes) by
helping them materially, cf. *Suppl.* 887, *Or.* 910–11, Eupolis fr. 129, Dem.
42.22 'those who are well off should show themselves χρήσιμοι to the citizens', Men. *Sam.* 15–16. The clash of social motives, and the positioning
of the Cyclops on the side of communal values (contrast *Od.* 9.114–15,
'[the Cyclopes] have no concern with one another'), is a witty updating
and revision of the Homeric text.

534 Athenaeus 2.36d, which survives only in epitome, cites the verse
πληγὰς ὁ κῶμος λοίδορόν θ' ὕβριν φέρει from Euripides, and it is perhaps
more likely that this is a variant version of 534 than a verse from another
play. The changes might have arisen from slips in quotation from memory or may rather be an 'acting' version which has at some time been
taken into written texts; the verse may have become quasi-proverbial.
The epitome cites the verse within a nest of passages on the effects
of wine and, in particular, on ὕβρις resulting from excessive drinking;
Athenaeus' source cannot here be identified, but the variant version

would seem to have arisen at a relatively early date. It is not impossible that Euripides' verse originally contained elements of both versions. The bad effects of excessive drinking and rowdy revelling is a common theme of literature, notably comedy, cf. Epicharmus fr. 146, Ar. *Wasps* 1253–5, Eubulus fr. 93, from the *Semele or Dionysos* (with Hunter 1983: 187–9), Alexis fr. 160.

πυγμάς is more colourful than πληγάς, better suits the Cyclops' reply, and picks up the theme of 229; cf. further Pratinas, *PMG* 708.8 κώμωι μόνον θυραμάχοις τε πυγμαχίαισι νέων, Ar. *Wasps* 1386 ὑπώπια, Eubulus fr. 93.8 (on the worsening effects of each additional bowl of wine) ἕκτος δὲ κώμων, ἕβδομος δ᾿ ὑπωπίων. For πληγάς, which may be inflicted by a staff as well as by fists, cf. esp. Ar. *Wasps* 1298, 1323–5, 1422, etc.

λοίδορόν τ᾿ ἔριν: cf. Alexis fr. 160.5, λοιδορεῖσθαι as a stage (before violence) in drunken behaviour. The alternative to ἔρις, ὕβρις, which can cover both insulting words and violence, is very frequently cited in such contexts, cf. Panyassis fr. 17–18 Bernabé (= 20, 22 West), Ar. *Wasps* 1303, 1319, Eubulus fr. 93.7, [Arist.]. *Probl.* 30.953b4; if L read λοίδορόν θ᾿ ὕβριν and the text of Ath. λοίδορόν τ᾿ ἔριν, the former would certainly be the standard text of this verse.

φιλεῖ: cf. 537, *IA* 1000–1 στρατὸς γὰρ ἀθρόος … / λέσχας πονηρὰς καὶ κακοστόμους φιλεῖ, Pind. *Nem.* 9.48 ἡσυχία δὲ φιλεῖ/μὲν συμπόσιον. In such statements φιλεῖν amounts to 'is characterised by'; φιλεῖν followed by an infinitive is also common in generalisations of this kind.

535 'Yes, I am drunk, but nevertheless no one [or 'No one'] would lay a hand on me!'. No one (in their right mind) would presumably ever pick a fist-fight with the Cyclops, but – in keeping with the pattern of this whole scene – he is now characterised by the reckless bravado of the very drunk. So too, the confession of drunkenness is a familiar part of the literary portrayal of those under the influence, cf., e.g., Pl. *Symp.* 212e (Alcibiades), Eubulus fr. 123.

ἔμπας 'all the same, nevertheless', cf. LSJ s.v. II.

οὔτις will presumably have reminded some of the audience at least of Odysseus' trick in *Od.* 9, cf. 549–50; once again, the Cyclops' words echo and foreshadow the familiar Homeric material.

536 Odysseus speaks as the Cyclops' teacher and there is no need to see, with, e.g., Rossi 1971a: 30 n.67, a distortion of the proverbial οἴκοι μένειν χρὴ τὸν καλῶς εὐδαίμονα (Aesch. fr. 317, Soph. fr. 934).

ὦ τᾶν: this common address (of unknown etymology) here characterises 'friendly' advice, cf. *Hcld.* 321, 688, Dodds on *Ba.* 802, Collard 2018: 97–8 (~ Stevens 1976: 42–3), Dickey 1996: 158–60; in other contexts it may suggest impatience or frustration. At Soph. *Ichn.* 104 it is used by one member of the satyr-chorus to another.

537 The Cyclops caps Odysseus' generalisation with a matching quasi-proverbial utterance; the monster already knows some sympotic 'rules', cf. 532–3n.

ἠλίθιος with the meaning 'stupid' occurs only here in Euripides and not in Aeschylus or Sophocles; [Aesch.] *PV* 1061 gives the only extant example of the verb ἠλιθιοῦν.

538 Cf. 708, *GP*² 153 for δέ ... γε in 'retorts and lively rejoinders'. Odysseus trumps the Cyclops' claim, with σοφός emphatically placed at verse-end to surpass ἠλίθιος, in what amounts to another mini-demonstration of sympotic 'capping', cf. 532–3n. Odysseus' success is marked by the first signs of hesitation from the Cyclops.

μεθυσθείς: aor. pass. participle of μεθύσκειν, cf. 167; the passive is used like intransitive μεθύω.

539–40 Silenos' advice is driven as much by a desire not to have to share the wine as by a wish to aid Odysseus' plot. An exchange between individual satyrs at Soph. *Ichn.* 104–5 is verbally very close to these verses: τί δρῶμεν ... /πῶς δοκεῖ; δοκεῖ πάνυ.

τί δρῶμεν ...; amusingly suggests the crisis of a tragic moment, cf. *Hipp.* 782, *IT* 96, *El.* 967, etc.; however different the mood (cf. Soph. *Ichn.* 104), this decision will indeed determine the Cyclops' wretched future.

541 Odysseus now adds a further reason for staying put – the grass outside the cave offers a splendid setting for drinking; καὶ μήν indicates assent to what has just been said and adds a further argument, cf. Ar. *Lys.* 206, *GP*² 353–4. Odysseus' words evoke the pleasures of an outdoor drinking-party, often described in literature and depicted in art, cf. Pl. *Rep.* 2.372b5, Theocr. 7.133–55, Ap. Rhod. *Arg.* 1.453–9, Lucian, *VH* 2.14, Cazzato 2016. 543 shows that the verse cannot be spoken by the Cyclops as a reason to invite his colleagues to join him, with 'adversative' καὶ μήν (*GP*² 357, so Masarrachia 1994: 60–2); if spoken by the Cyclops, the verse could only mark agreement with Silenos and show that the Cyclops is yielding to the pressure (so, e.g., Rossi 1971a: 31).

λαχνῶδες τοὔδας ἀνθηρᾶς χλόης 'the ground is thick/shaggy with flowering greenery'. The genitive, regular with verbs meaning 'be full of' (Smyth §1369), probably depends upon λαχνῶδες, cf. Soph. *El.* 895–6 περιστεφῆ ... ἀνθέων, *OT* 83 πολυστεφὴς ... δάφνης, rather than upon τοὔδας, 'the ground of flowering greenery is thick'. Kirchhoff's ἀνθηρᾶι χλόηι simplifies the construction, but is unnecessary.

τοὔδας: i.e. τὸ οὖδας, cf. Hipponax fr. 118.5 West τοὖς, i.e. τὸ οὖς. καὶ μήν is, however, very often reinforced by γε, and Porson's γ' οὖδας may be correct.

542 That it is pleasant to drink in the sun is not a strong reason not to invite the other Cyclopes to join him or to go on a κῶμος; he presumably means that the Cyclops should stay and enjoy the sun before it gets dark. For the time-setting of the play cf. 214n.

πρός ... θάλπος ἡλίου 'in (lit. facing) the warmth of the sun'; the simple πρὸς τὸν ἥλιον is more common. Just as the sympotic instruction of the Cyclops has elements in common with the similar lessons offered to Philocleon in Ar. *Wasps* (cf. next n.), so here we may compare Bdelycleon urging upon his father the pleasures, including judging in the sunshine, of having his own court at home (*Wasps* 771–5).

543 Bdelycleon similarly teaches his father how gentlemen recline at Ar. *Wasps* 1208–13. Later scholars knew that, in the time of Homer, heroes sat, rather than reclined, on festive occasions (cf. Ath. 1.17f, Fraenkel 1950: III 754), but the humour here resides in turning the Cyclops into an Athenian gentleman, not in the anachronism *per se*. In the satyric *Syleus*, Heracles invites the eponymous monster to some heavy drinking, κλίθητι καὶ πίωμεν· ἐν τούτωι δέ μου/τὴν πεῖραν εὐθὺς λάμβαν᾽ εἰ κρείσσων ἔσηι (fr. 691).

μοι: 'ethic' dative, here best translated 'please', cf. 43n.

544 ἰδού: cf. 153–4n.

545 δῆτα 'then', i.e. now that I am lying like this ..., cf. *Andr.* 84, *Hcld.* 667, *GP²* 269. The mixing-bowl should be 'in the middle' (547), in the centre of the drinkers' field of vision.

546 Silenos' excuse is comically absurd: who is likely to be 'passing by'? Here again (cf. 153–4, 669–90nn.) excitement at the prospect of drinking wine is expressed by verse-division ('*antilabē*'). The lively, almost slapstick action of the 'symposium' of Silenos, the Cyclops, who is worried that Silenos is drinking too much of the wine, and an increasingly impatient Odysseus is brought out by four further *antilabai* at 558, 560, 565, 568.

καταβάληι 'knock over'.

547 κλέπτων is often used of doing something on the sly, cf. 552 λάθραι, LSJ s.v. IV, but here 'stealing', an important theme of the play (cf. above p. 81. on the *hypothesis*, 223n.), is just as appropriate.

κάτθες: i.e. κατάθες, with apocope of the disyllabic prefix, as often.

ἐς μέσον: the positioning of the mixing-bowl 'in the middle', in full view of all the symposiasts, was an important element, and manifestation, of the principles of equality and openness – the symposiasts too spoke 'into the middle' (Theognis 495, etc.) – which were central to sympotic ideology, cf., e.g., Ford 2002: 39–45.

548 Cf. *Od.* 9.355–6 δός μοι ἔτι πρόφρων καί μοι τεὸν οὔνομα εἰπὲ/αὐτίκα νῦν. The Cyclops, however, now also behaves like a 'modern' symposiast in asking the identity of his fellow 'guests', cf. Critias fr. 6.1–7 West, Call. fr. 178.14.

χρὴ καλεῖν: according to the Homeric script, the Cyclops 'has to' call Odysseus 'No Man', cf. 194.

549 χάριν δὲ τίνα λαβών σ' ἐπαινέσω; 'What favour will I obtain and thank you [for obtaining it]?; ἐπαινέσω is more likely to be future indicative than aorist subjunctive. Odysseus' reply virtually completes the Homeric reworking which 548 had begun, cf. *Od.* 9.356 ἵνα τοι δῶ ξείνιον ὧι κε σὺ χαίρηις; it is as though the Euripidean Odysseus insists on going through every important move of the Homeric script. In Cratinus' version (above pp. 5–7), Odysseus seems also to have forced the Cyclops to follow the Homeric script, cf. fr. 145 τῆ νῦν πῖθι λαβὼν ἤδη, καὶ τοὔνομά μ' εὐθὺς ἐρώτα.

550 Cf. *Od.* 9.369–70 Οὖτιν ἐγὼ πύματον ἔδομαι μετὰ οἷσ' ἑτάροισι,/τοὺς δ' ἄλλους πρόσθεν.

ὕστερον: comparative and superlative forms are often interchanged in MSS, and Hermann's ὕστατον (cf. the Homeric πύματον) may well be correct.

θοινάσομαι: cf. 233n.

551 Silenos' sarcasm, delivered presumably from beside the mixing-bowl behind the Cyclops, draws the Cyclops' attention to what he is up to.

552 οὗτος, when used as a vocative, is a peremptory form of address, 'Hey!', often to an inferior, cf. *Alc.* 773 (Heracles to a slave), Collard 2018: 86 (~ Stevens 1976: 37–8), Dickey 1996: 154–8. It is very common in comedy.

553 The second metron consists of two tribrachs, perhaps suggestive of Silenos' embarrassment and/or haste.

οὗτος, i.e. the wine, amusingly corrects the Cyclops' rather different use of the same word in 552. Silenos is probably drinking straight from the mixing-bowl, as satyrs are not infrequently depicted in vase-painting.

ἔκυσεν: cf. 172–4n. In the satyric *Omphale* of Achaios (*TrGF* 20 F 33.1), the chorus-leader or one of the satyrs declares ὁ δὲ σκύφος με τοῦ θεοῦ καλεῖ πάλαι.

καλὸν βλέπω 'I have a lovely look in my eyes', not (as many translators) 'I look lovely, I look handsome', cf. 511, Hes. *Theog.* 911 (the Graces) καλὸν ... δερκιόωνται, Anacreon, *PMG* 360.1 ὦ παῖ παρθένιον βλέπων, Praxilla, *PMG* 754 ὦ διὰ τῶν θυρίδων καλὸν ἐμβλέποισα/παρθένε, LSJ s.v. βλέπω II, K–G I 309. The implication, however, which will soon be elaborated, is that Silenos is indeed both καλός and a suitable sexual partner (ἐρώμενος). The satyrs' deluded belief in their own sexual attractiveness is a familiar motif of satyr-play, cf. Laemmle 2013: 399–402.

554 The newly civilised Cyclops understands the need for reciprocity in erotic relationships, cf., e.g., Sappho fr. 1, Theognis 352, 1094, Xen. *Symp.* 9.6, *CEG* 530.2 φιλοῦντα ἀντιφιλοῦσα τὸν ἄνδρα Ὀνήσιμον. Full erotic reciprocity is not usually associated with paederastic relationships (and the aroused Cyclops will shortly have no interest in Silenos' emotional consent), but the classical construction of paederasty certainly encouraged the ἐρώμενος to feel φιλία for the ἐραστής, cf. Dover 1978: 49–54. Silenos does indeed love wine, he is φίλοινος, cf. Theognis 873–4 (an address to wine) οὐδέ σε πάμπαν/οὔτε ποτ᾽ ἐχθαίρειν οὔτε φιλεῖν δύναμαι.

κλαύσηι 'You'll be sorry', a warning, accompanied by a veiled threat of violence, to Silenos to desist from what he is doing, rather than (as Silenos takes it, cf. next n.) an observation about relationships, 'It will end in tears when you show love to someone who does not love you'. For this colloquialism, common in *Cycl.*, cf. *Andr.* 577, *Hcld.* 270, LSJ s.v. κλαίω I 2, Collard 2018: 49–50 (~ Stevens 1976: 15–16).

φιλῶν picks up Silenos' ἔκυσεν and thus means 'kissing', though the ambiguity opens the way to Silenos' response.

οὐ φιλοῦντα σέ specifically denies Silenos' claim that the wine had kissed him: no, it was Silenos doing the kissing, cf. 172–4n.

555 οὐ μὰ Δί᾽: Silenos amusingly takes the Cyclops' threat (κλαύσηι) literally: 'No by Zeus, this will not bring me the tears [of an abandoned lover], because …' The transmitted ναὶ μὰ Δί᾽ would mean 'Yes by Zeus, the wine does φιλεῖν me, because it desires (ἐρᾶν) me', which would either be a restatement of the claim that the wine kisses (φιλεῖν) Silenos or a kind of comic *a fortiori* argument, in which Silenos would (pretend to) understand the Cyclops' οὐ φιλοῦντα σέ not as 'which does not kiss you' but as 'which does not love you'; the denial with Diggle's οὐ seems much more pointed.

ἐρᾶν: the 'desire' of the lover is often opposed to the 'love' which both parties may feel, cf. 554n., Pl. *Phdr.* 255e1–2, Xen. *Hiero* 11.11.

ὄντος καλοῦ: according to Silenos, the wine makes the classic declaration of the ἐραστής to his beloved, 'Boy, you are καλός', cf. Theognis 1259, Call. *Epigr.* 28.5 (= *HE* 1045), Dover 1978: 111–24.

556 The Cyclops warns Silenos that when the latter passes him the cup it has to be full, i.e. Silenos should not have sampled it first. As οἰνοχόος (560), one of Silenos' tasks is to fill the cups from the mixing-bowl. Epicharmus fr. 72 (from *Cyclops*) suggests a very similar scene φέρ᾽ ἐγχέας ἐς τὸ σκύφος.

557 Silenos bends over the mixing-bowl again to drink, although ostensibly to check that the mixture is as ordered.

πῶς ... κέκραται; 'In what proportions [lit. how] is it mixed?' Common strengths, water to wine, were 2:1, 3:2, 5:2 and 3:1, cf. Plut. *Mor.* 657c, Ath. 10.426b–7c, Page 1955: 308, Hobden 2013: 48; satyrs of course preferred their wine neat or, at least, very strong, cf., e.g., Achaios, *TrGF* 20 F 9, Laemmle 2013: 441–3. In *Od.* the wine which Odysseus received from Maron was to be drunk in the mixture 20:1 (*Od.* 9.208–10); *Cycl.* draws a veil of silence over such an improbable detail.

οὖν marks a new stage in the action, i.e. 'Given that I will pass you a full cup, I must inspect …', *GP*² 426.

φέρε: cf. 8n.

558 ἀπολεῖς 'You'll kill [me]!', a common comic exclamation, cf. Ar. *Ach.* 470 (the exasperated Euripides), *Eccl.* 775, *Pl.* 390. With the Cyclops' growing impatience for a drink, caused by Silenos' deliberate delays, we may compare Kinesias' sexual frustration, caused by the apparently endless excuses of his teasing wife Myrrhine, in Ar. *Lys.*, cf. 936 ἄνθρωπος ἐπιτρίψει με, 952 ἀπολώλεκέν με κἀπιτέτριφεν ἡ γυνή. In Aristias, *TrGF* 9 F 4, from the satyric *Cyclops*, the Cyclops says to Odysseus ἀπώλεσας τὸν οἶνον ἐπιχέας ὕδωρ, a verse that later at least became proverbial. This has led to claims both that Euripides is here indebted to Aristias and that, by ἀπολεῖς, the Cyclops means (or also means) 'you will destroy [the wine by mixing water with it]', cf., e.g., Rossi 1971a: 36–7; it would be difficult for the audience to appreciate this, given how commonly the exclamation ἀπολεῖς is used.

οὕτως 'without further ado', cf. *Alc.* 680, LSJ s.v. IV.

οὐ μὰ Δί': like Myrrhine in Ar. *Lys.*, Silenos finds another reason for delay: as a proper symposiast, the Cyclops requires a garland. The transmitted ναὶ μὰ Δί', 'Yes [I shall give you the wine], not before …' seems less witty than Silenos' fussy negatives, but doubts about the true text remain. Diggle suggested νὴ Δί' οὐ πρίν and Blaydes οὐ μὰ Δία πρίν.

559 γεύσωμαί τέ τι 'and I get a taste' seems more knowingly ironic (cf. 153–5n.) than γεύσωμαί τ' ἔτι 'and I taste some more', but either interpretation of the transmitted text is possible.

560 The second metron contains a split 'comic' anapaest (above p. 37), again in Silenos' mouth.

οἰνοχόος ἄδικος 'The wine-pourer is unjust!'; the third-person exclamation seems more pointed than ὦ οἰνοχόος ἄδικος. In a 'real' symposium such an exclamation would presumably be intended for the ears of fellow-symposiasts, and ἄδικος might well have been the sympotic *mot juste* for (real or believed) misbehaviour by the wine-pourer; for criticism of wine-pourers cf. Call. fr. 178.18–19.

<οὐ> μὰ Δί': it seems funnier for Silenos to deny the charge, and hence to repeat the beginning of his preceding intervention at 558, but <ναὶ> μὰ Δί' is not impossible.

561 ἀπομακτέον δέ σούστίν 'But you must wipe your mouth' (during which time Silenos presumably drinks again). It may well have been normal practice to wipe food remnants off the mouth and beard before drinking (ἀπομάσσω also gave rise to the noun ἀπομαγδαλία, bits of bread on which symposiasts wiped their hands), but this may have been particularly necessary in the case of the Cyclops, given the nature of his recent meal. The transmitted ἀπομυκτέον, 'you must wipe your nose', need not mean that the Cyclops actually has a runny nose (cf. Plaut. *Asin.* 796–8) – it could simply be another of Silenos' absurd delaying tactics – and is not impossible here. Clem. Alex. *Paed.* 2.2.21 (cf. 2.7.60) lists 'constant spitting and blowing your nose (ἀπομύσσεσθαι) and rushing off to relieve yourself' as symptoms of sympotic excess (he perhaps remembers Xen. *Cyr.* 1.2.16, 8.8.8). In a summary of one of Euripides' satyric *Autolykos*-plays Tzetzes describes Silenos as 'snub-nosed, toothless, bald and with a runny nose (μυξῶδες)' (*Autolykos* T iv Kannicht, cf. Laemmle 2013: 120–1); the theme may therefore have had some topicality in satyr-play.

σούστίν: i.e. σοί ἐστίν, cf. 251–2n.

ὡς λήψηι πιεῖν: cf. 257n. For ὡς with the future indicative in a purpose clause cf. *Ba.* 784, Smyth §2203.

562 ἰδού: cf. 153–4n.

καθαρόν: the Cyclops' lips and beard may be 'clean', but they are anything but 'pure' (cf. already 35); καθαρόν is often found in cultic contexts for 'ritual purity'. The term appears three times in 14 verses in Xenophanes' famous description of an ideal symposium (fr. 1 West), and it may have a sympotic resonance here.

563 θές νυν τὸν ἀγκῶν᾽ εὐρύθμως 'Now place your elbow elegantly ...' The Cyclops has been lying down since 543, but now Silenos teaches him to prop himself on one elbow in the approved sympotic manner, cf. Call. fr. 191.43 μόλις δ᾽ ἐπάρας ὡς πότης ἐπ᾽ ἀγκῶνα.

εὐρύθμως evokes the ethos of the elite symposium in which the symposiasts themselves are 'on display', cf. Ar. *Wasps* 1210 εὐσχημόνως, Pl. Com. fr. 47, an instruction to play the *kottabos*-game εὐρύθμως.

ἔκπιε: an aorist imperative, cf. *Od.* 9.347 Κύκλωψ, τῆ, πίε οἶνον, Men. fr. 138 K–T; the alternative form, ἔκπιθι with long second syllable, is used in 570. The indicative ἔκπιεν is used of the Cyclops at *Od.* 9.353, 361.

564 Text and interpretation are disputed. It is clear that, up to the caesura, Silenos takes another drink, and it is often assumed that the point of the second half of the verse is that he has drained the cup, so that he is no longer actually drinking; hence Nauck's οὐκέτι. This interpretation, however, hardly suits the Cyclops' reaction in 565. Others assume that the difference between the two halves of the verse is that, during or after the verse, Silenos hides his head while drinking, either within the cup or mixing-bowl (Diggle 1994: 6–7), which would make for an almost slapstick scene of visual and acoustic effects, or behind it (Kovacs); it is clear from the Cyclops' alarm that Silenos has not finished drinking at the end of 564. This is one of a number of instances in this scene where uncertainties of text and stage-action go together. Other proposals include οὐχί με (Seaford) and χὥσπερ μ᾽ οὐχ ὁρᾶις (Austin and Reeve 1970: 9).

565 ἆ ἆ, τί δράσεις;: cf., e.g., *Andr.* 1076 (with Stevens' n.). As that example shows, the future tense does not mean that the person addressed (here Silenos) is not already doing what has alarmed the speaker, cf. the common τί λέξεις; (*Med.* 1310, Barrett on *Hipp.* 353), Radt 1985: 112.
ἡμύστισα 'I knocked it back', cf. 417n. For the *antilabē* see 546n.

566 λάβ': the implied object is either the drinking-cup (σκύφος) or the mixing-bowl itself. The transmitted participle is not impossible (cf. 14–15n.), but γε has very little sense, and correction to τε imposes also the imperative λαβέ. The Cyclops' words have the effect of getting the familiar story back on track, after Silenos threatened to ruin it by drinking all the wine.

567 Odysseus reacts to being put back in charge of drinking arrangements, but the stage-action which led to this mysterious utterance can no longer be reconstructed with certainty. Part of the meaning must be that Odysseus knows very well the strength of this particular wine, cf. 557 n. In 520 (where see n.). Odysseus claimed to be τρίβων with wine, and this verse seems to be a variation of that claim.
γοῦν marks that assent to the Cyclops' proposal is reasonable, cf. *GP*² 452–3.
ἄμπελος: i.e. ἡ ἄμπελος.

568 φέρ' ἔγχεόν νυν: cf. Epicharmus fr. 72 (the *Cyclops*) φέρ' ἐγχέας ἐς τὸ σκύφος, above p. 4, 556n. For the *antilabē* see 546n.
σίγα μόνον 'just be quiet!', cf. 161, 219, 476n.

569 'That's a difficult thing you've said [i.e. being silent], when one drinks a lot [of wine]'. [Arist.], *Probl.* 30.953b2–3 notes that wine-drinking makes men 'more chatty' (λαλίστεροι) and then even more wine turns them into orators (ῥητορικοί).
ὅστις ἄν with the subjunctive is commonly not introduced by a pronominal antecedent in generalising statements and is perhaps best translated as 'in a case where', cf. *El.* 816–17, *Hel.* 942–3, K–G II 441, Kannicht on *Hel.* 267–72. There is no need to understand, e.g., <ἐκείνωι> ὅστις.
πολύν: sc. οἶνον, cf. 573, Theocr. 18.11 with Gow's n.

570 Odysseus now hands the Cyclops a cup of wine.
μηδὲν λίπηις recalls *Od.* 9.292 (the Cyclops' first meal of Odysseus' comrades) ἤσθιε δ' ὥς τε λέων ὀρεσίτροφος, οὐδ' ἀπέλειπεν.

571 'The drinker must expire along with the drink'. συνθνήισκειν occurs nowhere else and may be a 'drinking term' familiar to Euripides' audience but not to us; although the Cyclops will not 'die' in the course of the play, there is presumably ironic menace in Odysseus' choice of word. Odysseus insists that the Cyclops drink the cup in one go; Greeks called this 'drinking ἀπνευστί', lit. 'without drawing breath' (cf. 417n.), an expression which may have given rise to the notion of 'death'. The later Alexandrian scholar Didymus described the pentameter of an elegiac couplet as unable to keep pace with the hexameter but 'running out of breath and being extinguished with' (συνεκπνέοντα καὶ συναποσβεννύμενον) the dead commemorated in elegy (cf. Brink 1971: 165).

σπῶντα: cf. 417n., 573.

572–7 The staging envisaged by the transmitted text is again disputed. 572 (παπαῖ κτλ.) need not imply that the Cyclops has already started drinking, as σοφόν is more naturally taken as a reaction to Odysseus' 'instruction'; 572 would in fact follow very well after 573–5 in which Odysseus has explained the remarkable powers (the σοφία ?) of wine, although παπαῖ is perhaps better separated from ἰοὺ ἰού. A plausible staging is that the Cyclops starts drinking and drains the cup while Odysseus is speaking 573–5 or in a pause after 575.

572 Cf. previous n. for a possible transposition of this verse.

παπαῖ: cf. 503, above p. 35.

τὸ ξύλον τῆς ἀμπέλου: why the Cyclops uses this apparent periphrasis for wine is unclear; Arnott 1972: 28 suggests that συνεκθανεῖν leads him to play on ξύλον as a reference to wooden instruments of torture or execution (LSJ s.v. II 3). No easy emendation suggests itself: an expression with ῥοή would suit very well (cf. 123, *Ba.* 281), but the corruption would be very difficult to explain.

573–4 Odysseus adapts his description to what he has heard from the Cyclops at 323–31.

γε emphasises the claim of the μέν clause, cf. *GP*² 159–60.

πολύν: cf. 569n.

τέγξας ἄδιψον νηδύν 'soaking your stomach till its thirst is removed', cf. 326–8n. ἄδιψον, which is found in medical treatises, is here proleptic, cf., e.g., Aesch. *Pers.* 298 ἄνανδρον τάξιν ἠρήμου θανών;

βαλεῖ: the subject is wine, understood from πολύν in the previous verse, rather than ὁ Βάκχιος in 575.

575 Odysseus' forced antithesis between 'the wet' and 'the dry' plays upon a traditional association of the former with good health and life and the latter with weakness and death, cf., e.g., *El.* 239, Hes. *WD* 586–8, Soph. *El.* 819, *Phil.* 954, Lloyd 1966: 44–6. That 'the Bacchic one' could dry you out is a paradox with which Odysseus teases the Cyclops (cf. *Ba.* 276–83); the idea seems to be that, if you do not take your thirst away completely by drinking everything you are offered, you will be punished by raging thirst and wasting.

576 ἰοὺ ἰού: cf. 464n.

577 ὡς ἐξένευσα μόγις 'How narrowly I swam out!', i.e. I just managed to drain the cup without expiring (cf. 571). ἐκνεῖν may be used metaphorically of safe escape (cf. *Hipp.* 470, *IT* 1186), but here the literal idea of 'swimming' in the wine ('the wine-dark sea') is important, cf. 677, Petr. *Sat.* 39.1 *'hoc uinum' inquit 'uos oportet suaue faciatis. pisces natare oportet'*. The Homeric Cyclopes have no ships and presumably cannot swim (cf. Theocr. 11.60), but the Cyclops is now fully in the spirit of the symposium, where the language of seafaring was very much at home, cf. 362n., Slater 1976, Nünlist 1998: 317–25.

ἄκρατος: both the literal (cf. 149) and metaphorical uses of ἄκρατος resonate, as also at 602; for the latter cf. Soph. fr. 941.4–5 ἵμερος/ἄκρατος, Pl. *Laws* 7.793a2–3 τὸν λύπης καὶ ἡδονῆς ἀκράτου βίον. The χάρις which attends wine-drinking at the symposium is about to be transposed into a drunken fantasy of the Χάριτες, cf. Dionysius Chalcus fr. 1.3 West Χαρίτων ἐγκεράσας χάριτας.

578–80 The effect of drink on the Cyclops is a mixture of familiar experience (the sky reels) and of delusions appropriate to the Cyclops' sense of self-importance (heavenly visions), cf. Pentheus' delusions at *Ba.* 918–21, Seaford 1981: 273; for the blurred vision of drunkenness cf. Ar. *Pl.* 1047–8 'His experience is the opposite of [all] others: apparently, when drunk, his vision is sharper'. The Cyclops is presumably still reclining on the ground (cf. 586n.) and so he probably now stares up at the sky in a drunken stupor.

ὁ δ' οὐρανὸς ... φέρεσθαι 'I think the heavens are rushing along, mingled with the earth'. Clement of Alexandria too notes that one of the effects of drunkenness is that 'everything seems to wheel around in a circle' (κύκλωι ... περιφέρεσθαι, *Paed.* 2.2.24). The reeling sky is described in language which evokes the idea of the (sexual) 'mingling' of heaven and earth both at the beginning of time, cf. fr. 484, Hes. *Theog.* 132–3, Aesch. fr. 44, and in the ordinary functioning of nature, cf. fr. 898.9–11, 'the awesome heaven, when filled with rain, is made by Aphrodite to desire to fall into the earth; and when the two of them mingle (συμμιχθῆτον) in unity ...'

τοῦ Διὸς ... τὸν θρόνον: the Olympians sit upon θρόνοι as early as Homer (for Zeus cf. *Il.* 1.536, 8.442), and the move to Ganymede in 582 might suggest that the Cyclops' fantasy is of all the Olympians feasting together (as, e.g., at the end of *Il.* 1). Nevertheless, some of Euripides' audience may have thought of Pheidias' monumental Zeus at Olympia, where the god sits on a lavishly decorated θρόνος (Call. fr. 196.23, Paus. 5.11.1), on which are carved *inter alia* the three Χάριτες (Paus. 5.11.7). For the literary evidence for Pheidias' Olympian Zeus cf. *DNO* II 221–70.

τὸ πᾶν ... δαιμόνων ἁγνὸν σέβας: cf. Soph. *OT* 830 θεῶν ἁγνὸν σέβας, *Phil.* 1289 ἁγνὸν [Wakefield: ἁγνοῦ] Ζηνὸς ὑψίστου σέβας.

581 Just as the prospect of wine had instantly turned Silenos' thoughts to sex (169–71), so the tipsy Cyclops is immediately aroused. With a truly

satyric delusion (cf. 553n.), the Cyclops fancies that (all!) the Graces are
flirting with him and that he has to beat off their advances, just as the
Theocritean (and sober) Cyclops claims that many girls are after him
(Theocr. 11.76–8); both sets of females are figments of the Cyclops' imagination. It may well be, however, that the drunken Cyclops here mistakes
the ugly satyrs for the beautiful Graces, just as old Silenos is about to play
the role of the young Ganymede; [Arist.], *Probl.* 30.953b16–18 observes
that someone who has been drinking will kiss people 'whom no sober
person would kiss, whether because of their appearance or their age'. For
the satyrs in 'feminine' roles cf. above pp. 31–2.

οὐκ ἂν φιλήσαιμ'· 'I will not kiss [you]', addressed to the Graces. Refusal
is regularly expressed by a negative with ἄν and the optative, cf. Ar. *Frogs*
830, K–G I 233–4, Smyth §1826. These words are often understood as a
question, 'Shouldn't I kiss them?', but that seems far less funny than that
the Cyclops should address the figures of his delusions.

αἱ Χάριτες πειρῶσί με 'The Graces are flirting with me', addressed either
to Odysseus or to the audience or to no one in particular. Hesiod made
the Graces the daughters of Zeus and an Oceanid, and gave them the
names Aglaie, Euphrosune and Thalia (*Theog.* 907–9); for other versions
of their parentage cf. Schol. Flor. on Call. fr. 7 (Harder 2012: 1.138).
Hesiod describes their highly seductive appearance: 'From their eyes
limb-loosening desire flows down as they gaze; from under their brows
their look is lovely' (*Theog.* 910–11); the Cyclops takes this eroticism as
directed at himself.

πειρῶσι: a standard verb for unwanted sexual attention, more usually
applied to men 'harassing' women or boys, cf. Ar. *Knights* 517, *Peace* 150,
Henderson 1991: 158, LSJ s.v. A IV 2.

582–3 ἅλις: lit. 'Enough!', i.e. 'Stop it!', cf. *Hel.* 1581, Soph. *Aj.* 1402,
Collard 2018: 66–7. Various attempts have been made to integrate ἅλις
syntactically with what follows, but none convinces.

Γανυμήδη ... τὰς Χάριτας 'I shall take my rest/lie in bed with this Ganymede here more pleasantly than with the Graces'. The deluded Cyclops
takes a parting shot at the (imaginary) Graces: not only does he scorn
their advances, but he will have more fun anyway with a male sexual partner. It was assumed from an early date, if not already in Homer (cf. *Il.*
20.231–5, *HHAphr.* 202–6), that Zeus's interest in his beautiful Phrygian
wine-pourer was paederastic, cf. *Or.* 1392 Γανυμήδεος ... Διὸς εὐνέτα, *IA*
1049–50 Διὸς/λέκτρων τρύφημα φίλον, Dover 1978: 196–7.

583 It seems impossible that the Cyclops should swear by the rejected
Graces (i.e. νὴ Χάριτας) in affirming his preference for a 'Ganymede', and
the transmitted κάλλιστα νή presumably arose by correction after κάλλιον ἤ
had been falsely divided as κάλλιο νή.

583-4 A contrast or choice between paederastic and heterosexual pleasures was to become a staple of Hellenistic and later literature (cf. Asclepiades, *AP* 12.17 (= *HE* 988–91), Meleager, *AP* 5.208 (= *HE* 4046–9), Ovid, *AA* 2.683–4, Ach. Tat. 2.35–8, Ath. 13.601d–6b); for an earlier period cf. Trag. Adesp. fr. 355.2–3 (satyric?) πρὸς θῆλυ νεύει μᾶλλον ἢ ἐπὶ τἄρ-σενα;/ὅπου προσῆι τὸ κάλλος, ἀμφιδέξιος, Cratinus fr. 163 μισεῖς γὰρ πάνυ τὰς γυναῖ-/κας, πρὸς παιδικὰ δὲ τρέπηι νῦν, Laemmle 2013: 383–91. Paederastic themes presumably played a significant role in Sophocles' satyric Ἀχιλλέως ἐρασταί (cf. esp. fr. 153). According to one later biographical tradition, Sophocles (T 75) was φιλομεῖραξ, whereas Euripides (T 107a–b) was φιλο-γύνης. The Cyclops' preference here, which in part is an amused rejection of the choral foreshadowing at 511–18, is perhaps to be understood as in keeping with the paederastic ideology of the elite symposium, cf. Dover 1978: 149–51, though how he exercises it lacks the sexual subtlety on which elite symposiasts prided themselves, to judge by the sympotic literature which survives; what actually happened at elite symposia may of course have been uncomfortably close to the Cyclops' designs on Silenos. Sympotic practice is one area in which *Cycl.* holds up a satyric mirror to the audience.

πως adds an ironic note of knowing choice; the sophisticated Cyclops can now reflect upon his own sexual preferences.

τοῖς θήλεσιν: for the neuter cf. *Her.* 536, Trag. Adesp. fr. 355 (cited above).

585 γάρ marks Silenos' question as 'surprised and incredulous' (*GP²* 77), cf. 153–4n.

ὁ Διὸς … Γανυμήδης 'Zeus's Ganymede'; the meaning is obvious, but the slightly unusual expression (which, by itself, might erroneously suggest 'G., son of Zeus') is influenced by παιδικοῖσι in the previous verse: Ganymede was Zeus's παιδικά, i.e. beloved boy (LSJ s.v. παιδικός III 2).

586 ναὶ μὰ Δί': the Cyclops' oath throws Silenos' incredulousness back at him.

ἁρπάζω is the standard verb used in descriptions of abduction to be followed by rape; for Ganymede cf., e.g., *HHAphr.* 203. The present tense suggests that the Cyclops here stands up and grabs hold of Silenos.

'κ τῆς Δαρδάνου 'from the [land/city] of Dardanos', cf. *Hcld.* 140 ἐκ τῆς ἐμαυτοῦ. Homer makes Dardanos Ganymede's great-grandfather (*Il.* 20.219–35), cf. *IA* 1049 ὁ Δαρδανίδας of Ganymede. The Cyclops' behaviour now manifests his belief that he is the equal of Zeus in every respect (cf. 320–31).

587 ἀπόλωλα at the opening of the verse has a mock-tragic resonance, cf. Soph. *Phil.* 742, 745, 923.

σχέτλια ... κακά 'wretched misfortunes', cf. *Suppl.*1074, *El.* 1170, Ar. *Pl.* 856. At *Od.* 9.295 σχέτλια ἔργα are the eating of Odysseus' comrades by the Cyclops; the outrage here will be of a different kind.

πείσομαι 'I shall suffer'; though the usage is rarely attested in the classical period, there is little doubt that πάσχειν could suggest 'be buggered, be the "passive" partner in male anal intercourse', and that sense resonates here, cf. 597, Ar. *Thesm.* 201 (παθήματα), Sandbach on Men. *Dysk.* 891.

588 μέμφηι belongs to the language of erotic relationships, cf. Theocr. 2.9, Call. *Epigr.* 42.1 (= *HE* 1075, a comastic poem).

κἀντρυφᾶις, i.e. καὶ ἐντρυφᾶις, is somewhere between 'come over all coy with ...' and 'act haughtily towards ...'; for similar uses of simple τρυφᾶν cf. LSJ s.v. III.

πεπωκότι 'because I am drunk'; the transmitted πεπωκότα, to be taken with ἐραστήν, would leave κἀντρυφᾶις as a parenthesis, and this seems very awkward. A lover's drunkenness is likely to make the beloved more resistant and with olding, because the lover is both less reticent about his desperate sexual need (cf. Pl. *Phdr.* 240e5–7) and less able to impose himself physically.

589 'I/you shall see X bitter' is a very common way of saying 'The business X will end up very badly for me/you', with πικρόν functioning as a predicative adjective, cf. *Alc.* 258, *Ba.* 357, Hom. *Od.* 17.448, Kannicht on *Hel.* 448, Austin and Olson on Ar. *Thesm.* 853. The superlative πικρότατον here heightens the comic effect, cf. Ar. fr. 614 (context unknown) πικρότατον οἶνον τήμερον πίηι τάχα. Silenos is the very last figure for whom wine should be 'bitter', cf. 148–56; that earlier scene of pleasure is here reversed.

590–5 Now that the Cyclops and Silenos have entered the cave, Odysseus turns to remind the satyrs of what they have to do; the style of address is flattering. The speech is the structural equivalent of *Od.* 9.376–7: 'I encouraged all my comrades with words, lest someone shrink back in fear'.

590 Διονύσου παῖδες: the satyrs are 'children of Dionysos', in something of the same way that doctors are 'children of Asclepios' (Pl. *Rep.* 3.407e5–408a1). For L's unmetrical Διωνύσου cf. 204n.

εὐγενῆ amusingly calls attention to the very obscurity of the satyrs' γένος.

591 ἀνήρ: i.e. ὁ ἀνήρ, the Cyclops.

τῶι δ' ὕπνωι: the article may be another (cf. 592n.) evocation of the Homeric story which the plot follows, 'the sleep we are expecting', cf. 454. There seems no reason for τῶι δ' Ὕπνωι, as a reference to the god of sleep (cf. 601), and Blaydes suggested τῆιδ', 'here'.

παρειμένος 'relaxed by', 'overcome by', the perf. pass. participle of παρ-ίημι, cf. *Her.* 1043, *Or.* 881.

592 Odysseus knows what will happen 'soon' because it is in the Homeric script, cf. *Od.* 9.373–4 (when the Cyclops has fallen asleep) φάρυγος δ' ἐξέσ-συτο οἶνος/ ψωμοί τ' ἀνδρόμεοι.

593 †ὠθεῖ has presumably intruded by mistake from the verse above (ὠθήσει), and no restoration can be more than plausible. Diggle suggested καπνὸν πνέων or πνέων καπνόν, Murray καπνούμενος and Napolitano κεκαυμένος (cf. 457).

594 παρηυτρέπισται, 'has been made ready' (cf. *IT* 725), functions not just as information for the satyrs, but also as dramatic anticipation for the audience, cf. *El.* 1142 κανοῦν δ' ἐνῆρκται καὶ τεθηγμένη σφαγίς. We can imagine, if we wish, that Odysseus did what was necessary to prepare the weapon (cf. 455–7) during the singing of 483–518. For the augment in παρηυ- cf. 2n.

κοὐδὲν ἄλλο πλήν 'and [there is] nothing else [to do] except ...', cf. *Andr.* 746, Soph. *OC* 573. This 'remaining act' will, of course, prove too much for the satyrs.

595 ὄψιν: cf. 458–9n.

ὅπως ἀνὴρ ἔσηι 'Show yourself a man!'; exhortations are commonly expressed by ὅπως with the future, cf. 630, Xen. *Anab.* 1.7.3 ὅπως οὖν ἔσεσθε ἄνδρες ἄξιοι τῆς ἐλευθερίας, Smyth §1920, 2213. ἀνήρ, like 'man' in English, is often given the resonance of 'real man', 'a man worthy of the name', cf. *Alc.* 957, *El.* 693, Hdt. 7.210.2, LSJ s.v. IV, Diggle 2004: 467; addressed to a group of satyrs, who will in any case never 'grow up', the exhortation is wrily amusing, cf. Soph. *Ichn.* 366–7.

596 Any claim by the notoriously cowardly and pleasure-loving satyrs to be steadfast and dependable will not be believed by anyone.

πέτρας: cf. *Od.* 17.463–4 (Odysseus when struck by a stool hurled at him by Antinoos) ὁ δ' ἐστάθη ἠύτε πέτρη/ἔμπεδον. In other contexts such language refers to hard-heartedness and imperviousness to reason and pity, rather than to steadfastness, cf. *Med.* 1279–80, *Il.* 16.35.

κἀδάμαντος: i.e. καὶ ἀδάμαντος. Poets use 'adamant' as a wondrously hard metal like steel which is associated with gods, cf. Hes. *WD* 147, *Theog.* 239, Troxler 1964:19–21, West on *Theog.* 161. Related terms appear three times in [Aesch.] *PV*, but otherwise never in tragedy.

597–8 The satyrs are keen to get Odysseus back where the action is, but they themselves will stay outside.

παθεῖν: cf. 587n.

ἀπάλαμνον 'awful, unlawful, outrageous', a word not otherwise found in drama; the satyrs draw a discreet veil over what will happen to Silenos. Arnott 1972: 28 suggests a pun on the literal meaning 'without hands'.

ὥς σοι τἀνθάδ᾽ ἐστὶν εὐτρεπῆ '[Be assured] that things here [i.e. our role] are ready'; the satyrs pick up Odysseus' language of readiness (594) to suggest that they will play their full part.

599–607 Cf. 350–5n. There is a similar invocation by a departing character at *Phaethon* fr. 781.268–9 (= 268–9 Diggle).

599–600 ἄναξ Αἰτναῖε: Hephaistos' forge was sometimes said to be under Etna (cf. [Aesch.] *PV* 366–7), but more commonly on the Lipari islands off the north-east coast of Sicily or elsewhere on Sicily, cf. Call. *h.* 3.46–9, Hunter on Ap. Rhod. *Arg.* 4.761–2. At Pind. *Pyth.* 1.25 Typhos, the giant buried beneath Etna, sends up Ἀφαίστοιο κρουνούς.

γείτονος κακοῦ goes both with ὄμμα and with ἀπαλλάχθηθ᾽, 'be rid of'. On the perils of bad neighbours cf. Hes. *WD* 346–8, Call. *h.* 6.117. There is an amusing banalisation in urging the god to get rid of a troublesome neighbour, as one might an acquaintance who lives locally.

λαμπρόν: cf. 486, 462 φαεσφόρωι.

ἅπαξ 'once for all'.

601 Cf. Electra's invocation to πότνια Νύξ/ὑπνοδότειρα τῶν πολυπόνων βροτῶν at *Or.* 174–5; for an invocation to Sleep in very different circumstances cf. Soph. *Phil.* 827–31. Sleep, not necessarily personified, also played a significant role in Odysseus' blinding of the Cyclops in *Od.* (cf. 9.372–3).

Νυκτὸς ἐκπαίδευμ᾽: Sleep is already a child of Night in Hesiod (*Theog.* 211–12, 758–9). ἐκπαίδευμα, which occurs only here, lays emphasis upon the child as an object of parental rearing, cf. 276, Pl. *Crito* 45c10; the simple παίδευμα is used both in this literal sense (*Hipp.* 11, *El.* 886–7) and for rather looser connections (*Andr.* 1100–1, fr. 24b.4).

602 ἄκρατος: cf. 577n.

θηρί: the satyrs use this term for the Cyclops at 658.

θεοστυγεῖ: cf. 396n.

603 Cf. 107n. Elsewhere, Odysseus is prepared to admit that the Trojan War was not necessarily 'most glorious', cf. 280–5.

604 αὐτόν τε ναύτας τ᾽ ... Ὀδυσσέα 'Odysseus himself and his sailors'; for the second object intervening between parts of the first cf. *Her.* 774–6, Ar. *Frogs* 587–8, K–G I 80, Diggle 1994: 208. 'Sailors' assigns a very subordinate role to the comrades, cf. 98n., *Od.* 8.162.

605 'Gods and men' are very frequently paired in 'polar expressions' which seek to cover all eventualities (cf. *Andr.* 163, *Hipp.* 675), but here there is point to the dichotomy. The Cyclops has no concern (cf. the repeated οὔ μοι μέλει in 322, οὐδέν μοι μέλει 331) with either god or man: he blasphemes against one (cf. 316–35) and eats the other.

ὑπ᾽ ἀνδρός 'through the agency of a man', cf. *Med.* 487. The expression amounts to 'Do not allow ... to be destroyed by a man ...' Coming immediately after θηρὶ τῶι θεοστυγεῖ, the designation of the Cyclops as 'a man' shows up Odysseus' rhetorical posturing for what it is.

θεῶν is scanned as a single syllable by synizesis, cf. 231n.

606–7 Depending on the rhetorical context, τύχη and the gods may be said either to work together or to be different, and sometimes competing, forces, cf. fr. 901 ('does τύχη or δαίμων determine human affairs?'), *Hec.* 488–91 ('does τύχη or Zeus watch over human affairs?'), Dover 1974: 138–41, Mikalson 1983: 59–62, Battezzato on *Hec.* 488–9. In the Hellenistic period Τύχη became a prominent literary theme and was also the object of cult in very many places; its prominence in the later plays of Euripides (e.g. *Ion* 1512–15) foreshadows that rich afterlife. Already in the classical period Τύχη is treated as a god when the emphasis is upon the power she wields (cf. Aesch. *Ag.* 664); in Soph. *Ichn.* 79–80 Silenos prays to θεὸς Τύχη καὶ δαῖμον ἰθυντήριε to allow him to succeed (τυχεῖν) in his current undertaking.

ἤ 'or', i.e. 'otherwise', cf. LSJ s.v. A I 3; this may be the only such example in drama.

τὰ δαιμόνων: 'the affairs of the gods' differs here very little from 'the gods', cf. Soph. *OT* 977 τὰ τῆς τύχης.

608–23 THIRD STASIMON

The chorus sing a lively trochaic and dactylic song of pleasure at what is about to happen; at the end they express again their longing to escape to Dionysos. Somewhat comparable is, again (cf. introductory n. on 356–74), *Ba.* 977–1023 where the chorus take pleasure in imagining Pentheus' punishment and also use a periphrastic style to describe the victim, like ξενοδαιτυμών here (610), cf. 609n., *Ba.* 980–1, 995–6 = 1015–16.

The colometry of the song is uncertain (hence the disturbance in the line-numbering), and we have printed Diggle's distribution; for alternative arrangements cf. Meriani 1996, Cerbo 2015: 79–80:

– ᴗ – – ᴗ – ᴗ		
λήψεται τὸν τράχηλον	*tr dim (syncopated)*	608
– ᴗ – ᴗ – ᴗ –		
ἐντόνως ὁ καρκίνος	*tr dim cat (lekythion)*	
– ᴗᴗ – ᴗᴗ – ᴗᴗ – ᴗ –		
τοῦ ξενοδαιτυμόνος· πυρὶ γὰρ τάχα	*4da*	610
– – ᴗ – ᴗ – ᴗ –		
φωσφόρους ὀλεῖ κόρας.	*tr dim cat (lekythion)*	
– – – ᴗ – ᴗ – ᴗ –		
ἤδη δαλὸς ἠνθρακωμένος	*sp lekythion*	

– ᴜ ᴜ – ᴜᴜ– ᴜᴜ – ᴜ ᴜ		
κρύπτεται ἐς σποδιάν, δρυὸς ἄσπετον	*4da*	615
– ᴜ – ᴜ – ᴜ – – ᴜ–		
ἔρνος. ἀλλ’ ἴτω Μάρων, πρασσέτω,	*tr trim (syncopated)*	
– ᴜ ᴜ – ᴜᴜ– ᴜ ᴜ –		
μαινομένου ’ξελέτω βλέφαρον	*da tetr cat (D²)*	
– – ᴜ – ᴜ– ᴜ –		
Κύκλωπος, ὡς πίηι κακῶς.	*ia dim*	
– – – ᴜ ᴜ– ᴜᴜ – – ᴜ ᴜ–		
κἀγὼ τὸν φιλοκισσοφόρον Βρόμιον	*da pent cat (sp D²)*	620
ᴜ – ᴜ – ᴜ – ᴜ–		
ποθεινὸν εἰσιδεῖν θέλω,	*ia dim*	
– – – ᴜ – ᴜ–ᴜ –		
Κύκλωπος λιπὼν ἐρημίαν·	*sp lekythion*	
– – ᴜ – ᴜ –ᴜ –		
ἆρ’ ἐς τοσόνδ’ ἀφίξομαι;	*ia dim*	

608 Willink 2001: 528 suggested λήψεταί <γε> to produce unsyncopated trochaics, but the emphatic particle is certainly not needed here.

609 ἐντόνως 'fiercely, vehemently'.

καρκίνος, lit. 'crab', is a term for a kind of tongs or pincers used by smiths and other metalworkers to grasp hot metal, cf. Philip, *AP* 6.92.3 (= *GP* 2716), Pancrates, *AP* 6.117.1, Ath. 10.456d–e. The non-metaphorical term is πυράγρα, and Hephaistos' πυράγρη at *Il.* 18.477 is glossed by the A and D scholia as ὁ χαλκευτικὸς καρκίνος. 'The crab will seize the neck of him who feasts on strangers' is a vividly riddling image which suits the fondness of satyrs (and satyr-drama) for riddles and oracular language, cf. Laemmle 2013: 428–35. The satyrs here evoke the blacksmith simile of *Od.* 9.391–4 (cf. 469–71n.), but whereas there the smith dipped blazing metal into cold water to temper it, here the satyrs imagine that the smith's tongs will grasp the Cyclops' neck and (presumably) then hold his head in the fire; in fact, it will be a red-hot brand which is drilled into the Cyclops' eye. The satyrs repeat their focus on the Cyclops' head at 647. The cue for the satyrs' vivid image is Odysseus' prayer to Hephaistos, the blacksmith god of Etna (cf. 599–600n.), but they move from imagining the god himself at work to treating 'Hephaistos' as a simple metonymy for 'fire', cf. 610; γάρ effects the transition from one version of Hephaistos to another. For the metonymy, which occurs as early as *Il.* 2.426, cf. Arnott 1996: 455–6.

610–12 τάχα and ἤδη are further temporal markers which remind us of the Homeric script, cf. above pp. 19–20.

610 ξενοδαιτυμόνος: cf. 658 θηρὸς τοῦ ξενοδαίτα.

611 φωσφόρους … κόρας: cf. 462 with 460–4n.

615 κρύπτεται ἐς σποδιάν 'is hidden in the ash'; the verb refers to a set-tled state rather than to the act of being concealed, cf. *Her.* 263, *Hel.* 606. ἐς with the accusative here embraces both the previous motion into the ash and the current position, cf. *Suppl.* 1206–7, K–G I 543, Smyth §1659.
δρυός: cf. 383–4n. The stake is olive-wood (455).
ἄσπετον 'huge, mighty', cf. *Od.* 9.319–24, the description of the Cyclops' massive staff. The adjective is suitably epic; the only other occurrence in Euripides is *Tr.* 78 (also epic in resonance – the storm which will wreck the Greek fleet).

616 ἴτω Μάρων: the chorus urge the wine (141–3n.) to do its/their work. Cf. *Ba.* 977 ἴτε θοαὶ Λύσσας κύνες κτλ., 992 ἴτω δίκα φανερός κτλ.

618 μαινομένου: the Cyclops is 'crazed' not just because of his culinary habits, but also (paradoxically) because he is an opponent of Dionysos, the god of true μανία, cf. 168n., *Ba.* 399–400, 981, 999–1000, etc. At Pl. *Laws* 6.773d1 μαινόμενος is used of unmixed wine (cf. Hunter 2012: 170–1), and hence Meriani 1996 defends the transmission here; it is, however, much more pointed for the satyrs to call the Cyclops 'crazed', as this serves as justification for his punishment.

619 ὡς πίηι κακῶς 'so that his drinking has a miserable end'; the mean-ing is not very different from Silenos' last desperate exclamation (589).
620–3: cf. 76–81n.
620 φιλοκισσοφόρον 'who loves to wear the ivy'; κισσοφόρος is a standard epithet of the god, cf. Pind. *Ol.* 2.27, Ar. *Thesm.* 988 (with the n. of Austin and Olson). Ivy is very closely associated with Dionysos and his worship-pers in both art and literature, cf. 620, *Ba.* 177, 205, *HHDion.* 40–1, Dodds on *Ba.* 81, Blech 1982: 183–210, Laemmle 2013: 175–6. Κισσός is found as a satyr-name on vases cf. Kossatz-Deissmann 1991: 156–7.
Βρόμιον: cf. 1n.
622 ἐρημίαν: cf. 22, 116. For the satyrs, as for the Odysseus of *Od.*, the land of the Cyclops represents a negation of all sociability; it is the empti-est (and driest) of deserts.
623 τοσόνδ': i.e. to the happy state described in the immediately pre-ceding verses.

624–55 FOURTH EPISODE

Odysseus unexpectedly re-emerges from the cave to tell the satyrs to keep quiet and that now is the time to help him with the blinding. The satyrs make all kinds of absurd excuses for inaction, but finally offer to sing an efficacious magical song instead of providing physical help; Odysseus returns into the cave to carry out the blinding with his men.

624 Not dissimilar is Ar. *Peace* 310–18 (a scene which has often been considered quasi-satyric) where Trygaios desperately tries to get the chorus of farmers to keep quiet so as not to attract Polemos' attention. At *Hipp.* 565–8 Phaedra, who is on stage, commands the chorus to keep quiet (σιγήσατ', ὦ γυναῖκες) so that she can hear what is being said inside the *skēnē*, there too (cf. *Cycl.* 630–41) the plea for silence will be followed by an exchange which exploits the fact that the chorus cannot leave the *orchēstra* to support the heroine (*Hipp.* 575–80). Davidson 2000: 26 suggests that Odysseus' command here is 'the indirect offspring' of places in the second half of *Od.* where the hero needs to tell those who know his identity not to give it away by excessive joy (e.g. *Od.* 21.226–9), cf. 476n.

θεῶν is scanned as a single syllable by synizesis, cf. 231n.

θῆρες is not otherwise explicitly used of the satyrs in *Cycl.*(cf. 117n.), but cf. Soph. *Ichn.* 221 (also spoken by a character brought out by the satyrs' noise); in that play Silenos calls the satyrs κάκιστα θηρῶν ὀνθία and κάκιστα θηρίων (147, 153). Cf. further Voelke 2001: 54–61, Laemmle 2013: 436–40.

625 ἄρθρα στόματος 'the joinings of your mouths'; ἄρθρα (< ἀραρίσκειν) is where parts of the body 'fit together'. Sophocles extends the idea by referring to feet as ἄρθρα ... ποδοῖν and eyes as ἄρθρα ... κύκλων (Soph. *OT* 718, 1270). The periphrasis here shows the high-status Odysseus seeking to impose himself upon the noisy chorus. At *Or.* 183–5 Electra, protective of the sleeping Orestes, begs the chorus, σῖγα/σῖγα φυλασσομένα/στόμα τὸ σὸν ἀκέλαδον κτλ.

οὐδέ 'not even', with οὐ ... οὐδέ then added in the following verse, cf. *GP*² 194. Satyrs are the very last creatures one should try to keep quiet or still (cf. 220–1).

626 σκαρδαμύσσειν 'blink', the most minimal of bodily movements. [Arist.] *Physiog.* 813a20–1 observes that habitual eye-movers (σκαρδαμύκται) are cowardly; this would certainly suit the satyrs, but we do not know how familiar this piece of physiognomic lore was.

627–8 τὸ κακόν, 'the monster', 'the pest', is probably accompanied by a gesture or glance towards the cave, cf. Ar. *Birds* 931 τουτὶ ... τὸ κακόν (the wandering poet). Odysseus' expression also allows the proverbial wisdom to resonate that it is better not to 'wake' old troubles ('let sleeping dogs lie'), cf. Theognis 423, Soph. *OC* 510, Denniston on *El.* 41–2.

ἔστ' ἄν ... πυρί 'until the sight in the Cyclops' eye has had its contest with the fire'. The principal difficulty resides in ἐξαμιλληθῆι, which others understand, though without good parallels (*Or.* 431 is very uncertain), as 'be rooted out' or 'be forced out', with ἐξ- perhaps governing ὄμματος, 'forced out from the eye', cf. fr. 752c.1 πρὸς αἰθέρ' ἐξαμίλλησαι κόρας (with Bond 1963: 57). It seems, however, best to understand the compound verb as here differing very little in meaning from the simple ἁμιλλᾶσθαι.

629 The satyrs snap their mouths shut and are 'all attention'. Despite 'gulping down the air in our jaws', the stress is on their silence, rather than on holding their breath; being satyrs, however, they require a whole verse to profess their silence.

ἐγκάψαντες: the verb is otherwise restricted to comedy before the Hellenistic period.

630 For this form of command cf. 595n.

ἄψεσθε τοῦ δαλοῦ χεροῖν 'take the torch in your hands'. At *Od.* 9.379, the Homeric equivalent of these verses, ἄψασθαι is used of the stake itself and means 'catch alight' (LSJ s.v. ἅπτω B I); such verbal play was to become a staple of later poetry.

631 ἔσω μολόντες: this is no more possible for the satyr-chorus than for any tragic chorus, cf. 624n.; they will be kept in the *orchēstra* by both stage-convention and cowardice, cf., e.g., Arnott 1972: 25–6, Laemmle 2013: 214–15. At *Hec.* 1042–3 the chorus briefly consider entering the *skēnē* to help Hecuba; for the relation between that scene and *Cycl.* cf. above pp. 43–4.

διάπυρος: cf. *Od.* 9.379 διεφαίνετο δ᾽ αἰνῶς. Odysseus means of course that the sharp end of the brand is now glowing hot (cf. 456–8), but it is wrily amusing that he urges the satyrs to pick up something which is 'glowing hot'.

καλῶς: cf. 344n.

632–4 replay 483–6, but any enthusiasm has long since passed; the satyrs now seek to buy time. Cf. further 635–41n.

οὔκουν 'Why then don't you ...?', cf. 241, *GP*² 431.

τάξεις: at *Od.* 9.331–3 Odysseus orders his men to draw lots for who will help him in the blinding, cf. above p. 10.

πρώτους probably means 'at the front [of the stake]', i.e. nearest the Cyclops, rather than 'first' in time, cf. 483–4. These satyrs will be stationed (cf. τάξεις) 'in the front rank'.

καυτόν, 'burned', cf. 457 κεκαυμένον; the adjective does not otherwise appear before Aristotle, and the conjecture cannot be considered certain.

μοχλόν has not previously been used of the stake, but it comes from Homer, cf. *Od.* 9.332, 378.

τῆς τύχης 'this success, the happy outcome', cf. *IT* 1067 ὡς ἂν καὶ σὺ κοινωνῆις τύχης, *Hel.* 1409, LSJ s.v. III 1.

κοινώμεθα: cf. 471; there the satyrs 'wanted' to share in the blinding, but it is really a share of the success which they want, cf. Laemmle 2013: 213.

635–41 Whereas 632–4 are most naturally given to the chorus-leader, it is clear that these seven verses are spoken by at least two and perhaps more individual choreuts, speaking either for themselves or as representatives of small groups of satyrs (the plural pronouns allow both interpretations).

Lines 635–6 and 637 are clearly spoken by different satyrs, and 638–9 and
640b–41 are most likely spoken by the same satyr (καὶ ... γε in 640 almost
guarantees this). It is unclear whether these last verses are spoken by the
same satyr who spoke 635–6, the arrangement which we have followed
here, or by a third party. If there are only two (A and B), then after B
has tried to outdo A by claiming lameness, A retorts that he too has that
complaint and, after Odysseus (or another satyr) has objected, A adds yet
another reason for incapacity (he cannot see). There is no certain way to
choose between assigning the verses to two or three (or more) speakers,
and the text allows more than one staging. The satyrs' typical display of
cowardice was in any case presumably accompanied by lively movement in
the *orchēstra* as they try to move as far away from the *skēnē* as possible. The
scene, moreover, offers a satyric take on the impossibility of the chorus leaving the *orchēstra* to take part in action behind the *skēnē*, cf. Laemmle 2019a.

Individual satyrs also speak in a scene of very lively action at Soph. *Ichn.*
100–23, and cf. *Inachos* fr. 269c.20–4. The most famous tragic instance of
such a breaking-up of the collective choral voice is the futile debate and
inaction of the chorus of old men at Aesch. *Ag.* 1348–71, as they hear the
king's death-cries from within. For a very different use of multiple choral
voices cf. *Alc.* 77–112.

635–6 ἡμεῖς μέν ... ὠθεῖν 'I/we are standing in front of the door too far
away to shove ...'

μέν emphasises the preceding pronoun, '[I don't know about you], but
I certainly ...', cf. *GP*² 360. The second choreut or group then picks this
up in 637 with δέ.

μακροτέρω ... ὠθεῖν is an easily understood compression of μακροτέρω
<ἢ ὥστε> ὠθεῖν, cf. K–G II 503–4, Smyth §2007; infinitives are very regu-
larly attached to positive adjectives to fill out the sense, cf. 678, *Hcld.* 744
κακὸς μένειν δόρυ, K–G II 10. The comparative adverbial form μακροτέρω is
otherwise first attested in Aristotle, and μακροτέραν (Cobet) or μακρότερον
(Musgrave) may be correct; the transmitted μακρότεροι cannot stand, as
μακρός used of people (or satyrs) means 'tall'.

ἐσμεν ... ἐστῶτες: for this common periphrastic form cf. 381n., Smyth
§1961.

τῶν θυρῶν is not an absurd way to refer to the cave-entrance, but it
might thicken the metatheatrical play here: this satyr is a long way from
the central 'double-door' of the *skēnē*.

ὠθεῖν ἐς τὸν ὀφθαλμὸν τὸ πῦρ is a down-to-earth variant of the Homeric
μοχλὸν ... ὀφθαλμῶι ἐνέρεισαν (*Od.* 9.382–3).

637 δέ ... γ' marks a 'retort and lively rejoinder' (*GP*² 153), cf. 708:
'[You might be too far away], but *I* ...'

638–9 ἆρ' is inferential, 'if that is the case, then …', cf. *GP²* 45.

τοὺς γὰρ πόδας … ἐσπάσθημεν 'from standing we have received a sprain [lit. "have been wrenched, dislocated"] in our feet [acc. of respect]', cf. Hdt. 6.134.2 τὸν μηρὸν σπασθῆναι.

640 The incredulous question in the first half of the verse must be spoken either by Odysseus (as in L, followed here) or perhaps by another satyr, whether B or a third choreut; if it is spoken by a satyr, the point will be to undermine a rival claim to be excused from service with Odysseus. It is, however, far more likely that Odysseus should here express his incredulity than that one satyr (or group of satyrs) should openly seek to undermine the claims of another.

καὶ … γ' 'Yes, and …', cf. 178.

641 ἡμῖν offers a far more natural construction than the emphatic genitive.

κόνεος ἢ τέφρας: the alternative is a mark of improvisation. -εος is a metrically convenient genitive of nouns in -ις which is not uncommon in drama, cf. πόλεος (*Ion* 595, *Or.* 897), K–B I 442. **ποθέν** varies οὐκ οἶδ' ἐξ ὅτου (639), again indicative of improvisation.

642 'As allies, these men are worthless and nothing'. The verse, which the satyrs (or at least the chorus-leader) clearly hear, is either addressed to the audience or to no one in particular; in the latter case, the audience may even so feel itself addressed, cf. above p.36 n.118.

κοὐδέν: cf. 355, 667, *Andr.* 700, Ar. *Eccl.* 144, LSJ s.v. οὐδείς II 2. Hesiod already referred to the γένος οὐτιδανῶν Σατύρων καὶ ἀμηχανοέργων (fr. 10a.18 = 10.18 Most). Others take οὐδέν with σύμμαχοι, 'allies in no way'. For the common theme of the satyrs' cowardice cf., e.g., Soph. *Ichn.* 148–52, 168–72.

643–8 are presumably spoken by the chorus-leader, who resumes his normal role as spokesperson.

643–4 The satyrs' concern with what would happen to their backs perhaps recalls the idea of the Cyclops as a cook with meat-cleavers and spits (241–2, 302–3, 393, etc.). For the alternation of singular and plural verbs cf. above p. 24 n.72.

ὁτιή: this colloquial Attic form occurs nowhere in tragedy, if Aesch. fr. 281a.9 is satyric (cf. OSC 298–305).

ἐκβαλεῖν: Solon fr. 27.2 West uses this verb of 'losing' teeth naturally, but here it suggests the idea of 'spitting out' broken teeth after a beating (cf. Thphr. *HP* 4.8.4).

645 αὕτη refers to the substance of the ὁτιή clause, but takes its gender from πονηρία, cf. K–G I 74.

646–8 In place of offering physical help, the satyrs offer an 'Orphic spell' which will make the blazing torch leap into the Cyclops' eye all by itself. There were very close and traditional links between Orpheus and the satyrs' god, Dionysos (cf., e.g., *Hipp.* 953–4, West 1983: 15–18, 24–6, Burkert 1985: 296–301), and Orpheus is obviously the right figure to invoke to ask part of a tree (cf. 455) to move by itself, as trees, rocks and animals followed in the wake of his music (*Ba.* 560–4, *IA* 1211–13, Ap. Rhod. *Arg.* 1.23–31, etc.). A satyr is depicted listening to Orpheus' music on Attic vases of the mid-fifth century (*LIMC* s.v. Orpheus nos. 22–5, KPS 65). Satyrs had long had close connections with magic and supernatural powers (e.g. Aesch. fr. 281a.20, Soph. fr. 1130.12–14), and tempting though it may be to take this claim as nothing more than one more piece of satyric ἀλαζονεία, there is no clear evidence that we should do so. Lines 656–62 certainly do not look like an 'Orphic spell', but the Cyclops' immediate cry of 663 suggests that the satyrs' 'spell' has indeed played its part in the blinding, cf. Griffith 2015: 33. The scenario which the satyrs imagine has something in common with such scenes of magic as Medea's destruction of the bronze giant Talos through incantations and powerful emanations (Ap. Rhod. *Arg.* 4.1665–88) and the 'Kiln' song in which 'Homer' shows how he will summon spirits and magic-workers such as Circe to smash all the pottery inside a kiln if the potters do not pay him for singing for them (*OCT Homer*, Vol. 5, pp. 264–5, West 2003: 391–3). For a suggestive and speculative account of *Cycl.* 646–8 see Faraone 2008. The satyr-chorus seem to express an interest in ἐπωιδαί also at Aesch. fr. 281a.20.

646 ἀλλ᾽ οἶδ᾽ may itself evoke the style of magical incantation, cf. *HHDem.* 229–30, Faraone 2008: 136–7.

ἐπωιδὴν ... ἀγαθὴν πάνυ: cf. Ar. fr. 29 τελέει δ᾽ ἀγαθὴν ἐπαοιδήν (a comic oracle perhaps referring to a love-charm). Faraone 2008: 135–6 suggests that 'very good incantation' is a variant of τελεία ἐπαοιδή, a phrase found repeatedly in surviving incantations (cf., e.g., Brashear 1979: 262–4, 268). It is presumably mere coincidence that the only Homeric example of ἐπαοιδή occurs at *Od.* 19.457, where the sons of Autolykos staunch the bleeding of Odysseus' wound inflicted by the boar 'with an incantation'; here the satyrs will help Odysseus to cause terrible bleeding. πάνυ appears only here in Euripides; although there are occasional tragic uses, it seems to have been largely colloquial in tone, cf. Dettori 2016: 195–6, Collard 2018: 54–5, and there are further satyric examples at Aesch. fr. 47a.825 and Soph. *Ichn.* 105.

647 ὥστ᾽ is the standard, and perhaps universal, conjunction to introduce a consecutive infinitive in Euripides, cf. Diggle 1981: 8–9.

κρανίον, 'skull', a diminutive formed from κάρα, does not occur in tragedy, cf. 683; the resonance is somewhat derogatory, cf. *Il.* 8.84 (a horse, the only occurrence in Homer), Pind. *Isthm.* 4.54.

648 ὑφάπτειν probably just means 'set ablaze' (cf. *Tr.* 1274, *Or.* 1618, *Ba.* 778), without the connotation of furtiveness often found in compounds with ὑπο-.

μονῶπα: cf. 21n.

παῖδα γῆς: elsewhere in *Cycl.*, the Cyclops is, as in Homer, a son of Poseidon, but Hesiod made the Cyclopes the children of Gaia and Ouranos, in a passage (*Theog.* 139–46) which, like the present verse, stresses their single eye; for the links between the different Cyclopes known to mythology cf. Fowler 2013: 53–6, Buxton 2017. By calling the Cyclops a 'child of earth' the satyrs assimilate him to the Titans and the earthborn Giants whose rebellion was crushed by Zeus. We might even think specifically of Typhon, the giant buried beneath Mount Etna (cf.7n.): like him, the Cyclops will be burned up (cf. 663); OSC on 659–60 suggest that τυφέσθω … τύφετ' ὤ evoke Typhon's name (cf. Call. *h. Delos* 141), and Typhon is described as κεραυνῶι Ζηνὸς ἠνθρακωμένος at [Aesch.] *PV* 372 (cf. *Cycl.* 663). The 'Orphic' myth of Dionysos' dismemberment by the Titans may also be relevant, cf. Bernabé 2003, Faraone 2008: 139–41. The chthonic connections of another opponent of Dionysos, Pentheus, are stressed in *Ba.*, cf. Dodds's n. on 537–44.

649–50 Odysseus knows all about satyrs (cf. 99–100) and perhaps too all about satyr-drama; this verse self-consciously points to the constant character of the chorus. Now Odysseus has seen one further example to confirm what he already knows.

οἰκείοις φίλοις: i.e. the surviving men in the cave, cf. 378n. For the thought cf. *Andr.* 985–6 τὸ συγγενὲς γὰρ δεινόν, ἔν τε τοῖς κακοῖς/οὐκ ἔστιν οὐδὲν κρεῖσσον οἰκείου φίλου.

652–3 ἀλλ' οὖν … γ' 'Well, then, at any rate …', after the rejection of one possibility, cf. *GP²* 444.

ἐπεγκέλευε 'cheer us on'. This compound occurs certainly only here (cf. *El.* 1224), but ἐπικελεύειν is well attested in this sense, cf. *Ba.* 1088, Xen. *Cyn.* 6.20; this last passage shows that the corresponding noun is κέλευ(σ)-μα, cf. Soph. *Ichn.* 231 κέλευμα … κυνηγετῶν.

ὡς εὐψυχίαν … κτησώμεθα: lit. 'so that by your encouragements, I may acquire the courage of my comrades', i.e. 'so that your encouragements will make my comrades εὔψυχοι', cf. Soph. *Phil.* 1281. Odysseus presumably turns to re-enter the cave at this point and does not hear 654–5.

654 ἐν τῶι Καρί: a proverbial expression for allowing someone else to take all the real risk, cf. Archilochus fr. 216 West, Cratinus fr. 18, Pl. *Laches* 187b, *Euthyd.* 285c, Philemon fr. 17. The proverb was variously explained from the fact that Carians were the first mercenary soldiers and from the general worthlessness of Carians (cf. Hesych. κ 820); that the satyrs

5 COMMENTARY 655   237

should refer this proverb to the 'heroic' Odysseus is in keeping with their general attitude to him.

655 'As far as encouragements go, let the Cyclops smoulder'.

κελευσμάτων is often seen as a sign (and cf. 653) that the song which follows imitates the rhythmical chanting of the κελευστής who calls time to the rowers on a boat, cf., e.g., fr. 752g.12, *IT* 1405, Aesch. *Pers.* 397, Casson 1971: 300–2, Rossi 1971a: 22, Hamilton 1979: 291. The song does in at least one point pick up the ship-making simile of 460–1 (cf. 661n.), and it is clearly related to work-songs more generally, but there is no textual sign that the 'orders' of the κελευστής are relevant here.

656–62 FOURTH STASIMON

While Odysseus and his men get to work, the chorus sing a short iambo-choriambic song urging them on; the song was presumably accompanied by miming of the actions involved. The song has links to what we know of ancient work-songs, for which cf., e.g., Ar. *Peace* 459–69, 486–96, 517–19, Lambin 1992: 131–80, Karanika 2014; the ship-building simile of *Od.* 9.382–6 (cf. 460–4n.) describes a situation during which a work-song might have been sung. In the parallel scene of *Hec.* (cf. above pp. 43–4), while Hecuba attacks Polymestor behind the *skēnē*, the chorus sing a short song celebrating the fact that he is to be justly punished.

The song is metrically, and to some extent textually, uncertain. We have accepted a transposition by Diggle which gives clear metre at the head of the song:

⏑ – ⏑ –		
ἰὼ ἰώ·	*ia*	
– – ⏑ – – ⏑ ⏑ –		
ὠθεῖτε γενναιότατα,	*ia choriamb* (*wil*)	656
– ⏑ – – ⏑ ⏑ –		
σπεύδετ᾽, ἐκκαίετ᾽ ὀφρὺν	^ *ia choriamb*	
– – – ⏑ ⏑ – –		
θηρὸς τοῦ ξενοδαίτα.	*pherecratean*	
– ⏑ – – ⏑ –		
τύφετ᾽ ὤ, καίετ᾽ ὤ	2 *cretics*	
⏑ – ⏑ – – ⏑ ⏑ –		
τὸν Αἴτνας μηλονόμον.	*ia^ ch* ('aeolic heptasyllable')	
– – – ⏑ – – ⏑ ⏑ – –		
τόρνευ᾽ ἕλκε, μή σ᾽ ἐξοδυνηθεὶς	*ia^ pherecratean* (?)	661
– – ⏑ ⏑ – –		
δράσηι τι μάταιον.	*reizianum*	

In 657 Willink 2001: 529 keeps γεννιότατ' ὠθεῖτε as a 'hypercatalectic extension of the reizianum', but Diggle's transposition arguably gives better word-order.

In 661, the suggested pattern does not seem impossible in this context, but transposition of the imperatives would give an order which both follows a general rule that, in such asyndetic pairs, the second verb is at least as long as the first (Diggle 1994: 99–100, Willink 2001: 529–30) and also follows the order of sense (first 'pull' then 'whirl', cf. 661–2n.):

```
_ ᴗ _ _ ᴗ _    _ ᴗ ᴗ _ _
```
ἕλκε τόρνευε, μή σ' ἐξοδυνηθεὶς   tr pherecratean

In 661 Kovacs adopts the omission of σε found in apogr. Par.:

```
_    _ _ ᴗ _ ᴗ ᴗ _
```
τόρνευ' ἕλκε, μὴ 'ξοδυνη-   wil
```
_    _ _ ᴗ ᴗ _ _
```
θεὶς δράσηι τι μάταιον.   pherecratean

For further discussion cf. Dale 1981: 69, Willink 2001: 529–30.

656 ἰὼ ἰώ is a typical satyric shout, cf., e.g., Soph. *Ichn.* 88, 213, *Inachos* fr. 269c.25; a song of encouragement at *Or.* 1353 begins ἰὼ ἰὼ φίλαι.

γενναιότατα 'most bravely', 'like real heroes'.

657 ὀφρύν: cf. *Od.* 9.389 πάντα δέ οἱ βλέφαρ' ἀμφὶ καὶ ὀφρύας εὗσεν ἀυτμή, Theocr. 11.31–2.

658 θηρός: cf. 602.

ξενοδαίτα, which occurs nowhere else, is a variant of ξενοδαιτυμόνος in 610; cf. ξεινοδαΐκτας of the monstrous Kyknos at *Her.* 391, Pind. fr. 140a.56, Laemmle 2013: 286. -δαίτα is a Doric genitive of a noun in -ας (i.e. -ης): -αο contracts to -α.

659 τύφετ' ὤ, καίετ' ὤ: the exclamatory ὤ is to be taken with the preceding imperative, cf. 52, *Alc.* 234, Fraenkel on Aesch. *Ag.* 22. As transmitted, the third-person imperatives would lack an obvious subject.

καίετ' bears the sense of the preceding compound ἐκκαίετε, as regularly, cf. Renehan 1969: 77–85, 1976: 11–27.

660 τὸν Αἴτνας μηλονόμον 'the herdsman of Etna', perhaps also suggesting the 'Aitnaian (i.e. monstrous) herdsman', cf. 395n.

661–2 τόρνευ' ἕλκε 'whirl <and> pull'. The satyrs recall the ship-building image of 460–3. τορνεύειν, lit. 'turn on a lathe', here replaces κυκλεῖν in 463 and δινεῖν, the verb Homer uses twice of 'whirling' the stake in the Cyclops' eye (*Od.* 9.384, 388); that δινεῖν, δινωτός, etc. could also be used in connection with lathes (cf. Blümner 1879: 333) perhaps suggested the

substitution here, and cf. *Od.* 5.249–50 (Odysseus building the raft) ὅσον
τίς τ᾽ ἔδαφος νηὸς τορνώσεται ἀνὴρ/φορτίδος εὐρείης. ἕλκε will refer to 'pulling'
on the straps used to drive the drill (cf. 460–4n.). Others interpret the
two imperatives as a reference to pottery rather than ship-building; iconographic evidence, however, suggests that the potter's wheel was turned
manually by an assistant, and ἕλκειν does not seem a natural verb with
which to describe such an action, cf., e.g., Noble 1988: 21 with Figure 6,
Sparkes 1991: 14–15, Williams 2009: Figures 2–3. *Ba.* 1066–7, a very difficult passage in which both τόρνος and ἕλκειν occur, has been interpreted
as referring to the operation of a pole-lathe in which a spinning wheel
would 'drag' on a pole by means of a cord (cf. Palmer 1946, Willink 1966:
237–9), but there is no explicit evidence for such a technique in classical
Athens, and such an interpretation of that passage seems very improbable, cf. Diggle 1998. Willink 2001: 529 suggested τόρνευε <πᾶς>/ἕλκε to
ease the transition to the second person singular; better perhaps (cf. the
metrical analysis above) would be ἕλκε τόρνευε <πᾶς> (2*cr*).

μή σ᾽ ἐξοδυνηθείς ...: ἐξοδυνᾶν occurs only here; the ἐκ- has intensive force
to mark the extremity of the Cyclops' pain, cf. *Od.* 9.415 Κύκλωψ δὲ στενά-
χων τε καὶ ὠδίνων ὀδύνῃσι κτλ. σε is not strictly required, and its omission
gives identifiable metre (cf. 656–62 n.), but the satyrs' expression of concern is more pointed with it than without it, and the metrical argument is
not decisive here.

τι μάταιον might seem rather mild for the Cyclops' likely reaction to his
suffering, but μάταιος may be used of very serious actions or words (cf.,
e.g., Aesch. fr. 281a.19, Soph. *Tr.* 565, 587), so here 'outrageous', rather
than 'empty, vain'.

663–709 FIFTH EPISODE

The blinded and screaming Cyclops is taunted by the chorus who play
a kind of 'blind man's buff' with him, as he tries to lay his hands on the
Greeks. Odysseus joins in and reveals his true name to the Cyclops, who
then recalls an old prophecy he had once received about Odysseus. As the
Greeks and the satyrs escape, the Cyclops clambers up through his cave to
hurl rocks at his tormentors.

663–8 At some point during these verses the Cyclops appears at the
entrance to the cave; on the possible change to his mask at this point cf.
above p. 30. It seems almost certain that 663 at least is delivered while the
Cyclops is still out of sight behind the *skēnē*, for this allows a semi-parodic evocation of tragic practice, most notably of Agamemnon's death-cries at Aesch.
Ag. 1343–6 and perhaps also of the imitation of that scene at *Hec.* 1035–40.

The similarities between *Hec.* and *Cycl.* are particularly striking (see esp. 663 ~ *Hec.* 1035, 665 ~ *Hec.* 1037, 666 ~ *Hec.* 1039) and have led to much speculation about the relation between the two plays, cf. above p. 43–4.

663 offers a more articulate Cyclops than his Homeric predecessor, cf. *Od.* 9.395 σμερδαλέον δὲ μέγ᾽ ὤιμωξεν, περὶ δ᾽ ἴαχε πέτρη. The cry clearly evokes tragedy, and specifically Agamemnon's cry at Aesch. *Ag.* 1343, ὤμοι πέπληγμαι καιρίαν πληγὴν ἔσω.

κατηνθρακώμεθ᾽ 'I have been reduced to ash', cf. 648n. on Typhon; at Soph. *El.* 58 this compound is used of a cremated corpse. Such a comically elaborate verb, emphasised by use of the poetic plural, comes close to some Lucianic descriptions of Empedocles, cf., e.g., *Ikaromen.* 13 Ἐμπεδοκλῆς ἀνθρακίας τις ἰδεῖν καὶ σποδοῦ πλέως καὶ κατωπτημένος, *VH* 2.21 Ἐμπεδοκλῆς ... περίεφθος καὶ τὸ σῶμα ὅλον ὠπτημένος, *Peregrin.* 1; the story of Empedocles' leap into Mount Etna is first attested for Heraclides Ponticus (second half of fourth century, fr. 93–95A Schütrumpf = Empedocles P29 Laks–Most), but may have been extrapolated earlier from Empedocles' own poems. The Sicilian philosopher might have offered Euripides another link between the volcano and consumption by fire.

ὀφθαλμοῦ σέλας: accusative of respect; the remarkable expression (cf. fr. 472e.14 of the fire in a beloved's eyes) suggests the *pathos* of what has happened.

664 The malicious request to the Cyclops to cry out again (with Markland's certain αὖ) plays on the tragic pattern where death-screams are indeed repeated, cf. Aesch. *Ag.* 1345, Soph. *El.* 1415–16 (also in imitation of Aesch. *Ag.*, cf. Finglass ad loc.). The satyrs and the audience will both relish conformity to the tragic type; the sound of the Cyclops' anguish is music to the satyrs' ears, cf. 443–4.

ὁ παιάν: one form of paean was a song celebrating victory (cf. Aesch. *Sept.* 635, *Ch.* 343, Thucyd. 2.91.2, *RE* 18.2348, Rutherford 2001: 45–7), and here the satyrs sarcastically describe the Cyclops' cry of pain as a victory-song (for Odysseus and themselves). For choral pleasure at such cries within the *skēnē* cf. *Antiope* fr. 223.47–55, *Her.* 749–56; both those scenes thematise the workings of justice, as Odysseus is soon to do.

τόνδ᾽ 'that one you just sang', cf. K–G I 644.

666 Cf. *Hec.* 1039 (Polymestor) ἀλλ᾽ οὔτι μὴ φύγητε λαιψηρῶι ποδί.

οὔτι μὴ φύγητε: οὐ μή with the aorist subjunctive expresses strong denial, cf. Smyth §1804, 2755.

667 χαίροντες 'scot-free', lit. 'rejoicing', cf. *Med.* 398, *Her.* 258, *Or.* 1593, LSJ s.v. II, Collard 2018: 66.

οὐδὲν ὄντες: cf. 642n. At *Od.* 9.515 (also after the blinding) the Cyclops describes Odysseus as ὀλίγος τε καὶ οὐτιδανὸς καὶ ἄκικυς; the D-scholia on *Il.* 1.231 gloss οὐτιδανός as οὐδενὸς λόγου ἄξιος, which is certainly how the

Cyclops views Odysseus. Unfortunately for him, his tormentor was not οὐδέν but Οὖτις.

667–8 'For standing at the gates of this cave I shall fit my hands <to it>'. In *Od.* the blinded Cyclops sits down in the doorway (εἰνὶ θύρηισι) of the cave and stretches out his arms (χεῖρε πετάσσας) in order to catch any Greek who tries to escape (9.417–18); Euripides' Cyclops tries a similar stratagem, but standing rather than sitting. The difference is in part driven by the fact that we see a human actor playing the Cyclops and are not listening to Odysseus' narrative of a monster the size of a mountain.

φάραγγος τῆσδ': the deictic presumably accompanies the actual stretching out of his arms. The text is however uncertain. The transmitted τάσδ', 'these arms', is very little different in performative effect to 'this cave'; other suggestions, which involve the paradox of a blind man's deixis, include ταῖσδ' (Kirchhoff), 'these gates …' (which does not imply a reference to the other entrance, 707n.), and φάραγγι τῆιδ' (Seaford), 'I shall fit my hands to this cleft'.

669–90 The chorus' dialogue with the blinded Cyclops is characterised by lively stage-action – parodic, cruel, and verging on slapstick. The scene has thirteen instances of *antilabē*, i.e. division of a verse between two or more speakers. This occurs as an intensifying device in all forms of Greek dramatic dialogue, usually embedded in (or in close proximity to) stichomythic exchanges, cf. 261n.; for exceptions cf., e.g., *Andr.* 1077, *Hec.* 1127, *Ba.* 966–70, Soph. *Phil.* 54, 733. In *Cycl.*, all such verses but one (682n.) have a single change of speaker, as is normal in tragedy (Soph. *Phil.* 753 and the satyric *Ichn.* 205 have three changes). Several tragedies of Euripides have relatively long sequences of trochaic tetrameters divided between different characters (*Ion* 530–62, *Or.* 774–98, *IA* 1345–68), but the longest such trimeter sequence in *Cycl.* (681–6) is only six verses. It is, however, the third in a series of snatches of dialogue marked by *antilabē* and of increasing length (2 – 4 – 6 lines, 669–70, 672–5); such a formalised pattern might itself originate in, or point to, the game of 'blind man's buff' which is played out on stage (cf. 679–90n.).

669 τί χρῆμ' 'Why …?', cf. *Hcld.* 646 τί χρῆμ' αὐτῆς πᾶν τόδ' ἐπλήσθη στέγος, *Alc.* 512, *El.* 831. For the use of τί χρῆμα in place of τί cf. Collard 2018: 60 (~ Stevens 1976: 22). The mocking satyrs here play the role of the Cyclops' fellow-Cyclopes in Homer, cf. 445–6n., *Od.* 9.403–6.

αὐτεῖς: a high-style verb (in Ar. only at *Lys.* 717 in paratragedy) with the colloquial τί χρῆμα; heightens the mockery. αὐτεῖν is also used by the chorus-leader in the Aeschylean scene which is in the background here (*Ag.* 1344, cf. 663n.).

670 αἰσχρός γε φαίνηι 'You certainly look ugly!'; γε emphasises the adjective, cf. *GP*² 127. <ὤν> is, as often, to be supplied with φαίνηι.

κἀπὶ τοῖσδέ γ' 'And, moreover, on top of this …', cf. *GP*² 157.

672–3 replay the Homeric exchange between the Cyclops and the other Cyclopes, *Od.* 9.407–12. The repeated inferential ἄρ, 'in that case', mocks the Cyclops' failure to understand what has happened.

ἀπώλεσ': the transmitted ἀπώλεσεν offers a third-foot anapaest split across change of speaker, cf. above p. 37.

ἠδίκει: the imperfect indicates that the sense of wrong continues into the present, 'has been wronging you'.

με τυφλοῖ βλέφαρον 'blinds me in the eye', the so-called 'accusative of part and whole', cf. *Ba.* 619, Smyth §985. The present tense reworks *Od.* 9.408 Οὖτίς με κτείνει.

674 †ὡς δὴ σύ†: the Cyclops presumably said something implying that he was very certainly blind, but no suggested reconstruction is more than possible: ψεύδηι σύ (Diggle 1981: 38 n.1) is the most attractive suggestion (πῶς φὴις σύ;, Stinton 1977: 140); for a survey of earlier emendations cf. Diggle 1971: 49. Dindorf suggested deleting the whole verse, but it is perhaps better that the Cyclops should have a little longer to realise that he is being mocked. Some have kept the transmitted text and understood that a retort by the Cyclops is either interrupted (*GP*² 229) or 'left incomplete by aposiopesis' (Mastronarde 1979: 64 n.37).

675 σκώπτεις: cf. Ar. *Pl.* 973, Men. *Dysk.* 54, etc.

ὁ δ' Οὖτις, 'that Mr No Man', evokes the Homeric story, as does Odysseus' corresponding question at 129.

676 ὁ ξένος: Odysseus has been ὁ ξένος *par excellence* ever since the Phaeacian books of *Od.* The tables are truly turned: it used to be the Cyclops who 'destroyed' ξένοι.

μ' ἀπώλεσεν: the position of the enclitic, third in the sentence after an intervening subordinate clause, is very unusual, but cf. *Andr.* 551, *Hipp.* 1154.

677 ὁ μιαρός: a common comic term of abuse, cf. Ar. *Frogs* 466 καὶ μιαρὲ καὶ παμμιαρὲ καὶ μιαρώτατε, *Thesm.* 649, Collard 2018: 154–5; for other satyric instances cf. fr. 673.2, Soph. *Ichn.* 197.

κατέκλυσεν, 'drowned, swamped', continues the nautical language and images to describe drinking, cf. 576n., Petr. *Sat.* 21.6 *uino etiam Falerno inundamur*, Slater 1976; the Cyclops has been 'sunk', as was feared by the drunken young men in a famous story told by Timaeus (*FGrHist* 566 F 149 = Ath. 2.37b–e). A character in Xenarchus fr. 2 describes himself as a sailor who has (ironically) been 'destroyed and sunk' (ἀπώλεσε … καὶ κατεπόντωσεν) by too many toasts to 'Zeus the Saviour'. There are many examples of such language and imagery in the chapter on the dangers of 'shipwreck from drinking' (*Paed.* 2.2.22) by Clement of Alexandria (*Paed.* 2.2.19–34): 'The heart is swamped (περικλύζεται) by excessive drinking, the quantity of wine is like the menacing sea, in which the body has been sunk (βεβυθισμένον) like a ship and gone down to the depths of disorder, overwhelmed by the huge waves of wine …' (*Paed.* 2.2.28).

678 is best understood as an ironically sympathetic observation by the chorus.

παλαίεσθαι βαρύς 'hard to wrestle against, difficult to defeat in wrestling', cf. 635–6n. For wine as a tricky wrestler cf. Eubulus fr. 93.12, Plautus, *Pseud.* 1250–1. At *Ba.* 800 Pentheus exclaims ἀπόρωι γε τῶιδε συμπεπλέγμεθα ξένωι; the verb is a 'metaphor from wrestling' (Dodds ad loc.), but it is unclear how live that metaphor was: is Pentheus too wrestling with Wine?

679–90 This scene, in which the satyrs taunt the Cyclops by playing a kind of 'blind man's buff' with him, has obvious analogies to the taunting of the blinded Polymestor in *Hec.*, cf. above pp. 43–4; the fooling of the Scythian archer at Ar. *Thesm.* 1217–26, which is marked by lively *antilabai* (1218, 1220) also has some similarities to this scene, cf. above p. 24 n. 70. The closest Homeric analogy is *Od.* 9.456–7 where the blinded Cyclops wishes that his ram could speak and tell him 'where that man is hiding from my strength'. 'Blind man's buff' was called μυίνδα or χαλκῆ μυῖα, 'bronze fly', to make a connection with μύειν, 'to close the eyes' (cf. Hesych. μ 1813). 'They bind the eyes of one child with a sash; he spins around (περιστρέφεται) and says "I shall hunt a bronze fly". The others answer "You will hunt, but you won't catch", and they beat him with whips made of reed until he catches one of them' (Pollux 9.123, cf. 9.113, Herodas fr. 12.1, Eustath. *Hom.* 1243.30–3). ποτέρας τῆς χερός (681), ἐν δεξιᾶι σου (682) and πρὸς τἀριστερά (686) are presumably versions of phrases from the game. We have followed L and most editors in assigning all the choral utterances to the chorus-leader, but it cannot be ruled out that, in imitation of the children's game, different members of the chorus speak in 682 (perhaps two different choreuts), 684, 685, 686. Seidensticker 2010: 228 noted that from 669 to 688 there are fifteen choral remarks and attractively suggested that each was delivered by a different choreut, cf. above p. 26. In a long poem on children published in 1806, the theologian Friedrich Adolph Krummacher explicitly compared the blindfolded child in 'blind man's buff' to the blinded Polyphemos looking for the Greeks (Krummacher 1806: 209, 280); his note does not refer to Euripides, but it is hard to believe that he was unacquainted with *Cycl.*

679 Cf. *Hec.* 1064–5 (Polymestor) ὦ κατάρατοι,/ποῖ καί με φυγᾶι πτώσσουσι μυχῶν;

θεῶν is scanned as a single syllable by synizesis, cf. 231n.

680 ἐπήλυγα: probably 'overhanging', 'screening'. The word appears nowhere else, but ἐπηλυγάζειν (or -ίζειν) means 'cover, overshadow' and the middle can denote (so LSJ) 'use as a hiding-place'. Pollux 9.113 notes that in the game of μυίνδα (679–90n.) the other children 'hide' (κρυφθέν- τας) from the 'blind man'.

681–2 The Cyclops' frenzied distress leads to two successive breaches of Porson's Law (cf. above pp. 37–8).

681 λαβόντες 'occupying, taking possession of', cf. *Suppl.* 652, *IT* 962. **ποτέρας τῆς χερός;;** a local genitive, cf. [Aesch.] *PV* 714, Hdt. 5.77.4, Smyth §1448.

682 The only line in *Cycl.* with two *antilabai*, cf., e.g., *Alc.* 391, 1119, *Her.* 1418, 1420, here perhaps marking the climax of a cluster of such verses during 'blind man's buff' (cf. 669–90n.).

683–4 ἔχεις;; the simple verb without an expressed object allows the Cyclops' unexpected answer, cf. *Suppl.* 818, Soph. *Aj.* 875–6 (with Finglass' n.).

κακόν γε πρός κακῶι 'Yes, woe upon woe!', cf. *Hipp.* 874, Soph. *OC* 595.

τὸ κρανίον/παίσας κατέαγα 'I struck my head and smashed it'; the noun (cf. 647n.) goes both with the participle (as object) and with the verb (as accusative of respect), cf. Alciphron 3.18.1 τί δακρύω ... ἢ πόθεν κατέαγα τὸ κρανίον κτλ.; for the construction cf. Ar. *Pl.* 545, Diggle on Theophr. *Char.* 27.10. Blaydes suggested τοῦ κρανίου (cf. Ar. *Ach.* 1180, *Wasps* 1428, Lucian, *Timon* 48, K–G I 345), but that is unnecessary. The phrases in Lucian and Alciphron need not derive from this verse, but may do so. Cf. further Magnelli 2003: 196–7, above pp. 50–1.

κατέαγα: this perfect from κατάγνυμι is active in form but standardly passive in meaning. The penultimate vowel is long; the comic anapaest perhaps suits the lively 'low' action.

καί σε διαφεύγουσί γε: a belated and mocking answer to 679.

685 οὐ τῆιδέ πηι, τῆιδ' εἶπας; 'Didn't you say here somewhere, over here?', cf. *Rhes.* 689. The text is not certain. West 1981: 68 suggested punctuating οὐ τῆιδέ πηι· τῆιδ' εἶπας; 'Not anywhere this way – did you mean this way?'

686 πῆι γάρ; 'Where then?'; for γάρ in a surprised question cf. 153–4n.

περίαγου: middle imperative; the compound does not appear in tragedy. This may well be another echo of actual phrases from the χαλκῆ μυῖα game, cf. περιστρέφεται in Pollux' description (679–90n.). Biehl suggests that the verb puns on Κύκλωψ, 'Mr Circle', and that 687 shows that the Cyclops understands the joke.

687 οἴμοι γελῶμαι: there is a touch of paratragedy to the Cyclops' lament, cf. Aesch. *Eum.* 789, 819, Soph. *Ant.* 839 (Antigone cries οἴμοι γελῶμαι, but specific parody (so, e.g., Duchemin ad loc.) seems very improbable). For the habitual Greek fear of being laughed at cf., e.g., *Med.* 797, 383, Soph. *Ant.* 483, *Ajax* 382, Ar. *Ach.* 1081, *Peace* 1245.

688 Odysseus and his men have now got safely away, but the taunting of the blind man (οὗτος, cf. τόδε 690) continues.

ἀλλ' οὐκέτ': cf. *Hel.* 1229, where, with Jackson's transposition, it is also preceded by a complaint of κερτομία.

689 Cf. *Hec.* 1124 (Polymestor) ἢ γὰρ ἐγγύς ἐστί που;

ὦ παγκάκιστε: cf. *Med.* 465 (Medea to Jason), *Hipp.* 682 (Phaedra to the Nurse), *Suppl.* 513; the address does not occur in Ar.

τηλοῦ σέθεν: the last *antilabē* in the play, and perhaps Odysseus' contribution to 'blind man's buff' (cf. 679–90n.).

690 φυλακαῖσι φρουρῶ 'I keep a watchful guard on'. Odysseus is now his own bodyguard; the phrase is suggestive of military 'guarding', cf. *Rhes.* 764–5. φυλακὰς φυλάττειν is the more usual phrase (Xen. *Anab.* 2.6.10, Dem. 7.14, etc.).

Ὀδυσσέως: on the revelation of the name to the Cyclops cf. 103n.

692 μ' drifts to the normal second position for an enclitic pronoun ('Wackernagel's Law'), even though it then precedes the participle governing it, cf. *El.* 264, *Ion* 324. The transmitted γε would be assentient, 'Yes, the one which …', with <με> understood, just as apogr. Par. felt compelled to add it to the text.

ὠνόμαζ': the imperfect is idiomatic in such expressions, cf. *Suppl.* 1218, Fraenkel on Aesch. *Ag.* 681.

Ὀδυσσέα: the hero proudly repeats his name, cf. *Od.* 9.504–5 where he gives the Cyclops 'the full works': 'tell [anyone who asks who blinded you] that it was Odysseus, sacker of cities, son of Laertes, who dwells on Ithaca'. Kovacs 1994: 157–8, however, regards the repetition of the name as 'surprisingly weak' and suggests that the text is corrupt.

693 The idea of vengeful punishment for the Cyclops is present in *Od.* (cf. 9.317, 479), and picked up by Virgil (*Aen.* 3.638 *laeti sociorum ulciscimur umbras*), but the motif is much more pronounced in *Cycl.* (and in satyr-play more generally, cf. 441–2n.). In *Hec.*, where there is no 'escapeplot', the motif dominates the confrontation of Hecuba and Polymestor, cf. 1024, 1052–3, 1253–4, 1258.

694 'Our burning of Troy would be a wretched thing …'; for this use of κακῶς cf. *Hcld.* 171, and for Odysseus' appeal to the memory of the Trojan War cf. 198–200. Dobree's καλῶς would be ironical: 'A fine thing would be …' Cobet suggested ἄλλως, 'in vain, pointless'.

διεπυρώσαμεν: this is the only occurrence of this compound before Hellenistic prose. The verb, rather than, say, 'we sacked', is chosen because of what has happened to the Cyclops; it is perhaps more likely that it is a true plural and refers to 'the Greeks' as a whole (cf., e.g., 178, 282, 286–96), rather than a poetic singular referring to Odysseus alone.

The transmitted first-person singular middle would be in keeping with Odysseus' epic sense of his role at Troy (cf., e.g., *Od.* 1.2, 8.494–5, 9.502–5), and may be correct, but the error could easily have arisen from the following verse.

695 ἐτιμωρησάμην is followed by a double accusative, cf. *Alc.* 733. In Homer Odysseus taunted the Cyclops with punishment from Zeus and the other gods (*Od.* 9.479).

696–8 Cf. *Od.* 9.507–12. The Homeric prophet Telemos plays no part here, presumably as Euripides is now bringing everything to a very swift and hectic dramatic close. The motif here follows not just epic, but also Euripidean tradition: the tragedies regularly contain prophecy of the future as part of the dramatic closure, cf. Mastronarde 2010: 187–8.

αἰαῖ: cf. *Od.* 9.506–7 οἰμώξας … ὦ πόποι κτλ.

παλαιός picks up the Homeric παλαίφατα (*Od.* 9.507, 13.172). The adjective perhaps refers also to the fact that the oracle is now 'old' for the time of the play, i.e. it belongs to the Homeric story, cf. Laemmle 2013: 344. ἀρχαῖος of the Cyclops at Theocr. 11.8 has a similar double sense.

ἐκπεραίνεται 'is being fulfilled', cf. *Ion* 785, *Ph.* 1703, Ar. *Wasps* 799.

Τροίας ἀφορμηθέντος: this is not explicitly stated in the Homeric prophecy, and Euripides has perhaps been influenced by Hermes' prediction to Circe that she would be visited by Odysseus ἐκ Τροίης ἀνιόντα (*Od.* 10.332).

698–700 In *Od.* the Cyclops prays to Poseidon to make Odysseus' return both long delayed (ὀψέ) and wretched, 9.532–5; here the motif is included within the oracle which the Cyclops claims to have received: he and the audience all know of Odysseus' wanderings at sea. In the background perhaps lies Teiresias' very similar prophecy to Odysseus at *Od.* 11.100–17.

τοι 'I warn you', 'believe me', emphasising the certainty of the threat, cf. *Ba.* 516, *GP*² 537, 540.

δίκας ὑφέξειν: a standard phrase, also in prosaic legal language, cf. *Hec.* 1253, *El.* 698, LSJ s.v. ὑπέχω II 3.

ἐναιωρούμενον 'drifting on …', the only example of this compound outside medical prose; the simple verb can mean 'hover', 'be in suspense'.

701 κλαίειν σ' ἄνωγα: cf. 172–4n., 318–19n., 340; Odysseus, who does not normally stoop to comic or vulgar language (cf. above p. 36), throws the Cyclops' words back at him. ἄνωγα raises the expression above the purely colloquial, cf. 340n.

δέδραχ' ὅπερ λέγεις 'I have [already] done what you say <I will do>', namely drift on the sea for a long time. Odysseus thinks he is on the home-leg, but he is in fact only at the beginning of his troubles (cf. *Od.* 9.82–106). δέδραχ' may, however, seem too positive and active a verb for 'drifting on the sea' (cf. *Hec.* 1048), and others retain the transmitted λέγω, referring it either to Odysseus' proclamation of vengeance in 695 or to κλαίειν σ' ἄνωγα: Odysseus has already made the Cyclops very sorry, cf. Seaford 1982: 165.

702 νεὼς σκάφος: cf. 85n.

703 ἥσω 'I shall launch', a very unusual use of the simple ἵημι; Hdt. uses ἀφίημι in this sense at 5.42.2.

πόντον Σικελόν: the 'Sicilian sea' is that part of the Mediterranean east of Sicily stretching towards Greece, cf. *El.* 1347, Zuntz 1955: 66–7. As Ithaca might, on some reckonings, lie within that sea, Schumacher proposed εἰς for ἔς τ', but nothing seems to be gained by the change.

πάτραν: Odysseus' last word in the play expresses what has always mattered to him most, cf. 103, 277, *Od.* 9.21, 505, etc.

704 οὐ δῆτ': cf. 198n.

τῆσδ' ἀπορρήξας πέτρας 'breaking off a piece of this rock', partitive genitive, cf. Smyth §1341. The participle comes from *Od.* 9.481, but Euripides has downsized considerably: in Homer, the Cyclops first breaks off the peak of a mountain (9.481) and then 'a much bigger rock' (9.537).

705 αὐτοῖσι συνναύταισι 'your fellow-sailors and all', a common use of datives with αὐτός, cf. *Med.* 164, Smyth §1525, LSJ s.v. αὐτός I 5.

βαλών: cf. *Od.* 9.482, 539.

706 In *Od.* the Cyclops does not have to climb up to higher ground as the cave is at the edge of the land, presumably overlooking the sea (*Od.* 9.182–3).

707 '... climbing on foot through this second entrance'. The Cyclops now reveals that the cave has in fact an opening at the back, cf. *Od.* 13.103–12 (the 'cave of the Nymphs'); Odysseus' men could just have escaped that way (cf. Zwierlein 1967: 453 n.2), but that would certainly have spoiled the fun. ἀμφιτρής is found only here and at Soph. *Phil.* 19 δι' ἀμφιτρῆτος αὐλίου of Philoctetes' cave; it is impossible that the two instances are unconnected, and it is normally assumed that Euripides here imitates, for the comic delight of the audience, a device of a very recent Sophoclean play, cf. above pp. 40–1, Marshall 2001: 236–8. Unlike in *Cycl.*, the two entrances of the cave are strongly thematised in *Phil.*, cf. *Phil.* 16, 19, 159, 952, which makes a borrowing by Sophocles from *Cycl.* very unlikely. Philoctetes on the volcanic island of Lemnos is a further model for the Cyclops on Sicily.

As transmitted, ἀμφιτρής is here used as an elliptical noun, whereas it is adjectival in Sophocles; Kirchhoff removed the anomaly by suggesting πέτρας for ποδί at verse-end, but ποδί has excellent parallels (*El.* 489–90, *Hec.* 1263, Schmidt 1975, Diggle 1981: 36–7) and its removal does not carry conviction. The linguistic anomaly may perhaps calls attention to the borrowing from *Phil.* (cf., e.g., Dale 1969: 129). Diggle's lacuna after this verse still deserves serious consideration.

προσβαίνων 'climbing', cf. Beare 1905: 70–2, LSJ s.v. 2–3.

708–9 The satyrs rush off to 'hitch a lift' with Odysseus and thus exchange (they hope) servitude to the Cyclops for the blessed and familiar servitude to Dionysos, cf. 23–4n., Hunter 2009: 57. We shall see their future (τὸ λοιπόν) next time we watch satyr-drama. Olson 1988 argues that, in finding an Odysseus who has wine, the satyrs have indeed been reunited with Dionysos, which had been the purpose of their quest (cf. 13–14). It seems unlikely, however, that any member of the audience will have worried about the fact that the satyrs have not found the abducted god: he will, in any case, have long since freed himself, and if he wants to be reunited with the satyrs, he will be.

δὲ ... γε marks a lively retort to the Cyclops, cf. 538n.: 'We are no longer your slaves ...'

συνναῦται: when we first heard of the satyrs, they were rowers commanded by Silenos (13–17); as the play ends, they have swapped one commander for another – but it is always Dionysos whom they really serve.

τοῦδ' Ὀδυσσέως: the final deictic mocks the blind Cyclops for the last time, cf. 667–8n.

Βακχίωι: the play ends as it had begun with the god's name, and both play and tetralogy end with an acknowledgement (and perhaps gesture) to the god whose image presides over the theatre.

WORKS CITED

Ambrose, Z.P. 2005. 'Family loyalty and betrayal in Euripides' *Cyclops* and *Alcestis*: a recurrent theme in satyr play' in Harrison 2005: 21–38

Arnott, P.D. 1961. 'The overworked playwright' *Greece and Rome* 8: 164–9

Arnott, W.G. 1972. 'Parody and ambiguity in Euripides' Cyclops' in *Antidosis. Festschrift für Walther Kraus*, Vienna: 21–30

1996. *Alexis, The Fragments*, Cambridge

Austin, C. and Olson, S.D. 2004. *Aristophanes, Thesmophoriazusae*, Oxford

Austin, C. and Reeve, M.D. 1970. 'Notes on Sophocles, Ovid and Euripides' *Maia* 22: 3–18

Bain, D. 1977. *Actors and Audience*, Oxford

1981. *Masters, Servants and Orders in Greek Tragedy*, Manchester

Bakker, E.J. 2013. *The Meaning of Meat and the Structure of the Odyssey*, Cambridge

Bakola, E. 2010. *Cratinus and the Art of Comedy*, Oxford

Barrett, W.S. 2007. *Greek Lyric, Tragedy, and Textual Criticism. Collected Papers*, Oxford

Bary, C. 2012. 'The ancient Greek tragic aorist revisited' *Glotta* 88: 31–53

Battezzato, L. 1995. *Il monologo nel teatro di Euripide*, Pisa

2000. 'Synizesis in Euripides and the structure of the iambic trimeter: the case of θεός' *Bulletin of the Institute of Classical Studies* 44: 41–80

2018. *Euripides, Hecuba*, Cambridge

Baumbach, M. and Dümmler, N. eds., 2014. *Imitate Anacreon! Mimesis, Poiesis and the Poetic Inspiration in the Carmina Anacreontea*, Berlin

Beare, J.I. 1905. 'Miscellanea' *Hermathena* 13: 70–86

Belardinelli, A.M. et al. eds. 1998. *Tessere. Frammenti della commedia greca: studi e commenti*, Bari

Bentein, K. 2016. *Verbal Periphrasis in Ancient Greek*, Oxford

Bernabé, A. 2003. 'Autour du mythe orphique sur Dionysos et les Titans: quelques notes critiques' in D. Accorinti and P. Chuvin eds., *Des Géants à Dionysos*, Alessandria: 25–39

Bernsdorff, H. 2016. 'Anacreon and Athens' *Zeitschrift für Papyrologie und Epigraphik* 198:1–13

Bers, V. 1974. *Enallage and Greek Style*, Leiden

Biehl, W. 1977. 'Die qualitative Formgestaltung der trimetrischen Stücke in Euripides' *Kyklops*' *Hermes* 105: 159–75

1986. 'Zwei Textprobleme in Euripides' Kyklops' *Philologus* 130: 175–83

Biles, Z.P. and Olson, S.D. 2015. *Aristophanes Wasps*, Oxford.

Bing, P. 2014. '*Anacreontea* avant la lettre: Euripides' *Cyclops* 495–518' in Baumbach and Dümmler 2014: 25–45

Blech, M. 1982. *Studien zum Kranz bei den Griechen*, Berlin

Blümner, H. 1879. *Technologie und Terminologie der Gewerbe und Künste bei Griechen und Römern*, Vol. II, Leipzig

Boardman, J. 1989. *Athenian Red Figure Vases. The Classical Period*, London

Bond, G.W. 1963. *Euripides, Hypsipyle*, Oxford

Bosher, K. ed. 2012. *Theater outside Athens. Drama in Greek Sicily and South Italy*, Cambridge

Bowie, A. 1997. 'Thinking with drinking: wine and the symposium in Aristophanes' *Journal of Hellenic Studies* 117: 1–21

Brashear, W. 1979. 'Ein Berliner Zauberpapyrus' *Zeitschrift für Papyrologie und Epigraphik* 33: 261–78

Breitenbach, W. 1934. *Untersuchungen zur Sprache der euripideischen Lyrik*, Stuttgart

Bremmer, J. 2006. 'A Macedonian maenad in Posidippus (AB 44)' *Zeitschrift für Papyrologie und Epigraphik* 155: 37–40

Brink, C.O. 1971. *Horace on Poetry. The 'Ars Poetica'*, Cambridge

Burkert, W. 1983. *Homo Necans. The Anthropology of Ancient Greek Sacrificial Ritual and Myth*, Berkeley, CA

1985. *Greek Religion*, Oxford

Burzacchini, G. 1979. 'Eur. *Cycl.* 320–31' *Quaderni Urbinati di Cultura Classica* 32: 65–8

Butler, A.J. 1930. *Sport in Classic Times*, London

Buxton, R. 1994. *Imaginary Greece*, Cambridge

2017. 'Landscapes of the Cyclopes' in G. Hawes ed., *Myths on the Map*, Oxford: 52–64

Carey, C. 2011. 'Alcman: from Laconia to Alexandria' in L. Athanassaki and E. Bowie eds., *Archaic and Classical Choral Song*, Berlin: 437–60

Carpenter, T.H. 1997. *Dionysian Imagery in Fifth-Century Athens*, Oxford

Carpenter, T.H. and Faraone, C.A. eds. 1993. *Masks of Dionysus*, Ithaca, NY

Cassio, A.C. 2000. 'Esametri orfici, dialetto attico e musica dell'Asia Minore' in A.C. Cassio, D. Musti and L.E. Rossi eds., *Synaulía. Cultura musicale in Grecia e contatti mediterranei*, Naples: 97–100

2002. 'The language of Doric comedy' in A. Willi ed., *The Language of Greek Comedy*, Oxford: 51–83

Casson, L. 1971. *Ships and Seamanship in the Ancient World*, Princeton, NJ

Cazzato, V. 2016. 'Symposia *en plein air* in Alcaeus and others' in Cazzato, Obbink and Prodi 2016: 184–206

Cazzato, V., Obbink, D. and Prodi, E.E. eds. 2016. *The Cup of Song*, Oxford

Ceccarelli, P. 1998. *La pirrica nell'antichità greco romana*, Pisa and Rome

2004. 'Dancing the *pyrrhichē* in Athens' in Murray and Wilson 2004: 91–117

Cerbo, E. 2015. 'Metro e ritmo nel dramma satiresco (V–IV a.C.)' *Seminari Romani* 4: 71–117

Cerri, G. 1976. 'Nota testuale a Eur. *Cycl.* 147' *Rivista di Filologia e Istruzione Classica* 104: 139–43

Chantraine, P. 1945. 'Grec κομψός' *Revue des Études Grecques* 58: 90–6

Citti, V. 1994. *Eschilo e la lexis tragica*, Amsterdam

Clarke, M. 2004. 'The semantics of colour in the early Greek word-hoard' in L. Cleland, K. Stears and G. Davies eds., *Colour in the Ancient Mediterranean World*, Oxford: 131–9

Clements, A. 2013. '"Looking mustard": Greek popular epistemology and the meaning of δριμύς' in S. Butler and A. Purves eds., *Synaesthesia and the Ancient Senses*, Durham: 71–88

   2014. *Aristophanes' Thesmophoriazusae. Philosophizing Theatre and the Politics of Perception in Late Fifth-Century Athens*, Cambridge

Collard, C. 2018. *Colloquial Expressions in Greek Tragedy. Revised and Enlarged Edition of P.T. Stevens's Colloquial Expressions in Euripides*, Stuttgart

Collins, D. 2004. *Master of the Game. Competition and Performance in Greek Poetry*, Washington, D.C.

Compton-Engle, G. 2001. 'Mock-tragic priamels in Aristophanes' *Acharnians* and Euripides' *Cyclops*' *Hermes* 129: 558–61

Conophagos, C.E. 1980. *Le Laurium antique et la technique grecque de la production de l'argent*, Athens

Coo, L. 2019. 'Satyric nostalgia in the Aeschylean tetralogy' in Coo and Uhlig 2019: 11–28

Coo, L. and Uhlig, A. eds. 2019. *Aeschylus at Play. Studies in Aeschylean Satyr Drama*, Bulletin of the Institute of Classical Studies Supplement 62.2, London

Copley, F.O. 1956. *Exclusus Amator. A Study in Latin Love Poetry*, Baltimore, MD

Cozzo, A. 1988. *Kerdos. Semantica, ideologie e società nella Grecia antica*, Rome

Cramer, J.A. 1841. *Anecdota graeca e codd. manuscriptis Bibliothecae Regiae Parisiensis*, Vol. IV, Oxford

Cropp, M. and Fick, G. 1985. *Resolution and Chronology in Euripides. The Fragmentary Tragedies*, London

Csapo, E. 2003. 'The dolphins of Dionysus' in E. Csapo and M.C. Miller eds., *Poetry, Theory, Praxis*, Oxford: 69–98

Csapo, E. and Slater, W.J. 1995. *The Context of Ancient Drama*, Ann Arbor, MI

Csapo, E. and Wilson, P. 2019. *A Social and Economic History of the Theatre to 300 BC. Vol. II. Theatre beyond Athens*, Cambridge

Curbera, J. 2019. 'An essay on satyr names' in R. Parker ed., *Changing Names. Tradition and Innovation in Ancient Greek Onomastics*, Oxford: 100–37

Dale, A.M. 1969. *Collected Papers*, Cambridge

　1981. *Metrical Analyses of Tragic Choruses*, Fasc. 2, *Bulletin of the Institute of Classical Studies* Suppl. 21.2, London

D'Alessio, G.B. 2016. 'Bacchylides' banquet songs' in Cazzato, Obbink and Prodi 2016: 63–84

　2020. 'Dancing with the dogs: mimetic dance and the hyporcheme (on *Pind. fr. 107 S-M = Simonides fr. 255 Poltera)' in P. Agócs and L. Prauscello eds., *Simonides Lyricus*, Cambridge: forthcoming

D'Alfonso, F. 2006. *Euripide in Giovanni Malala*, Alessandria

Davidson, J. 2000. 'Beware of the danger: a Homeric motif in fifth century drama' *Classica et Mediaevalia* 51: 17–28

Davies, J.K. 1971. *Athenian Propertied Families*, Oxford

Davies, M. 1999. 'Comic priamel and hyperbole in Euripides, *Cyclops* 1–10' *Classical Quarterly* 49: 428–32

　2000. 'Homer and Dionysus' *Eikasmos* 11: 15–27

Davies, M. and Finglass, P.J. 2014. *Stesichorus, The Poems*, Cambridge

Davies, M.I. 1990. 'Asses and rams: Dionysiac release in Aristophanes' *Wasps* and Attic vase-painting' *Metis* 5: 169–81

De Falco, V. 1935/6. 'Euripide, "Ciclope" – v. 141–143' *Dioniso* 5: 110–11

de Jong, I. 1991. *Narrative in Drama. The Art of the Euripidean Messenger-Speech*, Leiden

　2001. *A Narratological Commentary on the Odyssey*, Cambridge

Denniston, J.D. 1930. 'Notes on the Greek particles' *Classical Review* 44: 213–15

Descroix, J. 1931. *Le trimètre iambique. Des iambographes à la comédie nouvelle*, Macon

Dettori, E. 2016. *I Diktyoulkoi di Eschilo. Testo e commento*, Rome

Dickey, E. 1996. *Greek Forms of Address from Herodotus to Lucian*, Oxford

Diggle, J. 1971. 'Notes on the *Cyclops* of Euripides' *Classical Quarterly* 21: 42–50

　1972. 'Euripides, *Cyclops* 511–18 (and other passages)' *Maia* 24: 345–8

　1981. *Studies on the Text of Euripides*, Oxford

　1994. *Euripidea*, Oxford

　1998. 'Euripides, *Bacchae* 1063–1069' *Eikasmos* 9: 41–52

　2004. *Theophrastus, Characters*, Cambridge

　2005. 'Rhythmical prose in the Euripidean hypotheses' in G. Bastianini and A. Casanova eds., *Euripide e i papiri*, Florence: 27–67

　forthcoming. 'Thundering Polyphemus: Euripides, *Cyclops* 320–8' in A. Antonopoulos, M. Christopoulos and G. Harrison eds., *Brill's Companion to Satyr Drama*, Leiden

Di Marco, M. 1980a. 'Una parodia di Saffo in Euripide (*Cycl.* 182–186)' *Quaderni Urbinati di Cultura Classica* 34: 39–45

1980b. 'Eurip. "Cycl." 499' *Giornale Italiano di Filologia* 11: 47–54

2013. *Satyriká. Studi sul dramma satiresco*, Lecce

Dittenberger, W. 1915. *Sylloge inscriptionum Graecarum*, 3rd ed., Vol. I, Leipzig

Dodds, E.R. 1960. *Euripides Bacchae*, 2nd ed., Oxford

Dougherty, C. 1999. 'The double vision of Euripides' *Cyclops*: an ethnographic *Odyssey* on the satyr stage' *Comparative Drama* 33: 313–38

Dover, K.J. 1974. *Greek Popular Morality in the Time of Plato and Aristotle*, Oxford

1978. *Greek Homosexuality*, London

Drago, A.T. 2007. *Aristeneto, Lettere d'amore*, Lecce

Duncan, A. 2012. 'A Theseus outside Athens: Dionysius I of Syracuse and tragic self-presentation' in Bosher 2012: 137–55

Easterling, P. 1985. 'Anachronism in Greek tragedy' *Journal of Hellenic Studies* 105: 1–10

1994. 'Euripides outside Athens: a speculative note' *Illinois Classical Studies* 19: 7–87

1997a. ed. *The Cambridge Companion to Greek Tragedy*, Cambridge

1997b. 'A show for Dionysus' in Easterling 1997a: 36–53

2013. 'Sophocles and the wisdom of Silenus: a reading of *Oedipus at Colonus* 1211–48' in D. Cairns ed., *Tragedy and Archaic Greek Thought*, Swansea: 193–204

Eden, P.T. 1990. 'Some skewered gobbets in Euripides' in E.M. Craik ed., *'Owls to Athens'. Essays on Classical Subjects Presented to Sir Kenneth Dover*, Oxford: 25–9

Ekroth, G. 2017. 'Bare bones: zooarchaeology and Greek sacrifice' in Hitch and Rutherford 2017: 15–47

Ercolani, A. 2000. *Il passaggio di parola sulla scena tragica*, Stuttgart

Fantuzzi, M. 2014. 'Tragic smiles: when tragedy gets too comic for Aristotle and later Hellenistic readers' in R. Hunter, A. Rengakos and E. Sistakou eds., *Hellenistic Studies at a Crossroads*, Berlin: 216–33

Faraone, C.A. 2008. 'Mystery cults and incantations: evidence for Orphic charms in Euripides' *Cyclops* 646–8?' *Rheinisches Museum* 151: 127–42

Fedeli, P. 1983. *Catullus' Carmen 61*, Amsterdam

Feeney, D. 2013. 'Catullus 61: epithalamium and comparison' *Cambridge Classical Journal* 59: 70–97

Fellmann, B. 1972. *Die antiken Darstellungen des Polyphemabenteuers*, Munich

Fletcher, J. 2012. *Performing Oaths in Classical Greek Drama*, Cambridge

Fongoni, A. 2014. *Philoxeni Cytherii testimonia et fragmenta*, Rome

Ford, A. 2002. *The Origins of Criticism*, Princeton, NJ

2011. 'Dionysos' many names in Aristophanes' *Frogs*' in Schlesier 2011b: 343–55

Fowler, R. 2013. *Early Greek Mythography*, Vol. II, Oxford

Fraenkel, E. 1950. *Aeschylus, Agamemnon*, Oxford

Gagné, R. 2016. 'The world in a cup: ekpomatics in and out of the symposion' in Cazzato, Obbink and Prodi 2016: 207–29

Gargiulo, T. 1994. 'Eur. *Cycl.* 235' *Eikasmos* 5: 103–8

Garner, R. 1990. *From Homer to Tragedy. The Art of Allusion in Greek Poetry*, London

Ghali-Kahil, L. 1955. *Les enlèvements et le retour d'Hélène dans les textes et les documents figurés*, Paris

Gomme, A.W. 1948. 'Thucydides notes' *Classical Quarterly* 42: 10–14

Gould, J. 1973. 'Hiketeia' *Journal of Hellenic Studies* 93: 74–103

Graf, F. 1974. *Eleusis und die orphische Dichtung Athens in vorhellenistischer Zeit*, Berlin

Grégoire, H. 1948. 'La date du *Cyclope* d'Euripide' *L'Antiquité Classique* 17: 269–84

Griffith, M. 2015. *Greek Satyr Play. Five Studies*, Berkeley, CA

Guthrie, W.K.C. 1969. *A History of Greek Philosophy*, Vol. III, Cambridge

Gutzwiller, K. 2014. 'Anacreon, Hellenistic epigram, and the Anacreontic poet' in Baumbach and Dümmler 2014: 47–66

Gygli-Wyss, B. 1966. *Das nominale Polyptoton im älteren Griechisch*, Göttingen

Hall, E. 1988. 'When did the Trojans turn into Phrygians? Alcaeus 42.15' *Zeitschrift für Papyrologie und Epigraphik* 73: 15–18

1989. *Inventing the Barbarian*, Oxford

2006. *The Theatrical Cast of Athens*, Oxford

Halliwell, S. 2012. '*Amousia*: living without the Muses' in I. Sluiter and R.M. Rosen eds., *Aesthetic Value in Classical Antiquity*, Leiden: 15–45

Halperin, D. 1983. *Before Pastoral. Theocritus and the Ancient Tradition of Bucolic Poetry*, New Haven, CT

Hamilton, R. 1979. 'Euripides' Cyclopean symposium' *Phoenix* 33: 287–92

Hanink, J. 2008. 'Literary politics and the Euripidean *Vita*' *Cambridge Classical Journal* 54: 115–35

Harder, A. 2012. *Callimachus, Aetia*, Oxford

Harrison, G.W.M. ed. 2005. *Satyr Drama. Tragedy at Play*, Swansea

Hedreen, G. 1994. 'Silens, nymphs, and maenads' *Journal of Hellenic Studies* 114: 47–69

Heinemann, A. 2016. *Der Gott des Gelages*, Berlin

Henderson, J. 1991. *The Maculate Muse*, 2nd ed., Oxford

Heydemann, H. 1885. *Dionysos' Geburt und Kindheit*, Halle

Hinz, V. 1998. *Der Kult von Demeter und Kore auf Sizilien und in der Magna Graecia*, Wiesbaden

Hitch, S. and Rutherford, I. eds. 2017. *Animal Sacrifice in the Ancient Greek World*, Cambridge

Hobden, F. 2013. *The Symposion in Ancient Greek Society and Thought*, Cambridge

Hordern, J.H. 2002. *The Fragments of Timotheus of Miletus*, Oxford

Hunter, R. 1983. *Eubulus, The Fragments*, Cambridge

  1999. *Theocritus. A Selection*, Cambridge

  2006. *The Shadow of Callimachus*, Cambridge

  2008. *On Coming After. Studies in Post-Classical Greek Literature and its Reception*, Berlin and New York

  2009. *Critical Moments in Classical Literature*, Cambridge

  2012. *Plato and the Traditions of Ancient Literature. The Silent Stream*, Cambridge

  2017. 'Callimachus, *Aitia* Fragments 173 and 43' in D. Sider ed., *Hellenistic Poetry. A Selection*, Ann Arbor, MI: 186–212

  2018. *The Measure of Homer*, Cambridge

  2020. 'John Malalas and the story of the Cyclops' in C. Meliadò, G.B. D'Alessio, L. Lomiento, and G. Ucciardello, eds., *Il potere della parola*, Alessandria forthcoming

Hunter, R. and Laemmle, R. 2019. 'Enkelados: Callimachus fr. 1.36' *Classical Philology* 114: 493–8

Hunter, R. and Uhlig, A. eds. 2017. *Imagining Reperformance in Ancient Culture*, Cambridge

Hunter, V.J. 1994. *Policing Athens*, Princeton, NJ

Imperio, O. 1998. 'Callia' in Belardinelli 1998: 195–256

Irwin, E. 1974. *Colour Terms in Greek Poetry*, Toronto

Itsumi, K. 1982. 'The "choriambic dimeter" of Euripides' *Classical Quarterly* 32: 59–74

Jackson, J. 1955. *Marginalia Scaenica*, Oxford

Jameson, M. 1971. 'Sophocles and the Four Hundred' *Historia* 20: 541–68

Janko, R. 1985. 'ΑΥΤΟΣ ΕΚΕΙΝΟΣ: a neglected idiom' *Classical Quarterly* 35: 20–30

Jouan, F. and Van Looy H. 1998. *Euripide Tome VIII. Fragments 1ʳᵉ partie*, Paris

Kaibel, G. 1895. 'Kratinos' Ὀδυσσῆς und Euripides' Κύκλωψ' *Hermes* 30: 71–88

  1899. *Comicorum graecorum fragmenta* I, Berlin

Kannicht, R. 1996. 'Zum Corpus euripideum' in C. Mueller-Goldingen and K. Sier eds., ΛΗΝΑΙΚΑ. *Festschrift für Carl Werner Müller*, Stuttgart and Leipzig: 21–31

Karanika, A. 2014. *Voices at Work. Women, Performance, and Labor in Ancient Greece*, Baltimore, MD

Kassel, R. 1991. *Kleine Schriften*, Berlin

Kilmer, M. 1993. *Greek Erotica on Attic Red-Figure Vases*, London

Konstan, D. 1990. 'An anthropology of Euripides' *Kyklops*' in Winkler and
    Zeitlin 1990: 207–27
Konstantinidou, K. 2014. 'Oath and curse' in A.H. Sommerstein and I.C.
    Torrance eds., *Oaths and Swearing in Ancient Greece*, Berlin: 6–47
Kossatz-Deissmann, A. 1991. 'Satyr- und Mänadennamen auf Vasenbildern
    des Getty-Museums und der Sammlung Calm (Basel) mit Addenda zu
    Ch. Fränkel, *Satyr- und Bakchennamen auf Vasenbildern* (Halle 1912)'
    Greek Vases in the J.- Paul Getty Museum 5:131–99
Kovacs, D. 1994. *Euripidea*, Leiden
Kowalzig, B. and Wilson, P. eds. 2013. *Dithyramb in Context*, Oxford
Kranz, W. 1933. *Stasimon*, Berlin
Krummacher, F.A. 1806. *Die Kinderwelt. Ein Gedicht in vier Gesängen*,
    Duisberg and Essen
Laemmle, R. 2007. 'Der eingeschlossene Dritte. Zur Funktion des
    Dionysos im Satyrspiel' in A. Bierl, R. Laemmle and K. Wesselmann
    eds., *Literatur und Religion. Wege zu einer mythisch-rituellen Poetik bei den
    Griechen*, Berlin and New York: I 335–86
    2013. *Poetik des Satyrspiels*, Heidelberg
    2014. 'Das Satyrspiel' in B. Zimmermann and A. Rengakos eds., *Die
    Literatur der klassischen und hellenistischen Zeit*, Munich: 926–67
    2017. 'Satyrspiel' in *Handwörterbuch der antiken Sklaverei*, Band 3,
    Stuttgart: 2499–2501
    2018. 'Zur Autor- und Stückzuweisung von P.Oxy. 1083 fr. 1 (S. **F
    1130 R.)' *Zeitschrift für Papyrologie und Epigraphik* 208: 44–66
    2019a. 'Precarious *choreia* in satyr play' in Coo and Uhlig 2019: 29–48
    2019b. 'Atalante *philandros*: teasing out satyric innuendo (Sophocles fr.
    1111 Radt = Hermogenes, *On Ideas* 2.5)' *Classical Quarterly* 69
    forthcoming 'Courtship and its discontents in Greek literature'
Laemmle, R. and Scheidegger Laemmle, C. 2012. 'Homer on Kithairon:
    dramatic and narrative representation in the *Bacchae*' *Classical Journal*
    108: 129–58
Lamari, A. ed. 2015. *Reperformances of Drama in the Fifth and Fourth Centuries
    BC*, Berlin
Lambin, G. 1992. *La chanson grecque dans l'antiquité*, Paris
Larson, J. 2001. *Greek Nymphs. Myth, Cult, Lore*, Oxford
LeVen, P. 2014. *The Many-Headed Muse*, Cambridge
Lissarrague, F. 1990. 'Why satyrs are good to represent' in Winkler and
    Zeitlin 1990: 228–36
    2013. *La cité des satyres*, Paris
Lloyd, G.E.R. 1966. *Polarity and Analogy*, Cambridge
Lloyd, M. 1999. 'The tragic aorist' *Classical Quarterly* 49: 24–45
Lourenço, F. 2011. *The Lyric Metres of Euripidean Drama*, Coimbra

Lowe, J.C.B. 1973. 'γ' ἄρα, γ' ἄρα and τἄρα' *Glotta* 51: 34–64

Luppe, W. 1996. 'Zur "Lebensdauer" der Euripides-Hypotheseis' *Philologus* 140: 214–24

Maas, M. and Snyder, J.M. 1989. *Stringed Instruments of Ancient Greece*, New Haven, CT

Magnelli, E. 2003. 'Un nuovo indizio (e alcune precisazioni) sui drammi "alfabetici" di Euripide a Bisanzio tra XI e XII secolo' *Prometheus* 29: 193–212

Marquart, R. 1912. *Die Datierung des euripideischen Kyklops*, Dissertation, Leipzig

Marshall, C.W. 2001. 'The consequences of dating the *Cyclops*' in M. Joyal ed., *In altum. Seventy-Five Years of Classical Studies in Newfoundland*, St John's: 225–41

Martin, G. 2018. *Euripides, Ion*, Berlin

Masaracchia, E. 1994. 'Note al *Ciclope* di Euripide' *Quaderni Urbinati di Cultura Classica* 48: 41–66

Masciadri, V. 1987. 'Autolykos und der Silen: eine übersehene Szene des Euripides bei Tzetzes' *Museum Helveticum* 44: 1–7

Mastromarco, G. 1998. 'La degradazione del mostro: la maschera del Ciclope nella commedia e nel dramma satiresco del quinto secolo a.C.' in Belardinelli 1998: 9–42

Mastronarde, D.J. 1979. *Contact and Discontinuity*, Berkeley, CA
  1989. 'Lautensach's Law and the augment of compound-verbs in EY-' *Glotta* 67: 101–5
  2002. *Euripides, Medea*, Cambridge
  2010. *The Art of Euripides*, Cambridge
  2017. 'Text and transmission' in L. McClure ed., *A Companion to Euripides*, Malden, MA: 11–27

Maxwell-Stuart, P.G. 1981. *Studies in Greek Colour Terminology*, Vol. I ΓΛΑΥΚΟΣ, Leiden

Mayer, M. 1887. *Die Giganten und Titanen in der antiken Sage und Kunst*, Berlin

McClure, L.K. 1995. 'Female speech and characterization in Euripides' in F. de Martino and A.H. Sommerstein eds., *Lo spettacolo delle voci*, Bari: II 35–60

Melero, A. 1984. 'La muerte de Encelado: una parodia satírica' *Estudios clásicos* 87: 159–66

Meriani, A. 1996. 'Euripide, *Cycl.* 608ss.' *Quaderni Urbinati di Cultura Classica* 53: 67–72
  1999. 'Il *Ciclope* di Euripide: osservazioni sulla colometria dei manoscritti' in B. Gentili and F. Perusino eds., *La colometria dei testi poetici greci*, Pisa and Rome: 157–68

Meuli, K. 1946. 'Griechische Opferbräuche' in *Phyllobolia für Peter von der Mühll*, Basel: 185–288

Meurig Davies, E.L.B. 1949. 'Two notes on Euripides' *Classical Review* 63: 49

Michaelides, S. 1978. *The Music of Ancient Greece. An Encyclopaedia*, London

Mikalson, J.D. 1983. *Athenian Popular Religion*, Chapel Hill, NC
1991. *Honor Thy Gods. Popular Religion in Greek Tragedy*, Chapel Hill, NC

Miller, M.C. 1997. *Athens and Persia in the Fifth Century B.C. A Study in Cultural Receptivity*, Cambridge

Millis, B.W. and Olson, S.D. 2012. *Inscriptional Records for the Dramatic Festivals in Athens*, Leiden

Montiglio, S. 2011. *From Villain to Hero. Odysseus in Ancient Thought*, Ann Arbor, MI

Morrison, J.S. and Williams, R.T. 1968. *Greek Oared Ships 900–322 B.C.*, Cambridge

Most, G.W. 2014. 'τὸν Ἀνακρέοντα μιμοῦ: imitation and enactment in the *Anacreontics*' in Baumbach and Dümmler 2014: 145–59

Muecke, F. 1984. 'Turning away and looking down: some gestures in the *Aeneid*' *Bulletin of the Institute of Classical Studies* 31: 105–12

Müller, C.W. 1997. *Philoktet. Beiträge zur Wiedergewinnung einer Tragödie des Euripides aus der Geschichte ihrer Rezeption*, Stuttgart and Leipzig

Mureddu, P. 1993. 'Il "multiforme Odisseo": appunti sulla figura e sul ruolo del protagonista del *Ciclope*' in R. Pretagostini ed., *Tradizione e innovazione nella cultura greca da Omero all'età ellenistica*. Rome: II 591–600

Murray, P. and Wilson, P. eds. 2004. *Music and the Muses*, Oxford

Napolitano, M. 1992. 'Euripide, *Cycl.* 14–15' *Bollettino dei Classici* 13: 117–23
2005. 'Appunti sullo statuto letterario del *Ciclope* di Euripide' *Dioniso* 4: 42–55

Nesselrath, H.-G. 1990. *Die attische Mittlere Komödie*, Berlin and New York

Nisbet, R.G.M. and Hubbard, M. 1978. *A Commentary on Horace: Odes II*, Oxford

Noble, J.V. 1988. *The Techniques of Painted Attic Pottery*, 2nd ed., London

Norden, E. 1913. *Agnostos Theos*, Stuttgart

Nünlist, R. 1998. *Poetologische Bildersprache in der frühgriechischen Dichtung*, Stuttgart

Obbink, D. 1993. 'Dionysus poured out: ancient and modern theories of sacrifice and cultural formation' in Carpenter and Faraone 1993: 65–86

Olson, S.D. 1988. 'Dionysus and the pirates in Euripides' "Cyclops"' *Hermes* 116: 502–4

Orth, C. 2009. *Strattis. Die Fragmente*, Berlin
Osborne, R. 1998. *Archaic and Classical Greek Art*, Oxford
 2011. *The History Written on the Classical Greek Body*, Cambridge
O'Sullivan, P. 2005. 'Of sophists, tyrants, and Polyphemos: the nature of the beast in Euripides' *Cyclops*' in Harrison 2005: 119–59
Paganelli, L. 1978/9. 'Note al *Ciclope* euripideo' *Museum Criticum* 13/14: 197–202
 1979. *Echi storico-politici nel 'Ciclope' euripideo*, Padua
 1980. Review of Ussher 1978, *Gnomon* 52: 425–9
 1981. 'Polifemo, Sileno e le Cariti (Eur. *Cycl.* 578–84)' *Emerita* 49: 139–43
Page, D.L. 1955. *Sappho and Alcaeus*, Oxford
Palmer, L.R. 1946. 'Mortar and lathe' *Eranos* 44: 54–61
Pàmias i Massana, J. and Zucker, A. 2013. *Eratosthène de Cyrène, Catasterismi*, Paris
Parker, L.P.E. 2016. *Euripides, Iphigenia in Tauris*, Oxford
Parry, M. 1971. *The Making of Homeric Verse*, Oxford
Pechstein, N. 1998. *Euripides Satyrographos*, Stuttgart and Leipzig
Peigney, J. 2015. 'La guerre de Troie dans le discours d'Ulysse à Polyphème chez Euripide (*Cyclope*, 285–312)' in S. Dubel, A.-M. Favreau-Linder and E. Oudot eds., *À l'école d' Homère. La culture des orateurs et des sophistes*, Paris: 105–14
Pendrick, G.J. 2002. *Antiphon the Sophist. The Fragments*, Cambridge
Pickard-Cambridge, A. 1962. *Dithyramb, Tragedy and Comedy*, 2nd ed. rev. by T.B.L. Webster, Oxford
 1968. *The Dramatic Festivals of Athens*, 2nd ed. rev. by J. Gould and D.M. Lewis, Oxford
Platnauer, M. 1960. 'Prodelision in Greek drama' *Classical Quarterly* 10: 140–4
Pötscher, W. 1998. 'Γλαύκη, Γλαῦκος und die Bedeuting von γλαυκός' *Rheinisches Museum* 141: 97–111
Polunin, O. and Huxley, A. 1965. *Flowers of the Mediterranean*, London
Power, T. 2010. *The Culture of kitharôidia*, Washington, D.C.
 2013. 'Kyklops *kitharoidos*: dithyramb and nomos in play' in Kowalzig and Wilson 2013: 237–56
 2018. 'New music in Sophocles' *Ichneutae*' in R. Andújar, T. Coward and T. Hadjimichael eds., *Paths of Song. The Lyric Dimension of Greek Tragedy*, Berlin and Boston: 343–65
Prauscello, L. 2017. 'Plato *Laws* 3.680b–c: Antisthenes, the Cyclopes and Homeric exegesis' *Journal of Hellenic Studies* 137: 8–23
Privitera, G.A. 1970. *Dioniso in Omero e nella poesia greca arcaica*, Rome
Pulleyn, S. 1997. *Prayer in Greek Religion*, Oxford

Radt, S. 1982. 'Sophokles in seinen Fragmenten' in *Sophocle*, Entretiens Fondation Hardt XXIX, Vandoeuvres and Geneva: 185–231
1985. 'Aristophanica' in W.J. Aerts et al. eds., ΣΧΟΛΙΑ. *Studia ... D. Holwerda oblata*, Groningen:103–18
Rashed, M. 2007. 'The structure of the eye and its cosmological function in Empedocles: reconstruction of Fragment 84 D–K' in S. Stern-Gillet and K. Corrigan eds., *Reading Ancient Texts. Essays in Honour of Denis O'Brien*, Leiden: I 22–39
Renehan, R. 1969. *Greek Textual Criticism. A Reader*. Cambridge, MA
1976. *Studies in Greek Texts*, Göttingen
Reynolds, L. and Wilson, N.G. 2013. *Scribes and Scholars*, 4th ed., Oxford
Richardson, N.J. 1974. *The Homeric Hymn to Demeter*, Oxford
Rijksbaron, A. 1991. *Grammatical Observations on Euripides' Bacchae*, Amsterdam
2007. *Plato, Ion or: On the Iliad*, Leiden
Robert, C. 1878. *Eratosthenis catasterismorum reliquiae*, Berlin
Robert, L. 1955. *Hellenica*, Vol. X, Paris
Rosenmeyer, P.A. 1992. *The Poetics of Imitation. Anacreon and the Anacreontic Tradition*, Cambridge
Rossi, L.E. 1971a. 'Il *Ciclope* di Euripide come κῶμος "mancato"' *Maia* 23: 10–38
1971b. 'Mondo pastorale e poesia bucolica di maniera: l'idillio ottavo del *corpus* teocriteo' *Studi Italiani di Filologia Classica* 43: 5–25
Rossum-Steenbeek, M. 1998. *Greek Readers' Digests? Studies on a Selection of Subliterary Papyri*, Leiden
Rusten, J. 1982. 'Dicaearchus and the *Tales from Euripides*' *Greek, Roman and Byzantine Studies* 23: 357–67
Rutherford, I. 2001. *Pindar's Paeans*, Oxford
Sansone, D. 2015. 'The place of the satyr-play in the tragic tetralogy' *Prometheus* 41: 3–36
Schadewaldt, W. 1926. *Monolog und Selbstgespräch*, Berlin
Schein, S.L. 2013. *Sophocles, Philoctetes*, Cambridge
Schironi, F. 2018. *The Best of the Grammarians. Aristarchus of Samothrace on the Iliad*, Ann Arbor, MI
Schlesier, R. 2011a. 'Dionysos' in M. Finkelberg ed., *The Homer Encyclopedia*, Malden, MA: I 210–11
ed. 2011b. *A Different God? Dionysos and Ancient Polytheism*, Berlin
Schmidt, M. 1976. *Die Erklärungen zum Weltbild Homers und zur Kultur der Heroenzeit in den bT-Scholien zur Ilias*, Munich
Schmidt, V. 1975. 'Zu Euripides, Kyklops 120 und 707' *Maia* 27: 291–3
Schöpsdau, K. 1994. *Platon Nomoi (Gesetze) Buch I–III*, Göttingen

Schumacher, R.W.M. 1993. 'Three related sanctuaries of Poseidon: Geraistos, Kalaureia and Tainaron' in N. Marinatos and R. Hägg eds., *Greek Sanctuaries. New Approaches*, London: 62–87

Scott, J.A. 1905. 'Additional notes on the vocative' *American Journal of Philology* 26: 32–43

Scullion, S. 2003. 'Euripides and Macedon, or the silence of the *Frogs*' *Classical Quarterly* 53: 389–400

Seaford, R. 1975. 'Some notes on Euripides' *Cyclops*' *Classical Quarterly* 25: 193–208

1981. 'Dionysiac drama and the Dionysiac mysteries' *Classical Quarterly* 31: 252–75

1982. 'The date of Euripides' *Cyclops*' *Journal of Hellenic Studies* 102: 161–72

1984. *Euripides, Cyclops*, Oxford

1987. '*Silenus erectus*: Euripides, *Cyclops* 227' *Liverpool Classical Monthly* 12: 227–8

1993. 'Dionysus as destroyer of the household: Homer, tragedy, and the polis' in Carpenter and Faraone 1993: 115–46

Seidensticker, B. 2010. 'Dance in satyr play' in Taplin and Wyles 2010: 213–29

Serrao, G. 1969. 'La parodo del "Ciclope" euripideo' *Museum Criticum* 4: 50–62

Shaw, B. 1982/3. '"Eaters of flesh, drinkers of milk": the ancient Mediterranean ideology of the pastoral nomad' *Ancient Society* 13/14: 5–31

Shaw, C.A. 2014. *Satyric Play. The Evolution of Greek Comedy and Satyr Drama*, Oxford

2018. *Euripides: Cyclops, A Satyr Play*, London

Sicherl, M. 1975. 'Die *editio princeps Aldina* des Euripides und ihre Vorlagen' *Rheinisches Museum* 118: 205–25

Simon, E. 1984. 'Ikonographie und Epigraphik: Zum Bauschmuck des Siphnierschatzhauses in Delphi' *Zeitschrift für Papyrologie und Epigraphik* 57: 1–22

Sittl, C. 1890. *Die Gebärden der Griechen und Römer*, Leipzig

Slater, W.J. 1976. 'Symposium at sea' *Harvard Studies in Classical Philology* 80: 161–70

Slenders, W. 2005. 'λέξις ἐρωτική in Euripides' *Cyclops*' in Harrison 2005: 39–52

Snell, B. 1935. 'Zwei Töpfe mit Euripides-Papyri' *Hermes* 70: 119–20

Snodgrass, A. 1998. *Homer and the Artists*, Cambridge

Sokolowski, F. 1955. *Lois sacrées de l'Asie Mineure*, Paris

1969. *Lois sacrées des cités grecques*, Paris

Spranger, J.A. 1921. *Codex Laurentianus XXXII.2, Euripides*, Florence

1939–46. *Euripidis quae in codicibus Palatino Graeco inter Vaticanos 287 et Laurentiano Conv. Soppr. 172 (olim Abbatiae Florentinae 2664) inveniuntur phototypice expressa*, Florence

Sparkes, B.A. 1962. 'The Greek kitchen' *Journal of Hellenic Studies* 82: 121–37

1975. 'Illustrating Aristophanes' *Journal of Hellenic Studies* 95: 122–35

1991. *Greek Pottery. An Introduction*, Manchester

Spies, A. 1930. *Militat omnis amans. Ein Beitrag zur Bildersprache der antiken Erotik*, Dissertation, Tübingen

Stanley-Porter, D.P. 1973. 'Mute actors in the tragedies of Euripides' *Bulletin of the Institute of Classical Studies* 20: 68–93

Stevens, P. 1976. *Colloquial Expressions in Euripides*, Wiesbaden

Stinton, T.C.W. 1975. 'Agamemnon 1127 and the limits of hyperbaton' *Proceedings of the Cambridge Philological Society* 21: 82–93

1977. 'Notes on Greek tragedy, II' *Journal of Hellenic Studies* 97: 127–54

Storey, I.C. 2005. 'But comedy has satyrs too' in Harrison 2005: 201–18

Sutton, D.F. 1974. 'Sophocles "Dionysiscus"' *Eos* 62: 205–11

1980. *The Greek Satyr Play*, Meisenheim am Glan

Taplin, O. 1977a. *The Stagecraft of Aeschylus*, Oxford

1977b. 'Did Greek dramatists write stage instructions?' *Proceedings of the Cambridge Philological Society* 23: 121–32

2007. *Pots and Plays*, Los Angeles, CA

Taplin, O. and Wyles, R. eds. 2010. *The Pronomos Vase and its Context*, Oxford

Thomas, O. 2015. 'Sophocles, seduction and shrivelling: *Ichneutai* fr. 316 Radt' *Classical Quarterly* 65: 364–5

Thomas, R. 1989. *Oral Tradition and Written Record in Classical Athens*, Cambridge

Thompson, D.W. 1932. 'Κτίλος' *Classical Review* 46: 53–4

Torrance, I.C. 2013. *Metapoetry in Euripides*, Oxford

2014. 'Ways to give oaths extra sanctity' in A. Sommerstein and I.C. Torrance, *Oaths and Swearing in Ancient Greece*, Berlin: 132–55

Travlos, J. 1988. *Bildlexikon zur Topographie des antiken Attika*, Tübingen

Trendall, A.D. 1967. *The Red-figured Vases of Lucania, Campania and Sicily*, Oxford

Trendall, A.D. and Webster, T.B.L. 1971. *Illustrations of Greek Drama*, London

Troxler, H. 1964. *Sprache und Wortschatz Hesiods*, Zurich

Turyn, A. 1957. *The Byzantine Manuscript Tradition of the Tragedies of Euripides*, Urbana

Usher, M.D. 2002. 'Satyr-play in Plato's *Symposium*' *American Journal of Philology* 123: 205–28

Ussher, R.G. 1978. *Euripides, Cyclops*, Rome

Van Wees, H. 2004. *Greek Warfare. Myth and Realities*, London

Voelke, P. 2001. *Un théâtre de la marge. Aspects figuratifs et configurationnels du drame satyrique dans l'Athènes classique*, Bari

von Reden, S. 1995. *Exchange in Ancient Greece*, London

von Straten, F.T. 1995. *Hiera kala. Images of Animal Sacrifice in Archaic and Classical Greece*, Leiden

Wackernagel, J. 1916. *Sprachliche Untersuchungen zu Homer*, Göttingen

Waltz, P. 1931. 'Le drame satyrique et le prologue du "Cyclope" d'Euripide' *L'Acropole* 6: 278–95

Wetzel, W. 1965. *De Euripidis fabula satyrica, quae Cyclops inscribitur, cum Homerico comparata exemplo*, Wiesbaden

West, M.L. 1966. 'Epica' *Glotta* 44: 135–48

    1981. 'Tragica V' *Bulletin of the Institute of Classical Studies* 28: 61–78

    1982. *Greek Metre*, Oxford

    1983. *The Orphic Poems*, Oxford

    1992. *Ancient Greek Music*, Oxford

    1997. *The East Face of Helicon*, Oxford

    2003. *Homeric Hymns, Homeric Apocrypha, Lives of Homer*, Cambridge, MA

White, J.W. 1912. *The Verse of Greek Comedy*, London

Wide, S. 1893. *Lakonische Kulte*, Leipzig

Wilamowitz-Moellendorff, U. von 1920. *Griechische Tragödien VIII. Euripides, Der Kyklop*, 2nd ed., Berlin

    1921. *Griechische Verskunst*, Berlin

Wilkins, J. 2000. *The Boastful Chef. The Discourse of Food in Ancient Greek Comedy*, Oxford

Williams, D. 2009. 'Picturing potters and painters' in J.H. Oakley and O. Palagia eds., *Athenian Potters and Painters*, Vol. II, Oxford: 306–17

Willi, A. 2008. *Sikelismos*, Basel

    2012a. '"We speak Peloponnesian": tradition and linguistic identity in post-classical Sicilian literature' in O. Tribulato ed., *Language and Linguistic Contact in Ancient Sicily*, Cambridge: 265–88

    2012b. 'Challenging authority: Epicharmus between epic and rhetoric' in Bosher 2012: 56–75

    2015. 'Epicharmus, the *Pseudepicharmeia*, and the origins of Attic drama' in S. Chronopoulos and C. Orth eds., *Fragmente einer Geschichte der griechischen Komödie, Fragmentary History of Greek Comedy*, Heidelberg: 109–45

Willink, C.W. 1966. 'Some problems of text and interpretation in the *Bacchae* II' *Classical Quarterly* 16: 220–42

2001. 'Notes on the parodos and other *cantica* of Euripides' *Cyclops*' *Mnemosyne* 54: 515–30

Wilson, N.G. 1966. Review of Zuntz 1965, *Gnomon* 38: 334–42

1983. *Scholars of Byzantium*, London

Wilson, P. 2010. 'The man and the music (and the choregos?)' in Taplin and Wyles 2010: 181–212

2017. 'A potted political history of the Sicilian theater' in H. Reid, D. Tanasi and S. Kimbell eds., *Politics and Performance in Western Greece. Essays on the Hellenic Heritage of Sicily and Southern Italy*, Iowa City, IA:1–31

Winkler, J.J. and Zeitlin, F. eds. 1990. *Nothing to Do with Dionysos?*, Princeton, NJ

Worman, N. 2008. *Abusive Mouths in Classical Athens*, Cambridge

Wright, M. 2005. *Euripides' Escape-Tragedies*, Oxford

2006. '*Cyclops* and the Euripidean tetralogy' *Cambridge Classical Journal* 52: 23–46

Yatromanolakis, D. 2007. *Sappho in the Making. The Early Reception*, Washington, D.C.

Zagagi, N. 1999. 'Comic patterns in Sophocles' *Ichneutai*' in J. Griffin ed., *Sophocles Revisited*, Oxford: 177–218

Zuntz, G. 1955. *The Political Plays of Euripides*, Manchester

1965. *An Inquiry into the Transmission of the Plays of Euripides*, Cambridge

Zwierlein, O. 1967. Review of Wetzel 1965, *Gnomon* 39: 449–54

INDEXES

satyrs, names of 96, 97, 127
sexuality in satyr-play 32–5, 83, 135–7,
    222–3
Silenos 32, 83–98; costume 29–30,
    133, 146–7; father of satyrs 33;
    separate from chorus 26–7; wisdom
    of 138
Sicily 5, 26, 44–5, 87, 91, 101–2,
    120–1, 123, 160
sikinis/sikinnis 32, 46, 95, 96, 98, 141
Sikinnos, slave of Themistocles 141
similes 19, 185–6, 194–5, 197, 209,
    229
Sisyphos 20, 119–20, 169
slavery, satyric motif 18, 84, 92, 248
Sleep (*Hypnos*) 227
Sophocles 1, 24, 26; satyr-plays 3, 35
    n.117, 38, 103, 144; *Philoctetes* 40–1,
    94, 114, 247
Sounion, Cape 158–9
stage-instructions (*parepigraphai*) 201
symposium, sympotic practice 17–18,
    188, 204–10, 210–25

Tainaron 158–9
Telemos 6, 246

tetralogies 2, 24, 43
Theatre of Dionysos 82, 199, 248
Theocritus 11, 101–2, 104, 204, 207
thyrsus 25, 108
Timotheus, lyric poet 8
Triton 153
Trojan War 20–1, 140, 156–8, 245
Tyche 11, 228
Typhoeus/Typhon 87, 165, 236
Tyro 167
Tyrrhenians 88–9
Tzetzes, John 3 n.11, 49 n.167

wealth, praise of 164
wedding-songs 205, 208–10
wind, north 167
wine, absence of 17–18, 145; and heat
    188; as Dionysos 17; as a wrestler
    205–6, 243; wine-tasting 130. See
    also Dionysos, mixing of wine and
    water
work-songs 102, 237

Zeus 21, 143, 164–7, 171, 172, 179,
    222, 224

INDEX OF PASSAGES DISCUSSED

For EU product safety concerns, contact us at Calle de José Abascal, 56–1°, 28003 Madrid, Spain or eugpsr@cambridge.org.

www.ingramcontent.com/pod-product-compliance
Ingram Content Group UK Ltd.
Pitfield, Milton Keynes, MK11 3LW, UK
UKHW020323140625
459647UK00018B/1986